The Property Tax, Land Use and Land Use Regulation

STUDIES IN FISCAL FEDERALISM AND STATE–LOCAL FINANCE

Series Editor: Wallace E. Oates, *Professor of Economics, University of Maryland and University Fellow, Resources for the Future, USA*

This important series is designed to make a significant contribution to the development of the principles and practices of state–local finance. It includes both theoretical and empirical work. International in scope, it addresses issues of current and future concern in both East and West and in developed and developing countries.

The main purpose of the series is to create a forum for the publication of high quality work and to show how economic analysis can make a contribution to understanding the role of local finance in fiscal federalism in the twenty-first century.

Titles in the series include:

The Property Tax, Land Use and Land Use Regulation

Edited by

Dick Netzer

New York University

STUDIES IN FISCAL FEDERALISM AND STATE–LOCAL FINANCE IN ASSOCIATION WITH THE LINCOLN INSTITUTE OF LAND POLICY

Edward Elgar
Cheltenham, UK • Northampton, MA, USA

#51983213

Published by
Edward Elgar Publishing Limited
Glensanda House
Montpellier Parade
Cheltenham
Glos GL50 1UA
UK

Edward Elgar Publishing, Inc.
136 West Street
Suite 202
Northampton
Massachusetts 01060
USA

A catalogue record for this book
is available from the British Library

Library of Congress Cataloguing in Publication Data
The property tax, land use, and land use regulation / edited by Dick Netzer.
　　　p. cm. — (Studies in fiscal federalism and state–local finance)
　　"In association with the Lincoln Institute of Land Policy."
　　1. Real property tax—United States. 2. Real property and taxation—United
States. 3. Land use—Law and legislation—United States. I. Netzer, Dick, 1928–
II. Lincoln Institute of Land Policy. III. Series.
　HJ4181.P724 2003
　333.73′17—dc21　　　　　　　　　　　　　　　　　　　　2003048547

ISBN 1 84376 328 1

Printed and bound in Great Britain by MPG Books Ltd, Bodmin, Cornwall

Contents

Figures

Tables

Contributors

Alex Anas, Department of Economics, State University of New York at Buffalo.

John E. Anderson, Department of Economics, University of Nebraska, Lincoln.

William T. Bogart, York College of Pennsylvania.

Paul Cheshire, Department of Geography & Environment, London School of Economics.

Peter F. Colwell, Department of Finance, University of Illinois at Urbana-Champaign.

Richard F. Dye, Department of Economics, Lake Forest College, and Institute of Government and Public Affairs, University of Illinois at Chicago.

William A. Fischel, Department of Economics, Dartmouth College.

John F. McDonald, College of Business Administration, University of Illinois at Chicago.

David F. Merriman, Department of Economics, Loyola University of Chicago, and Institute of Government and Public Affairs, University of Illinois at Chicago.

Robert H. Nelson, School of Public Affairs, University of Maryland.

Stephen Sheppard, Department of Economics, William College.

Geoffrey K. Turnbull, Department of Economics, Georgia State University.

Robert W. Wassmer, Graduate Program in Public Policy and Administration, California State University, Sacramento.

About the Lincoln Institute

The Lincoln Institute of Land Policy is a nonprofit and tax-exempt educational institution established in 1974. Its mission as a school is to study and teach land policy, including land economics and land taxation. The Institute is supported primarily by the Lincoln Foundation, which was established in 1947 by Cleveland industrialist John C. Lincoln. He drew inspiration from the ideas of Henry George, the nineteenth-century American political economist, social philosopher and author of the book, *Progress and Poverty*.

The Institute's goals are to integrate theory and practice to better shape land policy and to share understanding about the multidisciplinary forces that influence public policy. The Institute organizes its work in two departments: valuation and taxation, and planning and development. In addition we support a program on Latin American and Caribbean studies.

The Lincoln Institute seeks to improve the quality of debate and disseminate knowledge of critical issues in land policy by bringing together scholars, policy makers, practitioners and citizens with diverse backgrounds and experience. We study, exchange insights and work toward a broader understanding of complex land and tax policies. The Institute does not take a particular point of view, but rather serves as a catalyst to facilitate analysis and discussion of these issues – to make a difference today and to help policy makers plan for tomorrow.

Introduction

For at least 40 years, the various bodies of literature on the property tax, on land use and on land use regulation have contained references to and comments on the relation between the property tax and how land is used in places where the property tax is an important source of local government revenue (and where local government finance is of some consequence), and the relation between the property tax and land use regulation regimes. Often the references have been asides to the main argument of the work in question; in other cases, the relations have been explored more systematically. But it is fair to say that there is not a coherent exposition of some of the main issues, despite their importance.

That importance may be self-evident:

- It is obvious that a tax on structures must affect the uses of land, and the lack of revenue from a serious tax on the value of land that results in higher taxes on structures also affects land use.
- The revenue from a given rate of property tax is affected by the way land is used and, therefore, it is likely that local land use regulators will pay attention to that effect in their regulations.
- The efficiency and equity of the property tax are affected by land use, and the way land uses are regulated. These considerations should have a major impact on the way we conceive the American property tax: is it in the main a distorting tax on mobile capital that is likely to have a regressive incidence (as in the writings of Peter Mieszkowski and George Zodrow), or, in many places, a benefits tax that is quite close to being a land value tax in disguise (as in the work of William Fischel)?
- In the public policy realm, the reception to land value tax proposals is very much affected by land use issues, as we see conspicuously in debate on preferential assessments of selected types of land use.

The 10 essays that comprise the book begin with a stage-setting essay that models taxes on land and buildings in the context of a dynamic model of taxes on land and buildings (Anas). The remaining nine essays examine how various tax mechanisms and nontax alternatives that regulate land use complement or substitute for one another in their effects on land use. Two essays address the land use effects of variants of conventional property taxation, notably 'tax increment financing' (Dye and Merriman) and preferential assessments (Anderson), and a third looks at the land use effects of a widespread alternative local tax, the local sales tax (Wassmer). Three essays directly compare the land use effects of property taxes and direct regulation (Bogart; Cheshire and Sheppard; McDonald). The final three examine more radical institutional variants: the private community association as the mode of residential development (Nelson and Fischel, who see the issue quite differently) and the taxation of lot frontage rather than land value (Colwell and Turnbull).

Alex Anas, noting that static models of real estate markets, by pretending that all the land is available in the markets at all points in time, cannot answer the important questions relating to land value and building taxes. Instead, using a generalized perfect foresight model of real estate markets solvable by simulation, stripped down to its bare essentials, he shows that conventional property tax speeds up the demolition–reconstruction cycle, shortening the life span of buildings, thus resulting in excessive use of structural capital over time, while a tax on undeveloped land has the opposite effects. In the next stage, a different tax rate is levied on each type of undeveloped land and each type of building, the rates set to meet a desired revenue goal, recognizing the different price elasticities of demand and supply for these assets. The formulation is designed to calculate deadweight losses associated with optimal taxation schemes.

Richard Dye and David Merriman address a relatively new variant of property tax financing, tax increment financing, originally devised as a means of financing infrastructure in a defined (usually small) geographic area and thus speed development of that land. The resulting property tax revenue generated by the increased property values in the defined area is reserved for paying those infrastructure costs, mainly debt service on the bonds issued to finance the improvements, rather than being available for general local government purposes. The attraction is the local economic development and its spillovers. Dye and Merriman examine property value growth in Illinois municipalities (where the use of the device is very widespread). They find that the use of the device tends to shift the location of economic development, within municipalities as well as among them, and in many cases is not a positive-sum game.

John Anderson addresses a pervasive phenomenon in property taxation in the United States: preferential assessment for certain types of property, most commonly agricultural land. Typically, the preference for agricultural land takes the form of assessment on the basis of its value in its agricultural use, rather than its market value. As a result, the effective property tax rate is reduced for this type of property. This essay provides an overview of the impacts of preferential assessment and an investigation of alternative policies. Impacts include a wealth transfer to owners of property for which preferential assessment applies, effects on the timing and intensity of land development, and implications for horizontal and vertical equity of the property tax system. Several alternatives are examined, including classified property tax systems, purchase of development rights, conservation easements and graded tax systems.

Robert Wassmer considers an important alternative to property taxation in local finance. Local government in many American states use sales taxes; in some states the rate of the local portion of the sales tax is quite high. That makes the location of new shopping malls and other concentrations of retail activity of considerable importance to local decision makers. But is the volume of total retail sales and retail sales of two types of 'big-box' stores (car and home improvement) that occur outside the central cities of metropolitan areas influenced by the extent to which local governments raise revenue through sales taxes? Is the location of retailing influenced by growth controls? These are issues in California and elsewhere in the American West. The results of a regression analysis that controls for other factors that cause retail activity to locate outside central cities indicate that statewide reliance on some forms of revenue positively affect total retail sales and, even more, the two forms of 'big-box' retailing outside central cities. Some urban growth controls have the opposite effect – reducing decentralization.

William T. Bogart explores the extent to which zoning is equivalent to factor taxes in the impact on factor prices, local production and intrametropolitan trade. He models metropolitan areas as sets of smaller open economies. He concludes that zoning, a form of quality control, and factor taxes, a form of quantity control, are indeed partial substitutes, but also partial complements. While economists clearly prefer tinkering with prices to optimize outcomes, the American constitutional limits on the power of state and local government to tax in ways that can be deemed unlawful impediments to interstate commerce or 'taking' of property without compensation do constrain the use of factor taxes to achieve non-fiscal goals, while there is much more constitutional latitude in zoning. Bogart notes that there are numerous problems in comparing the two policy approaches that should be addressed in future research.

Cheshire and Sheppard examine some alternative policies for physically containing the growth of urban areas. A microsimulation provides a comparison between land use planning policies that enforce an urban growth boundary and tax policies that limit development at the urban periphery. The simulation uses data for a rapidly growing city in the south of England. It analyzes the welfare costs, distributional impact and effects on urban densities of alternative ways to achieve the degree of constraint currently observed. The authors find that the use of a tax on land could produce the same limitation on growth as existing regulatory policies, but with higher welfare levels at equilibrium. However, they find that the use of a tax designed to increase transportation costs, while capable of producing a compact urban form, would not raise welfare when compared to existing regulatory policies.

McDonald also compares local land use decisions and property taxation as policy instruments. His models connect these policy decisions to outcomes in the urban land and labor markets so that costs and benefits can be measured.

Robert Nelson and William Fischel address the land use control regime in the United States explicitly. They consider whether the rapid rise of private neighborhood associations in newly developed residential neighborhoods transforms the land use control regime and supplants local government provision of some public services. Nelson argues that it increasingly does just that, and in doing so renders some policy conflicts (as well as some of the issues discussed in this book) irrelevant.

Fischel views private neighborhood associations quite differently. He argues that these associations supplement, rather than displace, local government land use regulation. Homeowners appear to desire more, not less regulation, and therefore would oppose any proposal to substitute neighborhood associations for municipal governance. Less revolutionary reforms of local government, such as heightened judicial scrutiny of zoning under regulatory takings and more permissive rules for municipal secession and incorporation, might be more acceptable vehicles for reform and also would preserve local governments as mediating institutions in the American federal system

In another essay that 'thinks outside the box', Colwell and Turnbull consider transformation of the property tax from one on the *value* of parcels of real property to one on the *length of the frontage* of parcels. They point out that many social costs of urban development are related to the total length of lot frontage. They develop a model of a closed urban area with no location rents in which there are identical rectangular lots. They find that the frontage tax does address the social costs but does not reduce the total areas as much as some less efficient alternatives. The essay emphasizes that the concept of inefficient urban sprawl is not simply related to the total size of the urban area occupied by a given population, but rather to the configuration of developed lots and the relationship between lot configuration and the size of the urban area.

The essays in the book were presented at a conference sponsored by the Lincoln Institute of Land Policy held in January 2002. The discussants at that conference were: Karl Case, Wellesley College, Gary Cornia, Brigham Young University, Charles Leven, Washington University, Joyce Man, Indiana University, Wallace Oates, University of Maryland, Amy Ellen Schwartz, New York University, and Steven Sheffrin, University of California, Davis.

The papers were revised by their authors, who incorporated the suggestions and criticisms of those discussants. That would make including the discussants' presentations in this book redundant. There was one exception to this: Fischel (who had been scheduled as a discussant) wrote an essay presenting a different view of the issue that Nelson's essay discusses, rather than the usual brief discussant's critique. The Fischel essay appears here, in edited form.

All of us who participated in this venture are grateful to the Lincoln Institute and its staff for convening the conference and making it a rewarding and comfortable experience.

1. Taxes on buildings and land in a dynamic model of real estate markets

Alex Anas

1 INTRODUCTION

The Henry George (1879) *single tax* is a tax on land. But how should the tax be levied? The simplest example would be a lump sum tax on each unit of land to be paid regardless of what is to be done with that land and disregarding whether it is currently developed or not. Such a tax system is generally presumed to be neutral, as George had envisioned. And, it is presumed, one could vary the tax from one unit of land to the other: the implied tax rate as a proportion of land value would not have to be the same everywhere to achieve neutrality. But such a lump sum tax system – while probably deserving a lot more attention than it has received – would be considered inequitable unless it was related either to the *benefits received* by the owners of the land or to the landowner's *ability to pay*. Arguably, in an efficient capital market, the best measure of a landowner's ability to pay is his land value.

But can tax authorities or econometricians accurately measure the value of land covered with buildings? Mills (1998) has argued that they cannot. The consequences of inaccurate measurement could be quite severe. Consider the example of an owner of a building who is planning to demolish his building and sell the land because that is the most profitable action. Suppose that the tax authority, not knowing the land value, sets the lump sum tax on this owner so high that the after-tax value of the land that will be released by demolition becomes negative.[1] In a free society, if the owner were fully rational, he would abandon the building if all other alternatives yielded a negative return and if – by doing so – the tax could be avoided. Inducing abandonment in this way would be distorting and, hence, inefficient. To avoid the distortion and restore efficiency, owners could be forced to pay the tax even if abandoning. Knowing that they could so be forced, they would not abandon because they would reduce their losses by demolishing and selling the land. Such a prohibition of abandonment is a form of fascism. Alternatively, society could also restore efficiency by taking over and demolishing the abandoned building. Arguably, this is a form of socialism. To avoid both extremes, the tax authority and the building's owner could negotiate the tax down to some reasonable level. That, of course, is neither fascism nor socialism. But, at worst, it opens the door to corrupt dealings between landowners and tax authorities. At best, it increases the transaction costs involved in determining a reasonable tax. So we should look for land tax instruments that are easy to administer at arm's length and are based on observable measures of value.[2]

The modern literature on land taxation, implicitly recognizing the importance of tax schemes related to the ability to pay, has focused on ad valorem taxes that maintain proportionality between the tax paid and the 'true land value' so that all landowners faced the same tax rate. But all these modern attempts run into the basic question: 'What is the true land value that should be taxed?' Looking at the world, we see at least two types of land. The first is land that is undeveloped or vacant in the sense that there is no building on it. The second type of land is land that is occupied by a building of some sort or having minimal infrastructure improvements on it or near it, making it suitable for supporting buildings at a later date. Further scrutiny reveals additional complexity. The types of buildings as well as the types of vacant land that we see vary enormously in their underlying economics. There are, for example, tall buildings (such as skyscrapers) that are, for economic reasons, extremely unlikely to be demolished any time soon. Hence the land that they occupy is virtually locked out from the active market for land. There are, as well, shorter buildings in poor structural condition that are very likely to be demolished and could make their underlying land available for some other type of building to be constructed. Buildings can also be changed (from apartments to offices, for example) without affecting the underlying land or their structural density. To make a long story short, virtually every piece of land is a different type of land with a different propensity to remain in its present use or to become recycled into some other.

Looking at things in this way gives rise to a situation that is far different from George's idealized view. While it is still true that the aggregate supply of land is fixed for all practical purposes, the supply of vacant land at any one place is not at all fixed. More vacant land can be created by demolition of buildings and the supply of it is far from inelastic in general. Meanwhile, the supply of a particular type of building at a location can be very elastic or very inelastic depending – among other things – on the costs of construction, demolition and conversion without demolition, as well as the availability of vacant land nearby. These elasticities also depend on time horizons.

Given the above realistic way of looking at what we mean by a 'land market', what exactly is to be understood by a *single rate ad valorem tax on land value*? It is perhaps best to approach this question gradually by making a brief review of recently published modeling exercises by several urban economists who treated the response of an *entire* land market to different tax structures. These are the recent *static* models made by Mills (1998), Brueckner (2001) and Brueckner and Kim (2003) in which an idealized, homogeneous and instantly available land market exists by assumption. These authors examined the land tax in the context of the monocentric city of urban economics. They drew conclusions about the effects on physical city size and land use within such a city arising from a revenue-neutral switch from a conventional ad valorem property tax falling on land and structures at the same rate to a hypothetical pure ad valorem land tax falling on land only. Mills examined a monocentric city containing export-ing businesses only and open to the in- and out-migration of these busi-nesses. He showed that the switch to the land tax increased the capital per acre (structural density) that businesses would employ throughout the city. Because this increases the productivity of each acre, the rent–distance func-tion rises and the city expands in radius and in total output. Brueckner examined a city of housing consumers with a fixed total population and showed that the switch to a land tax causes the after-tax cost of capital to fall and thus the structural density of housing to rise on each acre. Dwelling sizes and total population being constant, the city shrinks in radius (less urban sprawl occurs). In Brueckner and Kim, it is shown that this result can be reversed if dwelling sizes are not constant. The lower after-tax cost of structural capital, arising from the switch to the single tax, increases the dwelling size demanded by each consumer while also increasing the struc-tural density of buildings. If the dwelling size effect dominates, there could be fewer households on each acre, even with taller buildings on each acre, and a city of a given total household population could expand in radius, causing more, not less, sprawl.

The above models being static, they cannot shed light on the dynamic effects of taxes. Dynamic analyses that can treat conversions involving buildings and land are needed. A paper by Arnott (1998) is a step in this direction and provides a good summary of earlier literature.[3] He consid-ered how to devise a neutral tax on a single developer/landowner rather than devise such a tax system for a whole land market. The developer in question has a unit of vacant land to build on and he decides, under perfect foresight, when to build and at what structural density. However, once he builds, the building remains undemolished forever. Arnott looks for a neutral tax in this context, a tax that is neutral with respect to the timing (when to develop the unit of vacant land) as well as the density of development, and also raises the desired revenue. He shows how to achieve such neutrality by the coordinated setting of three separate taxes, all related to some concept of value. The first tax is on the *pre-development value of the land*, defined as 'what the land is worth in its vacant state before it is developed'. The second tax is on the *post-development residual site value*, defined as 'property value minus the depreciated cost of the structure on the site'. The third tax is a subsidy on the structural capital employed on the site.

The purpose of the present chapter is to present a more general and complete theoretical framework and empirically useful modeling tool for analyzing alternative tax structures on buildings and land over an entire real estate market. Using such a framework in a dynamic context, it should be possible to devise alternative tax structures and make revenue-neutral comparisons among them, quantifying the deadweight losses of these alternative tax structures. Clearly, a dynamic model properly grounded in economic theory is the appropriate approach for such a research program. To this end, I will use the model that I have developed in earlier work with Richard Arnott, and I will modify it to deal with problems of property taxation and optimal property taxation.[4]

The chapter is organized as follows. Section 2 presents the structure of the model and the solution properties in the case where there are no taxes on buildings and land. (Appendix A is a technical appendix that explains how some of the relationships used in the model are derived.) Appendix B describes a computational algorithm (Anas and Choi, 2001) that was designed to solve the dynamic simulation model with exogenously specified taxes on building submarkets (or building types) and on land.

Then, in section 3, the model is stripped down to its bare essentials in order to investigate several of its simple properties in the presence of alternative taxation schemes for stationary state dynamics. By performing comparative statics on such a stationary state, we compare a tax on undeveloped land to a conventional property tax that falls on land and buildings at the same rate. It is shown that the conventional tax causes inefficient use of structural capital, because it speeds up the construction–demolition cycle, shortening the lives of buildings. In the *intensive margin* of building replacement, this results in excessive use of structural capital over time on each unit amount of land. But the conventional tax also works in the *extensive margin*, resulting in a lower stock of buildings (fewer units of land are developed). Hence, unlike what is commonly believed, the total amount of structural capital used over time would decrease only if the extensive margin effect dominated the intensive margin effect. Section 3 also shows that the tax on undeveloped land works in the opposite way, offsetting (even though imperfectly) the inefficiencies of the conventional tax. (These results are summarized in the text and the details of the analysis are presented in Appendix C.) The Mills or Brueckner models discussed earlier are static models and thus ignore the intensive margin of building replacement, although they treat the other intensive margin of structural density. The intensive margin of building replacement is also absent from Arnott's model which also treats structural density but does not consider demolition. In his model, development is clay-putty: once buildings are constructed they remain in place forever.

Section 4 presents a generalized optimal taxation problem that can be solved using an extended formulation of the dynamic model of section 2. In this formulation, there is a different tax rate on vacant land and on each building type and these taxes can be optimized for every year over a planning period. The 'optimal taxation problem' is a well-known textbook problem in economics. In this textbook version, it is recognized that the price elasticity of demand varies a great deal from commodity to commodity. Efficiency requires levying a higher tax rate on those commodities for which the demand is relatively price-inelastic and a lower tax rate on those for which the demand is relatively price-elastic. How does the setting of this textbook problem differ from that of the real estate market with land? It would be natural to view buildings in different submarkets and vacant land in different locations as being different commodities. As explained earlier, we also know that the price elasticities of demand for these buildings and land will differ, as will also the price elasticities of supply. In that sense, our problem is similar to the textbook problem but somewhat more complex. We leave solution of this optimal taxation problem to future work. Part of the research program is to embed the simulation procedure described in section 2 into a more general algorithm that can determine the optimal tax rates taking the interdependent demand and supply elasticities into account.

2   STRUCTURE OF THE MODEL

We now turn to a description of the simulation model.[5] The description presented here follows closely that in Anas *et al.* (2000).[6]

Basic Assumptions

Time consists of periods of equal length (years). Time t denotes the start of year t and time $t + 1$, the end of year t. $t = 0$ denotes the present (initial) year. Variables change only at the start or end of each year. The model incorporates idiosyncratic uncertainty on both the demand and the supply sides. For example, at the start of each year, consumers of buildings learn the idiosyncratic components of their tastes, earn incomes, choose their most preferred submarket and pay rents, while investors receive rents and bid on vacant land or building assets determining asset prices, prior to learning their idiosyncratic costs.[7] Idiosyncratic costs of maintenance for buildings for the year, are revealed a little after the start of a year, while costs of construction, structural conversion or demolition are revealed just before the end of a year. The timeline in Table 1.1 illustrates the sequence in investor and consumer actions and in the revelation of information within a year. The left side shows when a particular item of information is revealed and the right side shows the decisions that follow.

The building stock is divided into $k = 1 \dots K$ building types or submarkets. Each submarket represents a different combination of size (such as floor space), physical quality, structural density or location; $k = 0$ represents vacant land.[8] Buildings consist of structure and land. Buildings can be created from land via construction or from buildings of other types via structural conversions. Land is created by demolitions of buildings. m_{0k} is the lot size (or land needed per unit building) in submarket k and $\dfrac{1}{m_{0k}}$ is *construction density*. $m_{kk'}$, for $k > 0$, is the number of building units of type k, used up in the conversion process, to create one unit of type k', and $\dfrac{1}{m_{kk'}}$ is the $k \to k'$ *conversion density*. Of course, $m_{kk} = 1$ for all $k > 0$. The vector $\mathbf{S}_t = [S_{0t}, S_{1t}, \dots, S_{Kt}]$ is the stock (number of unit buildings[9]) in each submarket (or land for $k = 0$) in year t. The total amount of land (vacant plus occupied by buildings) is A_t and is exogenous for each t. We will normally assume that $A_t = A$ for each year t. $\mathbf{V}_t = [V_{0t}, V_{1t}, \dots, V_{Kt}]$ is the vector of asset prices for buildings and land in year t, and $\mathbf{R}_t = [R_{0t}, R_{1t}, \dots, R_{Kt}]$ is the vector of land and building rents (per unit building) in year t. The asset price of a unit building includes the value of the land on which the unit is built. The rent for vacant land, R_{0t}, is exogenously given for each t and the initial stock vector $\mathbf{S}_0$ is exogenous as an initial condition.[10] All other elements of the rent, stock and asset price vectors are endogenous for each t.

As noted, a unique feature of the model is that it treats stochastic heterogeneity at the level of individual agents on both the demand and the supply sides of the market. The chief reason for doing so is to achieve empirical realism in applied studies (for example, Anas and Arnott, 1993c,1994, 1997) as well as smooth computational solutions. On the demand side, consumers who belong to the same group differ in the idiosyncratic taste constants they attach to building submarkets. On the supply side, building units differ in idiosyncratic costs of maintenance for occupied and vacant units as well as in the costs of converting those units to land or to other units. Similarly, there are idiosyncratic costs in converting land to buildings.

We assume that each idiosyncratic utility or cost is a draw each year from the following double exponential distribution, known as the Gumbel and given by (1.1) below. We assume that all agents know the distribution of utility or cost and its mean for each alternative, but learn the value of their idiosyncratic deviation from the mean only after it is realized.

$$G(x < z) = \exp - [\exp - \gamma(z - \eta], \gamma > 0, \qquad (1.1)$$

where x stands for a random realization of idiosyncratic utility or cost. The distribution has mode η. We assume $E[x] = \eta + \frac{g}{\gamma} = 0$ (by imposing $\eta = -\frac{g}{\gamma}$) where $g = 0.5772$ is Euler's constant. The variance is $Var[x]$ $= \frac{\pi^2}{6\gamma^2}$; γ^2 is inversely proportional to the variance, and is called the *dispersion parameter* or the *heterogeneity coefficient*. As $\frac{1}{\gamma^2} \to 0$, idiosyncratic heterogeneity vanishes and all decision makers (consumers or investors) most prefer the same choice. And as $\frac{1}{\gamma^2} \to \infty$, idiosyncratic heterogeneity swamps nonrandom effects, making choices extremely heterogeneous. Then all choices are most preferred with the same probability.

Closure property of equation 1.1
The Gumbel distribution given by (1.1) has the property that it is closed under the maximization operation. Hence, if n random variates $(x_1, x_2, x_3, ..., x_n)$ are each i.i.d. with means $(X_1, X_2, X_3, ..., X_n)$ and dispersion parameter γ according to (1.1), then the random variate max $(x_1, x_2, x_3, ..., x_n)$ is also distributed according to (1.1) with mode $\frac{1}{\gamma} \ln\Sigma_{i=1...n} \exp(\gamma X_i) + \text{constant}$ and dispersion parameter γ. The proof is in Appendix A.

This closure property implies, for example, that the maximized objective in a population of maximizing agents has the same distribution as the *un*maximized objective has in the same population of agents. Thus aggregation across maximizing agents does not affect the ex post distribution of the maximized objective. This further implies that welfare comparisons can be made knowing that two different policies which affect individual objectives will not affect the variance of the maximized objective in the population of agents.

While the model will be stochastic at the level of consumers and investors as explained above, there is no uncertainty at the aggregate level. Hence rents, asset prices and stocks are all obtained as deterministic variables. Asset prices are deterministic because risk-neutral investors bid on buildings and on land before the uncertainty in costs is realized. Hence, at the time of bidding, investors are ex ante identical and make the same bids. The model solves for the expected stock distribution as a function of deterministic asset prices and for the expected allocation of households among submarkets as a function of deterministic rents.

Demand Side: Consumers

Consumers view submarkets as internally homogeneous. Hence they are indifferent about choice within a submarket. After learning his idiosyncratic realization of utilities for each submarket for that year, a consumer chooses the most-preferred submarket and randomly selects a unit building to rent within that submarket. Each consumer re-evaluates his choice at the start of each period and can costlessly relocate. We treat consumers as myopic and we assume that they neither borrow nor save. We divide them into $h = 1...H$ demand groups according to socioeconomic types (income, family size, age of household head or race). $\mathbf{N}_t = [N_{1t},...,N_{Ht}]$ is the exogenous vector of the number of consumers per year in each demand group; $\mathbf{y}_t = [y_{1t},...,y_{Ht}]$ is the exogenous income of a consumer in demand group h in year t;[11] $\mathbf{Y}_t = [Y_{1t},...,Y_{Kt}]$ is a vector of submarket qualities and β_h is the marginal utility of quality. Then, $\hat{U}_{hkt} = U_{hkt} + u_{hkt}$ is the utility a consumer enjoys from renting a unit building in submarket k in year t. $U_{hkt} = y_{ht} - R_{kt} + \beta_h Y_{kt}$ is the utility of submarket k which is common to all consumers of type h; u_{hkt} measures an idiosyncratic submarket-specific utility varying around mean utility U_{hkt} for consumers of type h. For each consumer of type h, idiosyncratic utilities $\mathbf{u}_h = [u_{h1t},..., u_{hKt}]$ are drawn from (1.1) at the start of each year with dispersion parameter δ_{ht} (that is, $\gamma \equiv \delta_{ht}$ in (1.1)). Then the probability that a type h consumer selects submarket k is $P_{hkt} = \text{Prob.}[U_{hkt} + u_{hkt} > U_{hst} + u_{hst}; \forall s \neq k]$, with $\Sigma_{k=1...K} P_{hkt} = 1$. Appendix A presents the proof that imposing (1.1) on each u_{hkt} (with mean 0) yields the multinomial logit choice probabilities:

$$P_{hkt}(\mathbf{R}_t) = \frac{\exp(\delta_{ht} U_{hkt})}{\Sigma_{z=1...K} \exp(\delta_{ht} U_{hzt})}; \Sigma_{z=1...K} P_{hzt} = 1. \tag{1.2}$$

Appendix A also proves that, under the closure property of (1.1) described above, the ex ante expected value of the maximized utility level (or expected consumer surplus) of a consumer in group h at the start of year t is:

$$\Psi_{ht}(\mathbf{R}_t) = E[\max(U_{hkt} + u_{hkt}; k = 1...K)] = \frac{1}{\delta_{ht}} \ln \Sigma_{z=1...K} \exp(\delta_{ht} U_{hzt}). \tag{1.3}$$

Supply Side: Investors

Investors are risk-neutral and perfectly competitive. As shown in Table 1.1, investors value buildings or land at the beginning of each year, knowing only the probability distribution of the idiosyncratic costs they will encounter later. Let $\mathbf{C}_t = [C_{kk't}]$ be the $(K+1) \times (K+1)$ matrix of expected k to k' conversion costs for $t > 0$, and let $\mathbf{c}_t = [c_{kk't}]$ be the corresponding $(K+1) \times (K+1)$ matrix of idiosyncratic conversion costs per unit of type k' building for $t > 0$, measured as a deviation from the expected cost. These

Table 1.1   Information and the actions of investors and consumers

Time	State of information	Investor and consumer actions
t	$\mathbf{R}_t, \mathbf{V}_{t+1}$ are revealed. Investors know the expected values $\mathbf{C}_t, \mathbf{D}_t$ of conversion and maintenance costs and their dispersions $\mathbf{\Phi}_t$ and $\mathbf{\phi}_t$.	Risk-neutral investors bid on housing units and land under perfect foresight on prices and under uncertainty about costs, determining asset prices $\mathbf{V}_t$, on the basis of $\mathbf{R}_t, \mathbf{V}_{t+1}, \mathbf{C}_t, \mathbf{D}_t, \mathbf{\Phi}_t$ and $\mathbf{\phi}_t$.
	Consumers earn their income $\mathbf{y}_t$ and know their taste premium values of housing submarkets $\mathbf{Y}_t$.	
$t + \varepsilon$	Idiosyncratic maintenance costs $\mathbf{d}_t$, for vacancy and occupancy are revealed for each housing unit as a draw from the double exponential with dispersions $\mathbf{\phi}_t$.	Investors decide, on the basis of rents, $\mathbf{R}_t$, and revealed maintenance costs, $\mathbf{D}_t + \mathbf{d}_t$, whether to keep a unit vacant or let it to a tenant.
	Idiosyncratic tastes $\mathbf{u}_t$ are revealed to consumers as draws from the double exponential with dispersions $\mathbf{\delta}_t$.	Consumers choose to rent in the most-preferred submarket, on the basis of net income $\mathbf{y}_t - \mathbf{R}_t$, taste premia, $\mathbf{Y}_t$ and the revealed idiosyncratic utilities $\mathbf{u}_t$.
$t + 1 - \varepsilon$	Idiosyncratic conversion costs, $\mathbf{c}_t$, are revealed for each feasible $k \to k' \in B(k)$ conversion of a unit, as a draw from the double exponential with dispersions $\mathbf{\Phi}_t$.	Investors undertake the most profitable conversion on the basis of the revealed conversion costs $\mathbf{C}_t + \mathbf{c}_t$ and $\mathbf{V}_{t+1}$.
$t + 1$	$\mathbf{R}_{t+1}, \mathbf{V}_{t+2}$ are revealed . . .	Risk-neutral investors bid on housing units and land . . .

Note: Timeline indicating flow of information and actions of market agents within one year: from time $t \to t + 1$ ($\varepsilon > 0$ is a very small constant).

are revealed right before the end of year t. Also let $\mathbf{D}_{ot} = [D_{1ot},...,D_{Kot}]$, $\mathbf{D}_{vt} = [D_{1vt},...,D_{Kvt}]$, be the expected maintenance costs for type k $(k>0)$ occupied and vacant units common to investors, with $\mathbf{d}_{ot} = [d_{1ot},...,d_{Kot}]$, $\mathbf{d}_{vt} = [d_{1vt},...,d_{Kvt}]$, the idiosyncratic deviations from the respective expected costs. These are revealed right after the start of year t. For each investor, the $-c_{kk't}$ and the $-d_{kot}$, $-d_{kvt}$ are drawn from (1.1) for each submarket and for land with dispersion parameters Φ_{kt} and ϕ_{kt}, and means 0, respectively. Let $\pi_{kot} = R_{kt} - D_{kot} - d_{kot}$ $(\pi_{kvt} = -D_{kvt} - d_{kvt})$ be the profits from keeping a type k unit $(k>0)$ occupied (vacant) during year t. Then the probability that a unit in submarket $k>0$ will be let to a consumer for year t is $q_{kot} = $ Prob. $[\pi_{kot} > \pi_{kvt}]$. The procedure of Appendix A gives the binomial logit:

$$q_{kot}(R_{kt}) = \frac{\exp\phi_{kt}(R_{kt} - D_{kot})}{\exp\phi_{kt}(R_{kt} - D_{kot}) + \exp\phi_{kt}(- D_{kvt})}; q_{kvt}(R_{kt}) = 1 - q_{kot}(R_{kt}). \quad (1.4)$$

From Appendix A, under the closure property, the expected profit of this occupancy decision at the start of year t is

$$\omega_{kt}(R_{kt}) \equiv E[\max(\pi_{kot}, \pi_{kvt})] = \frac{1}{\phi_{kt}}\ln[\exp\phi_{kt}(R_{kt} - D_{kot}) +$$

$$\exp\phi_{kt}(-D_{kvt})]. \quad (1.5)$$

For vacant land, we assume that it can always be rented for the exogenous land rent. Hence $\omega_{0t}(R_{0t}) \equiv R_{0t}$. Now note that year-end conversion profits from type k to type k' asset, discounted to the start of year t are $\Pi_{kk't} = \frac{V_{k't+1} - C_{kk't}}{(1 + r)m_{kk'}} - c_{kk't}$. The probability that an investor who holds asset type $k = 0,1,...,K$ at the start of year t will choose to convert to type k' just before the end of year t is $Q_{kk't} = $ Prob.$[\Pi_{kk't} > \Pi_{kst}; \forall s \in B(k)]$ for all $k' \in B(k)$, where $B(k)$ is the set of asset types to which a type k asset can be converted and $Q_{kk't} = 0$ for all $k' \notin B(k)$.

Figure 1.1 illustrates two (of many) possible ways of defining the sets $B(k)$, for three building types and land. We will refer to these as alternative *conversion technologies*. For realism, it should be assumed that $k \in B(k)$, for each k, so that it is always possible to keep a building at its current submarket state by incurring expenditure C_{kkt}. Figure 1.1a shows a quality hierarchy of buildings. Supposing that structural densities are the same for all these buildings, they differ only in structural quality. Buildings are constructed at the highest quality (quality 3 in the example of the figure) and, depending on the cost shocks experienced, can either stay in the same quality level or deteriorate only one quality interval per time period. Only the lowest quality buildings can be demolished. Thus a quality cycle is implied where buildings deteriorate gradually (and some faster than others,

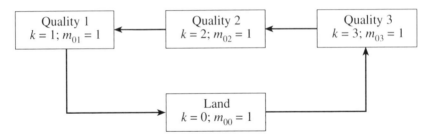

Note: Buildings are of the same structural density but differ only in quality. They deteriorate in quality, become demolished at the lowest quality and new housing is built at the highest quality: $B(0) = \{0,3\}$, $B(1) = \{0,1\}$, $B(2) = \{1,2\}$, $B(3) = \{2,3\}$.

Figure 1.1a   Quality cycle with constant structural density

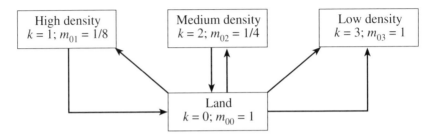

Note: Buildings do not deteriorate in quality. Buildings are of different structural densities that cannot be directly converted to one another. Each housing type can be demolished and any of the three types can be rebuilt in its place: $B(0) = \{0,1,2,3\}$, $B(1) = \{0,1\}$, $B(2) = \{0,2\}$, $B(3) = \{0,3\}$.

Figure 1.1b   Density cycle with constant quality

depending on idiosyncratic cost shocks experienced) until they are demolished and the new highest quality buildings are built on the land released by the demolition. So the owner of the lowest quality building can change his asset to a highest quality building over at least two periods: he demolishes in period 1 and builds the highest quality building in period 2. Figure 1.1b illustrates a situation in which there are three buildings that differ in structural density (unlike the first part of the figure) but not in quality. Each structural density can be demolished or constructed. To change from one structural density to another on the same land requires at least two periods: the existing structural density is demolished in the current period and the desired structural density is constructed in the next period.

The procedure of Appendix A now yields the following multinomial logit for year-end conversion probabilities in year t (that is, the probability that an owner of a type k asset will convert it to a type k' in year t):

$$Q_{kk't}(\mathbf{V}_{t+1}) = \frac{b(k',k)\exp\Phi_{kt}\dfrac{V_{k't+1} - C_{kk't}}{(1+r)m_{kk'}}}{\Sigma_{s=0,1...K}b(s,k)\exp\Phi_{kt}\dfrac{V_{st+1} - C_{kst}}{(1+r)m_{ks}}}; \Sigma_{k'=0,1...K}Q_{kk't} = 1. \quad (1.6)$$

where $b(k',k) \equiv 1$ if $k' \in B(k)$, and $b(k',k) \equiv 0$ if $k' \notin B(k)$. Those owners who undertake the conversion are those who draw (are shocked by) a low idiosyncratic conversion cost $c_{kk't}$. From Appendix A, applying the closure property, the expected discounted ex ante conversion profit from a type k unit at the start of t is:

$$\Omega_{kt}(\mathbf{V}_{t+1}) = E[\max(\Pi_{kk't}; \forall k' \in B(k))] = \frac{1}{\Phi_{kt}} \ln \Sigma_{s=0,1...K} b(s,k)\exp\Phi_{kt}$$

$$\times \frac{V_{st+1} - C_{kst}}{(1+r)m_{ks}}. \quad (1.7)$$

Dynamic Market Equilibrium

We will now define the dynamic market equilibrium problem for a real estate market as consisting of two phases. To do so, we must specify how the exogenous variables driving the market such as incomes, demand group populations and costs will be changing over time. Suppose that these variables change in some arbitrary pattern for an extended period, with each variable eventually settling on a stationary value thereafter. Then the response of the real estate market will consist of two phases. In phase 1, the real estate market adjusts to the arbitrary time profile of the exogenous variables, by evolving from the given initial stocks of buildings and vacant land to an eventual stationary state of stocks, rents and asset prices. This adjustment requires stocks, rents and asset prices to change year by year until they all become stationary at some terminal year T and remain stationary thereafter. This stationary phase is phase 2.

Solving the dynamic equilibrium problem requires doing three things, illustrated in Figures 1.2 and 1.3. First, one must solve for the stationary (phase 2) stocks, rents and asset prices and this is independent of any initial conditions. This phase 2 solution can be obtained conditional on the stationary values of the exogenous variables only. Second, one must solve for the non-stationary (phase 1) stocks, rents and asset prices given only the stationary asset prices obtained from phase 2 and the initial year stocks.

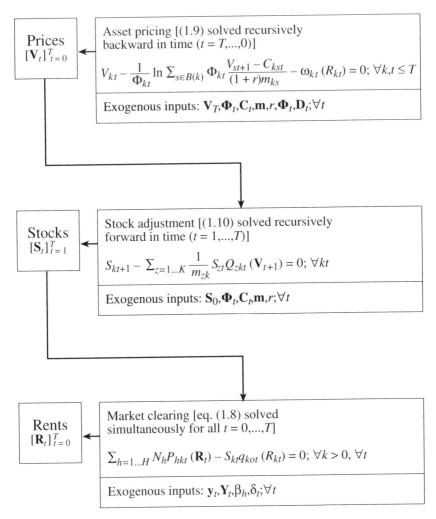

Figure 1.2   Block-recursive structure of dynamic housing market equilibrium

Third, one must pin down a reasonable approximation for the value of the terminal year T (that is, for the length of phase 1), so that stocks, rents and asset prices for T are sufficiently close to their stationary (phase 2) values. This is done simply by extending the non-stationary phase 1 until the difference between the year T and corresponding stationary variables is as small as possible (Figure 1.3). The algorithm that we have devised (Anas and Choi, 2001) and which is described in Appendix B in fact implements

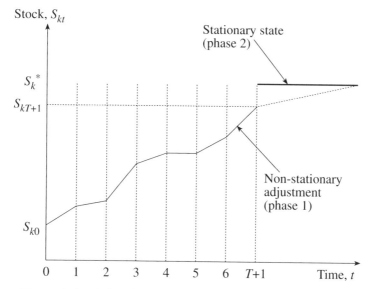

Note: The terminal period gap in stock of type k with predetermined terminal period T, is $|S_k^* - S_{kT+1}|$, where S_k^* is the stationary equilibrium stock; the longer the choice of terminal time period, T, the smaller the gap becomes.

Figure 1.3   Stock adjustment and terminal gap

this solution procedure. In this section, we will just focus on the formal statement of this two-phase dynamic equilibrium problem so that the solution procedure's basic structure can be seen and discussed in more detail.

Phase 1 (finite horizon non-stationary dynamic equilibrium)
Given the initial stock vector $\mathbf{S}_0$, the exogenous vacant land rent series R_{0t}, $t = 0,1,2...T$, all other exogenous vectors, matrices, sets $B(k)$ and a vector of end-of-terminal-year asset prices, $\mathbf{V}_{T+1}$, a dynamic equilibrium $[\mathbf{S}_t, \mathbf{V}_t, \mathbf{R}_t]_{t=0}^T$ satisfies (1.8), (1.9) and (1.10):

$$\Sigma_{h=1...H} N_{ht} P_{hkt}(\mathbf{R}_t) - S_{kt} q_{kot}(R_{kt}) = 0; \, k = 1,...,K; \, t = 0, 1,...,T. \quad (1.8)$$

$$V_{kt} - \Omega_{kt}(\mathbf{V}_{t+1}) - \omega_{kt}(R_{kt}) = 0; \, k = 0,1,...,K; \, t = 0, 1,...,T. \quad (1.9)$$

$$S_{kt+1} - \Sigma_{z=0,1,...K} \frac{1}{m_{zk}} S_{zt} Q_{zkt}(\mathbf{V}_{t+1}) = 0; \, k = 0,1,...,K; \, t = 0, 1,...,T. \quad (1.10)$$

Phase 2 (infinite horizon stationary dynamic equilibrium)
Removing the time subscripts, and letting $\mathbf{R}$ and $\mathbf{V}$ denote the rents and year-end asset prices respectively and letting $\mathbf{S}$ be the stationary stocks, the

dynamic equilibrium conditions in the stationary state ($t > T$) are written as:

$$\Sigma_{h=1...H} N_h P_{hk}(\mathbf{R}) - S_k q_{ko}(R_k) = 0; \; k = 1,...,K. \quad (1.11)$$

$$V_k - \Omega_k(\mathbf{V}) - \omega_k(R_k) = 0; \; k = 0,1,...,K. \quad (1.12)$$

$$S_k - \Sigma_{z=0,1,...,K} \frac{1}{m_{zk}} S_z Q_{zk}(\mathbf{V}) = 0; \; k = 0,1,...,K. \quad (1.13)$$

Anas *et al.* (2000) have used a concave mathematical programming approach to prove that the above two-phase problem has a solution that is a welfare maximum (that is, Pareto efficient). We now turn to a sketch of the solution procedure. Note that there are *3K + 2* equations for each *t < T* and for the stationary state. These equations have a block recursive structure, as shown in Figure 1.2. Equations (1.8) (and (1.11)) are the *market-clearing* conditions and state that the quantity of building units demanded equals the supply of building units offered for rent in each submarket and each year. Given some sequence of stocks, $[\mathbf{S}_t]_{t=0}^T$, these can be solved simultaneously for tentative equilibrium market-clearing rents $[\mathbf{R}_t]_{t=0}^T$. Equations (1.9) are the *zero profit* conditions or *asset bid–price* equations. They state that the asset prices are determined by competitive bidding such that zero ex ante economic profits accrue to each investor at the start of each year (or, equivalently, a normal expected rate of return equal to the exogenous interest rate, *r*, is earned.) Given the terminal asset prices $\mathbf{V}_{T+1}$ and the rents $[\mathbf{R}_t]_{t=0}^T$ from the previous step, equations (1.9) can be solved simultaneously for each *t* by backward recursion, for $t = T, T-1, T-2,...,1,0$, to find tentative equilibrium asset price series $[\mathbf{V}_t]_{t=0}^T$. Equations (1.10) are the Markovian *stock adjustment* equations. For each *t*, there are *K + 1* such equations, but one becomes redundant by the assumption that the total (vacant plus built-up) land is a time-invariant constant, A: $\Sigma_{z=0,1,...,K} m_{0z} S_{zt} = A$.[12] Given the asset prices $[\mathbf{V}_t]_{t=1}^T$, (1.10) are solved by forward recursion for $t = 1,...,T-2, T-1,T$ to calculate new stocks $[\mathbf{S}_t]_{t=1}^T$. In an iterative solution algorithm, one revisits (1.8) with these new stocks, repeating the loop, (1.8)→(1.9)→(1.10)→(1.8)→... (see Figure 1.2). The process continues until (1.8), (1.9) and (1.10) are jointly satisfied for all *t*.

3   COMPARISON OF THE CONVENTIONAL TAX WITH A TAX ON UNDEVELOPED LAND

It is helpful to examine the role of property taxation within the model presented in section 2. In order to do so, it is helpful to analyze initially a version of the model stripped down to its bare essentials. Suppose, for example, that $K=1$ (only one type of building exists). Then the model simplifies to a simple housing–land cycle (as in Anas and Arnott, 1993a, or its neoclassical version in Anas and Arnott, 1993b). In any one year, some buildings are constructed on vacant land (if the investor owning the land is shocked by a low construction cost) while other buildings are demolished to create vacant land (if the owner is shocked by a low demolition cost or a high maintenance cost). At stationary state, the flow of constructions must equal the flow of demolitions in each year so that the stock of vacant land and the stock of buildings is constant over time. Given this situation, which is the simplest version of the model, we can analyze the effects of a variety of tax schemes on the market. We will here examine two cases. One is the conventional ad valorem property tax that is levied at the same rate on both assets (vacant land and buildings). The other is a tax on vacant land only. What are the effects of such taxes on the *land-to-building-to-land* conversion cycle? What are their effects on the rent for buildings and on the asset prices of land and of buildings?

The Conventional Property Tax

With only one building type and only one land market, the model equations simplify as follows. We also assume that all buildings are fully occupied (no vacancy rate). The tax is assumed paid at the beginning of each year:

$$D(R_1) - S_1 = 0, \tag{1.14}$$

$$(1+\theta)\,V_0 - \frac{1}{\Phi_0}\ln\left(e^{\Phi_0\frac{V_0-C_{00}}{1+r}} + e^{\Phi\frac{V_1-C_{01}}{1+r}}\right) - R_0 = 0, \tag{1.15}$$

$$(1+\theta)\,V_1 - \frac{1}{\Phi_1}\ln\left(e^{\Phi_1\frac{V_1-C_{11}}{1+r}} + e^{\Phi_1\frac{V_0-C_{10}}{1+r}}\right) - R_1 = 0, \tag{1.16}$$

$$S_0 Q_{01} - S_1 Q_{10} = 0, \tag{1.17}$$

$$S_0 + S_1 - A = 0. \tag{1.18}$$

Let us review the notation. $D(R_1)$ is any downward-sloping aggregate demand function for building units as a function of the rent for buildings. As explained earlier, R_0, the rent on vacant land, is exogenous and could be taken as zero without any loss of generality. A is the total amount of land available, with S_0 and S_1 the stocks of vacant land and buildings, respectively. The structural density of buildings is assumed to be unity and there is no loss of generality since there is only one building type. V_0 and V_1 are the asset prices for vacant land and for a unit building, respectively. Q_{01} and Q_{10} are the construction and demolition probabilities, respectively (namely, the probabilities that in any one year a unit building will be demolished, releasing a unit amount of land and the probability that a unit amount of vacant land will be built on, creating a unit building). These probabilities are given by the following binary logit models:

$$Q_{01} = \frac{e^{\Phi_0 \frac{V_1 - C_{01}}{1 + r}}}{e^{\Phi_0 \frac{V_1 - C_{01}}{1 + r}} + e^{\Phi_0 \frac{V_0 - C_{00}}{1 + r}}} \text{ and } Q_{10} = \frac{e^{\Phi_1 \frac{V_0 - C_{10}}{1 + r}}}{e^{\Phi_1 \frac{V_0 - C_{10}}{1 + r}} + e^{\Phi_1 \frac{V_1 - C_{11}}{1 + r}}} \qquad (1.19)$$

It is useful to rewrite these as follows, by dividing numerator and denominator with the second exponential in the denominators:

$$Q_{01} = \frac{e^{\Phi_0 \frac{V_1 - V_0 - (C_{01} - C_{00})}{1 + r}}}{1 + e^{\Phi_0 \frac{V_1 - V_0 - (C_{01} - C_{00})}{1 + r}}} \text{ and } Q_{10} = \frac{e^{\Phi_1 \frac{V_0 - V_1 - (C_{10} - C_{11})}{1 + r}}}{1 + e^{\Phi_1 \frac{V_0 - V_1 - (C_{10} - C_{11})}{1 + r}}} \qquad (1.19')$$

This second way of writing things shows explicitly that the probability of construction on vacant land is an increasing function of the difference between the asset price of a building and the asset price of land, and that the probability of demolition is an increasing function of the difference between the asset price of land and the asset price of a building. C_{00}, C_{10}, C_{01}, C_{11} are the average (non-idiosyncratic) costs of vacant land maintenance, demolition, construction and unit building maintenance, respectively; Φ_0 and Φ_1 are the dispersions of the idiosyncratic costs associated with land and buildings, respectively; r is the interest rate and θ is the property tax rate.

Equation (1.14) is the market-clearing condition ensuring that the demand for buildings equals the stock; (1.15) and (1.16) are the after-tax asset price equations for land and buildings, respectively. These equations state that assets (vacant land and buildings) are valued in such a way that investors make only a normal rate of return after taking into account taxes, rents and expected profits from future conversions. Equation (1.17) is the stationary state condition stating that the expected quantity of buildings that are demolished and the expected quantity of vacant land that is developed are equal. Finally, (1.18) ensures that buildings and vacant land do not exceed the given total land units, A.

Equations (1.14)–(1.18) comprise a five-equation system that must be solved for R_1, V_0, V_1, S_0, S_1. This problem easily yields to conventional comparative static analysis. Appendix C provides the details. The key for deriving the result is first to show that $\frac{dR_1}{d\theta} > 0$. It states that an increase in the ad valorem tax rate increases the rent on buildings. Using this in equation (1.14), it follows that $\frac{dS_1}{d\theta}<0$: the property tax results in a lower

stock of buildings. Hence, from (1.18), $\frac{dS_0}{d\theta}>0,$ which establishes that

more land is held vacant. Now note from (1.17) that $\frac{S_0}{S_1}=\frac{Q_{10}}{Q_{01}}.$ Since the left

side is increased by a higher θ, so the right side must increase also. It is also

easy to establish the intuitive results that $\frac{dV_0}{d\theta}<0$ and $\frac{dV_1}{d\theta}<0$: the

property tax reduces the value of vacant land and of buildings. More

important for the result we are about to establish, $\frac{d(V_1-V_0)}{d\theta}<0.$

This means that the tax increases the value of vacant land relative to the value of a unit building. Therefore the rate of construction falls and the rate of demolition rises, as one can see by inspection of (1.19′) and this is consistent with the stock of vacant land increasing at the expense of the stock of buildings. Because the rate of demolition increases while the rate of construction falls, the average age of standing buildings falls. Hence, as pointed out earlier, the conventional property tax – operating in the intensive margin – speeds up the demolition–construction cycle, shortening the life span of buildings while, in the extensive margin, the property tax reduces the building stock.

   This finding enriches the conventional view of the property tax. It is widely recognized that the property tax increases the cost of structural capital relative to the cost of land. This fact has been widely touted by observing that developers would use less structural capital relative to land when constructing buildings on a given amount of land. But this perspective comes from models in which demolition and reconstruction are ignored. Our finding says that, *ceteris paribus*, buildings would not last as long with a conventional property tax as without it. Hence, because the conventional property tax encourages more demolitions and subsequent reconstruction, it causes an excessive use of structural capital over time. If this excessive use of capital over time in the intensive margin outweighs the reduced use of capital due to fewer buildings in the extensive margin (or due to lower structural density), then the property tax increases rather than decreases the total use of capital over time.

A Tax on Vacant Land

Next we will assume that there is only one tax and it is levied on vacant land. This is same as the *ad valorem tax on pre-development land value* encountered in the literature. Note, first, that this will change only equations (1.15) and

(1.16). In the case of (1.16) the tax rate θ disappears (set it to zero) since buildings are not taxed. In (1.15) there is actually no change and θ is now replaced by θ_0, which now stands for the tax rate levied on vacant land value. The effects of this tax on vacant land value are the opposite of the effects of the conventional tax analyzed above. It is easy to grasp intuitively and easy to prove analytically that the tax decreases the stock of vacant land because it increases the cost of holding vacant land. Hence the tax increases the stock of buildings: $\dfrac{dS_0}{d\theta_0} < 0$ and $\dfrac{dS_1}{d\theta_0} > 0$. Since the stock of buildings increases, rent falls: $\dfrac{dR_1}{d\theta_0} < 0$. Both building and vacant land asset prices fall: $\dfrac{dV_0}{d\theta_0} < 0$ and $\dfrac{dV_1}{d\theta_0} < 0$, but the value of a building is increased relative to that of land: $\dfrac{d(V_1 - V_0)}{d\theta_0} > 0$. Therefore the rate of construction rises and the rate of demolition falls. Thus this unconventional tax on vacant land slows down the demolition–reconstruction cycle, lengthening the life span of buildings. The average age of standing buildings increases. Hence, because this unconventional tax on vacant land encourages fewer demolitions and subsequent reconstruction, it discourages an excessive use of structural capital over time. The effects of the tax on vacant land are then the opposite of those of the conventional property tax.

4   AN OPTIMAL TAXATION PROBLEM FOR REAL ESTATE MARKETS

How would the dynamic equilibrium formulation studied in section 2 change in the presence of taxes on buildings and land? Note, first, that the formulation captures most key variables that are active in real estate markets. It is possible, within this framework, to introduce a variety of tax/subsidy instruments on the following, for example: (a) rents, (b) asset prices, (c) costs of construction, demolition, maintenance and other conversions, (d) net revenues of investors in buildings and land (that is, profit taxes) and (e) option values. Furthermore, in each case, taxes can be lump sum or ad valorem. (For example, a lump sum tax becomes due when a particular conversion is made or an ad valorem tax on conversion profits is levied.) Thus it is possible – in principle – to pose a very general problem in which optimal tax policies are selected by picking and choosing from a large menu of such tax instruments that can be treated within the model.

Special assumptions that are built into the model will limit conclusions we may draw about the effects of some taxation schemes. For example, the model treats real estate consumers as having linear-in-income utility functions.[13] Hence there would be no income effects from certain taxes/subsidies on consumers (such as income taxes). The same result holds on the supply side as well, because we have modeled investors as risk-neutral.

To keep things simple, we will here focus only on ad valorem taxes on asset prices. Thus suppose that θ_{kt} is the tax rate on a type k asset (vacant land or building) in year t. Then each asset of type k has a tax cost of $\theta_{kt}V_{kt}$. Equation (1.9), the asset-bid price (or asset valuation) equation, now becomes modified if we deduct the cost of the tax (assumed paid at the beginning of each year). This modified equation is

$$V_{kt} - \frac{1}{1+\theta_{kt}}[\Omega_{kt}(\mathbf{V}_{t+1}) + \omega_{kt}(R_{kt})] = 0. \tag{1.9'}$$

The revenue raised in year t is then $\Sigma_{k=0}^{K}\theta_{kt}V_{kt}S_{kt}$. We can now set up a welfare optimization problem over the infinite time horizon $t=0,1,2...T$, $T+1$, $T+2,...\infty$, where T is the terminal time T of phase I.

$$\text{Maximize } \tilde{Z} = \Sigma_{t=0}^{T}\frac{1}{(1+r)^t}\Sigma_{h=1}^{H}N_{ht}\Psi_{ht}(\mathbf{R}_t) + \frac{1}{(1+r)^T r}\Sigma_{h=1}^{H}N_{hT}\Psi_{hT}(\mathbf{R}_T)$$

$$+\Sigma_{k=0}^{K}V_{k0}S_{k0}. \tag{1.20}$$

with respect to $[S_{0t}, S_{1t},...,S_{Kt}]$ for $t=1,...,T$, $[V_{0t}, V_{1t},...,V_{Kt}]$ for $t=0$, $1,...,T$, $[R_{1t},...,R_{Kt}]$ for $t=0, 1,...,T$ and $[\theta_{1t},...,\theta_{Kt}]$ for $t=0, 1,...,T$ given all exogenous variables including the initial stocks S_{k0} for $k=0,...,K$ subject to the constraints:

$$\Sigma_{h=1\cdots H}N_{ht}P_{hkt}(\mathbf{R}_t) - S_{kt}q_{kot}(R_{kt}) = 0; k=1,...,K; t=0, 1,...,T. \tag{1.21}$$

$$(1+\theta_{kt})V_{kt} - \Omega_{kt}(\mathbf{V}_{t+1}) - \omega_{kt}(R_{kt}) = 0; k=0,1,...,K; t=0, 1,...,T. \tag{1.22}$$

$$S_{kt+1} - \Sigma_{z=0,1,...,K}\frac{1}{m_{zk}}S_{zt}Q_{zkt}(\mathbf{V}_{t+1}) = 0; k=0,1,...,K; t=0, 1,...,T. \tag{1.23}$$

$$\Sigma_{h=1,...,H}N_{hT}P_{hkT}(\mathbf{R}_T) - S_{kT}q_{koT}(R_{kT}) = 0; k=1,...,K. \tag{1.24}$$

$$(1+\theta_{kT})V_{kT} - \Omega_{kT}(\mathbf{V}_T) - \omega_{kT}(R_{kT}) = 0; k=0; 1,...,K. \tag{1.25}$$

$$S_{kT} - \Sigma_{z=0,1,...,K}\frac{1}{m_{zk}}S_{zT}Q_{zk}(\mathbf{V}_T) = 0; k=0,1,...,K. \tag{1.26}$$

$$\Sigma_{k=0}^{K}[\Sigma_{t=0}^{T}\frac{1}{(1+r)^t}\theta_{kt}V_{kt}S_{kt} + \frac{1}{r(1+r)^{T+1}}\theta_{kT}V_{kT}S_{kT}] - \Re = 0. \tag{1.27}$$

The objective function, which measures social welfare, consists of the three additive terms. Of these, the first is the non-stationary consumer surplus series of phase 1 discounted to the initial point in time. The second is the stationary phase (phase 2) consumer surplus series discounted to the initial point in time. Investors make zero profit in each year and, because this holds by the equations (1.22) and (1.25) of the dynamic market equilibrium, their profits need not be included in the social welfare function. However, the introduction of taxes will alter initial asset prices and, under the assumption that the tax policy is unanticipated, windfall gains or losses will accrue to asset holders at time $t=0$. Hence the level of *initial* asset prices must be included as the third additive term in (1.20). The constraints (1.24), (1.25) and (1.26) are the stationary market equilibrium conditions modified for taxes. They ensure that the stationary state is a market equilibrium conditional on the tax rates. Similarly, (1.21), (1.22) and (1.23) ensure that the non-stationary market equilibrium also holds conditional on the tax rates. The last constraint (1.27) requires that a present value tax revenue of $\Re>0$ be raised. Note that there is no restriction on the signs of the tax rates. Some can be negative (subsidies) while others are positive, but clearly at least one must be positive.

An alternative suboptimal formulation would require that pre-specified revenue constraints be met each year by a myopic tax planner: $\Sigma_{k=0}^{K}\theta_{kt} V_{kt}S_{kt}-\Re_t=0$ for year t. The suboptimality arises from the fact that the myopic tax planner cannot shift funds between periods but must balance his budget every period. This problem is considerably easier to solve because a present value budget need not be balanced across time periods. One could first solve the stationary state problem with the budget for that year imposed and would find the stocks, rents, asset prices and tax rates for the stationary state which maximized the stationary state's consumer surplus plus aggregate asset values. This would determine terminal asset prices conditional on terminal year optimal taxes. Then one would begin a loop of backward-in-time and forward-in-time recursions to find stocks and asset prices together with tax rates for each year by maximizing that year's objective and still meeting the revenue target for that year. This solution procedure is similar to the one without taxes discussed earlier (see Figure 1.2) except that taxes are also calculated at each step.

A comment is in order here about welfare comparisons (deadweight loss measurement) for dynamic optimal taxation problems such as those discussed above. Figure 1.4 illustrates the key point. Consider first curve I, the path of the discounted welfare level each year when there is no tax policy in place. This welfare path is Pareto efficient. Now introduce any tax policy such as those discussed above. To capture the uses of tax revenue, the present value tax revenue $\Re$ can simply be added to the optimized value of

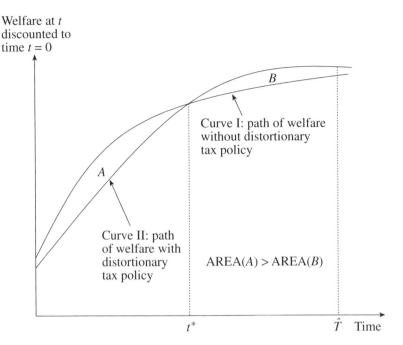

Welfare at *t*
discounted to
time *t* = 0

B

Curve I: path of welfare
without distortionary
tax policy

A

Curve II: path
of welfare with
distortionary
tax policy

AREA(*A*) > AREA(*B*)

t*　　　　　　　　　$\hat{T}$　Time

Note: Negative net benefits of a distortionary tax policy in the dynamic model with convergence to stationary state of time $\hat{T}$. In this example, positive net benefits occur after time *t**, including $\hat{T}$ at which time stationary state is reached, but these positive benefits are outweighed by the negative net benefits which occur in $0 < t < t^*$.

Figure 1.4　Welfare path comparisons

the consumer surplus plus initial asset values since, with linear utilities and risk-neutral investors, the redistribution of tax revenue does not affect the present value welfare level. Clearly, the optimal tax policy is distortionary (has a deadweight loss). Therefore, curve II is either below curve I for each *t*, or, in the case shown in Figure 1.4, curve II cuts curve I potentially several times (only once in the figure). In the case of the figure, area *A* must be larger than area *B* since the optimal tax policy must be distorting in present value terms. (An alternative possibility is that curve II starts above curve I but cuts it from above. In that case, the corresponding area *B* would have to be larger than the corresponding area *A*.) The case illustrated in the figure is interesting because the distortionary tax policy yields improved welfare some time in the future and, in particular, in the eventual stationary state. This possibility appears counterintuitive at first. But the reason for it has to do with the fact that the path of the building stock is changed by the tax policy. At any point in time, the building stocks on curve I and curve II will not be the same. One can think up the following scenario that would be a real example of this. Suppose that the optimal tax policy calls for high taxes on vacant land relative to taxes on buildings. This increases the investor's cost of holding vacant land which, in turn, causes buildings to be built early on so that the stock on curve II eventually exceeds the stock on curve I for the corresponding later time periods. This creates an inefficient abundance of buildings later on, causing rents to be lower and consumer surplus to be higher. Although consumer surplus is eventually higher on curve II, we know that the optimal tax policy causes a distortion in present value terms. Hence area B must be smaller than area A. The example of the figure illustrates the pitfalls of looking only at long-run benefits, ignoring the transient benefits along the adjustment path. It emphasizes that policies must be compared in terms of net present value benefits.

5 CLOSING COMMENTS

The algorithm described in Appendix B has been designed to examine the effects of ad valorem taxes on types of buildings and vacant land within the simulation model discussed in section 2. It calculates the deadweight losses arising from such tax systems with exogenously specified tax rates. The optimal tax policy problem posed in section 3 has not yet been implemented as an algorithm. When so implemented, it would allow direct derivation of the optimal tax policy and, hence, would allow us to investigate how optimal tax policies consisting of taxes on buildings and land should vary according to the circumstances of particular metropolitan land markets. Given that truly neutral and efficient taxes on land are controversial on the basis of equity, or simply difficult to implement, it is important to be able to compare the efficiency of alternative tax systems.

APPENDIX A: THE MULTINOMIAL LOGIT CALCULUS

A number of references are available detailing equivalent derivations of the multinomial logit model and the associated welfare measures: for example, McFadden (1974) or Anderson *et al.* (1992). This appendix follows the approach of the latter. Part (b), below, can also be proved by the approach of Small and Rosen (1981) who integrated the choice probability function to show that the expression in (b) is the (consumer or producer) surplus measure.

Derivation of the Multinomial Logit Model

Suppose that the payoffs (utilities or profits) of $i = 1,...,n$ discrete alternatives are measured by $X_i + x_i$, where each $-\infty < x_i < +\infty$ is distributed i.i.d. among the decision-making agents according to the cumulative density $G(\bullet)$ of the Gumbel given by (1.1), with dispersion parameter γ, and mode $\eta = -\dfrac{g}{\gamma}$ (mean zero). Then:

(a)   The probability that an agent most prefers alternative i is $Pr(i) = \dfrac{\exp \gamma X_i}{\Sigma_{j=1}^{n} \exp \gamma X_j}$;

(b) $E[\max(X_i + x_i)] = \dfrac{1}{\gamma} \ln \Sigma_{j=1}^{n} \exp \gamma X_j$.

Proof of (a)

The density function of (1.1) is $f(z) = \gamma[\exp - (\gamma z + g)]\{\exp - [\exp. - (\gamma z + g)]\}$. $Pr(i) = \text{Prob.}[X_i + x_i > \max \forall j \neq i\, (X_j + x_j)] = \displaystyle\int_{-\infty}^{+\infty} f(x_i) \prod_{j \neq i} G(x_j \leq X_i - X_j + x_i) dx_i$. We evaluate this, using the substitutions $a_i = \exp[-(\gamma x_i + g)]$ and $b_j = \exp(\gamma X_j)$. Then,

$$Pr(i) = \int_0^\infty \exp(-a_i) \prod_{j \neq i} \left[\exp\left(-\frac{a_i b_j}{b_i}\right)\right] da_i = \int_0^\infty \exp\left[-a_i\left(\Sigma_{j=1}^n \frac{b_j}{b_i}\right)\right] da_i$$

$$= \frac{-b_i}{\Sigma_{j=1}^n b_j} \left\{\exp\left[-a_i\left(\Sigma_{j=1}^n \frac{b_j}{b_i}\right)\right]\right\}_0^\infty = \frac{\exp(\gamma X_i)}{\Sigma_{j=1}^n \exp(\gamma X_j)}.$$

Proof of (b)

The procedure outlined in Anderson *et al.* (1992) is to derive the cumulative density, $H(w)$ of the random variable $w = \max \forall i (X_i + x_i)$ and then calculate its expected value as $E[w] = \int_{-\infty}^{+\infty} wH'(w)dw$. $H(w) = \prod_{i=1}^{n} G(x_i <$

$w - X_i) = \prod_{i=1}^{n} \exp[-k\exp(-\gamma w + \gamma X_i)] = \exp[-kF\exp(-\gamma w)]$, where $k =$
$\exp(\gamma\eta)$ and $F = \Sigma_{i=1}^{n}\exp(\gamma X_i)$. The density is $H'(w) = \gamma kFH(w)\exp(-\gamma w)$.
Before integrating we make the substitution $\bar{w} = \exp(-\gamma w)$.

Then $E[w] = \frac{1}{\gamma} \int_{\infty}^{0} \exp(-kF\bar{w})kF\ln\bar{w}d\bar{w} = -\frac{1}{\gamma}kF \int_{0}^{\infty} \exp(-kF\bar{w})\ln\bar{w}d\bar{w}$.

Rename $kF = s$ and use the Laplace transformation $\int_{0}^{\infty} e^{-st}\ln t\, dt =$

$-\dfrac{\ln s + g}{s}$ to integrate. Then $E[w] = \dfrac{1}{\gamma}(\ln kF + g) = \eta + \dfrac{g}{\gamma} + \dfrac{1}{\gamma}\ln\Sigma_{i=1}^{n}\exp(\gamma X_i)$

$= \dfrac{1}{\gamma}\ln\Sigma_{j=1}^{n}\exp(\gamma X_j)$, because $\eta + \dfrac{g}{\gamma} = 0$. Note that $H(w) = \exp[-kF\exp$

$(-\gamma w)]$ is a Gumbel with mode $\eta + \dfrac{1}{\gamma}\ln \Sigma_{j=1}^{n}\exp(\gamma X_j)$.

The choice probabilities (1.2), (1.4) and (1.6) are obtained by applying
the procedure of part (a). To get (1.2), the consumer choice probabilities,
define $X_i \equiv U_{hit}$ and $x_i \equiv u_{hit}$, $i = 1,\dots,K$ for each ht. To get (1.4), the occu-
pancy/vacancy probabilities, define $X_1 \equiv R_{kt}D_{kot}$, $X_2 \equiv -D_{kvt}$, $x_1 - d_{kot}$,
$x_2 \equiv -d_{kvt}$ for each kt. To get (1.6), the investor's conversion probabilities,
define $X_i \equiv \rho\dfrac{V_{it+1} - C_{kit}}{m_{ki}}$ and $x_i \equiv -c_{kit}$, all $i\epsilon B(k)$ and each kt. The expected
values (1.3), (1.5) and (1.7) are derived by applying the procedure of part
(b).

APPENDIX B: FORTRAN CODE FOR SOLVING DYNAMIC SIMULATION MODEL OF REAL ESTATE MARKETS WITH TAXES ON BUILDINGS AND LAND

Anas and Choi (2001) describe the FORTRAN code we have developed to solve dynamic real estate market problems described by equations (1.8)–(1.13), with exogenously specified tax rates. The algorithm is designed to solve problems conforming either to the commodity hierarchy cycle of Figure 1.1a or to the pattern of Figure 1.1b in which buildings differ according to structural densities. In each of these two cases, multiple land markets can be included, each land market containing potentially all building types.

Our algorithm first solves the phase 2 stationary equilibrium given the exogenous variables and calibrated parameters. Then the algorithm solves the first phase non-stationary dynamic equilibrium including an accurate time horizon truncation which determines T, the time at which the non-stationary phase converges to the stationary phase. The algorithm computes the deadweight losses of the pre-specified tax schemes.

Under a different operating option, the user specifies key data and key elasticities of demand and supply. Given these inputs, the dynamic simulation model calibrates itself and is then poised to perform simulations with these calibrated coefficients. A variety of exogenous inputs including taxes can be altered to explore their intertemporal effects on the real estate market.

APPENDIX C: COMPARATIVE STATIC ANALYSIS OF THE EFFECTS OF TAXES

The comparative static analysis of (1.14)–(1.18) with respect to θ is as follows:

$$
\begin{bmatrix}
D'(R) & 0 & 0 & 0 & -1 \\
0 & 1+\theta-\dfrac{Q_{00}}{1+r} & -\dfrac{Q_{01}}{1+r} & 0 & 0 \\
-1 & -\dfrac{Q_{10}}{1+r} & 1+\theta-\dfrac{Q_{11}}{1+r} & 0 & 0 \\
0 & -B & B & Q_{01} & -Q_{10} \\
0 & 0 & 0 & 1 & 1
\end{bmatrix}
\begin{bmatrix}
dR_1/d\theta \\
dV_0/d\theta \\
dV_1/d\theta \\
dS_0/d\theta \\
dS_1/d\theta
\end{bmatrix}
=
\begin{bmatrix}
0 \\
-V_0 \\
-V_1 \\
0 \\
0
\end{bmatrix},
$$

where $B=[S_0\Phi_0 Q_{01}Q_{00}+S_1\Phi_1 Q_{10}Q_{11}]/(1+r)$. The determinant of the system is:

$$
DET=(-B)(1+\theta-\dfrac{1}{1+r})+(Q_{10}+Q_{01})D'(R)\left[(1+\theta)(1+\theta-\dfrac{1}{1+r})+\right.
$$

$$
\left.\dfrac{Q_{10}(Q_{11}-Q_{01})}{(1+r)^2}\right]<0,
$$

assuming that $Q_{11}>Q_{01}$ or $Q_{10}+Q_{01}<1$ the sum of the construction and demolition probabilities is not extremely large. Calculating the effect on

rent we get: $\dfrac{dR_1}{d\theta}=\left(\dfrac{B}{-DET}\right)(V_1-V_0)\left(1+\theta-\dfrac{1}{1+r}\right)>0$ assuming that a

developed piece of land (land plus building) is worth more than an unde-

veloped one. From (1.14), it follows that $\dfrac{dS_1}{d\theta}<0$ and from (1.18) that $\dfrac{dS_0}{d\theta}$

>0. Since we have established that $d\dfrac{S_0}{S_1}>0$, it follows from (1.17) that $d\dfrac{Q_{10}}{Q_{01}}$

>0. Hence, from (1.19'), we can see by inspection that $\dfrac{d(V_0 - V_1)}{d\theta} > 0$ must

be true. Next, solving for $\dfrac{dV_1}{d\theta}$ and $\dfrac{dV_0}{d\theta}$, we find that $\dfrac{dV_0}{d\theta} = D'(R)\dfrac{Q_{01} + Q_{10}}{DET}$

$\left[-V_0(1 + \theta - \dfrac{Q_{11}}{1+r}) - V_1\dfrac{Q_{01}}{1+r} \right] + \dfrac{BV_0}{DET} < 0$ and $\dfrac{dV_1}{d\theta} = D'(R)\dfrac{Q_{01} + Q_{10}}{DET}$

$\left[-V_1(1 + \theta - \dfrac{Q_{00}}{1+r}) - V_0\dfrac{Q_{10}}{1+r} \right] + \dfrac{BV_1}{DET} < 0$. And, from these, $\dfrac{d(V_0 - V_1)}{d\theta}$

$= \dfrac{D'(R)(Q_{01} + Q_{10})}{DET}\left(1 + \theta - \dfrac{1}{1+r}\right)(V_1 - V_0) > 0$, which was inferred earlier.

The comparative statics with respect to the unconventional tax on land only follows a similar procedure and is intuitive given the above results. The matrix equation is:

$$
\begin{bmatrix}
D'(R) & 0 & 0 & 0 & -1 \\
0 & 1 + \theta_0 - \dfrac{Q_{00}}{1+r} & -\dfrac{Q_{01}}{1+r} & 0 & 0 \\
-1 & -\dfrac{Q_{10}}{1+r} & 1 - \dfrac{Q_{11}}{1+r} & 0 & 0 \\
0 & -B & B & Q_{01} & -Q_{10} \\
0 & 0 & 0 & 1 & 1
\end{bmatrix}
$$

$$
\begin{bmatrix}
dR/d\theta_0 \\
dV_0/d\theta_0 \\
dV_1/d\theta_0 \\
dS_0/d\theta_0 \\
dS_1/d\theta_0
\end{bmatrix}
=
\begin{bmatrix}
0 \\
-V_0 \\
0 \\
0 \\
0
\end{bmatrix},
$$

$DET = (Q_{01} + Q_{10})D'(R)\left\{ \left[\dfrac{(1 + \theta_0)(1 + r) - Q_{00}}{1+r} \right]\left[\dfrac{1 + r - Q_{11}}{1+r} \right] - \right.$

$\left. \left(\dfrac{1 - Q_{00}}{1+r}\right)\left(\dfrac{1 - Q_{11}}{1+r}\right) \right\} + B\left(\dfrac{1}{1+r} - (1 + \theta_0)\right), \dfrac{dR_1}{d\theta_0} = \left(\dfrac{B}{-DET}\right)(-V_0)$

$\left(\dfrac{1}{1+r} - 1\right) < 0$. From (1.14), it follows that $\dfrac{dS_1}{d\theta_0} > 0$ and from (1.19) that $\dfrac{dS_0}{d\theta_0}$

<0. Since we have established that $\dfrac{d\dfrac{S_0}{S_1}}{d\theta_0}<0$, it follows from (1.18) that

$\dfrac{d\dfrac{Q_{10}}{Q_{01}}}{d\theta_0}<0$. Hence, from (1.19′), we can see by inspection that $\dfrac{d(V_0-V_1)}{d\theta_0}<0$

must be true. Next, solving for $\dfrac{dV_1}{d\theta_0}$ and $\dfrac{dV_0}{d\theta_0}$, we find that $\dfrac{dV_0}{d\theta_0}=D'(R)$

$\dfrac{Q_{01}+Q_{10}}{DET}(-V_0)\left(1-\dfrac{Q_{11}}{1+r}\right)+\dfrac{BV_0}{DET}<0$ and $\dfrac{dV_1}{d\theta_0}=D'(R)\dfrac{Q_{01}+Q_{10}}{DET}(-V_0)$

$\dfrac{Q_{10}}{1+r}+\dfrac{BV_0}{DET}<0$. And, from these, $\dfrac{d(V_0-V_1)}{d\theta_0}=\dfrac{D'(R)(Q_{01}+Q_{10})}{DET}$

$\left(\dfrac{1}{1+r}-1\right)V_0<0$, which was inferred earlier.

NOTES

1. This is more likely to be the case if land value is a relatively small part of property value, as is the case in the United States.
2. Of course, the same pitfalls exist for taxes proportional to assessed values if those values cannot be accurately calculated, as they are unlikely to be for land occupied by buildings.
3. Earlier papers by Skouras (1978), David Mills (1981, 1982), Tideman (1982) and Wildasin (1982) debated the neutrality of alternative land taxes. Bentick (1979), Kanemoto (1985) and Turnbull (1988) focused on the effects of taxation on the timing and efficiency of development. But none of these authors considered demolition as we do in this chapter.
4. See Anas and Arnott (1991, 1993a, 1993b, 1993c, 1994, 1997) and Anas *et al.* (2000) for the earlier publications on this model and its empirical application.
5. The model is consistent with theory, but I refer to it as a 'simulation model' because simulation is the only practical way to solve it in the general case.
6. The model follows discrete choice theory. Despite my efforts over the years, the approach is still considered *unorthodox* within urban economics. But its enormous advantage is that it lends itself to direct empirical and numerical implementation of the theoretical models without sacrificing the theoretical form of the model equations (see Anas and Arnott, 1993c, 1994, 1997). This contrasts with *orthodox* urban economics where, with few exceptions, authors develop a theoretical model and then have to switch to some reduced form, vaguely related to the theoretical model, to test it empirically.
7. By 'building' we refer to any type of building such as single family home, apartment building, or office building. Consumers of buildings can be households or business establishments.
8. The model is here presented for a single land market, but in Anas and Arnott (1993c,

1994, 1997) it has been applied to metropolitan housing markets (such as Chicago) with two (city and suburban) land markets.
9. A 'unit building' is the quantity a building consumer wants to consume. In the case of housing consumers, a 'unit building' is a whole housing unit. In the case of business establishments, it could be viewed, for example, as a unit amount of floor space in a building.
10. That the vacant land rent is exogenous is analogous to the assumption of exogenous agricultural rent in the models by Mills (1998), Brueckner (1999), Brueckner and Kim (2000) or Arnott (1998) discussed earlier. Of course, there is no loss of generality in assuming that the rent for vacant land is zero.
11. For businesses, we may think of this as the net income before rent is paid, for example.
12. Lemma 2 in Anas *et al.* (2000) proves this redundancy of one of (1.10) for each t.
13. It is easy to change utility functions and allow income effects. See Anas and Arnott (1993c, 1994).

REFERENCES

Anas, A. and R.J. Arnott, 1991, 'Dynamic housing market equilibrium with taste heterogeneity, idiosyncratic perfect foresight and stock conversions', *Journal of Housing Economics*, 1(1), 2–32.

Anas, A. and R.J. Arnott, 1993a, 'Technological progress in a model of the housing–land cycle', *Journal of Urban Economics*, 34 (2), 186–206.

Anas, A. and R.J. Arnott, 1993b, 'A fall in construction costs can raise housing rents', *Economics Letters*, 41, 221–4.

Anas, A. and R.J. Arnott, 1993c, 'Development and testing of the Chicago prototype housing market model', *Journal of Housing Research*, 4, 73–130.

Anas, A. and R.J. Arnott, 1994, 'The Chicago prototype housing market model with tenure choice and its policy applications', *Journal of Housing Research*, 5, 23–90.

Anas, A. and R.J. Arnott, 1997, 'Taxes and allowances in a dynamic equilibrium model of urban housing with a size–quality hierarchy', *Regional Science and Urban Economics*, 27, 547–80.

Anas, A. and Y.J. Choi, 2001, 'Readme file for FORTRAN code designed to solve dynamic equilibrium in real estate markets with ad valorem taxes on buildings and land', working document, Department of Economics, State University of New York at Buffalo.

Anas, A., R.J. Arnott and T. Yamazaki, 2000, 'Existence, uniqueness and efficiency of dynamic housing market equilibrium', working paper, Department of Economics, State University of New York at Buffalo.

Anderson, S.P., A. de Palma and J.F. Thisse, 1992, *Discrete Choice Theory of Product Differentiation*, Cambridge, MA: MIT Press.

Arnott, R.J., 1998, 'Neutral property taxation', working paper, Department of Economics, Boston College.

Bentick, B.L., 1979, 'The impact of taxation and valuation practices on the timing and efficiency of land use', *Journal of Political Economy*, 87, 858–68.

Brueckner, J.K., 2001, 'Property taxation and urban sprawl', in Wallace E. Oates (ed.), *Property Taxation and Local Government Finance*, Lincoln Institute of Land Policy, 153–72.

Brueckner, J.K. and Hyun-A. Kim, 2003, 'Urban sprawl and the property tax', *International Tax and Public Finance*, 10, January, 5–23.

George, H., 1879, *Progress and Poverty*, New York: Robert Shalkenback Foundation, reprint 1970.

Kanemoto, Y., 1985, 'Housing as an asset and the effects of property taxation on the residential development process', *Journal of Urban Economics*, 17, 145–66.

McFadden, D., 1974, 'Conditional logit analysis of qualitative choice behavior', in P. Zarembka (ed.), *Frontiers in Econometrics*, New York, Academic Press, pp. 105–42.

Mills, D.E., 1981, 'The non-neutrality of land value taxation', *National Tax Journal*, 34, 125–9.

Mills, D.E., 1982, 'Reply to Tideman', *National Tax Journal*, 35, 115.

Mills, E.S., 1998, 'Economic consequences of a land tax', in Dick Netzer (ed.), *Land Value Taxation: Can It and Will It Work Today?*, Cambridge, MA: Lincoln Institute of Land Policy.

Skouras, A., 1978, 'The non-neutrality of land taxation', *Public Finance*, 30, 113–34.

Small, K.A. and H.S. Rosen, 1981, 'Applied welfare economics with discrete choice models', *Econometrica*, 49, 105–30.

Tideman, N.T., 1982, 'A tax on land *is* neutral', *National Tax Journal*, 35, 109–11.

Turnbull, G.K., 1988, 'Property taxes and the transition of land to urban use', *Journal of Real Estate Finance and Economics*, 1, 393–403.

Wildasin, D.E., 1982, 'More on the neutrality of land taxation', *National Tax Journal*, 35, 105–8.

2. The effect of tax increment financing on land use

Richard F. Dye and David F. Merriman

1 INTRODUCTION

A municipality may use tax increment financing (TIF) to promote economic development by allowing certain areas, designated as TIF districts, to use the tax revenue generated by increases in the assessed value of properties within them for investment in the district.[1] Unlike some other development incentives, TIF requires no explicit expenditure of local tax revenues. Also the opportunity to pledge incremental revenues provides access to borrowing that might otherwise not be available. In recent years TIF has become extremely popular among state and local governments around the United States. (For a general introduction to tax increment financing, see Klacik and Nunn, 2001, or Chapman, 1998.)

Despite the virtues mentioned above, TIF is controversial for a number of reasons. In most states overlapping local governments share the property tax base. In Illinois, for example, school districts, municipal governments and county governments all levy property taxes. Economic development that is favored by one type of government (for example, a municipality) will not necessarily benefit others (school districts). Illinois municipal governments can establish TIF districts with little input from other units of government. Some analysts have expressed concern that TIF may allow municipalities to appropriate school district revenue for their own purposes.

A second, even more fundamental, concern about TIF is that it may simply change the location of economic development rather than stimulate new growth. After state enabling legislation makes TIF possible, developers may persuade local governments to make concessions that otherwise would not have been available. Development may be relocated to TIF districts benefitting some areas only at the expense of others.

In a study of property value growth in municipalities in the six-county Chicago metropolitan area we found support for this view (Dye and Merriman, 2000). Our results showed that municipalities that host TIF districts grew less rapidly than those that did not. This conclusion was not overturned even after controlling for a wide variety of municipal characteristics and carefully considering the impact of selection bias caused by the fact that past growth may influence the decision to adopt TIF. We found empirical evidence that non-TIF areas of municipalities with a TIF district grew less rapidly than otherwise would be expected. This controversial conclusion, which is apparently at odds with some academic literature on this topic (for a review, see Man, 2001), drew heated criticism from some Illinois TIF advocates.

Dye and Merriman (2000) hypothesized that the slower growth in TIF-adopting municipalities was caused by inefficiently allocating government and private resources from the non-TIF to the TIF portion of municipalities. In this chapter we explore this hypothesis in more detail by using data on the type of TIF district and the type of property – commercial, industrial or residential – to focus explicitly on changes in land use. If our interpretation of the earlier results is correct, economic activity within TIF districts substitutes for activity outside the district. This suggests that TIF districts that are primarily industrial will depress industrial activity outside the district but may have little impact on commercial or residential land uses. Similarly, we expect that commercial TIF districts will primarily replace commercial activity in non-TIF areas. In this research we empirically study distortions in land uses as a result of TIF districts.

Our analysis has three different components, each with a different sample. First, we refit the six-county municipal analysis of our earlier paper with a sample that has more years of data and a few more municipalities. We extend the analysis of the expanded six-county sample to include information on the type of TIF district and look separately at different land use categories. Second, at the cost of some data limitations, we expand the sample to include most municipalities in all 102 Illinois counties. Third, we analyze a sample of annual observations on TIF districts in the Chicago metropolitan area over the last two decades. We examine within-district growth in equalized assessed value (EAV) by type of TIF district.

2   THE SIX-COUNTY MUNICIPALITY SAMPLES

In our earlier study we used data on 235 municipalities in the six-county Chicago metropolitan area for the period 1980 to 1995. With more recent data, we are able to expand the number of municipalities to 246 and the time period to 1980–98.

The dependent growth rate variables are constructed from three components: *available* municipal EAV, *base*-year TIF district EAV and the TIF district EAV *increment*. Since the municipal tax base, which we call available EAV, includes the frozen TIF base but not the TIF increment, *gross-of-TIF* EAV equals *available* EAV plus TIF *increment* EAV, and *net*-of-TIF EAV equals *available* EAV minus TIF *base* EAV.

In municipalities without a TIF, available EAV, gross EAV and net EAV are, of course, all equal. Dye and Merriman (2000) found that both the net-of-TIF EAV growth rate and the gross-of-TIF EAV growth rate in municipalities with TIF were lower than the available EAV growth rates of similar municipalities without a TIF. The relatively slow growth of net-of-TIF EAV led us to conclude that the existence of a TIF district reduces growth outside the TIF while the relatively slow growth of gross-of-TIF EAV led us to conclude that growth within TIF districts is not sufficient to compensate for reduced growth outside the TIF districts.

In the present study, our primary interest is in how TIF districts affect land uses. As explained below, we lack sufficient data to calculate net and gross EAV growth by land use. Thus our analysis in this chapter is largely confined to available EAV growth. Since available EAV excludes the TIF increment, its growth rate will be a lower bound on the growth rate of gross-of-TIF EAV.[2] Also, because available EAV includes the TIF base which, by definition, has a zero growth rate, the growth rate of available EAV will be less than that of net-of-TIF EAV. However, in our sample most TIF districts are quite small relative to the municipality so that available and net-of-TIF EAV will be very similar.[3] Thus our empirical results can be interpreted as indicating the impact of TIF districts on the growth of EAV in the area that is within the municipality but outside the TIF district.

The first row of Table 2.1 compares the growth rates of gross EAV for the 100 TIF-adopting and the 146 non-adopting municipalities in the period (1980 to 1984) before any of the municipalities in the sample had adopted TIF. In this period, EAV grew slightly faster for the municipalities that would later adopt TIF (4.66 versus 4.41 per cent per year). The second row of Table 2.1 indicates that in the period after all of the adopters in the sample had established TIF (1995 to 1998), gross EAV grew less rapidly for TIF adopters (5.20 versus 6.46 per cent per year). The last row of Table 2.1 shows that the net-of-TIF EAV growth rate for TIF adopters was even lower, suggesting that TIF district growth may come at the expense of property values within the host city but outside the designated development area. In summary, before any adjustment for the effects of other determinants, there is a negative relationship between TIF adoption and growth.

A systematic examination of the relationship between TIF and property value growth requires econometric controls for variables other than TIF that may affect growth. The econometric problem is made more difficult by the fact that establishment of a TIF district may be systematically related

Table 2.1   Mean annualized percentage growth rates in municipal EAV, six-county sample

	Dep. var.	TIF status group	
Period	Growth in	TIF adopters (N = 100)	Non-adopters (N = 146)
Pre-adoption (1980–84)	Gross* EAV	4.66	4.41
Post-adoption (1995–98)	Gross** EAV	5.20	6.46
Post-adoption (1995–98)	Net*** EAV	5.06	

Notes:
* Gross EAV equals available EAV for all municipalities in the pre-adoption period.
** In the post-adoption period, gross EAV equals available EAV plus the TIF increment for adopters, while gross EAV equals available EAV for non-adopters.
*** Net EAV equals available EAV minus the TIF base for adopters.

to a community's expectation about future property value growth. Anderson (1990) pointed out that municipalities that expect rapid property value growth have an incentive to adopt TIF in order to capture from overlying governments property tax revenue on the increment. Anderson used econometric techniques designed to control for sample selection bias resulting from the endogenous establishment of TIF districts. Similar econometric techniques have been used by Man and Rosentraub (1998), who found evidence of endogeneity in the establishment of TIF districts, and by Anderson and Wassmer (2000).

As in our earlier work (Dye and Merriman, 2000) we divide our data into three periods. We use data from the 1980–84 'pre-adoption' period to predict TIF adoption during the period from 1985 to 1995. Data from the end of the adoption period (1995) are used to predict growth in EAV in the 1995–98 'post-adoption' period. We use econometric methods that allow us both to test for sample selection bias and to estimate the impact of an endogenously determined TIF. [4]

Table 2.2 shows estimates of the effect of TIF on growth in gross and net EAV for the six-county sample, refitting the econometric specifications used in Dye and Merriman (2000) with a slightly larger number of municipalities and more recent (1995–98) post-adoption growth period. In all of the specifications the test statistic for sample selection bias (shown in the last column) is insignificant so that we cannot reject the hypothesis that TIF adoption is exogenously determined. Specifications 2.g.1 and 2.n.1 (where 'g' is for gross and 'n' is for net) include a single dummy variable for TIF adoption (and a number of control variables that are listed in the footnote

Table 2.2   TIF-effect estimates for the old and new six-county samples[a]

Spec. no.	Sample Municipalities	Growth period	Dep. var. Growth	TIF dummy[b]	TIF share	Years since	Selection Test variable[c]
2.g.1	246	1995–98	Gross EAV	−0.19 (0.12)			0.19 (0.19)
2.g.2	246	1995–98	Gross EAV	0.24 (0.14)	0.04 (1.18)	−0.07 (0.67)	0.04 (0.04)
2.n.1	246	1995–98	Net EAV	−0.64 (0.37)			0.72 (0.68)
2.n.2	246	1995–98	Net EAV	−0.01 (0.00)	0.15 (4.24)**	−0.13 (1.15)	0.16 (0.16)

Notes:
[a] Absolute values of z-ratios are in parentheses with ** for 5 per cent. Additional variables controlling for home-rule status, aggregate tax rate, population, income per capita, poverty rate, non-residential share of EAV, EAV per square mile, distance to the Chicago loop, and each of the collar counties (counties surrounding Chicago) were included but are not shown.
[b] Estimated simultaneously using methods described in Dye and Merriman (2000).
[c] Estimated simultaneously using methods described in Dye and Merriman (2000). A significant coefficient suggests that the TIF dummy is endogenously determined.

to the table). The coefficient on the TIF dummy variable is not significantly different from zero for growth in either gross or net EAV.[5]

In specifications 2.g.2 and 2.n.2 we control not only for the existence of a TIF but also for its size relative to the municipality (TIF share) and its age (Years since). Again we cannot reject the hypothesis that TIF adoption is exogenous. Since TIF existence, size and age are jointly determined and correlated, it is difficult to interpret the point estimates and statistical significance of individual coefficients. We used these coefficients to construct a Wald test of the hypothesis that a municipality that had a typical TIF (that is, one that was the mean TIF age of 7.15 years since adoption and mean TIF share of 7.28 per cent of EAV) would have the same EAV growth rate as an otherwise identical municipality without a TIF. The WALD statistics are insignificant (not shown, but 0.0003 for specification 2.g.2 and 0.012 for specification 2.n.2), giving us no basis to reject this hypothesis. In summary, our empirical analysis provides no evidence that TIF adoption raises either net or gross municipal EAV growth rates.

In this chapter we are primarily interested in the impact of tax increment financing on land use. We use the Illinois Department of Revenue's coding of municipal EAV data by type (residential, commercial and industrial) to calculate total municipal EAV by type. Unfortunately, the Illinois Department of Revenue does not code incremental EAV in the TIF district by type of property and county clerks do not code the base-year EAV of the TIF district by land use type. Therefore we cannot calculate either gross or net EAV by type. However, we do know something about land use within the TIF because the Illinois Department of Commerce and Community Affairs codes TIF districts by type: central business district (CBD), commercial, industrial, housing, and other or mixed use. Since we can calculate neither gross nor net EAV growth by land use we investigate whether available municipal EAV growth by land use varies systematically with the type of TIF district in the municipality.

The first two rows of Table 2.3 present results for all land uses combined. These specifications (3.a.1 and 3.a.2 where 'a' is for all available EAV) differ from those in Table 2.2 only because we have used as the dependent variable growth in available municipal EAV rather than the gross- or net-of-TIF EAV. In each case we cannot reject the hypothesis of an insignificant effect of TIF adoption on EAV growth. The third row, specification 3.a.3, starts to get at the question of the impact of tax increment financing on land use by including separate dummy variables for the particular types of TIF districts. Although all of the point estimates of the TIF-type dummies are negative, none is statistically significant.

In the next three rows (the 'r' specifications) of Table 2.3 the type of property in the dependent growth rate variable is narrowed to just residential EAV. The empirical results provide no evidence that TIF districts affect residential EAV. Although the coefficient on the years-since-adoption variable in specification 3.r.2 is negative and significant (other things being equal, older TIF districts reduce residential EAV growth) we cannot reject the hypothesis that a municipality with a TIF of mean age and size will experience the same residential EAV growth as a municipality without a TIF. In specification 3.r.3 we do not find evidence that a housing or any other kind of TIF increases residential EAV growth.

The next three rows of Table 2.3 (the 'c' specifications) present the TIF effect results for growth in commercial EAV.[6] In specification 3.c.1 a test statistic for selectivity bias is significant, indicating that TIF adoption is jointly determined with commercial EAV growth. Our estimated coefficients correct for the selectivity bias caused by this simultaneity. In specification 3.c.2 the coefficient on the TIF share variable is significantly positive, but a Wald test on the joint significance of the TIF dummy, TIF share and years-since-adoption variables indicates that a municipality with a typical TIF would not experience more rapid EAV growth than one without a TIF. In specification 3.c.3, the coefficient on commercial TIF

Table 2.3   Growth in available municipal property value, 1995–98, for the six-county municipality sample[a]

Spec. no.	Sample municipalities	Dep. var Growth in available EAV	TIF dummy[b]	TIF share	Years since	CBD TIF type	Commercial TIF type	Industrial TIF type	Housing TIF type	Other TIF type	Selection Test variable[c]
3.a.1	246	All land uses	-0.37 (0.23)								0.07 (0.07)
3.a.2	246	All land uses	0.10 (0.06)	0.05 (1.45)	-0.08 (0.73)						-0.12 (0.12)
3.a.3	246	All land uses				-0.71 (1.00)	-1.10 (1.44)	-0.17 (0.23)	-1.17 (0.73)	-0.59 (1.01)	0.23 (0.59)
3.r.1	246	Residential land uses	-0.05 (0.03)								-0.23 (0.20)
3.r.2	246	Residential land uses	1.50 (0.74)	0.01 (0.24)	-0.22 (1.79)*						-0.29 (0.26)
3.r.3	246	Residential land uses				-0.38 (0.46)	-0.40 (0.46)	0.32 (0.39)	-1.55 (0.85)	-0.25 (0.37)	-0.11 (0.25)
3.c.1	245	Commercial land uses	-5.65 (1.54)								3.95 (1.79)*
3.c.2	245	Commercial land uses	-5.39 (1.40)	0.31 (4.33)**	-0.12 (0.53)						2.83 (1.34)
3.c.3	245	Commercial land uses				-1.57 (1.02)	-3.90 (2.35)**	-2.71 (1.71)*	-4.18 (1.20)	-0.60 (0.47)	1.69 (2.00)**

Table 2.3 (continued)

Spec. no.	Sample municipalities	Dep. var Growth in available EAV[b]	TIF dummy[b]	TIF share	Years since	CBD TIF type	Commercial TIF type	Industrial TIF type	Housing TIF type	Other TIF type	Selection Test variable[c]
3.i.1	244	Industrial land use	10.53 (1.88)*								-6.20 (1.84)*
3.i.2	244	Industrial land use	7.23 (1.19)	-0.14 (1.28)	0.50 (1.40)						-5.63 (1.67)*
3.i.3	244	Industrial land use				0.29 (0.12)	0.14 (0.06)	-0.11 (0.04)	8.73 (1.62)	1.74 (0.88)	-0.76 (0.58)

Notes:
[a] Absolute values of z-ratios are in parentheses with ** for 5 per cent and * for 10 per cent significance. Additional variables controlling for fiscal structure, community type and location were included but are not shown (see notes to Table 2.2).
[b] Estimated simultaneously using methods described in Dye and Merriman (2000).
[c] Estimated simultaneously using methods described in Dye and Merriman (2000). A significant coefficient suggests that the TIF dummy is endogenously determined.

adoption type has an estimated negative impact on growth in commercial property. Since the dependent variable does *not* include the TIF increment, this suggests that commercial property growth within TIF districts may come at the expense of commercial property in the same town but outside the boundaries of the district. The cross-effect of industrial TIF adoption on commercial property growth is also negative in specification 3.c.3.

Finally, the last three rows of Table 2.3 (the 'i' specifications) show the TIF effect results for growth in industrial EAV. Again we find evidence of selectivity bias but correct for it with our estimation method. In specification 3.i.1, we find that TIF adoption significantly increases industrial EAV growth. The estimated effect is quite large: a municipality with a TIF has industrial EAV growth almost 11 per cent larger than a similar municipality without a TIF. In specification 3.i.2, each of the individual coefficients is statistically insignificant, but a Wald test indicates that their joint effect is positive and significant. Municipalities with a typical TIF district experience more rapid industrial EAV growth than similar municipalities without a TIF district. Surprisingly, even though the overall effect is significant, according to specification 3.i.3 there is no evidence that the type of TIF affects the growth of industrial EAV.

3   THE 102-COUNTY MUNICIPALITY SAMPLE

We now extend the analysis of the effect of TIF and TIF type on growth in municipal EAV from the six counties in the Chicago metropolitan area to all 102 counties in the state of Illinois. There are several additional data limitations for this sample. Because it requires collecting information from each separate county, we do not have base-year EAV for TIF districts in the 96 downstate counties. Thus we cannot measure the TIF share of EAV independent variable. We also cannot calculate the growth in net-of-TIF EAV dependent variable, even for all land use types combined. We do not have tax codes – a list of overlapping jurisdictions – for smaller, downstate municipalities; thus we cannot construct the same 'aggregate property tax rate' used as a control variable in our growth equations. Instead, we create a 'partial aggregate tax rate' from identifying just the municipality, the county, and the elementary and secondary school districts.[7]

Table 2.4 shows the raw pre- and post-adoption growth rates for the all-county sample. The same pattern emerges as in Table 2.2. The 205 TIF adopting towns grew more rapidly pre-adoption but less rapidly post-adoption than the 1037 non-adopters.

The first three rows of Table 2.5 (the 'a' specifications) present the results for growth in *all* available municipal EAV for the 1242 municipalities in the

*Table 2.4   Mean annualized percentage growth rates in municipal EAV,
102-county sample*

	Dep. var.	TIF status group	
Period	Growth	TIF adopters (N = 205)	Non-adopters (N = 1037)
Pre-adoption (1980–84)	Gross* EAV	3.31	1.86
Post-adoption (1995–98)	Gross** EAV	6.27	7.60
Post-adoption (1995–98)	Available EAV	5.19	

Notes:
* Gross EAV equals available EAV for all municipalities in the pre-adoption period.
** In the post-adoption period, gross EAV equals available EAV plus the TIF increment for
  adopters, but gross EAV equals available EAV for non-adopters.

102-county sample.[8] The results are striking. Specifications 5.a.1 and 5.a.2 show a significantly negative impact of TIF adoption on non-TIF property values. In specification 5.a.3, the coefficient on each dummy variable is negative but only 'other' TIF district type, with mixed or non-specified land uses, significantly reduces EAV growth. The results in Table 2.5 for residential property (the 'r' rows) are much the same as just seen for all land uses combined: a persistently negative effect of TIF adoption on EAV growth. Again TIF districts with 'other' land use types significantly reduce EAV growth.

The next three rows of Table 2.5 (the 'c' specifications) present the results for non-TIF commercial EAV for the 1238 municipalities in the statewide sample that include some commercial EAV. The TIF adoption dummy is insignificant in specification 5.c.1 and the TIF dummy and years-since-adoption variable (evaluated at the mean number of years) are jointly insignificant in specification 5.c.2. However, commercial property outside the TIF district is negatively affected by having a commercial use designated TIF district (specification 5.c.3). The effect is quite large: all else equal, a municipality with a commercial TIF experiences 3 per cent less commercial EAV growth outside the TIF according to our findings.

The final three rows of Table 2.5 (the 'i' specifications) present the results for non-TIF industrial EAV for the 1208 municipalities in the statewide sample that include some industrial EAV. In contrast with the Chicago metropolitan area sample, we find no evidence that TIF districts have a

Table 2.5 Growth in available municipal property value, 1995–98, for the 102-county municipality sample[a]

Spec. no.	Sample municipalities	Dep. var. Growth in available EAV	Independent variables							Selection Test variable[c]
			TIF dummy[b]	Years since	CBD TIF type	Commercial TIF type	Industrial TIF type	Housing TIF type	Other TIF type	
5.a.1	1242	All land uses	-2.77 (2.77)**							0.90 (1.58)
5.a.2	1242	All land uses	-3.52 (3.13)**		0.12 (1.46)					0.91 (1.60)
5.a.3	1242	All land uses			-0.88 (1.60)	-0.83 (1.17)	-0.07 (0.10)	-1.53 (1.47)	-1.35 (3.15)**	0.07 (0.27)
5.r.1	1242	Residential land uses	-2.38 (2.32)**							0.63 (1.07)
5.r.2	1242	Residential land uses	-2.59 (2.24)**	0.03 (0.40)						0.63 (1.08)
5.r.3	1242	Residential land uses			-0.58 (1.03)	-0.26 (0.36)	0.28 (0.40)	-1.63 (1.52)	-1.09 (2.48)**	-0.16 (0.57)
5.c.1	1238	Commercial land uses	-0.37 (0.16)							-0.27 (0.21)
5.c.2	1238	Commercial land uses	-1.27 (0.49)	0.14 (0.75)						-0.25 (0.19)
5.c.3	1238	Commercial land uses			-1.15 (0.91)	-3.00 (1.83)*	-2.31 (1.50)	-1.69 (0.70)	-1.29 (1.30)	0.47 (0.75)

47

Table 2.5 (continued)

Spec. no.	Sample municipalities	Dep. var. Growth in available EAV	TIF dummy[b]	Years since	CBD TIF type	Commercial TIF type	Industrial TIF type	Housing TIF type	Other TIF type	Selection Test variable[c]
5.i.1	1208	Industrial land use	1.30 (0.44)							−0.97 (0.57)
5.i.2	1208	Industrial land use	−1.62 (0.48)	0.46 (1.89)*						−0.93 (0.55)
5.i.3	1208	Industrial land use			−1.78 (1.07)	−0.72 (0.34)	−1.86 (0.93)	−0.15 (0.05)	0.54 (0.42)	−0.05 (0.06)

Notes:
[a] Absolute values of z-ratios are in parentheses with ** for 5 per cent and * for 10 per cent significance. Additional variables controlling for fiscal structure, community type and location were included but are not shown (see note to Table 2.2 and endnote 8).
[b] Estimated simultaneously using methods described in Dye and Merriman (2000).
[c] Estimated simultaneously using methods described in Dye and Merriman (2000). A significant coefficient suggests that the TIF dummy is endogenously determined.

positive impact on the growth in industrial use EAV in the statewide sample.

4   THE SIX-COUNTY TIF DISTRICT SAMPLE

Our finding that the establishment of a TIF district apparently deters (or at least does not stimulate) economic activity in surrounding areas does not suggest a lack of development within TIF districts. In fact, our preferred explanation for our results involves increased economic activity in the TIF district – that development in TIF districts may substitute for (or displace) activity that otherwise would have occurred outside of the district.

We are interested in whether TIF districts that emphasize particular land uses (for example, industrial uses) might grow faster than others. We also wonder whether TIF districts in slow-growing communities might grow more slowly than districts in rapidly expanding communities. Finally, we want to know what happens to EAV growth in TIF districts as the districts age.

As discussed above, we were unable to obtain data about the base value of TIF districts outside the Chicago metropolitan area, so our analysis of TIF district growth is confined to the six-county Chicago metropolitan area sample. Descriptive statistics about our sample are given in Table 2.6. We have one or more EAV growth rates for 247 TIF districts that began in the years 1981 to 1997.[9] For the two TIF districts that began in 1981 we observe TIF increments in each of 17 years and calculate 17 annualized growth rates.[10] For the 24 TIF districts started in 1997 we have only one annual growth rate. For the average TIF district in our sample we have 6.7 years of growth rates.

The 'size of TIF base' row in Table 2.6 shows that the average TIF district in our sample has a base-year EAV of almost $11 million, but there is a very large variance. One TIF district has a base value of less than $500 while the City of Chicago's central loop TIF district has a base value of almost $1 billion. This huge variance in the size of TIF districts makes growth rates difficult to interpret.

Table 2.6 shows that 37 of the TIF districts in our sample are designated as central business district areas, 30 are designated as commercial land use, and 47 are designated as industrial land use. Only seven areas are designated as supporting housing development. Just over half of the TIF districts (51 per cent) are designated as supporting 'mixed' or 'other' land uses.

Just as there is great variety in TIF district base values there is great variety in TIF district growth rates. Each TIF district has a range of annualized growth rates *over multiple years* of observation. To summarize the range of growth rates *across TIF districts*, Table 2.6 presents separate rows

Table 2.6   Descriptive statistics for the six-county TIF district sample

	Number	Per cent		
Year TIF started:				
1981	2	0.8		
1982	2	0.8		
1983	2	0.8		
1984	3	1.2		
1985	8	3.2		
1986	21	8.5		
1987	12	4.9		
1988	18	7.3		
1989	15	6.1		
1990	28	11.3		
1991	14	5.7		
1992	9	3.6		
1993	21	8.5		
1994	23	9.3		
1995	19	7.7		
1996	26	10.5		
1997	24	9.7		
Total	247	100		
Type of TIF:				
Central business district	37	15		
Commercial	30	12		
Industrial	47	19		
Housing	7	3		
Other	126	51		
Total	247	100		
Variable:	Mean	Std. dev.	Minimum	Maximum
Number of years of data on TIF growth	6.7	4.0	1	17
Size of TIF Base (nominal $)	$10982059	$63876330	$487	$988298550
Annualized TIF EAV growth (%):				
Maximum	41	71	0	471
Minimum	13	35	0	365
Mean	24	45	0	365
Annualized city EAV growth during TIF district's life (%):				
Maximum	5	3	0	17
Minimum	−0.11	0.37	−3	0
Mean	3	2	0	13

of descriptive statistics based on each district's cross-year maximum, minimum and mean annualized EAV growth rate. The average of the mean TIF EAV growth rate (that is, the mean district mean year annualized growth rate) was 24 per cent. The rate of EAV growth within TIF districts greatly exceeds the rate of growth in the cities that host the districts. We paired each TIF district with its host city and calculated the maximum, minimum and mean EAV growth rate in the city over the life of the district. During the life of the TIF the mean city had a mean year EAV growth rate of only about 3 per cent.[11] In the median city, host city EAV grew less than half as fast as EAV within its TIF district (calculations not shown).[12]

The large variance in TIF district base values and growth rates requires further discussion. TIF districts with little EAV can attain greater rates of growth than those with large bases. Almost any development activity in the TIF district with a base EAV of only $487 will result in a growth rate of several hundred per cent. For Chicago's loop TIF district with a base of almost $1 billion, growth of several hundred per cent would be nearly impossible. Figure 2.1a and Figure 2.1b plot the *maximum*-year annualized EAV growth in each TIF against its base. Figure 2.1a shows the 195 TIF districts with a base EAV of less than $10 million. All of the growth rates

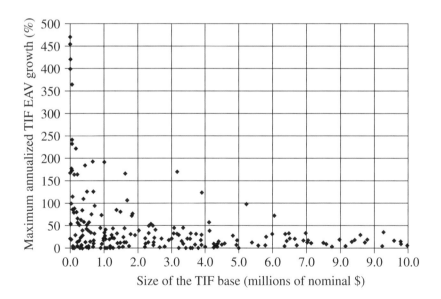

Note: TIF base less than $10 million, n = 195.

Figure 2.1a   Maximum annualized TIF EAV growth as a function of size of TIF base (1)

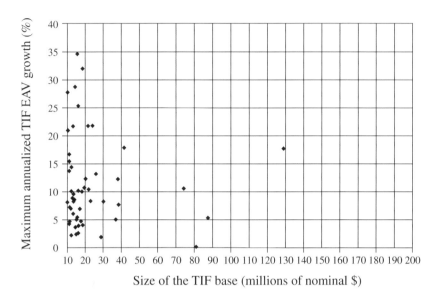

Note: TIFs with base of more than $10 million, n = 51, one TIF with base of almost $1 billion omitted.

Figure 2.1b   Maximum annualized TIF EAV growth as a function of size of TIF base (2)

above 200 per cent occur in TIF districts with a base of less than $170000. None of the TIF districts with a base of over $6.1 million has a maximum growth rate exceeding 50 per cent. Figure 2.1b shows the 51 TIF districts with a base EAV of between $10 and $200 million.[13] All of these TIF districts have maximum rates of growth of less than 35 per cent and there is no clear relationship between base EAV and rate of growth.

In our regression specification we include the natural log of the TIF base value in order to allow the size of the base EAV to affect the growth rate. However, inspection of Figures 2.1a and 2.1b indicates that the variance in growth rates is much larger among TIF districts with small bases than among those with large bases. For example, compare the variance in maximum annualized EAV growth rates among those TIF districts with a base of one-half million dollars (in Figure 2.1a) to the variance among TIF districts with a base of about $10 million (in Figure 2.1b). Growth rates in small TIF districts range from zero to 200 per cent, while in the larger districts growth rates range from about 2 to 30 per cent.

We do not know the reason for this pattern, but one contributing factor may be assessment practices. By law, the TIF base is the equalized *assessed* value in the district, not the *market* value of real estate. In some TIF districts real estate parcels may have an artificially low EAV because they have been purposely underassessed or because the municipal government or other tax-exempt organization owns them. If tax-exempt parcels are transferred to private owners or if underassessed parcels are reassessed to market value after TIF designation, we might observe high EAV growth rates even in the absence of any economic development. In TIF districts with relatively small bases these events might be especially significant and this could account for some of the high variance in growth rates. Unfortunately, our data set does not contain information about these kinds of events. Our statistical procedures (discussed in more detail below) are designed to account for the skewed variance in our dependent variable.

We conceptually decompose TIF district growth in order to provide a framework for our empirical analyses. By definition:

$$Y_i^{t+a} = (\pi_{t+a} + 1) Y_i^t e^{r_i^{t+a}a}, \tag{2.1}$$

where Y_i^k is the (nominal) assessed value of the real estate in TIF district i at year k ($k = t$ or $t+a$), t ($t = 1981$ to 1997) is the year the TIF district started, a ($a = 1$ to 18) is the age of the TIF district, π_{t+a} is the rate of 'inflationary' appreciation in real estate between year t and year $t+a$, and r_i^{t+a} is the 'real' average annual rate of growth of EAV in district i between year t and $t+a$.

We can rearrange equation (2.1) and take the log of both sides to get:[14]

$$G(i, t+a) = \Pi_{t+a} + r_i^{t+a}, \tag{2.2}$$

where $G(i, t+a)$ is the nominal average rate of growth of market value of real estate in TIF district i between year t and year $t+a$ and $\left(\dfrac{\pi_{t+a}}{a}\right) = \Pi_{t+a}$ is the average annual rate of real estate inflation between year t and $t+a$.

Our task is to model Π_{t+a} and r_i^{t+a} and estimate parameters that determine these growth rates. Rather than attempt to correct for inflation using a published price index, we assume that inflationary growth in TIF district real estate values is correlated with inflationary growth in real estate values in the surrounding area. When we control for EAV growth in the surrounding area we also control for inflationary growth in TIF district real estate values.

Non-inflationary, or real, growth in the value of TIF district could depend upon characteristics of t, a and i. That is, growth could depend upon the particular conditions in the start year 't', the age of the TIF district 'a', and 'site conditions' at the location of the ith TIF district.[15]

Interactions among these factors may also influence economic development.

We control for start year conditions that are common to all TIF districts in our sample by using a dummy variable for each start year. We control for the age of the TIF by using a continuous variable '*a*' to represent years since the TIF started. We have only limited information about site conditions, but can control for base EAV and the type of TIF district (that is, the land use in the district).

We do not have specific information about other site conditions such as the land area or transportation access to the TIF district.[16] However, we do know that many of the site characteristics of the TIF district are constant over its life. For example, a TIF district that has access to a major transportation thoroughfare at birth is likely always to have access to that thoroughfare. Because of this, a TIF district that has an unexpectedly high (or low) growth rate in one year is also likely to have an expectedly high (or low) growth rate in the next year. Similarly, the variance of the growth rate in some TIF districts may be systematically higher than in other districts.[17] We exploit this intuition in our estimation procedure.

We construct a panel data set. Each panel consists of observations of annualized growth rates in a single TIF district from the year the TIF began until 1998. The panels are pooled into a time-series cross-section data set. We estimate a generalized least squares (GLS) random effects model (Greene, 1993). This estimation procedure allows the error term for each TIF district to have a unique autocorrelation parameter and allows heteroskedasticity across districts.[18] By allowing error terms to be autocorrelated and by allowing the degree of autocorrelation to vary across TIF districts, we take into account the fact that some TIF districts may grow more rapidly (or slowly) because of particular site conditions that we cannot directly observe. By allowing for heteroskedasticity across districts, we take into account the fact that some TIF districts will have large (or small) variances in their growth rates for reasons we do not observe.

Our regression results are presented in Table 2.7. Specification 7.1 includes data on all 216 TIF districts for which we have an uninterrupted string of growth rates.[19] On average we observe about seven years of growth in each district, so that we have a total of more than 1500 observations. The coefficient on age indicates that a TIF district's growth rate falls by about 1 per cent each year it is in existence. This might be the result of TIF district administrators capitalizing on development opportunities early in the life of the district.

We control for inflationary growth in TIF district EAV by including host city EAV growth and its square as independent variables. We expect that, in the absence of TIF designation, EAV growth of areas within a city would

Table 2.7 *Growth in TIF property value, 1981–97, for the six-county TIF district sample*

Specification	7.1	7.2	7.3	7.4	7.5
Sample	All TIFs	All TIFs	CBD TIFs	Commercial TIFs	Industrial TIFs
Number of TIFS	216	216	32	29	40
Number of observations	1538	1538	327	224	226
Average number of obs. per TIF	7.12	7.12	10.22	7.72	5.65
Variable					
Age of TIF (years)	−0.01 (7.67)**	−0.01 (8.76)**	−0.003 (2.14)**	−0.01 (3.54)**	−0.01 (3.20)**
EAV growth rate in host city since TIF started	−0.23 (2.11)**	−0.32 (3.14)**	−0.78 (2.92)**	−1.39 (1.70)*	0.45 (0.89)
Square of EAV growth rate in host city since TIF started	2.07 (2.00)**	2.94 (2.86)**	4.40 (2.17)**	6.23 (0.76)	7.06 (0.66)
Natural log of TIF base	−0.10 (19.73)**	−0.10 (21.53)**	−0.004 (0.62)	0.29 (2.33)**	−0.06 (3.75)**
Central business district TIF	0.02 (1.54)				
Commercial TIF	0.004 (0.32)				
Industrial TIF	−0.04 (3.89)**				
Housing TIF	−0.09 (4.00)**				

Note: Absolute values of z-ratios are in parentheses, with ** for 5 per cent and * for 10 per cent significance; sample includes TIF districts with uninterrupted data on growth rates; dummy variables for year the TIF started were also included but estimates are not shown.

be correlated with citywide EAV growth. In light of our findings in previous sections of the chapter, we considered the possibility that citywide EAV growth might be an endogenous variable. However, replacing citywide EAV growth with a measure of areawide growth does change the qualitative results reported below.

TIF district growth is apparently influenced by growth in the host city in a complex way. The coefficient on EAV growth in the host city is significantly negative while the coefficient on the square of city EAV growth is significantly positive. According to specification 7.1, an increase in host city growth will *slow* growth in the TIF district if the city is growing by less than about 5.6 per cent but will raise TIF district growth thereafter.[20] According to Table 2.6, city EAV growth averages only 3 per cent. Thus, in most cases, an increase in city growth will lower TIF district growth. One explanation for this pattern might be that, when city growth is slow, economic development officers put additional effort into stimulating growth in TIF districts.

The most statistically significant control variable in this specification is the natural log of the TIF district base value. This coefficient implies that doubling the TIF base results in a 10 per cent decline in the *annualized* TIF district growth rate. Even after controlling for other factors, large TIF districts grow more slowly than small districts.

The next four variables in specification 7.1 are dummies that control for the type of land use activity in the TIF district. Central business and commercial TIF districts grow at about the same rate as the excluded category (mixed and other) while both industrial and housing TIF districts grow significantly more slowly. The relatively slow growth of industrial TIF districts is particularly disappointing for local development prospects since these districts often support activities that export goods to other regions. In contrast, commercial TIF districts are likely to substitute for development that otherwise would have occurred elsewhere in the region. Housing TIF districts are also likely to substitute for development that would have occurred elsewhere in the region. However, from a public policy point of view, a relocation of housing activity is generally the reason for a housing TIF district. In large cities, central business districts (CBDs) often produce specialized services that are exported from the region. However, in our sample, most of the CBD TIF districts are located in downtown areas of small suburban cities and compete with regional shopping malls rather than service producers in other regions. In summary, the most rapidly growing TIF districts appear to be those that relocate economic activity rather than increase development in the region.

Although we do not report them in Table 2.7, regression specifications 7.1 to 7.5 also include a series of dummy variables that control for the year each TIF was established. We find no evidence of a trend in these coefficients. It does not appear that more recently established TIF districts are growing either faster or more slowly than those established in past years.

Specification 7.2 uses the same sample as specification 7.1 but excludes the dummy variables to control for TIF district type. This specification is included as a transition to specifications 7.3, 7.4 and 7.5 and not because it is of independent interest. Dropping controls for TIF district type has little impact on the magnitude or significance of the other coefficients.

Specifications 7.3, 7.4 and 7.5 present separate regressions for CBD, commercial and industrial TIF districts. There were too few observations on housing-designated TIFs to estimate coefficients specifically for this type of TIF district. Specification 7.3 shows that the rate of growth in CBD TIF districts declines more slowly with age than for other types. This makes sense, because CBD TIF districts usually incorporate areas that are already economically mature. The opportunities for rapid growth early in the life of the TIF district are diminished. Even more notable is the insignificance of the coefficient on the natural log of the TIF base value in specification 7.3. There is no relationship between the initial size of a CBD-type TIF district and its growth rate.

Specification 7.4 uses data on 29 commercial TIF districts. The estimated coefficients on TIF district age are similar to those in specification 7.2. The coefficient on the log of the TIF base is positive, indicating that large commercial TIF districts grow faster than small districts. The point estimate of the coefficient on the host city's EAV growth is much larger (in absolute value) in specification 7.4 than in specification 7.2. The coefficient on the square of this variable is insignificant in specification 7.4. Commercial TIF districts are more competitive with growth in their host cities than other types of TIF district. Growth in the host city reduces growth in commercial TIF districts.

Specification 7.5 uses data on 40 industrial TIF districts and presents a dramatic contrast to specification 7.4. In particular, industrial TIF districts exhibit no evidence of competition with their host cities. The coefficients on the host city's EAV growth rate and its square are insignificant (and the point estimates are positive). Industrial TIF districts do not suffer when their host cities grow more rapidly.

5 CONCLUSION

Tax increment finance is an alluring tool. In the Chicago metropolitan area, assessed property value in TIF districts grew much faster than in their host cities. Proponents hope that TIF will stimulate stagnant areas and lead to a virtuous cycle of growth that will benefit the entire city. Our empirical analyses do not provide much evidence that this has occurred. Rather, we find that, even after controlling for other important factors and taking into account the self-selected nature of TIF imposition, the non-TIF areas of municipalities that use TIF grow no more rapidly – and perhaps more slowly – than similar municipalities that do not use TIF.

TIF has different impacts when land use is considered. We find evidence that commercial development in TIF districts directly substitutes for similar development outside the TIF district. In the Chicago metropolitan area, establishment of a commercial TIF district reduced commercial EAV growth by 3.9 per cent annually in non-TIF areas. Establishment of an industrial TIF also reduces commercial EAV outside the TIF district. When our sample includes municipalities across the entire state our results for commercial TIF districts are similar. We find additional evidence that the establishment of a TIF reduces residential EAV growth outside the TIF.

Industrial-use TIF districts may be fundamentally different from other TIF districts. The goods produced in industrial districts are generally exported from the region so that industrial development within TIF districts will not necessarily reduce industrial development elsewhere in the region. Our empirical analysis of industrial TIF districts is consistent with this line of reasoning. In most specifications we find that industrial TIF districts have no impact on EAV growth in non-TIF areas. However, we do find that, in the Chicago metropolitan area, establishment of an industrial TIF *increases* the growth of industrial EAV in the non-TIF portion of a municipality.

When we analyze the growth in individual TIF districts we find more evidence that the type of TIF district matters. Small TIF districts grew more rapidly than large districts, new TIF districts grew faster than older districts, and industrial use and residential use TIF districts grew less rapidly than other types of districts. The slow growth of industrial TIF districts is particularly disappointing because these districts provide the best opportunity for attracting new development to the region.

We also found that the growth rate in TIF districts in general and especially in commercial use TIF districts slows as municipal growth increases. This suggests that commercial TIF districts may be most successful in slow-growing municipalities. However, for industrial use TIF districts we find no evidence of an inverse relationship between host city and TIF district growth.

Our research suggests that policy makers should employ great caution in using TIF despite the lure of rapid development within the district. We find evidence that development within TIF districts, particularly commercial and residential development, substitutes for development elsewhere in the municipality. The design of TIF districts clearly matters, however. Small TIF districts grow more rapidly than large districts. Industrial TIF districts are less likely to substitute for development outside the TIF area.

NOTES

1. We thank Diane McCarthy for research assistance, Gib Bassett for econometric advice, and Joyce Man for valuable comments on an earlier draft. We gratefully acknowledge funding from the Lincoln Institute of Land Policy.
2. This statement assumes that the TIF increment grows at a faster rate than the rest of the municipality, which is generally true in our data (see Table 2.6.)
3. For example, if the TIF base is equal to 3.8 per cent of available EAV (the average observed in our data) and available EAV grows at 4.8 per cent per year (the average observed in our data) the net-of-TIF EAV growth rate will be about 5.0 per cent. Gross-of-TIF growth rates could be considerably higher depending upon the rate of growth of the increment and the number of years the TIF had been in existence.
4. The first-stage estimation of TIF adoption includes control variables for prior growth in EAV, prior growth in EAV squared, prior growth in population, prior growth in population squared, prior growth in per capita income, prior growth in per capita income squared, municipal tax rate, non-municipal tax rate, school aid formula range, population, per capita income, poverty rate, non-residential share of EAV, distance to the Chicago loop, and county. Variable definitions and details of our econometric methodology are discussed in Dye and Merriman (2000). As in our earlier study, we reject the hypothesis of sample selection bias in nearly all of our regression specifications. In each estimate below we report a test statistic for sample selection bias and coefficients estimates that allow for the endogeneity of TIF adoption. We have also run all models under the assumption that TIF adoption is determined exogenously. The basic qualitative results we report here are unchanged
5. Nor are the TIF dummy coefficients significant in the alternative specifications with exogenous TIF adoption. In contrast, our early study found a significant negative coefficient on the TIF dummy for the exogenous specification of net EAV, suggesting that municipalities that adopted TIF grew more slowly than would otherwise have been the case. While our provocative result of a significantly negative impact of TIF adoption on growth is not robust to the change in the sample and period, we still find that there is no positive impact of TIF adoption on the growth in citywide property values.
6. In the 'c' and 'i' specifications of Tables 2.3 and 2.5 a small number of observations are lost when growth in commercial or industrial property value starts from a zero base.
7. For the 246 northeastern municipalities for which we have both variables, the correlation between the aggregate tax rate and the partial aggregate tax rate is 0.98.
8. The list of control variables is slightly different from that for the six-county sample: home-rule status, partial aggregate tax rate, population, income per capita, poverty rate, non-residential share of EAV, EAV per square mile and dummy variables for each of five collar counties, for northern and southern Cook counties (which are assessed in different triennial cycles), and for each of the metropolitan areas in the state (with non-metropolitan counties the omitted category). There is no variable for 'distance from the Chicago loop' in the statewide model.
9. There are many more TIF districts (247) than municipalities that have adopted TIF (100) in the six-county sample, because some municipalities house more than one TIF district.
10. Calculated as the logarithm of current TIF EAV divided by the base value of the TIF, divided by the number of years since the TIF began.
11. The annualized city EAV growth during a TIF district's life reported in Table 2.6 should

      not be confused with the growth rates in municipal EAV reported in Table 2.1. The unit of analysis in Table 2.6 is the TIF district. This means that a city, such as Chicago, that has multiple TIF districts in multiple years is counted multiple times. Furthermore, in Table 2.6, city EAV growth rates are annualized over the varying life spans of the TIF district rather than over the periods given in Table 2.1.

12. Mean annualized TIF EAV growth is much larger than median annualized TIF EAV growth because a few TIF districts were outliers that grew at very high rates. This is discussed in more detail below.

13. The Chicago Loop TIF district with a base EAV of nearly $1 billion is not shown on the figure. This TIF district had a maximum growth rate of 2.5 per cent.

14. The derivation of equation (2.2) uses the fact that: $\ln(\Pi_{it+a} + 1) \cong \Pi_{t+a}$.

15. These conditions can be understood by an analogy with the factors that influence the economic well-being of a child. Site conditions (for example, parents' genetic endowment), year of birth (for example, children born in 1960 and who may have entered the job market at the depth of a recession in 1982) and age (years since birth) all may play a role in an individual's earnings.

16. For an analysis that has more specific controls for site conditions, see Bryne (2002).

17. For example, TIF districts with small base values are likely to have a bigger variance in their growth rates than those with large base values.

18. In preliminary analysis we estimated OLS and fixed-effects regressions specifications. The OLS specification was rejected on the basis of a strong correlation between the residuals and the predicted value of the dependent variable. The fixed-effects specification was rejected because the Breusch and Pagan (1980) Lagrange multiplier test of the null hypothesis that the variances of TIF specific constants were zero was rejected.

19. Twenty-four TIF districts are excluded from the sample because they began in 1997 and we have only one year of data on growth rates. In seven additional TIF districts one year of intermediate growth was missing. We discard these observations as well because the econometric technique we use to estimate the autocorrelation parameter requires a continuous string of growth rates.

20. Note that specification (7.1) implies that $G(i,t + a) = \text{constant} - (0.23 \times \text{CEAV}) + (2.07 \times \text{CEAV}^2)$, where CEAV is the host city's EAV growth. This implies that

$$\frac{\partial G(i,t+a)}{\partial CEAV} = 0 = -0.23 + (4.14 \times \text{CEAV*}) \Rightarrow \text{CEAV*} = \frac{0.23}{4.14} = 0.056.$$

REFERENCES

Anderson, John E., 1990, 'Tax Increment Financing: Municipal Adoption and Growth', *National Tax Journal*, 43, 155–63.

Anderson, John E. and Robert W. Wassmer, 2000, *Bidding for Business: The Efficacy of Local Economic Development Incentives in a Metropolitan Area*, Kalamazoo, MI: W.E. Upjohn Institute for Employment Research.

Breusch T. and A. Pagan, 1980, 'The Lagrange Multiplier Test and its Applications to Model Specification in Econometrics', *Review of Economic Studies*, 47, 239–53.

Bryne, Paul F., 2002, 'Determinants of Property Value Growth for Tax Increment Finance Districts', University of Illinois, Institute of Government and Public Affairs, Urbana, Illinois, working paper no. 102, February.

Chapman, Jeffrey I., 1998, 'Tax Increment Financing as a Tool of Redevelopment', in Helen Ladd (ed.), *Local Government Tax and Land Use Policies in the United States*, Cheltenham, UK and Northampton, MA: Edward Elgar, pp. 182–98.

Dye, Richard F. and David F. Merriman, 2000, 'The Effects of Tax Increment Financing on Economic Development', *Journal of Urban Economics*, 47, 306–28.

Greene, William H., 1993, *Econometric Analysis*, 2nd edn, New York: Macmillan Publishing Company.

Klacik, J. Drew and Samuel Nunn, 2001, 'A Primer on Tax Increment Financing', in Craig L. Johnson and Joyce Y. Man (eds), *Tax Increment Financing and Economic Development: Uses, Structures and Impact*, Albany: State University of New York Press, pp. 15–29.

Man, Joyce Y., 2001, 'Effects of Tax Increment Financing on Economic Development', in Craig L. Johnson and Joyce Y. Man (eds), *Tax Increment Financing and Economic Development: Uses, Structures and Impact*, Albany: State University of New York Press, pp. 87–99.

Man, Joyce Y. and Mark S. Rosentraub, 1998, 'Tax Increment Financing: Municipal Adoption and Effects on Property Value Growth', *Public Finance Review*, 26, 523–47.

3. Preferential assessment: impacts and alternatives

John E. Anderson

1 INTRODUCTION

Background

State and local governments in the United States provide for reduced property taxation of agricultural land and open space. The primary mechanism by which this is accomplished is preferential assessment. By preferential assessment we mean any aspect of a property tax system that provides that a lower assessment ratio be applied to specific classes of properties. Most often states provide preferential assessment for agricultural property with a use value assessment methodology. Under this method of assessing property, the highest and best use of the property is not used as the assessed value for tax purposes. Rather, the value of the property in its current use is the value designated for tax purposes. To the extent that market value and use value diverge, with use value being lower than market value, a tax preference is provided to that property. The effective property tax rate is the nominal tax rate times the assessment ratio – the ratio of assessed value to market value. By providing a preferential assessment, lowering assessed value in relation to market value thereby lowering the assessment ratio, the effective property tax rate is reduced.

Preferential assessment is pervasive, with nearly all of the states permitting use value assessment for agricultural land in particular. Valuing land in its agricultural use rather than in its highest and best use reduces the assessment ratio for properties where agriculture is not the highest and best use. The states of Wisconsin and Michigan are the only exceptions to the general rule that states permit some sort of preferential assessment for agricultural and open space land. Those states provide tax relief for agricultural land through circuit-breaker mechanisms in exchange for forgone development rights. Hence, all 50 states provide some sort of preferential property tax treatment for agricultural land and nearly all do so through preferential assessment in particular.

Justification

The fact that agricultural land is taxed at a rate below that of other types of property is indisputable. The remaining question is why agricultural land should be taxed at a lower effective rate than other classes of property. Various justifications are possible, although none is definitive. First, it may be that open space at the periphery of an urban area provides positive externalities appreciated by the general population. This may include the existence value of wildlife, open space and forests. If so, land markets may allocate too much land to developed use, ignoring the external benefits provided by agricultural use and open space. To correct for that misallocation it may be appropriate to provide a Pigouvian subsidy to agricultural land to ensure that the socially optimal amount of open space is retained. Anderson (1993c) investigates the potential use of Pigouvian taxes or subsidies to correct the optimal timing of land development in the presence of externalities. This argument is valid, but measuring the positive externality is difficult and properly designing a tax/subsidy scheme to correct for that externality would be challenging. Furthermore, this argument is probably not appropriate for agricultural land in locations far from urban areas. In pure farm country, it is difficult to make the positive externality argument without relying exclusively on an appeal to existence value on the part of urban residents. Ultimately, this rationale is rather inexact in providing specific guidance for the preferential treatment of agricultural land and open space.

Second, property taxes are used by local governments to finance the provision of local public goods, including education, road and bridge maintenance, and other local public services. Following the benefit principle, if agricultural landowners benefit to a lesser extent from the provision of these public goods and services, it may be proper to reduce the tax they are asked to pay for such services. This argument involves an implicit assumption that the median or decisive voter in the community is not a farmer. That is presumably the reason for the local government providing too many of the local public services from the farmers' point of view. While this may be true in the case of farmland near an urbanized area, it is probably not true in pure farm country. Even if the decisive voter is a farmer, there may be other explanations for the local government overproviding public services. Models abound in the public choice literature (such as the monopoly-agenda control model) that explain this phenomenon. Of course, this argument also relies on the benefit view of the property tax in maintaining that the level of taxation should be directly related to the benefits received by the property owner. The literature on property tax incidence is not conclusive on the question of whether the property tax is a benefits tax (entirely). Even so, this particular application of the benefit principle is not unique to the issue of property taxation. In many other areas of taxation we find significant groups of taxpayers who claim that they do not receive benefits in proportion to the taxes they pay. Such situations, if found to be compelling by the political process, usually lead to exemptions (either partial or full) or reduced rates of taxation. In other cases, the resolution is a cap on the tax, thereby limiting the amount of tax in order to prevent a divergence between the benefits received and the tax paid.

Third, it may be that federal government subsidies to farmers inflate land values through the capitalization of those subsidies into land value. In a recent debate over capping farm subsidies, for example, Senator Dorgan of North Dakota was quoted as saying that 'big government payments were driving up land prices' (Associated Press, 2002) With artificially high land values, state and local governments provide property tax relief by taxing at a lower effective tax rate. To gauge the magnitude of the effect, consider that the 1999 AELOS survey reported that government payments to 914116 farms in the USA amounted to $16.7 billion. The average payment of $18269, when capitalized as a perpetuity at a 5 per cent discount rate, is worth $365380 per farm. If those payments are at least partially capitalized into land value, making the land value higher than it would be otherwise, then local governments may perceive that they should tax a portion of the land value, but not the full market value in order to compensate. Of course, it must be recognized that use value assessment of agricultural land should include the capitalized value of the government farm payments, since that is an integral aspect of agricultural use of the land. Hence use value assessment would not properly compensate for the capitalized value of the subsidy stream. Nevertheless, by taxing use value rather than market value, local governments are reducing the effective rate of taxation and may be doing so in recognition that land value includes the capitalized value of farm subsidies.

Federal subsidies to farmers have the effect of raising net farm income. In a development timing model such as Anderson (1986) or Turnbull (1988) the effect of the subsidy stream is to delay development. That effect may be consistent with state and local government objectives, but it also causes property taxes to be higher. Higher property taxes on agricultural land have the effect of speeding development. In order to compensate for that effect, state and local governments may recognize the need to reduce the effective rate of taxation on agricultural land. Of course, it can be argued that there is a similar effect for residential property. Since the US income tax system does not tax the imputed rental value of owner-occupied housing there is a tax advantage that is capitalized into house values. Yet there is no preferential taxation of residential property because of this capitalization effect.

There are three possible rationales for taxing farmland at a lower rate than other classes of property. The first two arguments do not specify that preferential assessment is required, however. A lower effective tax rate can be accomplished by other means, such as a classified tax rate structure with agricultural land taxed at a lower rate. There are also arguments supporting higher effective tax rates applied to agricultural land and open space. The primary argument in this vein is based on the efficiency of taxing land value, generating no excess burden given the inelastic supply of land. If land is supplied inelastically while capital is supplied relatively elastically, economic theory indicates that we should tax land at a relatively high rate and structures at relatively low rate. While no one disputes this fundamental result, using this as a normative rationale for higher rates of land taxation is problematic. The policy implications of this view have been resisted since the time of Henry George.

Extent of Application

Morris (1998) has compiled a recent survey of the preferential assessment methods applied by the states, based on Aiken (1989) and Census of Agriculture sources. There are various applications of preferential assessment applied by the states: 19 states provide for preferential assessment only; 26 states provide preferential assessment with deferred taxation; five states provide preferential assessment with restrictive land use agreements and deferred taxation.

For a general overview of taxes on farmland in the USA, see Wunderlich and Blackledge (1994). Using a 1988 survey of taxes actually paid by individual farmland owners (the Agricultural Economics and Land Ownership Survey – AELOS), regardless of the assessment ratio applied, they found that the $5.1 billion in property taxes paid on agricultural land accounted for less than 5 per cent of US real property taxes. Property taxes averaged $6.08 per acre and $0.85 per $100 of value (owner-estimated). They examined whether preferential assessments affected the tax rates reported in the survey. Of the 19 states with preferential assessment (and no rollback) they found that nine states had effective tax rates below the median and 10 states had rates above the median. They concluded that the relationship between preferential assessment and tax rates applied in the states is not obvious. The most recent AELOS survey results (1999) report estimated real estate taxes of $8.56 per acre or $0.64 per $100 of value. The estimated market value of land and buildings per acre was $1371, up from $676 in the 1988 AELOS.

Literature

The literature on use value assessment dates back to the 1970s with the Barlowe *et al.* (1973) early summary of use value legislation, the Beattie and Ransom (1979) review of policy issues, the Gloudemans (1974) paper presenting the fundamental assessment issues, the Conklin and Lesher (1977) work on use value assessment as a means to slow urban growth, the Carman (1977) and Schwartz *et al.* (1976) work on California's early experience with use value assessment, and the Power and Cooke (1976) work on Florida's early experience with use value assessment.

As early experience with use value assessment grew, the literature turned to specific considerations of the effects, including the Bowman and Mikesell (1988) assessment uniformity work, the Chicoine and Scott (1983) analysis of farm-level data on use value assessment impacts, the Chicoine and Hendricks (1985) work on tax shifting due to use value assessment and implications for state school aid, and the Dunford and Marousek (1981) work on local tax shifts due to use value assessment. The Ferguson (1988) work on evaluating the effectiveness of use value assessment programs at that time also provided a useful framework for policy evaluation.

Most recently, research on use value assessment has included the Anderson (1993a) work analyzing the Michigan program, the Anderson (1993b) theoretical analysis of the impact on development timing, the Anderson and Bunch (1989) empirical work on preferential assessment and its impact on land values in Michigan, the Anderson and Griffing (2000) empirical analysis of parcel-level data in Nebraska comparing use value and market value, the Entreken (1994) practical insights for appraisers, the McFarlane (1999) theoretical synthesis of results to date on the effects of taxes on development, the Morris (1998) county-level empirical study of the rate at which farmland is being converted to developed uses and the impact of use value assessment in slowing that process, the Plantinga and Miller (2001) work on valuing the rights to future development, the Tavernier and Li (1995) work on the effectiveness of use value assessment in slowing land development, and the Wunderlich (1997) general survey of effects of preferential assessments.

2 IMPACTS

Potential impacts of preferential assessment of agricultural land include effects on the effective rate of taxation, the price of land, the timing of development, the intensity of development and other effects.

Preferential property tax rates, whether direct in the form of a classified tax system or indirect through preferential assessment ratios, should have an impact on land value. Reductions in property taxes should be at least partially capitalized into higher land values. Hence preferential assessment confers a windfall gain in wealth on agricultural landowners. From a public choice point of view, the popularity of preferential assessments throughout the country reflects the rent-seeking behavior of agricultural landowner-voters. Preferential assessment systems are simply one more way (in addition to set-aside programs, emergency payments, commodity price supports and so on) in which the farm lobby has been successful in obtaining benefits for farmers.

Basic Model of Land Value

The basic model of land value developed in Anderson (1993b; 1986) can be used to examine the issues related to preferential assessment. Suppose that a landowner has a pre-development net income stream described by the function $f(t)$. We can think of this as the farming net income generated by the land. Suppose that at time period $t = D$ a net income stream can be generated by a developed use of the land such as housing. The net income stream generated by the developed use of the land is captured by the function $h(t,D)$. Including D as an argument in this function permits the developed net income stream to depend upon the time that development occurs. The amortized development cost is included implicitly in the net income stream $h(t,D)$. There is no property tax in this basic model

Discounting at the rate r, the value of the property prior to development, $t < D$, is denoted $V(t,D)$ and given by the following equation:

$$V(t,D) = \int_t^D f(u)e^{-r(u-t)}du + \int_D^\infty h(u,D)e^{-r(u-t)}du. \qquad (3.1)$$

Including a property tax in the model, applied to the market value of the property at rate τ, we can write the value expression as

$$V(t,D) = \int_t^D f(u)e^{-(r+\tau)(u-t)}du + e^{-(r+\tau)(D-t)}\int_D^\infty h(u,D)e^{-(r+\tau)(u-D)}du. \qquad (3.2)$$

Notice that undeveloped land value depends upon the farming net income stream reflecting the farming use of the land up to period D. After that point, however, the value of the land reflects the developed net income stream. Hence the value of undeveloped property depends upon a mixture of net incomes due to farming and developed land use.

Once developed $t \geq D$, the value of the land is simply the second integral in equation (3.1) with lower limit of integration t. If we include a property tax applied to the market value of the property at the rate τ the property value expression can be written as

$$V(t,D) = \int_t^\infty h(u,D)e^{-(r+\tau)(u-t)}du. \tag{3.3}$$

This expression indicates that the value of the property is the present discounted value of the post-development net income stream where the discount rate used includes the property tax rate.

Model of Land Value with Preferential Assessment

To incorporate a preferential assessment rate we can modify the basic model of Anderson (1993b). Equation (3.1) was derived on the assumption that the value of the property for tax purposes was the market value reflecting highest and best use. With preferential assessment (or use value assessment) we must apply the tax to the property value reflecting farming use of the land. To do so, let us define $F(t)$ as the discounted farm net income stream:

$$F(t) = \int_t^\infty f(u)e^{-r(u-t)}du. \tag{3.4}$$

In the special case of constant farm income with $f(t) = f$ for all periods t, we have the case of a perpetuity and the farming value of the land is simply $F(t) = f/r$. This value is often called the use value of the land as it captures only the value in farming use. Technically, of course, the term 'use value' could apply to any current use of a property that is less than the highest and best use of that property. We use the term 'market value' to describe the value of a property in its highest and best use.

If the farmland is subject to a property tax applied at the rate τ, the value expression is simply modified by making the discount rate in equation (3.4) $(r+\tau)$. Hence the value of the farmland, in perpetual use as farmland, is the present discounted value of the net farm income stream, where the discount rate includes the property tax rate:

$$F(t) = \int_t^\infty f(u)e^{-(r+\tau)(u-t)}du. \tag{3.5}$$

It will also be convenient to define the developed property value in the period of development, $t = D$ as

$$H(D,D) = \int_D^\infty h(u,D)e^{-r(u-D)}du. \tag{3.6}$$

For time periods after development occurs, $t \geq D$, the value of land subject to preferential assessment for tax purposes can be written as $\tilde{V}(t,D)$:

$$\tilde{V}(t,D) \int_t^\infty [h(u,D) - \tau F(u,D)]e^{-r(u-t)}du. \tag{3.7}$$

In this case, the property tax is the rate τ applied to the farming value of the land, ignoring the potential developed value of the land. This differential equation can be solved to obtain the following value expression:

$$\tilde{V}(t,D) = \int_t^\infty h(u,D)e^{-r(u-t)}du - \tau\int_t^\infty F(u,D)e^{-r(u-t)}du. \tag{3.8}$$

This expression indicates that the value of the property when taxed on the basis of its use value is the present discounted stream of net income reduced by the present discounted value of the property tax payment stream where the tax is based on the preferential assessment.

Prior to development, $t < D$, the value of property subject to preferential tax assessment based on use value is given by the expression:

$$\tilde{V}(t,D) = \int_t^D f(u)e^{-(r+\tau)(u-t)}du + e^{-(r+\tau)(D-t)}\left[\int_D^\infty h(u,D)e^{-r(u-D)}du\right.$$

$$\left. - \tau\int_D^\infty F(u)e^{-r(u-D)}du.\right] \tag{3.9}$$

We will use the above expressions to investigate some of the implications of preferential assessment for undeveloped land that is subject to preferential assessment.

Implications

What are the implications of preferential assessment applied to undeveloped land? There are two primary effects to consider: the wealth effect due to the reduction in property tax that is capitalized into land value, and the development timing effect due to the reduced cost of holding undeveloped land. We consider each in turn.

Wealth effect

First, there is a gain in property wealth to the landowner that is represented by the difference between the property value under the preferential assessment regime and the property value under a non-preferential regime: $\tilde{V}(t,D) - V(t,D)$. Consider the case of an undeveloped piece of property where the difference in values can be written as

$$\tilde{V}(t,D) - V(t,D) = e^{-(r+\tau)(D-t)}\left\{\int_D^\infty h(u,D)[e^{-r(u-D)}\{1 - e^{-\tau(u-D)}\}]du\right.$$

$$\left. - \tau\int_D^\infty F(u)e^{-r(u-D)}du.\right\} \tag{3.10}$$

This expression captures the economic value (measured in period D) of the preferential tax treatment of the property. Since there is no preferential assessment prior to development in period D, the first term in curled braces on the right-hand side of the above equation is the present discounted value of the property tax stream (from period D forward) based on market value assessment. The second term on the right-hand side is the present discounted value of the property tax stream based on use value assessment. Hence the gain to the property owner is the present discounted value of the difference in the two property tax streams. The preferential assessment reduces the property tax liability of the property owner and raises the value of the property by the capitalized value of the tax savings. The size of the wealth effect depends upon the period of development, the post-development net income stream, the value of the property in farm use, and the property and the tax rate.

The wealth transfer is conferred on the original owner of the land and is therefore a one-time windfall. After that, the market mechanism takes account of the preferential taxation of the land and the market price is bid up. Subsequent owners of the property pay a price that includes the capitalized value of the preferential tax treatment when they buy the property. In an efficient real estate market, the after-tax rate of return will be equalized. Properties subject to preferential taxation will bring higher market prices. Those higher prices then generate higher property tax payments. In that sense, the wealth transfer issue is a one-time issue. Nevertheless, there are important equity implications to consider. The original owner may be treated differently from subsequent owners. Furthermore, two owners of identical properties may pay very different taxes, depending upon whether they are original or new owners.

Development timing effect
Second, there is an impact on the timing of land development. Anderson (1993b) has shown that use value assessment has the effect of delaying development, other things being equal. It is important to recognize, however, that the extent to which development is delayed depends upon a number of factors, including farming use value of the land relative to its value in potential developed use, and the rate of property taxation. The greater the divergence between the land's value in agricultural use and its value in developed use the more use value assessment delays development of the land. The greater the property tax rate, the more use value assessment delays development.

In the absence of preferential assessment, the first order condition for optimal timing of land development is given by:

$$H'(D)/H(D) = (r + \tau) - f(D)/H(D). \tag{3.11}$$

This condition specifies that, at the optimal time, the marginal benefit of waiting another period, given by the rate of increase in the developed value of the property, must be equal to the marginal cost of delaying development reflected by the discount rate including the property tax rate, adjusted for the pre-development farm net income that period. In the absence of a property tax and pre-development farm income, this rule collapses to the familiar Wicksellian conclusion that development should occur when the rate of increase in the value of the asset equals the interest rate.

With preferential assessment, the first order condition for the optimal time of development is modified to

$$H'(D)/H(D) = (r + \tau) - f(D)/H(D) - \tau F(D)/H(D)$$
$$- [(r + \tau)\tau/H(D)] \int_{D}^{\infty} F(u)e^{-r(u-D)}du. \qquad (3.12)$$

The effect of preferential assessment on development timing is clearly to delay development. The third and fourth terms on the right-hand side both reduce the opportunity cost of delayed development. The extent to which development is delayed depends upon two key factors: the farming use value of the land relative to the potential developed use, and the property tax rate. The greater the difference between use value and developed value, the more preferential assessment will delay development. Also the greater the property tax rate, the more use value assessment delays development. Of course, property tax rates have been declining over a long period of time in the USA as other revenue sources have become more important in state and local public finance. Consequently, the ability of preferential assessment to delay development may be eroded over time.

McFarlane (1999) and Turnbull (1988) have also analyzed the impacts of taxation on development, in terms of both the timing of development and the capital intensity of development. They have not, however, specifically examined the effects of use value assessment.

Empirical Evidence on the Effects of Preferential Assessment

One of the earliest and most important preferential assessment programs was the California Land Conservation Act of 1965 – the so-called 'Williamson' Act. That act permitted local governments to enter into contracts with private landowners in order to restrict parcels of land in agricultural or open space uses. In exchange for that use restriction, landowners were given the benefit of preferential assessment. The assessed value of the land was based on its farming or open space use, rather than on its full market value. In order to hold local governments harmless in this process, the state government provided transfers to compensate for the lost property tax revenue in the California Open Space Subvention Act of 1971. The Williamson Act Study Group (see Carter *et al.*, 1989), found that 65 per cent of the acreage in the Williamson Act was non-prime agricultural land. In fact, just 4.7 per cent of the land was prime agricultural land in urban areas. Proposition 13 then provided an interesting natural experiment on the effect of reduced property tax rates. When property tax rates fell from the 2.5 per cent to 3 per cent range that prevailed prior to Proposition 13 to less than 1 per cent after adoption of Proposition 13, there were widespread cancellations of contracts under the Williamson Act. The California evidence confirms our expectation from the above model that at low rates of property taxation the development timing delay is small. More generally, the California evidence indicates that preferential assessment provides no effective delay in land development timing.

Anderson and Griffing (2000) investigated the difference between market value and use value of agricultural land using two data sets for land values around Omaha and Lincoln, Nebraska. They estimated traditional negative exponential models of land value declining with distance from the central business district. The difference between market value and use value was found to decline with distance from the CBD, consistent with the pattern suggested in the Capozza and Helsley (1989) and Capozza and Sick (1994) spatial models of land value.

Anderson and Bunch (1989) analyzed the Michigan circuit-breaker program of property tax relief for agricultural land. They used cross section data and estimated a three-equation model of property tax credit levels, property tax rates and land values. Their analysis revealed that the combined property tax credits provided by the agricultural land retention program and the homestead circuit-breaker relief are capitalized into land values. Anderson (1993b) investigated both the capitalization of the tax relief into land value and the extent to which that property tax relief prevented the transition of land to developed use. He estimated models of land values and program participation rates and found that the property tax credits are partially capitalized into land value and that the circuit-breakers do not effectively retard land development. Enrollments in the land conservation program providing property tax relief are lower in those areas where potential development opportunities are greater. Urbanization pressure was also found to reduce program enrollments. Analysis of the Michigan program revealed that the credit program is not very effective in slowing the rate of land development, although it may provide an acceptable level of general assistance to farmers.

The most recent and comprehensive analysis of the way preferential assessment affects the rate of loss of farmland is that of Morris (1998), who compiled a pooled county-level data set using Census of Agriculture years

1959, 1964, 1969, 1974, 1978, 1982, 1987. Regressing the proportion of farmland lost in each county/year on a number of regressors, she found evidence that preferential assessment practices had an impact in slowing the rate of growth of farmland loss. According to her estimates, a gradual difference in rate of loss of farmland due to preferential assessment accumulates over a 20-year period to become approximately 10 per cent more of the land in a country being retained in agriculture than would have otherwise been retained. Of course, this finding does not mean that preferential assessment policies are necessarily economically effective. We do not have information about what that additional farmland retention cost. Without further information on the benefits and costs of preferential assessment policies, we cannot make an informed judgment on the economic efficacy of these policies.

3 ALTERNATIVES

What are the alternatives to preferential assessment of land? To answer this question, we must first clarify the intended purpose of preferential assessment. Various goals may be purported by advocates, including slowing development, preserving prime agricultural land, retaining open space and reducing the tax burden on farmers. Appropriate alternatives must be consistent with the intended goal of the preferential assessment program. Whether a wealth transfer or delay of development is the policy objective matters a great deal. In what follows we examine classified property tax systems, conservation easements, transfer or purchase of development rights, development impact fees and graded tax systems.

Classified Property Tax Systems

Rather than provide agricultural land with preferential assessment, the state could authorize local governments to administer a classified property tax system. With a classified system tax rates could differ among classes of property. This permits direct variation in rates rather than indirect variation through differences in the assessment method used. Since the effective tax rate is the product of the nominal tax rate and the assessment ratio, a reduction in the effective rate can be accomplished either directly through a lower nominal rate or indirectly through a lower assessment ratio. Why do most states prefer the indirect approach?

Suppose that we have a simple classified tax system with two different classes of property: farmland and developed land. There are two property tax rates; one applied to farmland τ_f and another applied to all other property τ, with $\tau_f < \tau$. All property is valued at market value for tax purposes. In this case, the value of property prior to development $(t < D)$ can be expressed as:

$$\tilde{V}(t,D) = \int_t^D f(u)e^{-(r+\tau_f)(u-t)}du + e^{-(r+\tau_f)(D-t)}\int_D^\infty h(u,D)e^{-(r+\tau)(u-D)}du. \quad (3.13)$$

Property value depends upon the discounted stream of net farm income (where the discount rate includes the farm property tax rate) plus the discounted value of the post-development net income stream (where the discount rate includes the post-development property tax rate). The difference between the property value given in equation (3.3) and this value under a classified property tax system represents the capitalized tax reduction. Of course, the tax advantage only comes from the lower tax while the land is used in farming. Once developed, the property is classified as such and the value becomes the developed value. The following expression captures the capitalized value of the tax advantage:

$$\tilde{V}(t,D) - V(t,D) = \int_t^D f(u)[e^{-(r+\tau_f)(u-t)} - e^{-(r+\tau)(u-t)}]du + [e^{-(r+\tau_f)(D-t)}$$
$$- e^{-(r+\tau)(D-t)}]\int_D^\infty h(u,D)e^{-(r+\tau)(u-D)}du. \quad (3.14)$$

This amount depends on the difference between the two tax rates and the length of time until development of the property. The greater the difference between the tax rates or the longer the time until development, the larger the capitalized value of the tax benefit provided by the classified system.

A state can provide a property tax reduction either indirectly through a lower assessment rate, thereby reducing the effective tax rate, or directly by a lower tax rate as in a classified tax system. Now, let us return to the question of why states all seem to prefer the indirect approach. There are several reasons that may motivate the preference for preferential assessments. First, this method permits case-by-case adjustments in assessed value and thereby permits customized effective tax rates. The local assessor is free to use discretion, within bounds, in determining the assessed valuation and thereby determining the effective rate of taxation. In a classified tax system, assessments are uniform and the only variation permitted is in the tax rates that apply broadly to entire classes of property. This is probably the primary reason why state and local governments prefer the indirect approach. Classified tax systems are blunt instruments with which to provide variations in effective property tax rates. Preferential assessments provide a much finer means by which to provide variation in effective tax rates.

Second, the state may prefer preferential assessment based on use value in order to distinguish between agricultural land that is used in farming and agricultural land that is used for other purposes as well. Consider the case of agricultural land that is also used for hunting purposes, for example. Preferential assessment may permit the local assessor to distinguish between agricultural land used solely for raising commodities from that land also used for commercial hunting purposes during part of the year. Use value assessment permits fine distinctions based on multiple uses. For this reason, it may be preferable to a classified tax system that would treat all agricultural land similarly. Finally, it may be that a classified tax system has a different incidence from that of a system of preferential assessment. Sonstelie (1979) demonstrates that the conventional wisdom about property tax incidence in a general equilibrium model is generally true of a classified system as well. If preferential assessment permits variation in the effective tax rate within a given class of property, however, there are additional incidence implications.

Conservation Easements

Rather than buy the land in its totality, with all the rights thereunto appertaining, why not buy a conservation easement? A conservation easement is a legal agreement restricting land use with implications for property valuation and taxation. Easements typically limit the development of housing subdivisions, non-farm development and other land uses deemed inconsistent with commercial agriculture. Property owners retain title to the property, but both their land use and the use of future owners of the property are restricted. Land can be bought and sold in market transactions, with the easement restricting land use. Conservation organizations often buy or accept donations of land with conservation easements. This legal means of restricting land use is quite effective, only alterable by a court of law through eminent domain proceedings or if the land changes and the conservation objectives become impossible to achieve.

Easements have the direct effect of reducing property value on the subject property and thereby reducing property taxes, given local tax rates. This effect operates regardless of the provision of use value assessment. Even under a market value assessment standard, a conservation easement reduces the market value of the property and thereby reduces the assessed value. Advantages include the fact that the property stays in private ownership and can be used for any purpose permitted by the easement restrictions. The restrictions continue from owner to owner over time. Surrounding property values may rise to some extent, if there are positive externalities generated by the open space provided by the easement. Estate taxes may also be reduced and property may pass more easily to heirs given the lower property value. If the conservation easement is donated to a land trust that donation may be treated as a charitable contribution, providing federal and state income tax deductions for the donor.

The simplest measure of the value of the conservation easement can be seen by considering the extreme case where all development rights are removed by the easement. In that case, the easement reduces the value of the property by the difference between equation (3.3) and equation (3.4), where the later equation is modified to include a property tax applied at the rate:

$$V(t,D) - F(t) = e^{-(r+\tau)(D-t)} \int_D^\infty h(u,D)e^{-(r+\tau)(u-D)}du - \int_D^\infty f(u)e^{-(r+\tau)(u-t)}du. \quad (3.15)$$

The effect of the conservation easement is to reduce the market value of the property by an amount that is the present discounted value of the developed use of the property less the farming use, from the point of development forward. This captures the opportunity cost of development for the landowner and represents the cost of the easement. We would expect compensation for such an easement to approximate this value.

Assessment or appraisal of easements is difficult since it is not clear which method of valuation is most appropriate. The comparable sales method can be used but requires an adequate number of appropriate comparables. Aside from the problem of the lack of data, there is an additional problem stemming from the fact that easement stipulations are not uniform, varying with each specific property case. Even if there are data on land sales with easements, how do you take into account the various different specifications on land use limitations imposed by the easements? It is difficult to control properly for the specific characteristics of the properties and the easements in applying the comparable sales method. Another method used is a before-and-after appraisal approach. The appraiser determines the value of the property before the conservation easement is created, with the property valued in its highest and best use assuming the full bundle of rights. Then the value of the property is recomputed on the assumption that the conservation easement has been put in place and the land use options have been restricted. In practice, there are often disputes over the highest and best use of the property prior to attaching the easement to the property.

Despite the various difficulties involved, conservation easements have become the major tool used by both public sector and private sector entities wishing to restrict conversion of farmland to developed use. Conservation easements are also used as a mechanism of land use restriction in other methods such as the transfer of development rights described next.

A related yet quite distinct approach is that of concurrence regulations which prevent development of land until infrastructure improvements such as water mains, streets, storm sewers and lights are installed. Florida has gained notoriety for using this approach to slow development and ensure that infrastructure improvements occur at the same time land is developed, rather than lagging behind development in a much more expensive process of retrofitting improvements after development occurs. Entreken (1994) provides insight on the implications of concurrence requirements for land value. He maintains that delays in the development process reduce land value and thereby constitute an unjust taking, although this conclusion is certainly open to challenge using the argument that it is properly within the state's interest to ensure an orderly development process.

Transfer or Purchase of Development Rights

Rather than provide property tax reductions in exchange for delayed development of agricultural land, why not transfer the development rights from areas where the community wants to slow or prevent development to other areas where development is acceptable? A community can purchase the rights to develop farmland from the owner, leaving all other land rights in the owner's hands. It then transfers those development rights to another parcel of land in an area where development is acceptable. The rights are generally transferred using the mechanism of a conservation easement. By a transfer of development rights (TDR) program the community purchases and holds development rights, slowing land development to its own prescribed pace or stopping development altogether. Compensation is provided for the landowner in exchange for the development rights. The community then applies land use regulations or growth control regulations.

Mills (1980) provides an early overview of markets for transferable development rights. He describes a typical TDR program as follows. A local government makes the decision to revoke the general right of landowners in the jurisdiction to develop land as they choose. Each landowner is assigned a number of development rights (DRs) with the number of rights assigned being proportional to the number of acres of land owned. Development in the jurisdiction is controlled by requiring DRs in exchange for permission to develop. The landowner must surrender DRs in exchange for the right to develop. Usually, higher density development requires more DRs. Through control of the number of DRs allocated to landowners, and the rate (price) at which those rights may be redeemed, the local government can control development. A landowner is not constrained to develop a given site at a predetermined density, however. The landowner may use DRs from another parcel to develop that site, forgoing development at the source site. Of course, development at a low density may free DRs to be used at another site. Mills established that the TDR mechanism provides for the same constructive land market intervention by the local government as is provided by direct land use controls, but it does not involve the inequitable distribution of development gains.

Experience with TDR schemes has revealed several important components of a successful TDR program. First, a designated land preservation zone must be designated. This is the sending area from which DRs will be sent to another designated area of the community where development is acceptable. DRs will be transferred from a no-growth zone to a growth zone of the community. Second, the designated growth area must be defined, within which development is permitted. Third, a pool of DRs legally severable from the remaining bundle of land rights (typical of fee simple ownership) must be assembled. Finally, the community must establish a procedure by which DRs are transferred from a property in the sending no-growth zone to another property in the receiving growth zone. A survey of TDR programs has been reported in Bredin (2000). That survey found 107 TDR programs in 25 states in the USA. The programs run the gamut from rural areas to large cities. Seven states have adopted statutes specific to farmland protection using TDRs.

TDRs are attractive because they appear to accomplish two complementary goals: open space preservation and compact development. In practice, TDR programs have proved difficult to implement, however, as it is often difficult to identify receiving areas open to high-density development. It is also difficult to establish guidelines for defining DRs in the sending and receiving areas and protect the integrity of the market for such rights. Difficulties arise in making the program understandable, equitable in administration and evasion-proof.

There have been two major court cases related to TDR programs argued before the Supreme Court. In the *Penn Central Transportation Co.* v. *City of New York* case in 1978, the Penn Central Co. owned a designated landmark building, Grand Central Terminal. A City of New York ordinance provided that the Landmarks Preservation Commission could designate landmark buildings and districts. Property owners whose property was in those districts were required to keep the exterior features of the buildings in good repair and have any plans for changes to building exteriors approved by the Commission. The ordinance also provided that unused development rights could be transferred to lots on the same block, across the street, or to nearby lots under the same ownership. The Penn Central Co. tried twice to build a 50-story office building above the terminal, but was denied by the Commission on both attempts. The Commission held that the skyscraper would be inconsistent with the turn-of-the-century design of the Grand Central Terminal. The court found that there was no taking. In the first place, the court said that the 'objective of preserving structures and areas with special historic, architectural, or cultural significance is an entirely permissible governmental goal'. Furthermore, the court held that there was no taking because the development rights were made transferable to at least eight other parcels in the vicinity of the terminal building. While the court acknowledged that those substitute rights may not have constituted just compensation if a taking had occurred, but 'the rights nevertheless undoubtedly mitigate whatever financial burdens the law has imposed'. The court also held that the company's reasonable expectation for the use of the property was that of the existing railway station, evidenced by leased commercial space.

A second case involving TDRs is that of *Suitum* v. *Tahoe Regional Planning Agency*. That case involved the owner of a parcel of land and the planning agency overseeing proposed development. All parcels of land within the watershed carrying runoff into Lake Tahoe were made off limits to development by the planning agency. In order to mitigate the impact on property owners, transfers of development rights were provided to other parcels suitable for construction. Ms. Suitum was denied the right to develop her property in the watershed area, but was offered a transfer of development rights. She claimed that the planning agency's denial of her right to develop was effectively a taking of her property without just compensation. The court found that the value of the rights was not essential to determine whether there had been a taking. TDRs were relevant only in setting the amount of compensation, not in determining whether there was a taking according to the court's ruling.

An alternative is the purchase of development rights (PDR). Communities have experimented with the outright purchase of development rights, with no transfer to another piece of land. The community simply buys the development rights from owners of land in a designated zone where growth is to be slowed or stopped. Landowners are offered a market-based price for the development rights to their land. The development rights are severed from the remaining bundle of rights and the community holds those rights. PDR programs are attractive because they do not involve a transfer to a receiving area. The community simply limits growth by purchasing and holding development rights. Difficulties arise in the determination of market-based prices to offer for the development rights, although few communities have experimented with alternative auction methods that may be effective in eliciting participation at appropriate prices. Research is needed on alternative auction methods that may facilitate PDR programs.

Development Impact Fees

An alternative to growth controls of various types is the application of development fees. The economic literature on impact fees includes Brueckner (1997), Delaney and Smith (1989), Gyourko (1991), McFarlane (1999), McMillen (1990), Singell and Lillydahl (1990), Skaburskis and Qadeer (1992) and Yinger (1998).

McFarlane has examined the impacts of taxes and fees on urban development. There are several ways in which a development fee may be applied, depending upon what is taxed. The fee may depend upon housing quantity, capital quantity, land quantity, value of development, or capital gain. McFarlane shows that many fees are neutral with respect to development timing when agricultural rents are zero. Second, he shows that taxes which are not imposed directly on the capital density of development (such as a tax on the income from agricultural land or a fee on land) have an indirect effect on density through their distortion of the timing of development. Third, he shows that location does not appear to be influential in determining the comparative static effects of fees as in the Turnbull (1988) model. Finally, he shows that the only fiscal instruments having the unambiguous effect of shrinking the size of the city are fees on land and housing. Such fees have the impact of increasing the capital density of development, however, and whether this impact is desirable depends upon the type of externalities that are present.

Brueckner (1997) developed a theoretical model within which to compare the effects of an impact fee and two types of cost-sharing schemes. His analysis demonstrates how a city's growth is affected by the switch from a cost-sharing scheme to an impact fee scheme. He also analyzes how the regime switch affects land values. Owners of developed land in a city that has grown beyond the population size where infrastructure can be provided at minimal cost per capita have an incentive to support the elimination of a cost-sharing scheme in favor of an impact fee scheme. They gain wealth in land value increases that occur with the switch in regime. Hence Brueckner shows how political pressure in favor of impact fee regimes is likely to occur where costs are rising in a perpetual sharing setting (where the interest cost of existing city infrastructure is shared among landowners). His most important result is that an impact fee scheme generates the efficient population path for the city (proposition 4). This result requires that land development timing be optimal. Empirical studies by Delaney and Smith (1989) and Singell and Lillydahl (1990) have found that house prices rose in both Florida and Colorado after the imposition of impact fees in those states. That finding is consistent with the Brueckner result that the value of developed land rises.

If a city has grown beyond the population at which infrastructure can be provided at minimal cost per capita, Brueckner's result confirms the conventional wisdom that a switch to an impact fee regime retards development. That conclusion is reversed, however, if the city switches early in its history. Let us suppose that we have a city which has reached that population already and adopts an impact fee regime. Assume that there is an exogenous cost of development C and an impact fee I applied at the point of development $t = D$. The value of the property is then

$$V(t,D) = \int_t^D f(u)e^{-(r+\tau)(u-t)}du + e^{-(r+\tau)(D-t)}\int_D^\infty h(u,D)e^{-(r+\tau)(u-D)}du$$
$$- [C + I]e^{-(r+\tau)D}. \quad (3.16)$$

The first-order condition for the optimal choice of development time D can be written as

$$H'(D)/H(D) = (r+\tau) - f(D)/H(D) - (C+I)(r+\tau)/H(D). \quad (3.17)$$

This condition states that at the optimal time for development D the rate of growth in the developed property value $H'(D)/H(D)$ must equal the discount rate including the property tax rate τ, minus a term reflecting the opportunity value of non-development $f(D)/H(D)$, and the conversion cost of development $(C+I)(r+\tau)/H(D)$. In the absence of development conversion cost and impact fee $C+I$, we know that the third term on the right-hand side of this first order condition is absent from equation (3.11). The marginal benefit of waiting an additional period is the rate of increase in the developed value of the property. The marginal cost of waiting is the forgone interest including property tax less the pre-development farm net income. The impact fee due at the time of development has the effect of reducing the marginal cost of delaying development and hence causes development to occur later.

The effect of the impact fee is clearly to delay the optimal time of development, other things being equal. The question we now want to investigate is whether an impact fee I can be chosen that provides the same development timing as preferential assessment provides. If we set this first-order condition equal to the first-order condition from the use value problem of Anderson (1993b) we obtain the following condition:

$$(C+I) = \tau F(D)/(r+\tau) + \tau \int_D^\infty F(u)e^{-r(u-D)}du. \quad (3.18)$$

These two conditions will be identical when the cost of conversion plus the impact fee equals the fraction $\tau/(r+\tau)$ of the farm value of the property at development time plus the discounted future property tax that would be applied to the farm value of the land in the future. We can solve for the impact fee $I*$ that will delay development by the same amount as use value assessment:

$$I* = \tau F(D)/(r + \tau) + \tau \int_D^\infty F(u)e^{-r(u - D)}du - C. \qquad (3.19)$$

Notice that the appropriate impact fee must depend upon the farm value of the property at the point of development and the discounted future stream of property taxes that would be applied to the farm value of the property. It must also be inversely related to the development cost. This is an odd impact fee, obviously, since it is designed to delay development by the same length of time as use value assessment.

Of course, even if we can ensure the same delay in development, the two policies differ in their impact on the value of the property and hence the landowner's wealth. While we could design an impact fee that would delay development in the same way that preferential assessment delays development, we cannot ensure that the effect on the property owner's wealth is identical. In fact, we know that preferential assessment increases the property owner's wealth, as demonstrated in equation (3.10), but an impact fee reduces the property owner's wealth. Hence, if the policy objective is to slow development, an impact fee is a viable mechanism, but if the objective is to transfer wealth to property owners, the impact fee is infeasible.

Are such development or impact fees schemes a viable alternative to preferential assessment? In terms of their impact on development timing, impact fees may accomplish the similar objective of slowing the rate of development. When we consider the impact on undeveloped land value, however, there is a clear difference in these policy approaches. Brueckner shows that, while the change in the value of developed land is unambiguously positive, the change in the value of undeveloped land is ambiguous, in general. A switch to an impact fee regime does not guarantee increased land value for undeveloped land. We know that a preferential assessment regime increases undeveloped land value. Hence, if we are primarily concerned with increasing the wealth of undeveloped landowners, an impact fee regime will not necessarily accomplish that goal.

Graded Tax Systems

Rather than apply a traditional property tax with a single rate imposed on both land and structures, why not tax land and structures at different rates? There are potential efficiency gains to a graded tax system, based on well-known results in the optimal tax literature. If there are clear differences in the price elasticities of demand and supply for land and structures, apply tax rates that are inversely proportional to the elasticities. More specifically, if land is supplied less elastically than capital, apply a higher tax rate to land and a lower tax rate to capital. While that is the standard prescription from the optimal tax literature, it is important to note that the simple inverse elasticity rule is derived by invoking the strong assumption that all cross-price elasticities are zero. Hence the general equilibrium nature of the problem is collapsed to a partial equilibrium problem in order to obtain a clean result. On this topic, see Atkinson and Stiglitz (1980) and Myles (1995).

Brueckner (1986) has provided a modern treatment of the economic impacts of site value taxation, an extreme case of a graded tax system where capital is taxed at a relatively low rate and land value is taxed at a high rate. He shows that the long-run effects of shifting to a graded tax system depend on the relative size of the tax zone to which the new regime applies and the degree of housing price exogeneity. If the tax zone covers a small portion of the city's housing market, so that prices can be considered exogenous, gradation of the tax system leaves the price of housing unaffected, but raises capital improvements per acre of land and the value of land. The increase in land value is surprising since the move to a graded tax system increases the direct tax burden applied to land. If the tax zone covers the entire city so that prices are endogenous, gradation of the tax system reduces the price of housing, raises capital improvements per acre of land and lowers land values (for reasonable values of the elasticity parameters). Land value falls because of the reduction in housing prices. Brueckner's results suggest that a small city in a large metropolitan area may be able to generate capital gains for landowners by a move to a graded tax system, but for a large city or a metropolitan move to a graded tax system landowners will suffer capital losses. Housing consumers, however, clearly benefit. Brueckner's short-run analysis of the spatial incidence of gains and losses of a move to a graded tax system reveals a counterintuitive result. The most intensively developed land parcels suffer windfall losses due to the higher tax, while the least intensively developed parcels reap windfall gains.

Anderson (1999; 1993d) has examined the effects of two-rate property tax systems on land development. He has shown that the move to a two-rate tax system (with a relatively higher rate applied to land) depends on the relationship between development timing and capital intensity in the land profit function of the developer. Effects may differ between decentralizing or declining urban areas as compared with centralizing or growing areas. Sufficient conditions for the claim that a two-rate tax system will speed development and increase capital intensity of development are as follows:

capital and time are strong complements and the elasticity of substitution between capital and land is small in the housing (development) production function.

Of course, a high rate of taxation applied to land and a low rate applied to structures would have an incidence that is contrary to the apparent attempt of preferential assessment systems to reduce the effective rate of taxation on farmland. The wealth transfer involved with preferential assessment was quantified in section 2. Aside from that wealth transfer there is also an efficiency effect of preferential assessment that operates through the land market. If the preferential assessment regime is effective, more land is retained in agriculture than would otherwise occur; unless that effect corrects for some market failure, the lower rate of taxation distorts the land market allocation of resources.

One possible approach is to correct for the wealth transfer conferred by preferential assessment through the use of a graded tax system. Since preferential assessment confers windfall wealth on agricultural landowners, that wealth can be recaptured through a higher tax applied to land.

Nechyba (1998; 2001) has developed a general equilibrium model in which tax reform raising land taxes and lowering capital taxes can be investigated. His simulations show that a revenue-neutral shift to land rent taxation would raise capital stocks, increase labor supply and output, and lower land values. Of course, the magnitude of these effects depends on the elasticities of substitution between factors; nevertheless the general pattern of effects is established for reasonable parameter specifications.

4   SUMMARY AND CONCLUSIONS

The practice of preferential assessment is pervasive and suggests that states generally want to provide lower effective rates of taxation for agricultural land. Slowing the rate of development, retaining prime agricultural land, preventing sprawl and other public policy objectives are given as rationales for this tax policy treatment of agricultural land. Whether preferential assessment is effective in these regards is an open question, given that there has been relatively little empirical research on the impacts of such tax policies. The recent work of Morris (1998) shows that, over time, preferential assessment may slow the rate of farmland loss. She shows that the initial reduction is small, but the effect strengthens over time. Whether that benefit justifies the cost of preferential assessment programs, in a given state or across the states, has not been determined, however.

Preferential assessment has impacts on the timing of land development and the wealth of landowners. The optimal length of time before development is greater, slowing the conversion of agricultural land to higher uses. Agricultural landowners also benefit from an increase in wealth due to the capitalized property tax reduction that accompanies preferential assessment. Hence there is a wealth transfer to agricultural landowners.

What are the alternatives? Classified property tax systems, conservation easements, transfer or purchase of development rights, development fees and graded tax systems are all potential alternatives to the prevailing method of providing preferential assessments. Each of these alternatives to preferential assessment have been examined and evaluated. Several of these alternatives provide more direct means of achieving policy goals than does the practice of preferential assessment.

REFERENCES

Aiken, J.D., 1989, 'State Farmland Preferential Assessment Statutes', technical report, University of Nebraska-Lincoln.

Anderson, John E., 1986, 'Property Taxes and the Timing of Urban Land Development', *Regional Science and Urban Economics*, 16, 483–92.

Anderson, John E., 1993a, 'State Tax Credits and Land Use: Policy Analysis of Circuit-Breaker Effects', *Resource and Energy Economics*, 15, 295–312.

Anderson, John E.,1993b, 'Use-Value Property Tax Assessment: Effects on Land Development', *Land Economics*, 69, 263–9.

Anderson, John E., 1993c, 'Urban Land Development, Externalities, and Pigouvian Taxes', *Journal of Urban Economics*, 33, 1–9.

Anderson, John E., 1993d, 'Two-Rate Property Taxes and Urban Development', *Intergovernmental Perspective*, Vol. 19, Washington, DC: U.S. Advisory Commission on Intergovernmental Relations (ACIR), pp. 19–20, 28.

Anderson, John E., 1999, 'Two-Rate Property Tax Effects on Land Development', *Journal of Real Estate Finance and Economics*, 18, 181–90.

Anderson, John E. and Howard C. Bunch, 1989, 'Agricultural Property Tax Relief: Tax Credits, Tax Rates, and Land Values', *Land Economics*, 65, 13–22.

Anderson, John E. and Marlon F. Griffing, 2000, 'Use-Value Assessment Tax Expenditures in Urban Areas', *Journal of Urban Economics*, 48, 443–52.

Associated Press, 2002, 'Senate Approves Cap on Farm Payments', 7 February.

Atkinson, Anthony B. and Joseph E. Stiglitz, 1980, *Lectures on Public Economics*, New York: McGraw-Hill Book Company.

Barlowe, Raleigh, James G. Ahl and Gordon Bachman, 1973, 'Use-Value Assessment Legislation in the United States', *Land Economics*, 49, 206–12.

Beattie, G. and R. Ransom, 1979, *Use Value Assessment: Its Causes, Its Characteristics, Its Effects*, Cambridge, MA: Lincoln Institute of Land Policy.

Bowman, John H. and John L. Mikesell, 1988, 'Uniform Assessment of Agricultural Property for Taxation: Improvements from System Reform', *Land Economics*, 64, 28–36.

Bredin, John B., 2000, 'Transfer of Development Rights: Cases, Statutes, Examples, and a Model', 2000 APA National Planning Conference.

Brueckner, Jan K., 1986, 'A Modern Analysis of the Effects of Site Value Taxation', *National Tax Journal*, 39, 49–58.

Brueckner, Jan K., 1997, 'Infrastructure Financing and Urban Development: The Economics of Impact Fees', *Journal of Public Economics*, 66, 383–407.

Capozza, Dennis R. and Robert W. Helsley, 1989, 'The Fundamentals of Land Prices and Urban Growth', *Journal of Urban Economics*, 26, 295–306.

Capozza, Dennis R. and Gordon A. Sick, 1994, 'The Risk Structure of Land Markets', *Journal of Urban Economics*, 35, 297–319.

Carman, Hoy F., 1977, 'California Landowners' Adoption of Use-Value Assessment Program', *Land Economics*, 53, 275–87.

Carter, Harold O. *et al.*, 1989, 'Report of the Williamson Act Study Group', California Department of Conservation, Office of Land Conservation.

Chicoine, David L. and Donald A. Hendricks, 1985, 'Evidence on Farm Use Value Assessment, Tax Shifts, and State School Aid', *American Journal of Agricultural Economics*, 67, 266–70.

Chicoine, David L. and J.T. Scott, 1983, 'Agricultural Use-Valuation Using Farm Level Data', *Property Tax Journal*, 2, 1–12.

Conklin, H.E. and W.G. Lesher, 1977, 'Farm Value Assessment as a Means for Reducing Premature and Excessive Agricultural Disinvestment in Urban Fringes', *American Journal of Agricultural Economics*, 59, 755–9.

Delaney, C.J. and M.T. Smith, 1989, 'Impact Fees and the Price of New Housing', *Journal of the American Real Estate and Urban Economics Association*, 17, 41–54.

Dunford, Richard W. and Douglas C. Marousek, 1981, 'Sub-County Tax Shifts Attributable to Use-Value Assessments on Farmland', *Land Economics*, 57, 221–69.

Entreken, H.C., Jr., 1994, 'Analysis of Land Value Under Differing Land Use Restrictions', *Appraisal Journal*, 62, 596–9.

Ferguson, J.T., 1988, 'Evaluating the Effectiveness of Use-Value Programs', *Property Tax Journal*, 7, 157–65.

Gloudemans, R.J., 1974, *Use-Value Farmland Assessments: Theory, Practice, and Impact*, Chicago: International Association of Assessing Officers.

Gyourko, J., 1991, 'Impact Fees, Exclusionary Zoning, and the Density of New Development', *Journal of Urban Economics*, 30, 242–56.

McFarlane, Alistair, 1999, 'Taxes, Fees, and Urban Development', *Journal of Urban Economics*, 46, 416–36.

McMillen, D.P., 1990, 'The Timing and Duration of Development Rate Tax Increases', *Journal of Urban Economics*, 28, 1–18.

Mills, David E., 1980, 'Transferable Development Rights Markets', *Journal of Urban Economics*, 7, 63–74.

Morris, Adele C., 1998, 'Property Tax Treatment of Farmland: Does Tax Relief Delay Land Development?', in Helen Ladd (ed.), *Local Government Tax and Land Use Policies in the United States*, Cheltenham, UK and Northampton, MA: Edward Elgar.

Myles, Gareth D., 1995, *Public Economics*, Cambridge: Cambridge University Press.

Nechyba, T.J., 1998, 'Replacing Capital Taxes with Land Taxes: Efficiency and Distributional Implications with an Application to the United States Economy', in D. Netzer (ed.), *Land Value Taxation: Can It and Will It Work Today?*, Cambridge, MA: Lincoln Institute of Land Policy.

Nechyba, T.J., 2001, 'Prospects for Land Rent Taxes in State and Local Tax Reforms', working paper, Duke University Department of Economics.

Plantinga, Andrew J. and Douglas J. Miller, 2001, 'Agricultural Land Values and the Value of Rights to Future Land Development', *Land Economics*, 77, 56–67.
Power, Fred B. and John P. Cooke, 1976. Market and Use Value: Florida's New Tax Assessment Law', *Growth and Change*, 7, 34–6.
Schwartz, S.I., David E. Hansen and T.C. Foin, 1976, 'Landowner Benefits from Use-Value Assessment under the California Land Conservation Act', *American Journal of Agricultural Economics*, 58, 170–78.
Singell, L.D. and J.H. Lillydahl, 1990, 'An Empirical Examination of the Effect of Impact Fees on the Housing Market', *Land Economics*, 66, 82–92.
Skaburskis, A. and M. Qadeer, 1992, 'An Empirical Estimation of the Price Effects of Development Impact Fees', *Urban Studies*, 29, 653–67.
Sonstelie, Jon, 1979, 'The Incidence of a Classified Property Tax', *Journal of Urban Economics*, 12, 75–85.
Tavernier, Edmund and Farong Li, 1995, 'Effectiveness of Use-Value Assessment in Preserving Farmland: A Search-Theoretic Approach', *Journal of Agricultural and Applied Economics*, 27, 626–35.
Turnbull, Geoffrey K., 1988, 'Property Taxes and the Transition of Land to Urban Use', *Journal of Real Estate Finance and Economics*, 1, 393–403.
Wunderlich, Gene, 1997, 'Land Taxes in Agriculture: Preferential Rate and Assessment Effects', *American Journal of Economics and Sociology*, 56, 215–28.
Wunderlich, Gene and John Blackledge, 1994, 'Taxing Farmland in the United States', U.S. Department of Agriculture, Economic Research Service, Agricultural Economic Report Number 679.
Yinger, J.,1998, 'The Incidence of Development Fees and Special Assessments', *National Tax Journal*, 51, 23–41.

4. The influence of local fiscal structure and growth control choices on 'big-box' urban sprawl in the American West

Robert W. Wassmer

1 INTRODUCTION

> Though forbidden to raise property taxes, [California] city governments do get sales taxes from stores. Result: what's called 'fiscalization of land use', meaning a wild scramble for retail base especially for mega auto malls and big-box retailers. The result's not just more suburban sprawl, but real ugliness, what California urban planning expert William Fulton describes as 'sales tax canyons bleak relentless [zones] designed not to encourage or facilitate community, but simply to empty passing wallets'. (Peirce, 1998)

This quotation, by a newspaper columnist represents what some observers in California and other states believe is a cause and effect relationship that generates profound social consequences. Municipalities that rely on local sales taxes for the provision of local services seek taxable retail sales not only for the consumption needs of their citizens, but also for the discretionary fiscal surplus it yields. Such local governments seek out new retail stores and draw retail sales away from central places in a metropolitan area where economics would have naturally caused such retail sales to occur were it not for local sales tax reliance. In policy discussions this issue has received increased attention due to the claim that this 'fiscalization of land use' contributes to urban sprawl. Salient to the motivation of this chapter is that all of this has occurred with little to no empirical evidence regarding the importance of local fiscal structure to land use decisions in a metropolitan area.

Given the renewed national interest in the United States in spatial patterns of urban growth, prominent urban economists such as Gordon and Richardson (1997), Mills (1999) and Brueckner (2000) have weighed in on the issue of urban sprawl with articles that summarize an economic approach to defining what constitutes smart urban growth. These economists emphasize that the metropolitan decentralization of people and economic activity in the USA has occurred for well over 50 years and has been driven in large part by population increases, real income increases and decreases in the real cost of automobile use. To most economists, decentralization is only an undesirable pattern of urban land use if the total costs it imposes upon a metropolitan region are greater than the total benefits generated from it.

Conversely, other analysts like Ewing (1997), Downs (1999) and Myers and Kitsuse (2000) have pointed out that a purely market-based approach to defining excessive spatial growth ignores the institutional environment in which economic actors in a metropolitan area make land use decisions. These analysts highlight the fact that government institutions influence local land use decisions and can generate or slow urban decentralization. The objective of this chapter is to determine whether the statewide structure of local public finance and the metropolitan use of urban growth boundaries work to further or deter retail decentralization in a metropolitan area. This chapter offers an extension of earlier work (Wassmer, 2002) on this issue, in that these influences are derived for two forms of 'big-box' retail (car and home improvement) sales.[1]

Fiscalization of land use implies that the system of local public finance influences local land use decisions. Regression analysis is used here to test whether the real dollar value of different forms of retail activity in a metropolitan area's non-central places is independently influenced by statewide measures of the structure of local government revenue reliance. This measure of the fiscalization of land use is appropriately sought after controlling for non-central place population, income, age distribution, farmland price, previous growth rate and the presence of different forms of urban containment.

The explanatory variables contained in the regression analysis, except those representing local revenue reliance and urban containment policies, represent factors that fittingly drive the non-central location of retail activity in a metropolitan area. From the social perspective of what is best for the entire region, local revenue reliance is a poor basis for determining retail location decisions. If local revenue reliance is found to increase non-central retail sales in a metropolitan area independently, it can be considered a cause of excessive retail decentralization or sprawl. At the same time, if the presence of an urban containment policy reduces non-central retail sales then it has achieved its stated policy goal of slowing the amount of retail decentralization that would have occurred without it.

The regression analysis that follows indicates that statewide measures of reliance by municipalities on some forms of own-source revenue exert a positive influence on the overall amount of non-central retail activity in metropolitan areas in the western USA over the period 1977 to 1997. Regarding local reliance on general sales taxation, this positive influence is much greater when non-central retail activity is measured in terms of car or building material sales. In addition, the continuing presence of some forms of urban containment reduces the overall amount of some forms of non-central retail activity. The negative influence of urban containment is also much larger when its influence is gauged in regard to big-box retail sales.

The concept of urban retail sprawl is developed in the next section of the chapter in a discussion of the ways that both planners and economists have thought about it. The third section grounds the regression analysis in theory by reviewing previous literature on the determinants of retail location in a metropolitan area. This section also discusses why the way that local governments raise revenue in a state could influence the intrametropolitan location of retail activity in that state, and how this influence is expected to be even greater on big-box forms of retail activity. Section 4 of the paper offers a description of differences in the degree of big-box retail decentralization in 47 metropolitan areas in the western portion of the USA. Section 5 provides background on the regression test used to determine whether statewide averages for municipal revenue reliance and/or the presence of urban containment policies exert measurable influences on the location of different forms of retail activity in a metropolitan area. The sixth section contains a discussion of the regression results. The implications of the research are in the concluding section.

2   URBAN RETAIL SPRAWL

Urban planners, and increasingly the general public, label undesirable forms of suburban land use with the term 'sprawl'. Observing this now common application, a few researchers have developed a list of land use characteristics that are most often associated with being so labeled. Downs (1999) defines urban sprawl by observable traits such as unlimited outward extension of new development, low-density developments in new areas, 'leapfrog' development, transport dominance by private cars, and strip commercial development. Myers and Kitsuse (2000) frame the issue of sprawl in terms of patterns of urban population density that produce undesirable social outcomes.

Ewing (1994) surveyed academic articles written on sprawl between 1957 and 1992 and found that low-density, strip, scattered and leapfrog are the forms of urban development most often labeled 'sprawl'. In his review he highlights the fine distinction between undesirable non-compact develop-

ment in a metropolitan area (sprawl) and desirable polycentric development (multiple centers in an urban area). Polycentric development, which
now characterizes most large metropolitan areas in the USA, is often more
efficient (in terms of clustering land uses to reduce trip lengths and reduce
congestion) than development in just one compact centralized pattern.
This is also the line of reasoning offered by economists who have written
on this issue. Planners and economists recognize that there are socially
beneficial reasons for activity to locate in non-central parts of a metropolitan area. Decentralized development should only fall under the pejorative
label of 'sprawl' to the degree that it is being driven by reasons that are
unlikely to promote social optimality.

The desire here is to test whether the fiscalization of land use influences
the amount of retail decentralization observed in a metropolitan area. A
regression analysis uses the real dollar value of aggregate retail activity and
two forms of big-box retail activity in non-central places as the dependent
variables. Suburban retail activity that is greater than warranted by economic factors coincides with other rudiments of how sprawl has been perceived: (1) a lower density of development in the metropolitan area's central
places, (2) greater possible leapfrog development at the urban fringe, (3)
greater car reliance for retail shopping, and (4) greater congestion and air
pollution generated in getting to retail shops that are farther away from the
customers that use them (central place citizens shopping in non-central
place locations).

3   THE LOCATION OF RETAIL ACTIVITY IN A METROPOLITAN AREA

If urban retail sprawl is defined as non-central retail activity that is greater
than non-central economic factors warrant, then knowing the relevant
economic factors that determine the intrametropolitan location of retail
activity is important. As summarized in Dipasquale and Wheaton (1996)
and O'Sullivan (2000), economic theory predicts that a profit-maximizing
retail firm chooses a specific location in a metropolitan area based upon
the location of its customers, transport costs, agglomeration economies
and the degree of scale economies in its particular form of retail production. In a metropolitan area with one central city, these factors push retailers that exhibit high and even moderate scale economies in production to
locate primarily in the central city. Retailers with relatively small-scale
economies in production base their intrametropolitan location on where
their customers reside and a division of the region into profitable market
areas. Big-box retailers are more likely to exhibit at least moderate scale

economies in production and thus, absent the fiscalization of land use, should be somewhat more likely to choose central place locations in a metropolitan area.

Between 1950 and 1990, the percentage of the US metropolitan population living in central cities fell from 64 to 38 per cent. The fraction of metropolitan retail employment in US central cities accordingly fell from about two-thirds in 1950 to a little less than one-half in 1990. This suburbanization of retail activity was caused by the migration of existing metropolitan residents from central cities to the suburbs, an overall increase in metropolitan residents and a greater percentage of them choosing to live in the suburbs, and falling car transport costs which reduced ties to a central shopping location.[2]

In a review of the economic thinking on the causes of metropolitan suburbanization, Mieszkowski and Mills (1993) find valuable insights offered by both the natural evolution and fiscal/social approaches. The natural evolution approach emphasizes the significance of income, population, transport and technological changes to determining the degree of decentralization in a metropolitan area. The fiscal/social approach is a generalization of Tiebout's (1956) model of 'voting with one's feet' and points to increased urban decentralization as partly the result of citizens' desires to form and fund more homogeneous communities. To do this, suburban communities use land use controls and subsidies to attract residents and business that offer a fiscal surplus and do little to damage the local environment.

Municipal revenue from retail activity, that in most instances requires a relatively small amount of local government services and generates relatively little environmental damage, offers a good choice of funding for local services. If suburban communities actively seek retail activity for the purpose of the fiscal surplus it generates, then greater statewide reliance on a municipal revenue instrument that generates a local fiscal surplus through greater local retail activity may generate greater retail decentralization. Local fiscal structure is unlikely to induce more retail activity in a metropolitan area, but it can induce changes in where it locates. Within a metropolitan area, non-central places draw retail activity greater than warranted by their population characteristics from the central places where historically it has been located.[3]

Other researchers have also recognized that local fiscal factors can contribute to the generation of urban decentralization. Harvey and Clark (1965) assert that local reliance on property taxation discourages the conversion of farmland to non-agricultural use because, once this is done, the land is subject to higher taxation. The hesitancy of jurisdictions to designate agricultural land for non-agricultural uses encourages leapfrog development. Misczynski (1986) popularized the use of the phrase 'fiscalization of land use' in California policy circles to describe what he increasingly expected to happen after California's post-Proposition 13 abandonment of property taxation as a discretionary source of local revenue. Innes and Booher (1999) point to the complex and fragmented system of local finance in California, with its heavy reliance on sales taxation as a source of local discretionary revenue, as the single most important factor driving local land use decisions in the state. Atkinson and Oleson (1996) believe the car to be the major culprit of sprawl, but maintain that this would not have been possible without complementary local finance policies. Kotin and Peiser (1997) have looked at public/private partnerships for high volume retailers and the degree to which municipalities benefit from them. In a monograph-length study of sales taxation in California, Lewis and Barbour (1999) conclude that local sales tax reliance has influenced local land use decisions in the state.

In addition, Brueckner and Kim (2000) demonstrate that the theoretical influence of local property tax reliance on the generation of metropolitan decentralization is indeterminate. Greater reliance on local property taxation reduces individual housing consumption, which raises population density and reduces urban sprawl. Concurrently, greater local property taxation reduces the intensity of land development, lowers population density and encourages urban sprawl. A simulation using reasonable real-world values suggests that the likely influence of greater local property taxation in generating urban sprawl, through its influence on capital use, is slightly positive.

Finally, Brueckner and Fansler (1983) conducted a relevant regression study of the determinants of the size of an urban area. Using 1970 data and relying on traditional urban theory, they regressed the Census-defined size in square miles of the 40 largest urbanized areas in the USA against the urbanized area's population, median income, rent paid on agricultural land and proxies for commuting costs. The empirical analysis that follows builds upon Brueckner and Fansler's study by including statewide measures of municipal revenue reliance in a regression designed to explain retail activity in non-central places in western US metropolitan areas. Before the method of doing this is described in greater detail, the next section of the chapter offers a description of areas included in the study and differences over time in their non-central place retail activity.

4   BIG-BOX RETAIL DECENTRALIZATION IN THE WESTERN UNITED STATES

An empirical study of the degree of metropolitan retail decentralization must begin with a unit of analysis. For this study it is the 61 metropolitan areas in what the Census Bureau defined in 1990 as the continental western United States, less the seven metropolitan areas in Idaho, Montana and Wyoming. The analysis is limited to metropolitan areas in the West for a few reasons. The first is that six of the eight states defined as western enacted statewide ballot box or legislative restrictions on the local use of property taxes between 1977 and 1997. Through Proposition 13 (1978), Measures 5 and 47 (1990 and 1996), and Amendment 1 (1992), California, Oregon and Colorado voters all used the citizen initiative to limit local property taxation. In Arizona, Nevada and Utah, state legislatures took similar steps.[4] These restrictions, which Sokolow (2000) classifies as harsher than in any other region in the USA, offer natural experiments by which to test the influence of changes in statewide municipal fiscal structure on metropolitan retail decentralization. Furthermore, most metropolitan areas in the western USA grew up in an era of rising populations, rising real incomes and declining transport costs. Metropolitan areas in Idaho, Montana and Wyoming are not included because the metropolitan development patterns in these three states are very different from those of the western states retained in the sample used here.[5]

Fifty-four metropolitan areas are used in the analysis. A metropolitan area consists of the relevant component counties in the 1990 Census definition of either a Metropolitan Statistical Area (MSA) or a Primary Metropolitan Statistical Area (PMSA).[6] Since the focus of this chapter is retail activity in suburban locations, the suburban area within a metropolitan area is the constituent counties in an MSA or PMSA, less the 'central places' included in the 1990 definition of urbanized areas in a metropolitan area.[7] Central places are considered by the Census to be the dominant employment and residential centers in each urbanized area. For instance, the suburban area in the San Diego MSA would be San Diego County less the cities of Coronado, Escondido and San Diego. Table 4.1 contains a list of the 54 metropolitan areas in the sample, the areas' component counties, and the central places that are excluded from these counties to create the definition of a metropolitan area's non-central places that is used here. This designation of suburbia is an attempt to account for the polycentric nature of most US metropolitan areas through the use of existing data sources.

The three dependent variables in the regression analyses that follow are (1) total retail sales, (2) building material sales, and (3) new and used car sales. Big-box retail sales are represented by building material and new/used car sales due to popular perceptions of what big-box is ('Home Depots' and 'Automalls') and the availability of comparable data for 1977, 1987 and 1997 for the 54 metropolitan areas under consideration.[8] Table 4.2 offers a comparison of the ratio of non-central place building material (car) sales to total metropolitan area building material (car) sales for the

Table 4.1   Urban area definitions for the western United States, 1990

Metropolitan area name	Counties in metropolitan area	Central places (cities) in metropolitan area	Metropolitan area name	Counties in metropolitan area	Central places (cities) in metropolitan area
Phoenix-Mesa AZ, MSA	Maricopa AZ, Pinal AZ	Mesa AZ, Phoenix AZ, Scottsdale AZ, Tempe AZ	San Diego CA, MSA	San Diego CA	Coronado CA, Escondido CA, San Diego CA
Tuscon AZ, MSA	Pima AZ	Tucson AZ	San Francisco CA, PMSA	Marin CA, San Francisco CA, San Mateo CA	San Francisco CA
Yuma AZ, MSA	Yuma AZ	Yuma AZ	San Jose CA, PMSA	Santa Clara CA	Gilroy CA, Palo Alto CA, San Jose CA, Santa Clara CA, Sunnyvale CA
Bakersfield CA, MSA	Kern CA	Bakersfield CA	San Luis Obispo-Atascadero-Paso Robles CA, MSA	San Luis Obispo CA	Atascadero CA, Paso Robles CA, San Luis Obispo CA
Chico-Paradise CA, MSA	Butte CA	Chico CA	Santa Barbara-Santa Maria-Lompoc CA, MSA	Santa Barbara CA	Lompoc CA, Santa Barbara CA, Santa Maria CA
Fresno CA, MSA	Fresno CA, Madera CA	Fresno CA	Santa Cruz-Watsonville CA, PMSA	Santa Cruz CA	Santa Cruz CA, Watsonville CA
Los Angeles-Long Beach CA, PMSA	Los Angeles CA	Lancaster CA, Long Beach CA, Los Angeles CA, Pasadena CA	Santa Rosa CA, PMSA	Sonoma CA	Petaluma CA, Santa Rosa CA
Merced CA, MSA	Merced CA	Merced CA	Stockton-Lodi CA, MSA	San Joaquin CA	Lodi CA, Stockton CA

Table 4.1 (continued)

Metropolitan area name	Counties in metropolitan area	Central places (cities) in metropolitan area	Metropolitan area name	Counties in metropolitan area	Central places (cities) in metropolitan area
Modesta CA, MSA	Stanislaus CA	Modesto CA, Turlock CA	Vallejo-Fairfield-Napa CA, PMSA	Napa CA, Solano CA	Fairfield CA, Napa CA, Vacaville CA, Vallejo CA
Oakland CA, PMSA	Alameda CA, Contra Costa CA	Alameda CA, Berkeley CA, Oakland CA	Ventura CA, PMSA	Ventura CA	San Buenaventura (Ventura) CA
Orange CA, PMSA	Orange CA	Anaheim CA, Irvine CA, Santa Ana CA	Visalia-Tulare-Porterville CA, MSA	Tulare CA	Porterville CA, Tulare CA
Redding CA, MSA	Shasta CA	Redding CA	Yolo CA, PMSA	Yolo CA	Davis CA, Woodland CA
Riverside-San Bernardino CA, PMSA	Riverside CA, San Bernardino CA	Hemet CA, Palm Desert CA, Palm Springs CA, Riverside CA, San Bernardino CA, Temecula CA	Yuba City CA, MSA	Sutter CA, Yuba CA	Yuba CA
Sacramento CA, PMSA	El Dorado CA, Placer CA, Sacramento CA	Sacramento CA	Boulder-Longmount CO, PMSA	Boulder CO	Boulder CO, Longmount CO
Salinas CA, MSA	Monterey CA	Monterey CA, Salinas CA	Colorado Springs CO, MSA	El Paso CO	Colorado Springs, CO
Denver CO, PMSA	Adams CO, Arapahoe CO, Denver CO, Douglas CO, Jefferson CO	Denver CO	Salt Lake City-Ogden UT, MSA	Davis UT, Salt Lake UT, Weber UT	Salt Lake City UT, Ogden UT
Fort-Collins-Loveland CO, MSA	Larimer CO	Fort Collins CO	Bellingham WA, MSA	Whatcom WA	Bellingham WA

MSA / PMSA	Component Counties	Component Places
Grand Junction CO, MSA	Mesa CO	Grand Junction CO
Greeley CO, MSA	Weld CO	Greeley CO
Pueblo CO, MSA	Pueblo CO	Pueblo CO
Las Vegas NV & AZ, MSA	Clark NV, Mohave AZ, Nye NV	Las Vegas NV
Reno NV, MSA	Washoe NV	Reno NV
Albuquerque NM, MSA	Bernalillo NM, Sandoval NM, Valencia NM	Albuquerque NM
Las Cruces NM, MSA	Dona Ana NM	Las Cruces NM
Santa Fe NM, MSA	Los Alamos NM, Santa Fe NM	Santa Fe NM
Eugene-Springfield OR, MSA	Lane OR	Eugene OR, Springfield OR
Medford-Ashland OR, MSA	Jackson OR	Medford OR
Portland-Vancouver OR, PMSA	Clackamas OR, Columbia OR, Multnomah OR, Washington OR, Yamhill OR, Clark WA	Portland OR, Vancouver WA
Salem OR, PMSA	Marion OR, Polk OR	Salem OR
Provo-Orem UT, MSA	Utah UT	Provo UT, Orem UT
Bremerton WA, PMSA	Kitsap WA	Bremerton WA
Olympia WA, PMSA	Thurston WA	Olympia WA
Richland-Kennewick-Pasco WA, MSA	Benton WA, Franklin WA	Kennewick WA, Pasco WA, Richland WA
Seattle-Bellevue-Everett WA, PMSA	Island WA, King WA, Snohomish WA	Auburn WA, Everett WA, Seattle WA
Spokane WA, MSA	Spokane WA	Spokane WA
Tacoma WA, PMSA	Pierce WA	Tacoma WA
Yakima WA, MSA	Yakima WA	Yakima WA

47 metropolitan areas in the sample for which data are available.[9] The top eight data rows in this table report the averages for each state, where available, using metropolitan area as the unit of observation.

As shown at the top of Table 4.2, for building material and car sales where multiple year averages are available, some western states (five out of 12 cases) experienced an increase in the percentage of these forms of big-box sales occurring in non-central locations relative to all metropolitan locations, while the other seven cases showed a decrease. Using only these figures it is hard to distinguish whether these forms of urban retail sprawl have increased or decreased over time, but, as indicated above, it is perhaps best to not designate an increase in the percentage of retail activity occurring in non-central places as sprawl if population, income and demographic shifts warrant such changes. In addition, there are many distinct metropolitan areas that experienced a decrease in the percentage of building material sales occurring in non-central places between 1987 and 1997 (Chico-Paradise, Sacramento, Denver, Bellingham and Tacoma) and even more for car sales (Chico-Paradise, Denver, Las Vegas, Medford-Ashland, Salem and Spokane). Other than that there is a great deal of variation in the degree of non-central place big-box retail activity occurring in western metropolitan areas and over time, it is hard to draw any specific conclusions from the information in Table 4.2. A regression analysis of the determinants of suburban retail activity is necessary to comprehend the causes of the observed variation.

5   STATEWIDE LOCAL REVENUE CHOICES AND RETAIL DECENTRALIZATION

The three dependent variables for the empirical study discussed next are the real values of retail sales, building material sales and car sales in non-central places for the available metropolitan areas described in the previous section.[10] For each of these dependent variables, where available, information is gathered from 1977, 1987 and 1997. The pooling of cross-section and time-series data permits variation in non-central retail sales to occur across metropolitan areas and within an area over time. These data allow a regression test of whether statewide averages for pertinent forms of own-source municipal revenue reliance exert any significant influences on the amount of non-central retail sales in a state's metropolitan areas. A model of what determines non-central retail sales in a metropolitan area is necessary to formulate this regression test. The model that follows builds upon the earlier work of Brueckner and Fansler (1983).

Economic theory indicates that the real dollar value of retail sales in the

Table 4.2   Distribution of building material and car sales for non-central places in metropolitan areas in the western United States

1990 Metropolitan area name	1977 Non-central places/metro. building mat. sales	1987 Non-central places/metro. building mat. sales	1997 Non-central places/metro. building mat. sales	1977 Non-central places/metro. car sales	1987 Non-central places/metro. car sales	1997 Non-central places/metro. car sales
Arizona average for MSAs	0.81		0.23		0.10	0.15
California average for (P)MSAs		0.59	0.51	0.50	0.53	0.45
Colorado average for (P)MSAs		0.40	0.38	0.20	0.35	0.33
Nevada average for MSAs		0.46	0.51		0.57	0.25
New Mexico average for MSAs		0.26	0.04			0.13
Oregon average for (P)MSAs			0.33	0.37	0.25	0.27
Utah average for MSAs			0.10	0.46	0.73	0.53
Washington average for (P)MSAs	0.65	0.55	0.48	0.35	0.34	0.38
Phoenix-Mesa AZ, MSA			0.265		0.201	0.216
Tucson AZ, MSA			0.189		0.000	0.081
Bakersfield CA, MSA			0.592	0.239	0.195	0.296
Chico-Paradise CA, MSA		0.538	0.258		0.473	0.406
Fresno CA, MSA			0.308		0.409	0.467
LA-Long Beach CA, PMSA			0.629		0.618	0.699
Orange CA, PMSA			0.670		0.708	
Ventura CA, PMSA	0.913			0.677	0.701	0.789
Merced CA, MSA			0.452		0.176	
Modesta CA, MSA						0.484
Redding CA, MSA			0.070			

Table 4.2 *(continued)*

1990 Metropolitan area name	1977 Non-central places/metro. building mat. sales	1987 Non-central places/metro. building mat. sales	1997 Non-central places/metro. building mat. sales	1977 Non-central places/metro. car sales	1987 Non-central places/metro. car sales	1997 Non-central places/metro. car sales
Sacramento CA, PMSA		0.803	0.704		0.781	0.877
Salinas CA, MSA		0.422		0.416		
San Diego CA, MSA						0.474
Oakland CA, PMSA					0.782	
San Francisco CA, PMSA	0.706	0.606	0.677	0.657	0.737	0.814
San Jose CA, PMSA						0.098
Santa Rosa CA, PMSA			0.497			0.160
Vallejo-Fairfield-Napa CA, PMSA						0.080
Visalia-Tulare-Porterville CA, MSA			0.782			
SLO-Atasc-Paso Robles CA, MSA			0.669			
San Barb-Santa Maria-Lom CA, MSA						
Stockton-Lodi CA, MSA			0.295		0.272	0.221
Boulder-Longmount CO, PMSA			0.118			0.383
Colorado Springs CO, MSA		0.080	0.597			0.153
Denver CO, PMSA		0.712	0.427		0.875	0.003
Fort Collins-Loveland CO, MSA				0.388	0.327	0.806
Grand Junction CO, MSA					0.194	0.391
Greeley CO, MSA				0.219		0.301
Pueblo CO, MSA				0.000	0.000	
Las Vegas NV & AZ, MSA			0.548		0.567	0.490

Reno NV, MSA	0.013			0.469	0.455	
Albuquerque NM, MSA					0.256	
Las Cruces NM, MSA				0.037		
Santa Fe NM, MSA	0.130					
Eugene-Springfield OR, MSA	0.340			0.334		
Medford-Ashland OR, MSA	0.202	0.222	0.368	0.330		
Salem OR, PMSA	0.263	0.287				
Provo-Orem UT, MSA	0.295			0.095		
Salt Lake City-Ogden UT, MSA	0.773	0.730	0.456			
Bellingham WA, MSA		0.255		0.252	0.417	
Bremerton WA, PMSA		0.304		0.556		
Olympia WA, PMSA		0.060		0.502		
Seattle-Bellevue-Everett WA, PMSA				0.668	0.681	
Spokane WA, MSA		0.366	0.333	0.388		0.551
Tacoma WA, PMSA		0.470	0.395	0.516		0.743
Yakima WA, MSA		0.276	0.326			

non-central portion of a metropolitan region increases as non-central population and real household income increase. Suburban retail activity may be slowed by a higher acquisition price for agricultural land upon which to build new retail centers. The availability of transport options can also influence where people in a metropolitan area shop. These four factors (population, income, price of agricultural land and transport options) are what Brueckner and Fansler (1983) expect to influence the size of an urbanized area.[11] With the exception of proxies for transport options, the model of suburban retail sales used here also relies on these same causal factors. Metropolitan transport options are excluded for two reasons: (1) demographics, population and income largely determine the transport options available in a metropolitan area, and (2) the influence of transport options on suburban retail activity is not the focus of this investigation. If metropolitan transport options were to be included as explanatory variables in the regression analysis, they would need to be considered a simultaneously determined variable and appropriately modeled.[12]

Further refinement of Brueckner and Fansler's model of urban size is necessary to assess accurately the influence of local government fiscal institutions on non-central retail activity. This is in the form of controlling for demographic differences in the type of population located in non-central places, previous decade's growth in non-central population, and any forms of urban growth controls that may be present. The model used to delineate the regression analysis is thus:

Retail Sales$_{i,t}$ = f (Income$_{i,t}$, Population$_{i,t}$, Previous Decade's Population Growth$_{i,t}$, Presence of Urban Containment Policy$_{i,t}$, Price of Agricultural Land$_{i,t}$, Percentage Population Less than Age 18$_{i,t}$, Percentage Population Greater than Age 64$_{i,t}$, Percentage Statewide Discretionary Municipal Revenue from Property Taxes$_{i,t}$, Percentage Statewide Discretionary Municipal Revenue from General Sales Taxes$_{i,t}$, Percentage Statewide Discretionary Municipal Revenue from Other Taxes$_{i,t}$), where i = 1, 2, 3, ..., or 54 (for each metropolitan area's non-central places) and t = 1977, 1987 or 1997.

The degree of statewide reliance on different forms of own-source municipal revenue can influence the amount of retail activity in non-central metropolitan places through local fiscal zoning and the offering of local economic development incentives. Municipal revenue reliance for a specific category is calculated as a percentage of locally generated revenue from sources most likely to be influenced by local land use decisions. The term used here to describe this form of local revenue source is 'discretionary'. Discretionary revenue sources include locally generated property taxes, general sales taxes, other taxes, and user charges/special assessments.[13] The term 'discretionary' also refers to the fact that, if a statewide policy were instituted to reduce percentage reliance on one of these local revenue instruments, the percentage reliance on one or all of the others would likely have to increase. Only three of the four discretionary revenue sources are accounted for in the regression model because the third, Percentage Statewide Discretionary Municipal Revenue from Charges, equals 100 per cent less the sum of the included three.

As widely documented elsewhere, municipalities and unincorporated areas of counties in the USA regulate local land uses with an eye on the fiscal bottom line.[14] Municipal and county governments in the USA also use local incentives to attract desirable land uses within their boundaries.[15] Both of these activities can result in greater local retail activity in a metropolitan area's non-central places than economic factors alone would dictate. Different degrees of statewide reliance, on different forms of own-source municipal revenue, could thus yield different amounts of fiscal surplus generated by local land devoted to retail activity. The greater the reliance on a municipal revenue source that generates a local fiscal surplus from local retail activity, the more likely that local officials zone for retail land uses and use local incentives to encourage taxable retail sales. In their study of the fiscal benefits that retailers offer cities in California, Kotin and Peiser (1997) include local sales taxes, property taxes and business license fees (which fall into the category of other taxes used above) as the three forms of city revenues that need to be accounted for.

The US *Census of Governments* divides municipal own-source revenue into two categories: current charges/miscellaneous revenue and taxes. The Census describes current charges as fees for specific local services delivered to a local citizen or business. For the purpose of this study, charges equal current charges plus special assessments. Special assessments are included with charges because of their Census definition as 'compulsory contributions collected from owners of property benefitted by special public improvements'. The Census includes interest earnings, special assessments, sale of property, and other general revenue under its definition of miscellaneous revenue. With the possible exception of special assessments, these forms of miscellaneous revenue are unlikely to generate a local fiscal surplus through greater retail activity and are excluded from the regression model.

The Census classifies municipal taxes in the forms of property, general and selective sales, individual income, corporate income, motor vehicle license, and other taxes. None of the eight western states considered here allows local personal or corporate income taxes. All other forms of local taxation, except motor vehicle taxes and selective sales taxes (on motor fuels, alcohol, tobacco and public utilities), are accounted for in the regression analysis because they offer the potential for a local suburban government to benefit from a fiscal surplus gained through the attraction of greater retail activity within its boundaries.[16]

Brueckner and Kim (2000) have theoretically shown that the expected influence of greater local reliance on property taxation on urban decentralization through capital use is uncertain. Aside from altering capital use, greater local reliance on property taxes can also encourage local land use decisions that are more likely to generate a fiscal surplus through property taxation (property tax revenue greater than the cost of local services required by the retail property). The influence that this has on suburban retail activity depends upon how retail trade does in generating a property tax fiscal surplus relative to alternative uses (housing or manufacturing) for a municipality's land.[17]

Throughout a state, greater average local reliance on general sales taxation as a source of discretionary local revenue offers a reason for suburban governments in the state to lure retailers away from traditional business districts in central place communities and increase the amount of retail sales in the suburbs. In support, through a survey of officials in 300 California cities that asked them to rank 18 different motivations for evaluating the desirability of various forms of development projects, Lewis and Barbour (1999) found that 'new sales tax revenues' always finished first or second in terms of the importance most often given. Interestingly, only the 36 central city officials in the sample systematically ranked sales tax considerations consistently lower. The lure of collecting other taxes, such as a license fee or other business tax, from retailers offers an additional motivation for non-central place governments to draw retail activity away from traditional central place locations.

Economic theory indicates that suburban income and population should exert a positive influence on suburban retail sales, while the influence of the price of agricultural land in the metropolitan area should be negative. After a previous decade's surge in population growth, retail developers may not have been able to keep pace with the amount of development specified by population, and retail sales may be smaller, holding other factors constant, in an area that previously experienced high population growth. Alternatively, developers may view high population growth in the past as an indicator of even greater growth expected for the future and consequently develop more than existing population and income itself would call for. Urban areas with a higher percentage of senior citizens or families with children are likely to exhibit different retail consumption patterns; however, the directions of these influences are uncertain.[18]

The regression model used to explain non-central retail activity in a metropolitan area also includes six explanatory variables that account for whether a certain type of Urban Containment Policy (UCP) exists in a metropolitan area and, if it does, how long it has been in existence. UCPs are commonly referred to as urban growth boundaries and are designed to slow the degree of decentralization in a metropolitan area that would have occurred over time. The presence of a UCP could thus reduce the amount of non-central retail activity in metropolitan areas where they are in place.[19]

The regression includes the three different types of UCPs cataloged by Nelson (2001) in his examination of these policies. The first type is 'closed-region containment'. Nelson defines this as covering the whole metropolitan area, explicitly preserving land at the urban fringe, and attempting to shift displaced development back to the center. The second type is 'open-region containment'. It also covers the whole metropolitan area, but does nothing explicitly to preserve open space at the fringe, although it does endeavor to shift development back to the center of the urban area. The final type of UCP is 'isolated containment'. By Nelson's definition, a policy of isolated containment does not exist on a metropolitan basis, intends only to preserve limited land outside some jurisdictional boundaries, and does nothing to shift development occurring outside these intrametropolitan boundaries back to the urban core.

As taken from Nelson, a description of the western metropolitan areas that had one of the three urban containment policies in place in 1997 is shown in Table 4.3. Further investigation yielded the recorded information on the approximate year that each of these UCPs began. Since development patterns are more likely to be constrained by an urban containment policy the longer it has been in place, the explanatory variables in the regression include three dummy variables for whether a type of UCP exists, and three other variables that account for the number of years since a certain UCP began in the metropolitan area.

The high level of variation in own-source municipal revenue reliance across states and across time is denoted by the values recorded in Table 4.4. For instance, on average between 1977 and 1997, municipal governments in New Mexico drew only 22.4 per cent of their discretionary local revenue from property taxation. The comparable figure for municipal governments in Oregon was 52.6 per cent. For general sales taxation over the same 20-year period, municipal governments in Oregon relied on it for none of their discretionary revenue, while municipal governments in Colorado gained 41.1 percent of their discretionary revenue from it. As well, within state variations over time for some states were large. In 1977, local governments in California drew 41.7 per cent of discretionary revenue from property taxation; by 1997, this value had fallen to 25.7 per cent. General sales taxation totaled 12.1 per cent of New Mexico's discretionary municipal revenue in 1977; by 1997 it had risen to 37.0 per cent. Nevada municipalities relied on

Table 4.3   Year that type of urban containment policy began in western metropolitan areas

Western metropolitan areas with an urban containment policy (UCP)	Type of UCP		
	Closed-region containment	Open-region containment	Isolated containment
Yuma AZ, MSA			1996
Chico-Paradise CA, MSA			1983
Fresno CA, MSA			1984
Sacramento CA, MSA			1993
San Diego CA, MSA	1979		
San Jose CA, MSA			1972
Santa Rosa CA, PMSA			1996
Vallejo-Fairfield-Napa CA, PMSA			1980
Visalia-Tulare-Porterville CA, MSA			1974
San Luis Obispo-Atascadero-Paso Robles CA, MSA		1981	
Santa Barbara-Santa Maria-Lompoc CA, MSA			1989
Yolo CA, PMSA			1987
Yuba City CA, MSA			1989
Boulder-Longmount CO, PMSA			1978
Fort Collins-Loveland CO, MSA			1980
Santa Fe NM, MSA		1991	
Eugene-Springfield OR, MSA	1982		
Medford-Ashland OR, MSA	1982		
Portland-Vancouver OR, PMSA	1979		
Salem OR, PMSA	1981		
Bellingham WA, MSA	1992		
Olympia WA, PMSA	1992		
Seattle-Bellevue-Everett WA, PMSA	1992		
Tacoma WA, PMSA	1992		
Yakima WA, MSA	1992		

Table 4.4   *Percentage statewide discretionary municipal revenue from component sources for western United States*

Year and state	Revenue from property taxes	Revenue from general sales taxes	Revenue from other taxes	Revenue from charges
1997 Arizona	15.6	39.0	5.5	39.9
1997 California	25.7	20.1	11.9	42.4
1997 Colorado	10.8	40.3	4.1	44.8
1997 Nevada	24.9	0.0	15.0	60.1
1997 New Mexico	14.6	37.0	2.7	45.7
1997 Oregon	46.7	0.0	12.7	40.6
1997 Utah	24.5	28.9	5.7	41.0
1997 Washington	24.5	22.0	10.5	43.0
1987 Arizona	18.7	36.0	5.5	39.8
1987 California	28.1	23.2	13.7	35.0
1987 Colorado	14.6	43.1	4.9	37.5
1987 Nevada	23.8	0.0	22.6	53.6
1987 New Mexico	18.3	31.5	2.6	47.6
1987 Oregon	55.7	0.0	7.2	37.0
1987 Utah	29.1	27.6	4.7	38.6
1987 Washington	25.9	22.5	12.1	39.5
1977 Arizona	25.5	43.4	3.9	27.2
1977 California	41.7	23.1	10.2	25.0
1977 Colorado	23.8	39.8	5.1	31.4
1977 Nevada	37.0	0.9	22.9	39.2
1977 New Mexico	34.3	12.1	8.7	44.8
1977 Oregon	55.3	0.0	8.0	36.7
1977 Utah	28.1	31.8	5.6	34.5
1977 Washington	31.5	18.4	12.4	37.7

other taxes for 22.9 per cent of their discretionary revenue in 1977; by 1997 this figure had fallen to 15.0 per cent.

The bottom of Table 4.5 lists the number of observations included in each of the three separate regressions. Owing to missing data, as shown in Table 4.2, there are respectively only 69 and 87 observations in the building material and car sales regressions. The descriptive statistics for variables included in the three regressions are also listed in Table 4.5. The non-central place values of median household income and population are calculated from the US Department of Housing and Urban Development's *State of the Cities Data System*.[20] Actual income values were not available for 1997

Table 4.5 Descriptive statistics for variables included in regression analyses

Variable description	Total retail sales mean (standard deviation)	Building material sales mean (standard deviation)	Car sales mean (standard deviation)
Respective dependent variable ($1 000 000s)	$3 844.121 ($7 017.489)	$395.151 ($605.331)	$1 089.884 ($1 935.023)
Real value median household income in non-central places	$41 801 ($8 543)	$43 077 ($8 713)	$43 255 ($8 588)
Population in non-central places	453 085 (730 899)	571 754 (870 910)	520 814 (779 437)
Previous 10-year percentage growth in non-central places	28.99 (19.01)	27.62 (17.42)	27.87 (17.60)
Dummy if closed-region urban containment in place	0.099 (0.300)	0.116 (0.322)	0.138 (0.347)
Years closed-region urban containment in place	0.894 (3.315)	not relevant	1.391 (4.050)
Dummy if isolated urban containment in place	0.130 (0.338)	0.159 (0.369)	0.161 (0.370)
Years isolated urban containment in place	1.35 (4.30)	1.72 (4.74)	1.83 (5.00)
Dummy if open-region urban containment in place	0.019 (0.136)	not relevant	not relevant
Years open-region urban containment in place	0.174 (1.421)	not relevant	not relevant

Real value agriculture products in metro area per acre in agric.	$860.85 ($891.76)	$984.21 ($978.01)	$850.10 ($804.72)
Percentage of population in non-central places under age 18	29.16 (6.43)	27.82 (7.72)	27.95 (7.10)
Percentage of population in non-central places over age 64	10.80 (3.10)	11.35 (3.12)	11.25 (3.04)
Percentage statewide discretionary mun. revenue from property taxes	29.14 (10.45)	26.19 (7.24)	27.88 (9.69)
Percentage statewide discretionary mun. revenue from general sales taxes	23.47 (11.36)	23.13 (9.89)	22.81 (11.22)
Percentage statewide discretionary mun. revenue from other taxes	10.03 (4.02)	11.25 (3.72)	10.67 (3.75)
Observations	161	69	87

and had to be extrapolated from the available 1979 and 1989 values. Interpolation from the available decennial Census years was also necessary to determine population and income values for 1967, 1977 and 1987. The 1997 population value is an estimate provided by the Census. Various editions of the US Census *City and County Databook* offer the data necessary to calculate the desired measures of metropolitan age distribution. Interpolation yields the 1977 and 1987 values, while extrapolation results in the values for 1997. An appropriate proxy for the real price of agricultural land in a metropolitan area's non-central places is the real value of agricultural products sold in the metropolitan area divided by the number of agricultural acres in the area. These amounts come from the US *Census of Agriculture.*

A concern for the regression analysis is how to control for non-measurable factors that are fixed in a given year across all areas, or fixed in a given area for all years, and can influence the real value of non-central retail activity. Since the factors fixed in a given year are likely related to the position of the national economy in the business cycle, a dummy variable for observations from 1987, and another dummy variable for observations from 1997, are included in all regressions.

To control for factors fixed across all observed years, but that vary by metropolitan area, a few regression options are available.[21] The first is the 'fixed effect' method of dropping the constant term and including a set of dummy variables representing each of the metropolitan areas in the sample. This allows different constant terms to control for the fixed contribution of the unmeasured characteristics of a specific area. A second option is to treat ignorance on the specific fixed contribution of an area to its retail sales in the same manner as the general ignorance represented by the regression's error term. Using this 'random effect' method, the regression's error is composed of the traditional component plus a second component that varies by each of the specific metropolitan locations in the sample. A final option is to do nothing to account for specific area effects. The regression results recorded in Table 4.6 use the fixed effect method based upon the results of statistical tests that indicate that it is preferred in at least two of the three regressions.

6   REGRESSION FINDINGS

All of the regression results in Table 4.6 use White's method of adjusting the regression coefficient's standard errors for possible heteroskedastic bias from an unknown source.[22] The regression entries in Table 4.6 first contain, in bold, the mean elasticity values for the statistically significant regression

coefficients.[23] Below these are the actual regression coefficients, and in parentheses are the coefficient's standard errors.[24] The statistical significance of the
F statistic, recorded at the bottom of the table, indicates that the group of area
dummies included in the fixed effect model, as a whole, exerts a significant
influence on the determination of total retail sales. The statistical significance
of the Lagrange multiplier statistic, also at the bottom of Table 4.6, indicates
that the use of the fixed or random effect model is preferred to simple OLS
for total and car retail sales. Based upon these test statistics, and the fact that
a Hausman test statistic (that would indicate whether the random effect
method is preferred) could not be calculated, the preferred results are from
the fixed effect regression model.[25]

As expected, non-central place population exerts a significant influence
on all forms of non-central place retail sales. A 1 per cent increase in suburban population from its mean results in anywhere from a 0.83 to 1.01 per
cent increase in real retail sales from its mean for the average metropolitan
area in the sample. Brueckner and Fansler (1983), using OLS for a single
cross-section of US metropolitan areas, record a slightly larger 1.10 per
cent increase in urbanized land area for a 1 per cent increase in urbanized
population.

Household income never exerted a statistically significant influence on
non-central retail sales.[26] Non-central places that experienced higher population growth in the previous 10-year period were more likely to exhibit
greater car sales. Another significant influence, that is non-fiscal in nature,
is that a 1 per cent increase in the price per acre of agricultural land in the
metropolitan area resulted in about a 0.14 per cent decrease in real aggregate retail sales. This is the expected effect of higher prices for suburban
land slowing suburban retail expansion.[27] Brueckner and Fansler (1983)
record a twice-higher elasticity of -0.20 for a similar explanatory variable's
effect on the size of urbanized land area, but recall that this came from a
regression analysis using a single cross-section and no controls for fixed
effects. In addition, a 1 per cent increase in the number of the non-central
population over age 64 yields about a 0.29 per cent increase in non-central
total retail sales. The magnitude of this influence (elasticity) on car sales
was about half as large. Perhaps not surprisingly, a greater percentage of
young people (perhaps owing to a greater number of new and remodeled
homes) in non-central places only exerted a positive influence on building
material sales.

Particularly notable are the regression coefficients calculated for the three
different forms of urban containment policies. The presence of a closed-
region urban containment policy (a metropolitan urban growth boundary
which preserves land outside it and attempts to shift demand for regional
development to within it) is correlated with about one billion more dollars

Table 4.6   Descriptive statistics and regression results, using real value of various types of metropolitan retail sales ($1000000s) in non-central places as dependent variables

Explanatory variables	Total retail sales, fixed effect, ordinary least squares	Building material sales, fixed effect, ordinary least squares	Car sales, fixed effect, ordinary least squares
1987 year dummy	−255.37 (204.05)	−469.91 (268.72)	57.07 (232.51)
1997 year dummy	−184.95 (288.14)	−416.02** (192.63)	74.86 (414.07)
Real value median household income in non-central places	−0.006 (0.019)	−0.016 (0.039)	0.013 (0.031)
Population in non-central places	**0.825** 0.007*** (0.001)	**1.013** 0.0007*** (0.0003)	**0.956** 0.002*** (0.001)
Previous 10-year percentage growth in non-central places	−0.847 (3.737)	−0.227 (2.239)	**0.367** 14.34** (6.67)
Dummy if closed-region urban containment in place	1031.15*** (374.84)	−94.74 (111.23)	894.82** (228.40)
Years closed-region urban containment in place	**−0.021** −89.53** (35.41)	not relevant	**−0.227** −177.91*** (35.10)
Dummy if isolated urban containment in place	122.22 (145.03)	74.01 (73.98)	487.16* (321.73)
Years isolated urban containment in place	−9.50 (9.38)	−8.66 (6.59)	**−0.079** −47.06** (32.09)
Dummy if open-region urban containment in place	−306.18 (239.90)	not relevant	not relevant

		not relevant	not relevant
Years open-region urban containment in place	**0.003** 72.79*** (23.20)	not relevant	not relevant
Real value agriculture products in metro area per acre in agriculture	−**0.135** −0.601*** (0.203)	−0.073 (0.059)	0.336 (0.396)
Percentage population in non-central places under age 18	0.727 (16.82)	**2.257** 32.06*** (11.64)	7.22 (15.24)
Percentage population in non-central places over age 64	**0.288** 102.73** (40.79)	27.81 (25.85)	**0.116** 163.56*** (49.32)
Percentage statewide discretionary municipal revenue from property taxes	17.92 (20.57)	−54.74 (45.23)	25.35 (37.01)
Percentage statewide discretionary municipal revenue from general sales taxes	**0.242** 39.60** (17.49)	**2.996** 51.19** (20.80)	**0.958** 45.76** (26.89)
Percentage statewide discretionary municipal revenue from other taxes	**0.282** 107.94** (45.28)	14.38 (48.19)	**1.698** 173.48*** (52.24)
Observations	161	69	87
R-squared statistic	0.995	0.988	0.982
Adjusted R-squared statistic	0.992	0.908	0.934
F-test statistic	7.022***	0.685	0.908
Lagrange multipler test statistic	36.81***	0.83	6.23**
White heteroskedasticity corrected	yes	yes	yes

Notes:

*** = statistically significant in two-tailed test at greater than 99 per cent confidence; ** = 91 to 99 per cent confidence; significant elasticities, calculated from means, in bold.

Data also includes dummy variables for each of the 54 metropolitan areas included in sample of non-central places. The regression coefficients for these area dummies are non-reported but are available from author upon request.

of aggregate retail activity in the metropolitan area's non-central places, and about $900 million more in car retail activity. But these effects cannot be observed in isolation, for the total retail and car sales regressions also reveal that, for every year that closed-region containment was in place, the real value of retail activity in non-central places (holding other causal factors constant) fell respectively by about $90 million and $178 million.[28] Though these yearly decreases are not that large relative to the average real values of total and car retail activity of $3.8 billion and $1.1 billion, after 10 years of closed-region urban containment, the resulting $0.9 billion and $1.8 billion reductions in non-central total retail and car sales are notable amounts.

The regressions indicate that a region that institutes a policy of closed-region containment at first exhibits more non-central retail activity; however, after 12 years (calculated by dividing 1031 by 90) it continually has less. The corresponding turning point for car sales is about 5 (894/178) years. These findings are as expected if regions with greater sprawl are more likely to adopt closed-region containment, and over time this policy of urban containment is effective at reducing decentralization. The increasing cumulative effect over time is likely due to outer development patterns being increasingly constrained the longer a given closed-region policy has been in place.

Isolated urban containment (open space preservation in place only at submetropolitan jurisdictional boundaries and no effort to direct development back to central places) exhibited no statistically significant influence on the amount of total and building material activity in non-central places. But notice that the car regression does indicate a pattern similar to the influence of closed-region urban containment. A western metropolitan area, holding other factors constant, that adopts isolated urban containment again has more non-central car retail activity ($490 million), but after about 10.5 (490/47) years it again has less. Owing to its less constraining nature, the yearly reduction in non-central car sales due to isolated urban containment is about one-fourth of the reduction experienced with closed-region containment.

The positive regression coefficient on the variable representing the number of years that open-region urban containments in place in the total non-central retail regression deserves explanation. Recall that this form of urban containment policy is less restrictive than the closed-region form since it does not attempt to preserve open space outside drawn boundaries. The adoption of such a policy in the San Luis Obispo-Atascadero-Paso Robles and Santa Fe metropolitan areas was likely a response to anticipated sprawl and a desire to do something about it. But as the regression indicates, without concentrated efforts to preserve open space at the fringe, open-region urban containment policies do not reduce the decentralization of retail activity. The positive coefficient on years of open-region urban containment is unlikely to be causal and is just picking up the increased retail decentralization that was anticipated in the earlier adoption of this ineffective policy.

Regression coefficients of equal interest are the ones relating to the way statewide measures of reliance on various forms of discretionary municipal revenue affect non-central retail sales. In all regressions the percentage of statewide discretionary municipal revenue from property taxes exerted no statistically significant influence on any of the three forms of non-central retail sales. Though the simulation finding of Brueckner and Kim (2000), and the additional motivation of suburbs seeking fiscal surplus, indicate an expected positive influence, there is also the possibility that property tax reliance discourages capital consumption, promotes greater density and reduces retail decentralization. These offsetting occurrences could be the reason for the insignificant influence that this variable exerts on non-central retail sales.

Alternatively, the percentage of statewide discretionary municipal revenue from general sales taxation exerted a significant positive influence on all three forms of non-central retail activity. For every 1 per cent increase in sales tax reliance, real retail sales in non-central metropolitan places in the West rose by 0.24 per cent. The detected influence of general sales tax reliance on building material sales was over 10 times as large, while a 1 per cent increase in sales tax reliance resulted in about a 1 per cent increase in non-central retail activity. Not surprisingly, these findings confirm the hypothesis that, if fiscalization of land use is occurring, the measurable influence should be greater on big-box forms of retail sales than on all retail sales.

Statewide reliance on other taxes, which include various types of business taxes and franchise/license fees, also yielded significant positive influences on non-central total and car retail sales. For every 1 per cent increase in reliance on these other forms of local taxation, total retail sales in non-central places rose by 0.28 per cent.[29] The comparable influence on car sales was again as expected for a big-box item: a 1 per cent increase in other tax reliance resulting in an elastic 1.7 per cent increase in non-central car sales.

7   IMPLICATIONS

The regression findings confirm the expectations of economic theory. Population, available land prices and demographics influence the real dollar amount of retail sales observed in non-central places in the western USA. The regression analysis also generated evidence in support of the fiscalization of land use for retail activity and the view that the more restrictive uses of urban growth boundaries reduce the decentralization of metropolitan retail sales. These effects are larger on the two chosen forms of big-box retail sales than for total retail. If urban retail sprawl is defined as retail activity that is greater in a metropolitan area's non-central places than the non-central places' population, population growth, demographics, land prices and income warrant, then this study has shown that two forms of local government revenue reliance contribute to a greater sprawl.

As an example, this empirical analysis demonstrates that a statewide shift in local own-source revenue towards greater reliance on sales taxation contributes to a further decentralization of total, building material and car retail activities in the state's metropolitan areas. Looking over the data offered in Table 4.4, reliance on general sales taxation as a source of discretionary municipal revenue greatly increased in New Mexico. In 1977, municipalities in New Mexico drew 12.1 per cent of their discretionary revenue from general sales taxation; by 1997, this measure had more than tripled to 37.0 per cent. The regression findings indicate that such a 306 per cent increase in reliance on general sales taxation is likely to have resulted in about a 74 per cent increase in the dollar value of total retail activity occurring in New Mexico's non-central metropolitan places.[30] Even more interesting is the finding that, owing to this increased local reliance on general sales taxation, New Mexico is expected to have about 9.2 times more building material retail activity in its non-central places and about 2.9 times more car retail activity. Other states in the American West, with the exception of Colorado and Washington, having reduced their municipal discretionary revenue reliance on sales taxation between 1977 and 1997, have experienced less non-central retail activity than would have likely occurred if these reductions had not happened.

Equally important is the consistent finding that the percentage of statewide discretionary municipal revenue from property taxes was found to exert no statistically significant influence on the decentralization of retail activity in a metropolitan area. It appears that the continuing shift in the USA away from local property taxation as a primary source of discretionary revenue, and towards other alternatives such as local sales taxation and other business taxes, has not independently contributed to increasingly decentralized metropolitan land use patterns.

A policy lesson that one may be tempted to draw from this analysis is that states interested in reducing urban retail sprawl in their metropolitan areas consider reducing their statewide municipal reliance on the general sales tax. Such a lesson needs to be tempered by the reality that most voters in the USA prefer sales taxation to alternative ways of raising local revenue.[31] The real connection between retail sprawl and local sales taxation comes from the local retention of a portion of the sales tax revenue generated in a jurisdiction that is greater than necessary to cover the costs of providing additional local services to retailers. If this fiscal surplus is eliminated, it is less likely that non-central places in metropolitan areas will continue to desire and draw retail activity from central places for purely fiscal reasons. A workable option would be to collect a portion of local retail sales revenue on a regional basis, and distribute it back to communities in the region on a per capita basis. The fiscalization of land use demonstrated here could be slowed if this portion was large enough to reduce the current fiscal surplus that communities enjoy by favoring retail trade in local land use decisions. California has considered such legislation in the form of Assembly Bill 680 (2001). AB 680, which beginning in 2003 would have put the growth in local sales tax revenue in the six-county Sacramento Region into a regional pot in which one-third would have been given back to the jurisdiction it came from, an additional one-third would also have been given back to the jurisdiction it came from if they were building their fair share of low-income housing, and the remaining one-third would have been shared on a per capita basis. Voted upon in the 2002 legislative session, it was not signed into law because of the political reality that jurisdictions accustomed to fiscal surplus generated through the encouragement of 'excessive' retail activity are loath to give it up.[32]

Avenues for future research on this topic include an expansion of the data set to include other metropolitan areas in the USA. Perhaps the influence of statewide local fiscal structure is greater in the less developed and more quickly developing West than in the rest of the country. It would also be valuable, as done in Brueckner and Fansler (1983), to use square miles in the urbanized area as the dependent variable in a regression study and check whether statewide local fiscal structure and the presence of urban growth boundaries exert similar influences on the geographic size of a metropolitan area.

NOTES

1. 'Big-box' is commonly used in the USA to describe retail outlets that generate a large amount of taxable retail sales per customer visit. In a normative sense many also use it as an interchangeable description of what they consider urban sprawl.
2. Lang (2000) also writes about the declining percentage of metropolitan office space in US central cities and refers to it as 'office sprawl'. In 1979, 74 per cent of US office space was in central cities; by 1999, the central city share of office space had dropped to 58 per cent.
3. This is a restatement of the most stringent hypothesis that Lewis and Barbour (1999)

believe must hold in order to prove empirically that the fiscalization of land use is occurring.

4. Sokolow (2000) offers a comprehensive survey of property tax limitation in the western United States. See Chapman (1998) for a summary of the local public finance consequences of California's 1978 passage of Proposition 13.

5. The largest central cities in each of these excluded states only had 1992 populations of 136000, 84000 and 52000, respectively.

6. A PMSA consists of integrated counties that are divisible into smaller integrated units that comprise one or more counties. An MSA consists of counties that are not divisible into smaller integrated units.

7. This approach should be considered conservative in regard to defining excessive decentralization because many would consider the location of retail activity in a place not a central place in 1977 and 1987, but classified as such in 1990, as sprawl.

8. Data gathering was complicated by the fact that the US Census Bureau switched from using Standard Industrial Codes (SIC) in 1987 to designate different types of retail activity, to North American Industrial Classification System (NAICS) codes in 1997. For many types of retail this switch made multi-year comparisons impossible. This was not a problem for new and used car sales that are represented by SIC 551 (motor vehicle dealers – new and used cars) in 1977 and 1987, and NAICS 4411 (automobile dealers – new and used) in 1997. Building materials is represented by SIC 521 and SIC 523 (building materials and supply stores) and SIC 525 (hardware stores) in 1977 and 1987, and NAICS 4441 (building materials and supply dealers) in 1997.

9. Table I in Wassmer (2002) offers similar information for aggregate retail sales for all 54 of the western state metropolitan areas in the full sample.

10. Alternative dependent variables would be the percentage of total retail (or building material or car) sales in a metropolitan area occurring in its non-central places (the values in the data columns of Table 4.2). A model of what determines this percentage contains the same explanatory variables as included in the model below except that some of the explanatory variables (population, household income and demographics) need to be in percentage form (non-central value relative to total value in the metropolitan area). Such a regression specification was tried and the results offered low overall explanatory power (R-squared) and little statistical significance of specific explanatory variables. As described next, using total retail (or building material or car) sales in non-central places as dependent variables lends itself to more direct modeling and the resulting regression analysis offers quite different results.

11. A mathematical description of the formal urban model that yields these four causal factors – originally developed by Muth (1969) and Mills (1972) – is contained in Brueckner and Fansler (1983).

12. As further evidence that this is appropriate, Brueckner and Fansler (1983) found their variable proxies for commuting cost (percentage of commuters using public transit and percentage of households owning one or more cars) never to be statistically significant factors in explaining the size of an urbanized area.

13. In 1997, these four sources of local revenue accounted for nearly 50 per cent of the total local revenue collected in the western states in the sample. Statewide average reliance on local revenue, rather than metropolitan averages or local reliance, is used to ensure the exogenous nature of these explanatory variables to each metropolitan area. Since pertinent land use decisions are made in the unincorporated portions of US counties, statewide municipal revenue reliance is intended also to proxy for the average reliance that counties in a state have upon these forms of local revenue.

14. Fischel's (1985) book *The Economics of Zoning Laws*, especially Chapter 14, offers an excellent introduction to zoning in the USA and the use of fiscal zoning described here. Ladd (1998) provides a recent summary of land use regulation as a local fiscal tool widely used in the USA.

15. See Bartik (1991) and Anderson and Wassmer (2000) for book-length descriptions of the use and influence of local economic development incentives in the USA. Lewis and

Barbour (1999, pp.73–4) describe the specific forms of local incentives that are available to local governments in California.

16. Business taxes and franchise/license fees are included in the category of Percentage Statewide Discretionary Municipal Revenue from Other Taxes. In most states, revenue from businesses make up more than half of the amount accounted for in this category, with the other half coming from various sources such as severance taxes, death taxes and gift taxes. It is impossible to account for business related fees separately because distinct business values are not given.

17. For the a priori purpose of predicting the expected influence of local property taxation on non-central retail activity, it would be informative to know the amount of fiscal surplus through property taxation generated by retail activity relative to alternative forms of local activity. Unfortunately, a search of the literature revealed no previous estimates of this and a full evaluation would require at least another paper-length treatment.

18. To account for the spillover of retail customers between contiguous metropolitan areas, a dummy variable representing such metropolitan areas was included in preliminary regressions. This dummy was never statistically significant in the ordinary least squares (OLS) and random effect models, and could not be included in the fixed effect regression model due to perfect colinearity. A separate dummy for whether a metropolitan area is a PMSA yielded similar results. Both of these dummies are excluded from the final regression analysis.

19. The approach taken here in measuring the influence of a UCP on non-central retail activity is conservative, given that a UCP's influence on decentralization may also affect the amount of population that exists in non-central places. This separate influence is not measured.

20. Available at *http://webstage1.aspensys.com/SOCDS/SOCDS_Home.htm.*

21. See Kennedy (1992, pp.222–3) for a further description of these possibilities.

22. See Kennedy (1992, ch. 8) for a description of heteroskedasticity and the problems it presents for regression analysis. White's method of correction is described on p.130.

23. Statistical significance is defined in the standard manner of greater than 90 per cent confidence in a two-tailed test.

24. The Total Retail Sales regression uses only 161 of the possible 162 observation (54 areas over three years) because the Yuba City CA, MSA was not in existence in 1977 and hence certain needed explanatory data could not be gathered for it.

25. There is also the specification issue of whether a log-linear functional form is more appropriate than the linear form. A log-linear form uses the log of the dependent variable and allows for non-linear relationships between explanatory variables and the dependent variable. This specification was tried and the result was less statistical significance for all regression coefficients and a few unexpected signs. Hence the decision to use the linear form recorded in Table 4.6.

26. The non-statistical significance of the income coefficient may be due to the fact that 1997 income values are extrapolated. To test this hypothesis, all regressions were rerun using only the 1977 and 1987 samples. Again the regression coefficients on median household income were statistically insignificant; hence the basis for the decision to use the full sample.

27. The negative impact of higher agricultural prices on slowing retail decentralization is only expected if the price of urban land in the area is held constant. Although there is no direct control for this in the regression equation, the fixed effect method of including dummies for year observation from and for each specific metropolitan area should offer reasonable proxies for this.

28. As shown in Table 4.2, there are only a limited number of observations on building material sales for western metropolitan areas that practiced a policy of closed-region urban containment. For this reason, perfect colinearity prevented the inclusion of a variable representing the number of years that closed-region policy was in place in the building material regression. The same is true regarding the dummy explanatory variable for the presence of open-region urban containment and the number of years that

open-region containment was in place for both the building material and car sales regressions.

29.   To measure the independent influence of Percentage Statewide Discretionary Municipal Revenue from Charges on non-central activity, this category replaced the general sales tax category in other fixed effect regression runs. The result for all three dependent variables was that the explanatory variable representing other taxes remained positive and statistically significant, the property tax variable continued to exert a statistically insignificant influence, while the charge variable also exerted no significant influence. Considering that the legal intent of charges is to generate little to no fiscal surplus, the insignificance of charges to non-central retail activity is as expected.

30.   This is calculated by taking the 306 per cent increase in sales tax reliance and multiplying it by the sales tax elasticity of non-central retail sales (0.242) recorded in Table 4.6.

31.   For a poll supporting this, see the Advisory Council on Intergovernmental Relations (1987).

32.   See Johnson (2000). California State Senator Dede Alpert, in support of her different spring 2000 bill that would have distributed new local sales tax revenue in a county on a per capita basis instead of the current *situs basis,* believed that 'Retail sprawl leads to urban sprawl, which leads to traffic, pollution, and generally a pretty poor quality of life for communities. These communities could otherwise have been balanced with jobs and housing located near each other, full services provided by each level of local government and less fighting and more cooperation between local leaders. It is not rocket science. It is the incentives.'

REFERENCES

Advisory Council on Intergovernmental Relations, 1987, 'Changing public attitudes on government and taxes', Washington, DC.

Anderson, J.E. and R.W. Wassmer, 2000, *Bidding for Business: The Efficacy of Local Economic Development Incentives in a Metropolitan Area*, Kalamazoo, MI: W.E. Upjohn Institute.

Atkinson, G. and T. Oleson, 1996, 'Urban sprawl as a path dependent process', *Journal of Economic Issues*, 30, 607–9.

Bartik, T.J. 1991, *Who Benefits from State and Local Economic Development Policies?*, Kalamazoo, MI: W.E. Upjohn Institute.

Brueckner, J.K. 2000, 'Urban sprawl: lessons from urban economics', mimeo, Department of Economics, University of Illinois at Urbana-Champaign.

Brueckner, J.K. and D.A. Fansler, 1983, 'The economics of urban sprawl: theory and evidence on the spatial sizes of cities', *Review of Economics and Statistics*, 65, 479–82.

Brueckner, J.K. and H.A. Kim, 2000, 'Urban sprawl and the property tax', mimeo, Department of Economics, University of Illinois at Urbana-Champaign.

Chapman, J.I., 1998, 'Proposition 13: some unintended consequences', Public Policy Institute of California, San Francisco, CA (available at *http://www.ppic.org /publications/occasional/chapman.occ.pdf*).

Dipasquale, D. and W.C. Wheaton, 1996, *Urban Economics and Real Estate Markets*, Englewood Cliffs, NJ: Prentice-Hall.

Downs, A., 1999, 'Some realities about sprawl and urban decline', *Housing Policy Debate*, 10, 955–74.

Ewing, R.H., 1997. 'Is Los Angeles-style sprawl desirable?', *American Planning Association Journal*, winter, 107–26.

Ewing, R.H., 1994, 'Characteristics, causes and effects of sprawl: a literature review', *Environmental and Urban Issues*, winter, 1–15.

Fischel, W.A., 1985, *The Economics of Zoning Laws: A Property Rights Approach to American Land Use Controls*, Baltimore, MD: Johns Hopkins Press.

Gordon, P. and H.W. Richardson, 1997, 'Are compact cities a desirable planning goal?', *American Planning Association Journal*, winter, 95–106.

Harvey, R.O. and W.A.V. Clark, 1965, 'The nature and economics of urban sprawl', *Land Economics*, 41, 1–9.

Innes, J.E. and D.E. Booher, 1999, 'Metropolitan development as a complex system: a new approach to sustainability', *Economic Development Quarterly*, 13, 141–56.

Johnson, K., 2000, 'Bills attack cities' sales tax reliance', *Sacramento Business Journal* (available at *http://www.bizjournals.com/sacramento/stories/2000/05/01/story5.html*).

Kennedy, P., 1992, *A Guide to Econometrics,* 3rd edn, Cambridge, MA: The MIT Press.

Kotin, A. and R. Peiser, 1997, 'Public/private joint ventures for high volume retailers; who benefits?', *Urban Studies*, 34, 1971–86.

Ladd, H.F., 1998, 'Land use regulation as a fiscal tool', in W.E. Oates (ed.), *Local Government Tax and Land Use Policies in the United States: Understanding the Links*, Cambridge, MA: Lincoln Institute of Land Policy.

Lang, R.E., 2000, 'Office sprawl: the evolving geography of business', *Survey Series*, Brookings Institution, Washington, DC.

Lewis, P. and E. Barbour, 1999, *California Cities and the Local Sales Tax*, San Francisco, CA: Public Policy Institute of California, (available at *http://www.ppic.org/publications/PPIC121/PPIC121.pdf/index.html*).

Mieszkowski, P. and E.S. Mills, 1993, 'The causes of metropolitan suburbanization', *Journal of Economic Perspectives*, 7, 135–47.

Mills, E.S., 1999, 'Truly smart smart growth', *Illinois Real Estate Letter*, summer, 1–7.

Mills, E.S., 1972, *Urban Economics*, 1st edn, Glenview, IL: Scott Foresman.

Misczynski, D.J., 1986, 'The fiscalization of land use', in J.J. Kirlin and D.R. Winkler (ed.), *California Policy Choices*, Sacramento, CA: School of Public Administration, University of Southern California.

Muth, R.F., 1969, *Cities and Housing*, Chicago, IL: University of Chicago Press.

Myers, D. and A. Kitsuse, 2000, 'The debate over future density of development: an interpretive review', Lincoln Institute of Land Policy Working Paper, Cambridge, MA.

Nelson, A.C., 2001, 'Urban containment policy', mimeo, Department of City and Regional Planning, Georgia Institute of Technology, Atlanta, GA.

O'Sullivan, A., 2000, *Urban Economics*, 4th edn, Boston, MA: Irwin McGraw-Hill.

Pierce, N.R., 1998, *The Planning Report*, July, available at The Metropolitan Forum Project's web site (*http://www.metroforum.org/article/pierce_071998.html*).

Sokolow, A.D., 2000, 'The changing property tax in the West: state centralization of local finances', *Public Budgeting and Finance*, spring, 85–104.

Tiebout, C.M., 1956, 'A pure theory of local expenditure', *Journal of Political Economy*, 64, 416–24.

Wassmer, RW., 2002, 'Fiscalization of land use, urban growth boundaries, and non central retail sprawl', *Urban Studies*, 39, 1307–27.

5. Is zoning a substitute for, or a complement to, factor taxes?

William T. Bogart

1 INTRODUCTION

Local land use controls restrict the amount of factors of production that can be used in various activities. As such, they are quotas on the import of factors of production. An alternative arrangement would be to impose a tariff on the import of factors of production, but this is unconstitutional. This chapter explores the extent to which zoning is equivalent to factor taxes in its impact on factor prices, local production and intrametropolitan trade.[1]

There are several interesting complications in the analysis. First, zoning is typically a discontinuous constraint on land use. Under a regime that sets a maximum floor–area ratio (FAR), any FAR that is less than the limit is unconstrained. By contrast, the most common factor taxes are more continuous. For example, an increase in property value will increase the property tax, all else being equal. Second, imposing a constraint in one municipality will affect behavior in other municipalities. Their actions will affect land values and trade patterns throughout the metropolitan area, not only in the municipality making the land use decision. Third, zoning is not permanent, but is subject to change. Thus we need to consider the dynamic process by which land use decisions are made, noting that the existing zoning regulations are only the starting point for future negotiations.

This chapter synthesizes previous models of trade and zoning to analyze the extent to which zoning is a complement to or substitute for factor taxes. The point that zoning can be thought of as a quantity control instead of a price control for externalities leads naturally to a consideration of the role of uncertainty in determining the preferred approach. This allows us to address the 'homevoter hypothesis' of Fischel (2001), in which he argues that a primary explanation for zoning is the desire of homeowners to reduce the variance of possible outcomes.

The remainder of the chapter proceeds as follows. Section 2 explores the links between zoning and factor taxes. Section 3 briefly reviews the nature and pattern of intrametropolitan specialization and trade. Section 4 presents a static model of zoning and taxes that allows us to analyze their interconnections. Section 5 extends the discussion to a dynamic setting. Section 6 concludes.

2   ON THE VARIETY OF CONNECTIONS BETWEEN ZONING AND TAXES

Both zoning and factor taxes affect the way in which land is used. One can distinguish two separate effects of zoning. Zoning and related land use restrictions (subdivision regulations, building codes, and so on) limit the extent to which land can be used to produce certain goods and services. As a result, zoning can have an influence on the pattern of intrametropolitan trade.[2] For example, forbidding an activity within a suburb that the suburb would otherwise have exported does not necessarily mean that the activity does not occur, only that the residents of the suburb will now have to import the activity from another suburb. Just because your town does not allow WalMart to locate there does not mean that there will be no WalMart in the region; it only means that your residents will be shopping at WalMart in another town. It is possible, in addition, that changing the pattern of intrametropolitan trade will change the pattern of trade between the metropolitan area and other metropolitan areas.

Zoning and related land use regulation has two effects on production of traded goods within a region. The first effect of zoning is to alter the factor intensity of production. We may call this effect 'intensive zoning' because it operates at the intensive margin of production. In models where capital and land are the factors of production, this effect is modeled as a reduction in the capital–land ratio.[3] Alternatively, it could be modeled as a reduction in the labor–land ratio. Regardless, intensive zoning lowers the density with which land can be used to produce goods and services.

The second effect of zoning is to allocate a maximum amount of land for use in production of a good. An example of analysis exploring this type of zoning is McDonald and McMillen (1998). We may call this effect 'extensive zoning' because it affects the extensive margin of production. Extensive zoning that is a binding constraint is in effect a maximum production level for the good. This observation makes one result immediate: if extensive zoning is binding on a good or service that would be exported from the municipality in the absence of zoning, then it is possible for that good to be imported in the presence of zoning.

Most analyses only include one of the two types of zoning. An interesting example is Fischel's book (1985), which remains an important benchmark in zoning analysis. His definition of zoning as the division of land into areas in which some activities are permitted and others prohibited is clearly based on extensive zoning. But his formal analysis of zoning uses the idea of trading property rights to the intensity of land development, an intensive zoning concept. Less formal analyses, such as Downs (1994), implicitly recognize that there are two effects and that they are connected. Downs argues that restrictive suburban zoning (minimum lot size restrictions, for example, which are a form of intensive zoning) leads to conversion of agricultural land to urban land use (a change in land use at the extensive margin). However, Downs does not have a formal model of the two effects of zoning. The model developed in section 4 includes both intensive and extensive zoning and embeds them in a familiar trade setting. It is suggestive of the type of model that needs to be further developed and empirically investigated.

It is true that zoning and factor taxes are substitutes in the sense that one can achieve similar results using either policy. However, they are also complements in the sense that the use of one can influence both the efficiency and the political desirability of the other. This is most clear in the Hamilton extension to the Tiebout model (described in section 3).

Intensive zoning leads to a reduction in the capital–land ratio in the production of traded goods. This is also the effect that a tax on capital would have. If the tax was imposed only on capital used in the production of one product, say office services (a 'partial factor tax' in the language of public finance economists), then the capital–land ratio (height of the buildings) in office services would decrease, all else being equal. If the tax were imposed on all capital, there would be a decrease in the capital–land ratio in all goods.

There are three important differences between the effects of imposing a tax on capital and the effects of intensive zoning. The first difference is that intensive zoning can have differential effects on different goods, whereas a general tax on capital would not. However, if the capital tax was imposed as a series of separate partial factor taxes, then the effects of intensive zoning on both goods could be replicated.

The second difference between a tax on capital and zoning is more substantial. A tax on capital does not impose an upper limit on the production of the capital-intensive good, as does zoning. Suppose there is a partial factor tax on office service production. This might reduce the desired density of employment to the point that the cost-minimizing/profit-maximizing employment pattern would be to have no office employment in the suburb, perhaps because only retail and manufacturing activity is the highest and best use for the land. Under a tax regime, such an outcome is possible. However, if some land is zoned for office activity rather than retail or industrial activity, zoning will have a different impact than the tax, as the retail and industrial users will be unable to convert the land from office use.[4]

The third important difference is that zoning is a discontinuous constraint on development that only affects sectors or projects where the landowner wishes to exceed the allowable density (in the case of intensive zoning). Factor taxes, on the other hand, alter the optimal mix of factors even in cases where zoning is not binding. Intuitively, the relative efficiency cost of the two policies will depend on the extent to which zoning imposes large constraints on a few sectors as opposed to structure and land taxes imposing marginal adjustments on all sectors. Zoning, in the terminology of Blinder and Rosen (1985), is a 'notch' constraint. The formal analysis in section 4 illustrates how this feature of zoning complicates the analysis not only of zoning itself but also of its interaction with factor taxes.

While zoning is therefore not completely equivalent to a tax on capital, it does have similar effects. This implies that some of the same principles can be applied to the general equilibrium effects of zoning as apply to the general equilibrium analysis of taxation. In particular, it is likely that, even if the municipality is 'small' relative to the rest of the metropolitan area, its zoning could nevertheless have an impact upon other municipalities. Bradford (1978) and Courant and Rubinfeld (1978) illustrate this possibility using tax policy. The logic of their analysis is that the local taxation of capital (in their papers via a tax, in our situation via zoning) will lead to the migration of capital elsewhere, which will in turn lower the overall return to capital in other places as its supply increases. Hence capital owners everywhere bear some of the burden of the restriction on the use of capital in one area. Hanson (1998) provides empirical verification of the interconnected nature of counties in the United States, and finds that the bulk of the direct impact of any changes in one county is concentrated in counties within the same metropolitan area.

In addition to these models of indirect impact, there is a considerable literature that analyzes municipal government decisions as strategic choices that affect and are affected by other municipal governments' decisions. Wilson (1999) surveys the literature on tax competition, in which local governments try to attract households and residents by strategically choosing tax and public service combinations. In the case of land use restrictions, Brueckner (1998) and Helsley and Strange (1995) are examples of papers that model the decisions of local governments as interrelated. Finally, there is a line of research in which environmental regulation decisions by local governments are analyzed to see whether the potential mobility of firms has an impact on policy. Glazer (1999) is a recent example of this type of research. An ambitious paper by Copeland and Taylor (2001) attempts to provide a unified theory of environmental regulation and international trade. This is the type of modeling effort needed in the zoning literature as well, as we attempt to understand the impact of land use regulations in jurisdictions that are open to trade with other jurisdictions in the same metropolitan area as well as with the rest of the world.

3 INTRAMETROPOLITAN SPECIALIZATION AND TRADE

There is local specialization in the production of goods and services for export to other areas, and there is local specialization in the production of goods and services for local consumption. There is also redundancy, not just in government services and utilities, but also in the form of diffuse service employment in the form of McDonalds, Walgreens, Dominos and urgent care medical facilities.

Specialization in Local Consumption Goods – the Tiebout Model

We can usefully think of the suburbs in a metropolitan area as small open economies. They are 'open' because they import and export goods and services to other economies. They are 'small' in the sense that their individual actions are unlikely to have a dramatic effect on the entire market for goods and services.

Countries import some goods and services, export some goods and services, and locally produce and consume some goods and services. The USA, for example, imports VCRs from other countries, exports corn to other countries and consumes soft drinks that are produced within the USA. What are the analogous products for the suburban economy? The most common export is labor – people that live in the suburb and work in another suburb or downtown. A typical import is retail services from a regional shopping mall. (The shopping mall represents an export activity for the suburb in which it is located.) Important locally produced services include housing and local government services.

Just because every suburb produces housing and local government services does not mean that every suburb is identical. Quite the opposite, in fact: local government services and the quality and density of the local housing stock are among the primary ways that different suburbs are distinguished from one another. The dominant approach among economists to analyzing suburbs focuses precisely on these differences. This approach is called the 'Tiebout model', after the economist who first proposed it.[5]

The Tiebout model assumes that people are free to choose the town in which they reside. Towns compete for residents by offering a bundle of public services financed by local taxes. Individuals then 'vote with their feet' and choose the combination of taxes and public services that is most appealing to them. The conclusion of the model is that suburbs will tend to consist of people who have similar tastes for public services, and further that the system will be efficient in that the local taxes are essentially a price for local public services.

The Tiebout model has been the basis for most economic research focused on local governments for the past 45 years. There is considerable evidence that suburbs are relatively homogeneous.[6] It is difficult to measure individual preferences for public goods, but we know that these preferences are correlated with other characteristics, such as age and income. Much of the literature has focused on measuring these other characteristics, and examining whether suburbs in metropolitan areas with a more fragmented local government structure are more homogeneous.[7]

An important assumption of the Tiebout model is that people are free to locate without worrying about their journey time to work places. This assumption of accessibility flies in the face of anecdotes about long drives and gridlock. However, the evidence is that commuting times have remained roughly constant or fallen slightly over the past few decades, with the journeys in most metropolitan areas averaging less than 25 minutes. Hence the assumption that households are free to locate without regard to their workplace is consistent with the observed patterns of commuting.[8]

The most important theoretical addition to the original Tiebout framework was provided by Hamilton (1975, 1976) who argued that communities could use zoning to ensure that people were unable to 'free-ride' and enjoy local public services. As Hamilton points out, the most common local tax is the property tax, which varies according to the value of your house. So households have an incentive to own a below-average market value house in a town that supplies a high level of local public services. Fiscal zoning, in which towns set a minimum house value, solves this problem. Of course, it is illegal for towns to set a minimum house value, but the combination of zoning, subdivision regulations and building codes can implicitly have the same effect. Mieszkowski and Zodrow (1989) say that the flexibility available to local governments is insufficient to make the property tax efficient. Fischel (1992) disagrees, arguing that zoning reflects local preferences and is not a major restriction on households.

There is considerable evidence that suburbs specialize in producing local government services for their residents. Because one facet of the local amenities is the restrictiveness of zoning, it is unsurprising that not every suburb will have extensive employment opportunities for its residents within its borders. Let us turn now to some evidence on how much specialization exists in the production of traded goods as well as the nontraded local public services.[9]

Specialization in Production: Evidence from Employment Centers

Economists and geographers have been studying the emerging structure of the twenty-first century metropolitan area for some time now. (See Anas *et al.*, 1998, for a survey.) There are two main questions that have been asked. First, how much employment is located in employment centers – areas with both large numbers of workers and high employment density – and how much is more diffused? Second, are the employment centers specialized or do they resemble each other in the mix of industries located there?

Answering these questions is a fundamental step towards developing a theory of the impact of zoning. However, assembling the data needed for such work is still extremely difficult, so most studies only look at one metropolitan area at a time. While this is useful, it handicaps attempts to compare results across metropolitan areas, as different authors sometimes use slightly different methodologies, and there are also inherent difficulties in generalizing from the largest metropolitan areas, such as Los Angeles or Chicago, that have been the subject of the most extensive analysis.[10]

A recent paper that looks at four comparable metropolitan areas is Anderson and Bogart (2001). The authors analyze Cleveland, St Louis, Portland and Indianapolis using a common definition of employment center and a common approach for measuring specialization. Their results strongly support the idea that there is a common structure among metropolitan areas. They find that the percentage of total employment located in employment centers, the size distribution of employment centers and the pattern of specialization of employment centers is similar in each of the cities they study.

If employment centers are specialized, then it must be the case that they export their goods and services to other employment centers and import goods and services from other employment centers. It makes no sense, in such a world, to think that we can study the economy of a suburb in isolation. Rather, each suburb is part of a system of interactions, and the economic theory of trade is vital to understanding the modern metropolitan area.

An interesting finding from the research on employment centers is that most jobs within metropolitan areas are not located within employment centers (Anas *et al.*, 1998, p.1443) Therefore we need to analyze 'dispersed' employment as well as employment that is concentrated in centers. Few suburbs are completely specialized in providing residential services, as most include at least some commercial or industrial activity. By considering the pattern of trade not only among centers but also among these other sources of production, we will increase our understanding of the complete pattern of economic activity within the metropolitan area.

We are familiar with the ideas of importing and exporting goods and services from one country to another. However, it might seem puzzling at first to think about how imports and exports occur within a metropolitan area. After all, there is no customs barrier, no currency conversion and no passport required when transporting products from one suburb to another. How, then, can we describe these activities as importing or exporting?

When we say that a good or service is exported from an area, all that we mean is that the area produces more of the good than it wishes to consume. The excess is sold to others, in other words exported. Similarly, an import occurs when an economy consumes more than it produces. These definitions of imports and exports apply whether the economy in question is a country, a metropolitan area, a part of a metropolitan area or even an individual.[11]

When we talk about employment centers within a metropolitan area trading with each other, much of the trade will occur using cars and trucks. My morning trip to work represents an export of labor services from the place I live and an import of labor services by the employment center where my university office is located. The telephone, email and fax machine also make it possible to export and import services without anyone leaving their office. The phone call from a manufacturing company in a suburb to their lawyer in downtown Cleveland represents an export of legal services from downtown and an import of legal services to the suburb.

Anderson (1999) uses data from household travel surveys to estimate the magnitude of trade in labor services among municipalities in the Cleveland area. He was able to identify communities that were net importers of labor, including 'edge cities', and communities that were exporters of labor, that is, 'bedroom suburbs'. The amount of trade is substantial, with about $20 billion in exports (and imports) of labor services among municipalities in five counties in 1994. One way of characterizing this research is that it makes 'invisible' trade (in services) visible, by focusing on the part of the trade that the researcher can observe. A weakness of this approach is the necessity to impute the dollar value of trade flows.[12] Interestingly, Anderson finds that a large fraction of the workers in an employment center tend to live in residential areas very near to that employment center. The monocentric city model, while not a good model of the overall metropolitan structure, is nevertheless a decent approximation of the area surrounding an employment center.

Zoning reduces the quantity and types of goods and services that are produced in a municipality. However, if the residents (households or firms) of the municipality demand those goods and services, then they must be obtained elsewhere. Thus zoning is not only a barrier to trade but also an encouragement to trade.[13]

This dimension of zoning again emphasizes the fact that it is inappropriate to restrict the analysis of zoning purely to the municipality that is implementing the zoning. Rather, the institution of restrictive zoning in one place inevitably spills over into the remainder of the municipality. To repeat our earlier example, a town that does not allow for 'big-box' retail development is simultaneously imposing the condition on the remainder of the metropolitan area that the roads linking its residents to the eventual location of the retail activity will be more congested.

4   A MODEL OF ZONING AND LOCAL TAXATION

A good model of zoning must include the impact of zoning on location decisions of firms and households and on the intrametropolitan trade among municipalities.[14] A good model of zoning must also include the explicit land use regulation but integrate it with local taxes, as in the Hamilton-Tiebout framework. Even these minimal requirements lead to a complicated model, and the further desirability of an explicitly dynamic framework makes it almost impossible to design a model that adequately captures the rich local government environment.

This chapter extends a model of zoning due to Fu and Somerville (2001) to include more than one jurisdiction and also to include taxes on land and structures.[15] The interested reader is encouraged to look at their article for some of the technical details of the derivation. The zoning analysis is then embedded in the familiar Heckscher–Ohlin model of trade, applied in this case to trade among municipalities within a metropolitan area. We will use the model as a framework for suggesting a productive direction for future research.

Let us begin by introducing some notation and considering the problem facing a developer of one piece of land in one town. Suppose that there are constant returns to scale in real estate development. In that case, the development density (floor–area ratio, or FAR) h, can be written as a function of the capital–land ratio, K/L. Any given FAR h is produced with a cost $c(h)$, where $c'(h) > 0$ and $c''(h) > 0$.

The market price for space p is assumed to be independent of density but to depend on location characteristics or amenities X. The price of land is represented by v. In the absence of taxes, we can write the profits per unit of land to a developer as

$$\pi = p(X)h - c(h) - v. \tag{5.1}$$

Suppose that there is a structures tax t applied to the gross receipts from development and a land tax l. (A 'standard' property tax would require t and l to be equal.) In that case the profits per unit of land are

$$\pi = p(X)h(1-t) - c(h) - v(1-l). \tag{5.2}$$

If there is free entry into the development market, then in equilibrium profits equal 0 and we can rewrite equation (5.2) to show the value of land as a function of density:

$$v = p(X)h[(1-t)/(1-l)] - c(h)/(1-l). \tag{5.3}$$

The optimum density for the developer will be where equation (5.3) is maximized, which will occur at a density h^* such that

$$v_h = p(X)[(1-t)/(1-l)] - c'(h)/(1-l) = 0. \tag{5.4}$$

There are three things to observe about equation (5.4). The first thing to observe is that any zoning regulation that restricts h will only be binding if it is imposed at a FAR less than h^*. If zoning is binding, then $v_h > 0$.[16] The second thing to observe is that the standard property tax ($t = l$) is distorting in this framework. The density chosen when $t = l > 0$ is lower than the density chosen when $t = l = 0$. This is true because $p(X)$ does not change (by assumption) as we change the tax rate, but $c'(h)/(1-l)$ increases as l increases. Since $c'(h)$ is increasing in h, the higher the tax rate, the lower the optimal density of development. Hence it is possible in theory to choose a tax rate such that the optimal density of development is equal to the density imposed by a direct regulation on FAR. This 'equivalence' result will be explored in more depth later. The third thing to observe is that a land tax imposed alone ($t = 0$, $l > 0$) is nondistorting, in that the optimal h does not change regardless of the level of l.

Equilibrium with Multiple Locations

The model developed above looks at one location in isolation. However, in practice zoning decisions in one place affect land use and location decisions elsewhere.[17] Let us now consider equilibrium conditions when there are two towns in which a developer could locate. Suppose that $X_1 > X_2$ so that town 1 is more attractive. For simplicity, we will write $p(X_2) = \gamma p(X_1)$, where $\gamma < 1$.

As soon as multiple locations are introduced, notation complicates the analysis. We will focus on some simple results to avoid getting lost in algebra. Suppose that there are no taxes and that both towns have restricted their FAR to the same density ($h_1 = h_2 \equiv h$). What will the equilibrium look like? It must be the case that profits per unit of land for the developer are equal in each location in order for both to be developed. From equation (5.3) above, we can derive

$$v_1 - v_2 = (1 - \gamma)p(X_1)h. \tag{5.5}$$

Equation 5.5 has a simple interpretation. The more attractive amenities in town 1 are capitalized into land values. This is a familiar result and one that is robust when the model is more complicated.

Now consider the case where $h_1 < h_2$, in other words, where town 1 has more restrictive zoning than town 2. We can think of this intuitively as the case of an attractive suburb (higher amenities and tighter zoning) relative to either a downtown or an unincorporated area on the outskirts of a metropolitan area. For simplicity, let us say that $h_1 = \eta h_2$, with $\eta > 0$. We can derive from equation (5.3) a result analogous to equation (5.5), viz:

$$v_1 - v_2 = p(X_1)h_2(\eta - \gamma) + [c(\eta h_2) - c(h_2)]. \tag{5.6}$$

The second term is negative as long as $\eta < 1$ because marginal costs are increasing. The first term will be positive if $\eta > \gamma$ and negative if $\eta < \gamma$. Since η is a measure of the restrictiveness of zoning and γ is a measure of the relative amenities in the towns, we can interpret this condition as indicating that land values in town 1 will continue to be higher than land values in town 2 if zoning in town 1 is not too restrictive relative to the value of the amenities.

Town 1 has the opportunity to choose how restrictive its zoning is, that is η. Suppose that the goal of the local government is land value maximization, as is often assumed in the literature. (For example, see Sonstelie and Portney, 1980.) Further, suppose that there is a marginal congestion cost $\lambda(h_1)$ imposed on the residents of town 1 by developments in the town. Developments in town 1 increase congestion costs because of the direct effect of the development on the residents, including the added traffic from residents of town 2. The overall level of development in the metropolitan area will also affect λ. If the metropolitan area already has a high level of dense development, the marginal cost of increasing the density in town 1 is assumed to be less. If we assume that it takes town 2's zoning decision as fixed when deciding on its own zoning, then we can use equation (5.6) to derive the optimum condition for town 1:

$$\partial(v_1 - v_2)/\partial\eta = p(X_1)h_2 - h_2 c'(\eta h_2) = \lambda(h_1). \tag{5.7}$$

Equation (5.7) boils down to a straightforward marginal benefit equals marginal cost calculation. It is introduced here as a benchmark for comparing the optimization problem facing town 1 when there are land and structure taxes in addition to zoning.

Speaking of taxes, it is now time to reintroduce them into the model. Let us begin with the case of a 'standard' property tax (recall, this means that the tax rates on land and structures are equal). Denoting the tax rates by t_1 and t_2 for towns 1 and 2, respectively, we can derive an analog to equation (5.6):

$$v_1 - v_2 = p(X_1)h_2[\eta - \gamma\{(1 - t_2)/(1 - t_1)\}] + [c(\eta h_2) - c(h_2)]/(1 - t_1). \quad (5.8)$$

What difference do the taxes make? Consider the case where $t_1 = t_2$. In that case, the first term in equation (5.8) is identical to the first term in equation (5.6), the situation with no taxes. However, the second term (which, recall, is negative) is larger in equation (5.8) than the second term in equation (5.6). If land in town 1 is more valuable than land in town 2 in the absence of taxes, the difference will be reduced in the presence of taxes. In fact, it is possible that land in town 1 could be more valuable in the absence of taxes but less valuable once taxes are considered. Will this make town 1 more or less likely to impose tighter restrictions in the presence of taxes than it would in the absence of taxes? Consider the optimization problem facing the town in the presence of taxes, as illustrated in equation (5.9):

$$\partial(v_1 - v_2)/\partial\eta = p(X_1)h_2 - [h_2 c'(\eta h_2)]/(1 - t_1) = \lambda(h_1). \quad (5.9)$$

For this equation to hold, it must be true that the η chosen in (5.9) must be less than the η chosen in (5.7). So all else being equal, property taxes make it less attractive for a town to allow development. This makes sense in this model, as the taxes are not used to increase the value of land (for example by providing valuable public services). Including some value resulting from the taxes could alter the impact of taxes on the optimal level of regulation from the town's point of view.[18]

Figure 5.1 illustrates the municipal land value maximization problem described in equations (5.7) and (5.9), although the terms have been rearranged a little. The marginal benefit is downward-sloping because $c''(h) > 0$. The marginal cost is upward-sloping as long as $\lambda''(h) > 0$, which we will assume.[19] Increasing taxes (from zero to a positive amount in Figure 5.1) reduces the increment to land value – because of the capitalization of the taxes – while leaving everything else unchanged. Hence taxes shift the marginal benefit curve down, leading to a lower density being chosen by the town.

Zoning, Taxes and Intrametropolitan Trade

Now that we have developed a model of land use decisions by developers and land use restrictions by municipalities, it is time to investigate the

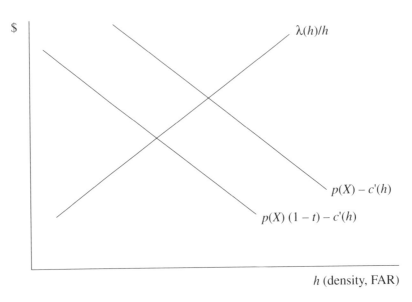

Figure 5.1   Land value maximization

implications for location of activity and trade within a metropolitan area. Suppose that there is a fixed amount of land in each town and that there is a fixed amount of capital to allocate to the towns.[20] For the moment, we will maintain the assumption that there is only one sector of production, so that there is only a single FAR to be determined. For trade to occur, there needs to be a variety of goods and services available, and we will extend the model to include this case after a couple more preliminaries are completed.

We will assume that town 1 imposes a FAR regulation while town 2 does not. This could reflect different political objectives in the two towns (town 2 is a central city or rural area that is trying to encourage development) or different political constraints (town 2 is an unincorporated part of a county that does not have zoning authority). Figure 5.2 illustrates the density in each town as a function of the regulation adopted in town 1. The density in town 1 is piecewise linear. When the constraint is binding, the density is equal to the constraint. Once the constraint is not binding the developers just choose the optimum (from equation 5.4) regardless of the level of η. Figure 5.2 is drawn assuming that the total level of capital in the metropolitan area allows both towns to be at their unconstrained optimum, but the basic logic remains even if the level of capital is allowed to vary.

As η, the parameter measuring the relative restrictiveness on land use in town 1, is increased (restrictiveness is decreased), the density in town 1

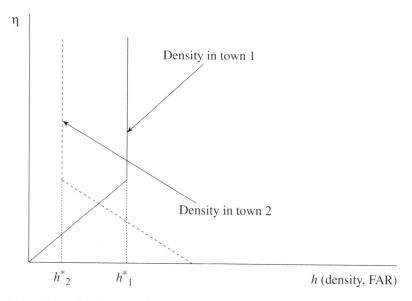

Figure 5.2   Density as a function of land use control in town 1 (no taxes)

increases towards its unconstrained optimum h^*_1. Because there is a fixed amount of capital and land, this means that the density in town 2 decreases. The unconstrained optimum density is greater in town 1 because of the maintained assumption that $X_1 > X_2$.[21]

Now consider the alternative situation, where there is a property tax but no zoning restriction. Figure 5.3 illustrates the relation between density and tax rates in town 1, holding the tax rate in town 2 fixed at 0. (We get this relation by solving equation (5.4) for the optimum density at the various tax rates.) The pattern is potentially more complicated (nonlinear relation between tax rate and density) than Figure 5.2 because the actual FAR will depend on firm decisions rather than just being at a quantity constraint. As drawn, the density of development in town 1 does not go to zero until the tax rate is 100 per cent. It is possible that all of the development would go to town 2 at a lower tax rate than 100 per cent, but the basic pattern of decreasing density with respect to the tax rate in the town will still hold.

Suppose that the tax rate in town 2 is not equal to zero, as will generally be the case. The only difference in the analysis is that the intercepts will vary. For example, if $t_2 > 0$ and $t_1 = 0$, the FAR in town 1 will be greater than h^*_1. Holding t_2 constant, though, the pattern we observe in Figure 5.3 will continue to hold even for $t_2 > 0$.

Figures 5.2 and 5.3 illustrate how density is determined in the presence

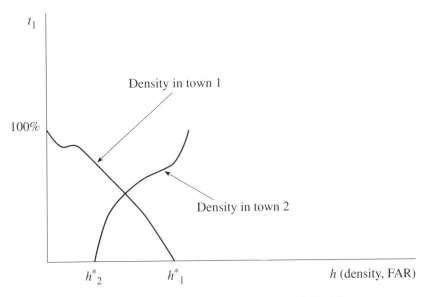

Figure 5.3   Density as a function of tax rate in town 1 (holding t_2
*   fixed at 0)*

of either zoning or taxes. In general, a town will have both a property tax
and a zoning law. In that case, the observed FAR is the *minimum* of the
zoning restriction and $h(t)$, the FAR chosen by a profit-maximizing developer given the tax rate. A town that wishes to restrict development thus has
two policy instruments at its disposal, the price instrument of the property
tax and the quantity instrument of the zoning restriction. These instruments are equivalent in the sense that a town can choose its FAR by setting
either one of the instruments. This is the clearest case for zoning and factor
taxes to be substitutes.

Now that we see how the FAR for each town is determined in the presence of zoning, taxes or both, we are ready to consider the impact of zoning
and factor taxes on intrametropolitan trade. All that needs to be done is to
extend the model to include more than one sector, so that the optimal FAR
will vary not only with X but also by sector. We expect that each town will
host activities from different sectors, creating opportunities for mutually
beneficial trade. Zoning and taxes can alter the location decisions of firms,
in turn changing the pattern of trade among towns in the metropolitan
area.

Formally, suppose that there are several sectors, each with a different
$c(h)$. Then the equilibrium condition in equation (5.4) will yield a different

h for each sector. A tax will affect the density in *all* sectors, while zoning (setting a maximum h, call it h_{limit}) will only affect sectors where $h^* < h_{limit}$. Figure 5.4 illustrates the impact of zoning and taxes when there are three sectors. Sector C, the least capital-intensive, is unaffected by the zoning limit, but is nevertheless affected by a property tax.[22]

The pattern of production will depend on the extent to which different sectors locate in different towns. The observed FAR in the town will be the weighted average of the FAR in each of the sectors there. If the towns differ, there is potentially reason for trade. Towns with higher density will trade the goods and services that they produce with towns with lower density. For example, a person might live in a bedroom suburb, commute to work as a banker in an office park in an edge city, and shop at a regional mall on the outskirts of the metropolitan area. This represents an export of labor services from the bedroom suburb that are used to produce exportable banking services from the edge city, and an export of retail services from the outskirts of the metropolitan area. Because the underlying model of factor location (land development) includes factor price equalization, this model is basically a version of the familiar Heckscher–Ohlin model of international trade.[23]

If communities were maximizing land value, why would we not just see one type of activity (the one with maximum land value)? There is not room here to provide the details of closing the model, but one would need to include the demand for households for various goods and services. In terms of the formal model, this would mean varying the bid-rent for each sector through $p(X)$ and making it endogenous in addition to varying the $c(h)$ function by sector.

Figure 5.2 illustrates the capital–land ratio in each town, which is a measure of 'intensive zoning'. As already noted, though, if there are a variety of productive activities, each of which has a different capital intensity, the municipal capital intensity is a weighted average of the capital intensities in each activity. So Figure 5.2 implicitly gives us some ideas about extensive zoning as well. If town 1 chooses to restrict its FAR to be less than that in town 2, then town 1 has effectively imposed a cap on the amount of capital-intensive production it will engage in. This provides a way in which public sector tax and regulatory decisions can influence the pattern of intrametropolitan trade, analogous to the way that local public expenditure decisions influence the pattern of trade in Wilson (1987).

Figure 5.4 is very similar to the types of diagrams that Blinder and Rosen (1985) use to analyze discontinuous 'notch' constraints in public sector activities. They point out that the efficiency cost of a notch relative to a continuous constraint (such as a tax) will depend on the extent to which activity is concentrated near to the notch. In Figure 5.4, for example, Sector C is not affected at all by the zoning constraint. Sector B is likely to have production efficiency affected by the notch, as the constraint is relatively close to the unconstrained optimum, so that the developer might well find it worthwhile to locate in the town even given the constraint. Sector A, on the other hand, is likely to be driven to another location in the metropolitan area, so the efficiency cost will depend on the attractiveness of the alternative location relative to the town that is imposing the zoning constraint.

A distortionary tax, on the other hand, has efficiency costs for each of the three sectors, as illustrated in Figure 5.4. The optimal density changes as the tax rate is increased, regardless of the capital intensity of the sector. Blinder and Rosen (1985) emphasize the comparison between the alternative policies, but in our application we can go even farther and note that the imposition of zoning can have an influence on the way we view the deadweight loss from property taxation. For instance, suppose that the zoning constraint exists and then a property tax is imposed. In that case, Sector B already has its FAR set below its optimum in the case of both zero taxes and positive taxes. In other words, there is no marginal efficiency cost to the tax, assuming that it does not lead the firms in Sector B to relocate.

Consider a further extension of Figure 5.4 in which each sector has a different zoning constraint.[24] In that case, the 'extra' deadweight loss of a property tax might be relatively small. This interaction between zoning and property taxes might help to explain the variance between the substantial

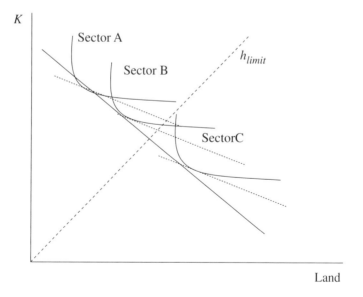

Figure 5.4   Sectoral density as a function of zoning and taxes

efficiency gains we expect from moving to a tax on land values with the relatively disappointing gains observed in practice. (See Oates and Schwab, 1997, for a thoughtful analysis of Pittsburgh's experience.) If firms are not completely free to adjust their behavior owing to the presence of zoning, the benefits of switching regimes are reduced.

As already noted above, in order to close the model we must determine the demand by households to consume the services produced by capital and land. We might also want to consider explicitly the commuting behavior of households as they combine their labor with capital and land to produce goods and services. (Anderson, 1999, is a first step in this direction.)

5   TOWARDS A DYNAMIC MODEL

The model sketched in section 4 is complex, but it is only a static analysis. Land use and land use regulation vary over time. This section discusses how the model could be extended to address topics in dynamic zoning already identified in the literature as important. It begins with a look at some comparative statics in the model, and then considers the question of land use regulation under uncertainty.

Changing Circumstances and Local Support for Infill Development

The decisions made today about zoning and taxes affect the land use decisions made today. Those decisions, in turn, influence who will have the opportunity to make land use decisions in the future. An important line of research has considered how the metropolitan economic structure and the local political situation coevolve. Baldassare and Wilson (1996) examine the changing support for growth controls in Orange County as the municipalities change. Peiser (1989) studies whether greater density results from zoning regimes that are relatively flexible or inflexible, emphasizing the importance of infill development in mitigating the 'sprawl' that results in the short run from a zoning regime that is flexible. Fu and Somerville (2001) provide a model of infill development that is explicitly aimed at identifying the links between local political decisions and the way in which land is used.

The formal model developed in section 4 emphasizes the relation between the decisions in the towns. This makes it possible to extend the questions posed by previous authors to the more general question of the pattern of development in a metropolitan area. Consider, for example, the impact of a change in the overall density of the metropolitan area on the decisions in a town. From Figure 5.1, we see that the marginal cost of development $\lambda(h)/h$ would shift out, leading to a higher density in that town. Of course, this change would affect not only the density in the town, but the pattern of trade with the rest of the metropolitan area and the land use decisions in other towns. The widespread use of referendum zoning, where substantial changes in land use have to be approved by the voters, provides a likely source for data on the changing sources of political support for zoning.

The 'Homevoter Hypothesis'

Fischel (2001) has argued that exclusionary zoning is often driven by the uncertainties that homeowners face when new developments enter their town. The formal model in this chapter is static and certain, so it does not allow us to analyze directly that question. We can, however, speculate on what an extension would look like.

Gatzlaff and Smith (1993) anticipate Fischel's argument and provide a formal model, albeit one lacking the rich institutional detail found in Fischel. Their basic point is that risk-averse households are more sensitive to unanticipated costs than to unanticipated benefits. Thus, even if the estimated mean impact of a development is accurate, it could be rational for households to oppose growth. They advocate using marginal cost pricing instead of using quantity controls in order to increase efficiency. This argument is a specific case of a more general result, to which we now turn.

Zoning is a restriction on the quantity produced of a good, while a tax on capital affects the price of the good. Because it imposes a maximum capital–land ratio in production, zoning is also like a maximum land price. There is a well-known result due to Weitzman (1974) that quantity controls are preferred to price controls in controlling the impact of negative externalities if and only if the benefits function has greater curvature than the cost function near the optimum. An interesting question is whether the theoretical justification of Weitzman is applicable to the practice of zoning in the USA. The three main situations where quantity controls are to be preferred are as follows. The first situation is where the cost curve is very flat, which would render prices almost useless as a control instrument. This does not seem to be the case with most land development. The second situation is where there is a 'kink' in the benefits curve, for example a point at which a situation goes from being tolerable to being intolerable. (Weitzman's example is a river that becomes too polluted for swimming.) This situation seems likely to occur in some cases, particularly in congested urban areas. The third situation is where a high degree of coordination is required. This situation is compelling only to the extent that developers are unable to act at a large enough scale to internalize coordination problems. Fischel (1994) provides an interesting case study of the ability of developers to allocate land use optimally.

One explanation for the prevalence of quantity controls, whether or not they are more efficient than price controls, is that quantities are more easily observed than prices, so that zoning is easier to administer. This is reasonably convincing in the case of a restriction on capital and conforms to the observation that neighbors identify most zoning violations. Glaeser and Shleifer (2001) provide a theoretical analysis of the use of quantity regulation that relies on the relative cost of enforcing quantity and price controls. A second, and quite plausible, explanation is that quantity controls are legal and price controls are not. A local regulation imposing a maximum land value would almost certainly be viewed as a taking (of private property by the state without compensation to the property owner), while local zoning laws that effectively impose a maximum land value have been upheld as long as there is some justification for them based on public welfare. Similarly, local tariffs on capital in various uses would almost certainly run afoul of the Commerce Clause. Classified property taxes, though, are a step in the direction of a price control.

Quantity controls might be relatively inefficient, but from the point of view of a town's residents they are better than nothing. Fischel's example of an 'equity insurance market' in which residents are insured against negative impacts from a new development can be thought of as a form of price control. The premium for the equity insurance is a price control facing a prospective developer, and such an approach might be more efficient than exclusionary zoning. Formal theoretical and empirical analysis of this topic is still in its infancy, but it is a promising area with the prospect of having an impact on public policy.

6   CONCLUDING COMMENTS

Is zoning a substitute for, or a complement to, factor taxes? The answer, clearly, is both. The challenge is to continue to explore the nuances of the relationship in order to better understand and inform public policy.

One issue that needs empirical investigation is the extent to which the 'notch' of zoning just implements the factor proportions that would result from taxes. Fu and Somerville (2001) have a creative approach to measuring the extent to which zoning regulations are binding. Their approach relies on the fact that the capital–land ratio incorporates all of the information about a site in the absence of binding zoning. Hence, if the site characteristics are significantly different from zero in a regression that includes the FAR, then the zoning constraint is binding. Their approach is implemented using data from Shanghai, China, but it would be instructive to consider US data as soon as possible.

This chapter has assumed (and I have argued at length elsewhere) that the appropriate way to model metropolitan areas is as a set of 'trading places' or small open economies. In order to better understand the pattern of trade and the impact of zoning and taxes on this trade, we need to construct 'current accounts' for municipalities. Anderson (1999) demonstrates that at least part of that empirical agenda is feasible, but his work relies on imputed data in addition to actual measurements. We need to do a better job of capturing the spatial nature of transactions.

Public expenditures on roads, stadiums and so on are nontariff barriers (or encouragements) to trade in the same way that zoning is. This chapter has completely neglected the expenditure side of the public sector because the discussion was already lengthy and unwieldy. The analysis of local public expenditures as trade policy takes on added relevance and urgency in a world of free trade in educational services – as how else could one describe the proliferation of charter schools, public school choice and vouchers? Further, the role of private entities such as homeowners' associations in providing substitutes for the local public sector is also likely to influence public support for both zoning and taxes. Wilson (1987) demonstrates how the Tiebout model of differences in public spending across municipalities implies a reason for trade in other goods and services. More fully integrating expenditures into the analysis of zoning and taxation will undoubtedly yield substantial payoffs in better understanding of metropolitan areas.

NOTES

1. One immediate difference between zoning and taxes is that taxes yield revenue for the local government. In most of the analysis in this chapter, I will not focus on this difference.
2. Fischel (2001) emphasizes that widespread exclusionary zoning developed contemporaneously with the first large-scale use of private cars by individuals and trucks by businesses. Because business activities became much more footloose as a result of the advent of trucks, he argues that zoning developed as a way for local homeowners to avoid the risk of an undesirable business locating nearby. See Moses and Williamson (1967) for an analysis of the impact of the truck on the location of business activity within metropolitan areas.
3. See McDonald (1978) for example. Sivitanidou and Wheaton (1992) analyze zoning as a restriction on the capital–land ratio in order to investigate the effects on factor prices. They find that zoning that is too rigorous can actually destroy the possibility of employment in a suburb. They also find that increasing the restrictiveness of zoning tends to benefit the owners of commercial land at the expense of workers – an 'artificial' scarcity of land has been created. Finally, they note the possible efficiency consequences of reducing agglomeration economies of scale.
4. Of course, this would provide an incentive for landowners to lobby for either a zoning variance or a reclassification of their property.
5. The economist was Charles Tiebout (1956). His original article has spawned an enor-

mous research literature that will be only briefly summarized here. An important modern interpretation and extension of Tiebout's work is Fischel (2001).

6. See Fischel (1985). Warner (1962) documents the extent of stratification in Boston suburbs as early as the late 1800s.

7. Bogart (1993) points out that the Tiebout process is only one reason that suburbs will tend towards homogeneity, in particular that they will attempt to exclude lower income households. He identifies four reasons for exclusion: fiscal zoning (exclude households that pay less in taxes than they consume in public services), public goods (exclude households that increase the cost of producing public services), consumption (exclude households that generate negative externalities, especially in housing) and political economic (exclude households that are likely to have systematically different preferences for public services than the politically dominant residents). He argues that it is impossible to distinguish among these reasons solely on the basis of the observation that certain types of households (low-income) are being excluded.

8. Hamilton (1989) observes that this empirical relation undermines the logic of the monocentric city model, in which households are assumed to trade off commuting time for land prices. If all parts of the metropolitan area are equally accessible for commuters, then commuting is not a sufficient explanation for intrametropolitan variation in land prices.

9. Public services are referred to as 'nontraded' because they are only available to the residents of the community. For example, only residents are allowed to send their children to the local public schools, and there are often restrictions on the use of public recreational facilities as well. On the other hand, 'traded' goods and services are available to anyone within the metropolitan area. For example, a shopping mall provides retail services to households throughout the region, not just people that live in the town where the mall is located.

10. See Giuliano and Small (1991) for an analysis of Los Angeles, and McMillen and McDonald (1998) for an analysis of Chicago.

11. At the individual level, I export economics lectures and import plumbing services. I also produce some goods and services for my own consumption, for example when I cook dinner for myself. Hanson (1998) empirically tests modern imperfect competition trade theories using data from counties in the USA. He finds that the economic spillovers resulting from a change in activity in one county are concentrated in nearby counties, which accords with the approach taken in this chapter of considering a metropolitan area in isolation.

12. Although Anderson (1999) only calculates commuting patterns, the travel data include other types of trips. It is possible to use the data to estimate trade in other services, such as retail, in addition to trade in factor services.

13. A book that explores in detail the link between local land use patterns and transportation patterns is Boarnet and Crane (2000). Most intrametropolitan trade is facilitated by car use, whether it is trade in labor services (that is, commuting) or trade in other goods and services.

14. A thoughtful paper on zoning by Levinson (1997), for example, suffers from the flaw that it treats the community's decision in isolation from the remainder of the metropolitan area.

15. Other models of interaction among communities include Brueckner (1998) and Helsley and Strange (1995). These models tend to focus on residential growth controls, while I want to think more broadly about the interaction of residential preferences and firm location.

16. This is intuitively clear, because the constraint binds only if the developer wishes to use the land more intensively. Algebraically, it follows from the assumption that the first term in equation (5.4) is invariant with respect to h while the second term is increasing with respect to h.

17. This is not only true in practice, but also true in theory, as Bradford (1978) and Courant and Rubinfeld (1978) demonstrate.

18. The result that the disposition of taxes and other payments can affect efficiency is well

19. known in the tax competition literature. For example, see Richter and Wellisch (1996). Any empirical implementation of this model would need to account for the use of the tax revenues. One way to interpret λ is as the *net* negative impact after accounting for the additional revenue from the new development.

19. The derivative of $\lambda(h)/h$ is positive as long as $h\lambda'(h) > \lambda(h)$, which will be true if $\lambda''(h) > 0$.

20. This is the typical setup for analysis of the impact of environmental regulation (see Glazer, 1999, for example). If we allowed the land area to vary, land use regulations would not bind as much. The extent to which land area can vary freely has been a subject of debate in the literature. See Henderson (1985) and Epple and Romer (1989) for two opposing views.

21. If town 2 is a central city, does it make sense that its unconstrained optimal density is less than that of town 1? Probably not, but it is not a key feature of Figure 5.2 that town 1's unconstrained density is higher than town 2's. The key is that the density in town 2 depends on the constraint in town 1.

22. How do we know that the property tax is distortionary? Recall that the optimum density in equation (5.4) is affected when the tax rate on structures equals the tax rate on land; in other words, when there is a standard property tax.

23. See Bogart (1998) for an exposition of trade theory analysis of metropolitan economic structure, including some preliminary discussion of the role of zoning in affecting intra-metropolitan trade. The Heckscher–Ohlin model is predicated on immobile factors of production. Land is clearly immobile, but capital is less obvious. Nechyba (2001) provides a succinct analysis of the relation between capital mobility and the incidence of the property tax, emphasizing that capital mobility is different in different sectors of production.

24. An interesting question, raised at the conference by Peter Colwell, is whether or not local governments impose nonbinding constraints. The answer to this question must be left hanging, but it clearly has implications for the extent to which the tax is distortionary.

REFERENCES

Anas, Alex, Richard Arnott and Kenneth Small, 1998, 'Urban Spatial Structure', *Journal of Economic Literature*, 36, 1426–64.

Anderson, Nathan, 1999, '"Trading Places": Measuring Trade in Labor Services Among Suburbs in Greater Cleveland', senior honors thesis, Department of Economics, Case Western Reserve University.

Anderson, Nathan and William T. Bogart, 2001, 'The Structure of Sprawl: Identifying and Characterizing Employment Centers in Polycentric Metropolitan Areas', *American Journal of Economics and Sociology*, 60, 669–91.

Baldassare, Mark and Georjeanna Wilson, 1996, 'Changing Sources of Suburban Support for Local Growth Controls', *Urban Studies*, 33, 459–71.

Blinder, Alan and Harvey Rosen, 1985, 'Notches', *American Economic Review*, 75, 736–47.

Boarnet, Marlon and Randall Crane, 2000, *Travel by Design: Urban Design and the New Transportation Planning*, New York: Oxford University Press.

Bogart, William T., 1993, '"What Big Teeth You Have!" Identifying the Motivations for Exclusionary Zoning', *Urban Studies*, 30, 1669–81.

Bogart, William T., 1998, *The Economics of Cities and Suburbs*, Upper Saddle River, NJ: Prentice-Hall.

Bradford, David F., 1978, 'Factor Prices May be Constant but Factor Returns are Not', *Economics Letters*, 1, 199–203.

Brueckner, Jan, 1998, 'Testing for Strategic Interaction Among Local Governments: The Case of Growth Controls', *Journal of Urban Economics*, 44, 438–67.

Copeland, Brian and Scott Taylor, 2001, 'International Trade and the Environment: A Framework for Analysis', working paper # 8540. National Bureau of Economic Research, Cambridge, MA.

Courant, Paul and Daniel Rubinfeld, 1978, 'On the Measurement of Benefits in an Urban Context: Some General Equilibrium Issues', *Journal of Urban Economics*, 34, 299–317.

Downs, Anthony, 1994, *New Visions for Metropolitan America*, Washington, DC and Cambridge, MA: Brookings Institution and Lincoln Institute for Land Policy.

Epple, Dennis and Thomas Romer, 1989, 'On the Flexibility of Municipal Boundaries', *Journal of Urban Economics*, 26, 307–19.

Fischel, William, 1985, *The Economics of Zoning Laws: A Property-Rights Approach to American Land Use Controls*, Baltimore: Johns Hopkins University Press.

Fischel, William, 1992, 'Property Taxation and the Tiebout Model: Evidence for the Benefit View from Zoning and Voting', *Journal of Economic Literature*, 30, 163–9.

Fischel, William, 1994, 'Zoning, Nonconvexities, and T. Jack Foster's City', *Journal of Urban Economics*, 35, 175–81.

Fischel, William, 2001, *The Homevoter Hypothesis: How Home Values Influence Local Government Taxation, School Finance, and Land-Use Policies*, Cambridge, MA: Harvard University Press.

Fu, Yuming and C. Tsuriel Somerville, 2001, 'Site Density Restrictions: Measurement and Empirical Analysis', *Journal of Urban Economics*, 49. 404–23.

Gatzlaff, Dean and Marc Smith, 1993, 'Uncertainty, Growth Controls, and the Efficiency of Development Patterns', *Journal of Real Estate Finance and Economics*, 6, 147–55.

Giuliano, Genevieve and Kenneth Small, 1991, 'Subcenters in the Los Angeles Region', *Regional Science and Urban Economics*, 21, 163–82.

Glaeser, Edward and Andrei Shleifer, 2001, 'A Reason for Quantity Regulation', *American Economic Review Papers and Proceedings*, 91, 431–5.

Glazer, Amihai, 1999, 'Local Regulation May Be Excessively Stringent', *Regional Science and Urban Economics*, 29, 553–8.

Hamilton, Bruce, 1975, 'Zoning and Property Taxation in a System of Local Governments', *Urban Studies*, 12, 205–11.

Hamilton, Bruce, 1976, 'Capitalization of Intrajurisdictional Differences in Local Tax Prices', *American Economic Review*, 66, 743–53.

Hamilton, Bruce, 1989, 'Wasteful Commuting Again', *Journal of Political Economy*, 97, 1497–504.

Hanson, Gordon, 1998, 'Market Potential, Increasing Returns, and Geographic Concentration', working paper # 6429. National Bureau of Economic Research, Cambridge, MA.

Helsley, Robert and William Strange, 1995, 'Strategic Growth Controls', *Regional Science and Urban Economics*, 25, 435–60.

Henderson, J. Vernon, 1985, 'The Tiebout Model: Bring Back the Entrepreneurs', *Journal of Political Economy*, 93, 248–64.

Levinson, Arik, 1997, 'Why Oppose TDRs? Transferable Development Rights Can Increase Overall Development', *Regional Science and Urban Economics*, 27, 283–96.

McDonald, John, 1978, 'The Estimation of the Impact of Residential Zoning on Land Values', *Economics Letters*, 1, 183–5.

McDonald, John and Daniel McMillen, 1998, 'Land Values, Land Use, and the First Chicago Zoning Ordinance', *Journal of Real Estate Finance and Economics*, 16, 135–50.

McMillen, Daniel and John McDonald, 1998, 'Suburban Subcenters and Employment Density in Metropolitan Chicago', *Journal of Urban Economics*, 43, 157–80.

Mieszkowski, Peter and George Zodrow, 1989, 'Taxation and the Tiebout Model: The Differential Effects of Head Taxes, Taxes on Land Rents, and Property Taxes', *Journal of Economic Literature*, 27, 1098–146.

Moses, Leon and Harold F. Williamson, Jr., 1967, 'The Location of Economic Activity in Cities', *American Economic Review (Papers and Proceedings)*, 57, 211–22.

Nechyba, Thomas, 2001, 'The Benefit View and the New View: Where Do We Stand, Twenty-Five Years into the Debate?', in Wallace Oates (ed.), *Property Taxation and Local Government Finance: Essays in Honor of C. Lowell Harriss*, Cambridge, MA: Lincoln Institute of Land Policy. pp.113–21.

Oates, Wallace and Robert Schwab, 1997, 'The Impact of Urban Land Taxation: The Pittsburgh Experience', *National Tax Journal*, 50, 1–21.

Peiser, Richard, 1989, 'Density and Urban Sprawl', *Land Economics*, 65, 193–204.

Richter, Wolfram and Dietmar Wellisch, 1996, 'The Provision of Local Public Goods in the Presence of Firm and Household Mobility', *Journal of Public Economics*, 60, 73–93.

Sivitanidou, Rena and William Wheaton, 1992, 'Wage and Rent Capitalization in the Commercial Real Estate Market', *Journal of Urban Economics*, 31, 206–29.

Sonstelie, Jon and Paul Portney, 1980, 'Take the Money and Run: A Theory of Voting in Local Referenda', *Journal of Urban Economics*, 8, 187–95.

Tiebout, Charles, 1956, 'A Pure Theory of Local Expenditures', *Journal of Political Economy*, 64, 416–24.

Warner, Sam Bass, Jr., 1962, *Streetcar Suburbs: The Process of Growth in Boston 1870–1900*, Cambridge, MA: Harvard University Press/MIT Press.

Weitzman, Martin, 1974, 'Prices *vs.* Quantities', *Review of Economic Studies*, 41, 477–91.

Wilson, John D., 1987, 'Trade in a Tiebout Economy', *American Economic Review*, 77, 431–41.

Wilson, John D., 1999, 'Theories of Tax Competition', *National Tax Journal*, 52, 269–304.

6. Taxes versus regulation: the welfare impacts of policies for containing urban sprawl

Paul Cheshire and Stephen Sheppard

1 INTRODUCTION[1]

One of the paradoxes of urban economic development is that resident households desire the personal consumption of space in all of its pleasant varieties, and strive to limit the indulgence of this desire exhibited by their fellow citizens. Each household seeks to consume private space as a location and surrounding garden for a residence, and can generally be expected to devote a considerable portion of income towards its acquisition. When others do this, however, the process is sometimes strenuously opposed and decried as 'sprawl'. The tension is made more severe in times of rising incomes and/or falling transport costs because these tend to encourage an increase in private consumption of land.

Part of the rationale for this tension is that private consumption of space is not the only way that space can generate utility for the household. Open space is an alternative use that is valued by nearby households. It may be available both in the form of a public good that is accessible to local households and in the form of private use (by other consumers or producers) that provides external benefits in the form of visual amenity or spatial separation from noxious uses. The public good nature of open space suggests that, without policy intervention, it will be underprovided.

Our central concern in this chapter is to examine some alternative policies for implementing development controls. We undertake a microsimulation to provide a comparison between land use planning policies that enforce an urban growth boundary and policies that limit development at the periphery using taxes. We parameterize our microsimulation using the structure of demand and policy implemented in a rapidly growing city in the south of England.

One (optimistic) way to understand the tension over urban development is to regard zoning and concerns over sprawl as part of the community struggle to ensure an optimal provision of the public benefits of open space. Of course, policies that limit urban development can also increase the wealth of the owners of residential property within the constrained communities, so that it is also possible that development controls are simply rent-seeking activities. The efficiency of the actual level of development control chosen is not addressed here but is taken as datum. It is the focus of the analysis reported in Cheshire and Sheppard (2002).

That households value both private land consumption and the different varieties of open space seems clear. Among others, Cheshire and Sheppard (1995) and (1998) have quantified the impact on land values and the structure of demand for accessible open space, inaccessible open space and private land consumption. Naturally, the fact that open space is valuable does not demonstrate that it is underprovided (or overprovided).

The *efficiency* of urban development is central to the concept of 'sprawl'. Brueckner (2001) and Brueckner and Kim (2000) take this as a starting point and provide a useful economic evaluation of the various reasons for public concern over 'sprawl'. It is worth noting the concerns they identify as the sources of the inefficiency associated with sprawl, because these indicate the relevant potential policy responses. The primary sources of economic inefficiency associated with sprawl are the loss of public good amenities arising from the development of open space at the periphery, and the increase in commuting (and associated pollution and congestion) that comes with low-density development.

A standard economic response would be to design policies that rely on taxation of any inefficient activities (whether commuting or development of peripheral land) in order to internalize the external costs. In Britain, and increasingly in the USA, land use policies have generally not relied on taxation. Instead direct regulation of land development has been employed. In the British context, this comes via the Town and Country Planning System that provides a national framework for local and regional regulation of land use and urban development. In the USA the call for 'smart growth' policies such as urban growth boundaries (UGBs) has become more pronounced, and such boundaries have been extensively applied in some areas. A useful taxonomy and discussion of these policies in the USA is presented in Downs (2001). In Britain, many of these policies have been employed for decades. We suggest that a closer examination of the UK context can contribute to our understanding of how such policies might work, and what alternatives are available.

There have been numerous proponents of the use of tax incentive policies for containing urban development. For example, American Farmland Trust (1997) advocates 'differential assessment' as a means of preserving land in agricultural use at the urban periphery. Essentially, this means application of lower property tax rates to land in agricultural use, and raising the rate if the land is converted to urban use. The difference between the agricultural and residential rate provides a direct tax on the process of urban land conversion at the periphery.

This sort of differential assessment is to some extent used in the UK, although the land use consequences are minimal because the levels of property taxation ('Council tax') are low even for land in urban use and are not directly related to the area of land used for residential purposes. Land in purely agricultural use (such as cropland) is not subject to rates, although 'non-agricultural' activities on farms are subject to business rates. Proposals have been put forward by the Department of Environment, Transport and Regions (2000) to provide reduced or eliminated taxation for these non-agricultural activities on small farms. Land in urban use (such as for residential purposes) is subject to a tax that varies with the value of the property (including structure) and across local authorities. The average annual tax over all authorities and types of residential properties is on the order of £650 (about $1000) per annum.

Commuting is also taxed (both in the UK and the USA) in the form of taxes on fuel and vehicles, and such increases in the operating cost per mile increase the incentives to live near the urban center (or at least near employment centers). Whether these taxes have a measurable impact on actual land use patterns is less obvious, but proponents of higher fuel taxation often cite the reduction in commuting and the more compact urban form such taxes would be expected to generate.

Both differential rates of land taxation and taxation on commuting seem to offer alternatives to the regulatory maintenance of an urban growth boundary. If we are to contemplate the policy alternative of using land taxation or taxation of commuting as an alternative mechanism for limiting urban sprawl, we must answer several questions:

- Is it possible? That is, can we find levels of taxation that, when applied in an urban context, produce an equilibrium that uses the same amount of land as is produced by the regulatory approach of the UGB?
- What levels of taxation are required (and, implicitly, would they be politically feasible)?
- Would these alternative policies increase or reduce the average welfare level compared to imposing a UGB?
- What are the potential distributional consequences of alternative policies?
- What impact might such taxes have on densities and the physical form of cities?

Our analysis below addresses these questions regarding the alternative policies of using differential land taxation and using ad valorem taxation on the 'operating costs' of transport as mechanisms to restrict the urban area to one that uses the same amount of land as is used in the status quo. One aspect of using taxation for such policies is the revenue raised. We assume that the revenues are spent locally with efficiency and equality (so that they are equivalent to an equal income transfer to each household that exhausts the total revenue raised). Other assumptions are clearly possible, including the polar extreme in which none of the tax revenues are returned to the community. Although they are not presented below, we have examined this polar extreme case and, while it is certainly less attractive from a welfare perspective, the basic quality of the results is not greatly affected.

Before proceeding to our analysis, we pause to inquire whether the welfare impacts or relative merits of alternative policies are either obvious or implied by theoretical considerations. An initial reaction might follow one of two opposing arguments. On the one hand, there is a relatively standard price theory argument indicating that imposing a tax on a commodity and then rebating the amount of the tax collected back to the consumer (equivalent to maximal efficiency in public expenditure) will never make the consumer better off. An alternative argument is derived from a focus on revenue raised from the tax and a comparison with the existing system. With a UGB or other planning constraint, the 'tax' imposed on urban residents is implicit. These come in the form either of more expensive land (and hence housing) resulting from the reduced supply of land for private residential consumption within the urban area, or of increased commuting costs resulting from choice of location outside the constrained area and commuting 'across the greenbelt' or from neighboring jurisdictions. The tax 'revenues' in this case are not used to provide local public goods, or rebated to all households within the urban area, but rather accrue as capital gains to owners of land with planning permission (many of whom may reside outside the urban area), as incomes for lawyers who specialize in planning appeals or as incomes to those who provide transport services. This argument suggests that, since the anti-sprawl tax policies we consider below incorporate local expenditure of tax revenues in the form of rebates, they must of necessity generate higher welfare for urban residents.

There are some difficulties with both of these arguments. The first argument compares the situation with constrained land use to a situation with unconstrained land consumption, and fails to consider the public good value of a reduction in urban sprawl. It also neglects redistributive impacts of tax policies. A tax on land in urban use, for example, may generate disproportionate revenue from more affluent consumers of housing with large lots. Equal rebates to each household (or public expenditures available to all residents equally) could provide a net transfer to lower income residents that results in an increase in average welfare levels.

The second argument may be excessively optimistic in expecting an inevitable increase in welfare. When choosing between anti-sprawl policies it might be helpful to ask which is likely to be associated with the least 'deadweight loss'. The relative elasticity of demand of the aspect of consumption that is taxed (whether explicitly or implicitly) will determine the cost of achieving any anti-sprawl benefits. In this situation it is possible that a policy regime may make inefficient use of 'revenues' but be preferable to an alternative that spends revenues more efficiently but generates them from a less efficient tax.

These observations suggest the appropriateness of using a microsimulation exercise as the basis of our analysis. The desirability of alternative policies will depend on the structure of demand and the distribution of income. These factors can be accounted for within the simulation, and the relative merits of alternative policies evaluated.

Our microsimulation utilizes a modified 'monocentric' model comprising individuals whose demand is based on the demand system whose estimates are presented below. While the model is similar to models familiar from the urban economics literature, it incorporates a variety of features that permit representation of some of the complexities of the actual urban area whose housing market and setting are used to estimate the structure of demand and parameterize the model. In the next section we describe these data, and in the third section we present our analysis of the structure of demand for house characteristics and neighborhood amenities. Making central use of the demand for private residential land, this structure is then used in sections 4, 5 and 6 to present estimates of the baseline level of land use regulation and to examine two fiscal alternatives to this regulation. Section 7 provides a summary of our results and some concluding remarks on the viability and desirability of these policy options.

2   DATA AND SETTING

Our data are drawn from the urban area of Reading, England. The city is located on the Thames about 35 miles west of central London. Reading is subject to considerable pressure for growth and residential development, and in response has adopted some of the most restrictive planning policies in the UK. With frequent high-speed rail links to London, proximity to Heathrow airport and other location advantages, the area has attracted a number of technology firms[2] and more generally follows the development patterns typical of prosperous, middle-size cities of the southeast of

England. Despite its proximity to London, Reading is a major employment center with more than 85 per cent of its employed residents working locally and a strong central business district employment concentration.

The city had in 1991 a metro area population of approximately 337000, comprising 129000 households. At the time of the 1993 survey, we estimate that there were 131370 households. Our initial sample of properties comprised over 870 separate structures. This provided a sample of approximately 20 per cent of the residential properties offered for sale by major estate agents in the autumn of 1993. Postal surveys with follow up were directed to each address in the sample to collect information on the actual sales price of the structure, and the income and demographic composition of the household. Responses from approximately 461 households were ultimately obtained, with complete response (including income and family structure) from 310 households.

Supplemental information on land use was assembled from Ordnance Survey resources and aerial photographs. Data on secondary school catchment areas and school quality were obtained from the local education authorities. Census data from 1991 were used for the ethnic and socioeconomic characteristics of local neighborhoods.

3   HEDONIC ANALYSIS OF DEMAND

In order to estimate the structure of demand for land and open space, we must first obtain estimates of the implicit prices of land and other structure and neighborhood attributes. We do this by estimating the modified linear Box–Cox hedonic price function given in equation (6.1). Note that the value function for urban residential land, specified in equation (6.2), is estimated directly as part of the hedonic price function. The land rent is 'monotonic' only in the sense that it is radially symmetric: land value must increase or decrease at the same rate in any given direction away from the urban center.

$$\frac{P^{\psi}-1}{\psi}=K+\sum_{i\in D}\beta_i\cdot q_i+\sum_{j\in C}\beta_i\cdot\left(\frac{q_j^{\lambda}-1}{\lambda}\right)+r(x,\theta)\frac{L^{\xi}-1}{\xi}, \qquad (6.1)$$

where

P	=	price of structure expressed as an annual cost,
q_i, q_j	=	structure or location-specific characteristics,
$K, \beta_i, \beta_j, \lambda, \psi, \xi$	=	parameters to be estimated,
L	=	quantity of land included with structure,
D	=	set of indices of characteristics which are dichotomous,

C   =   set of indices of characteristics which are continu-
                                ously variable,
$r(x,\theta)$ =   land rent function defined below,
λ, ψ, ξ =   the standard parameters of the Box–Cox functional
                                form.

$$r(x,\theta) = \beta_1 \cdot e^{x \cdot (\beta 2 + \beta 3 \cdot \sin(n \cdot \theta - \beta 4))},\qquad(6.2)$$

where
x =   distance from the city center,
θ =   angle of deflection from the city center,
n =   number of 'ridges' in land value, representing radial asymmetries,
β_i =   estimated parameters of land value function.

The estimated parameters for the hedonic price function are presented in Table 6A.1. Searching over a small grid (1–4) it was determined that a rent function with $n = 3$ ridges provided the best fit to the data. The estimated land value depends on the location and also the size of the lot and type of structure built upon it. For a structure matching the sample mean in all attributes (except location) the spatial structure of the land value function is illustrated in Figure 6.1. The surface is viewed from the southeast looking towards the northwest, and projected on the land value surface are the locations of sample observations and major transport routes. This measure of the value of land is essentially the price of 'land as pure space with accessibility'. Actual market prices of vacant land include the capitalized value of all the local amenities, neighborhood characteristics and local public goods to which occupation of the land gives access. As was shown in Cheshire and Sheppard (1998) these amenity values may exceed the value of land as pure space with accessibility.[3] The land tax analysed below is a tax on the value of 'land as pure space with accessibility' and so might most usefully be called a *pure land tax*.

Table 6A.2 provides some descriptive statistics for the sample and the estimated attribute prices and expenditure shares for structure and neighborhood attributes. These are used in estimating the demand system, which in turn is used as the basis of our microsimulation.

We begin with a basic Almost Ideal Demand System linearized in the fashion suggested by Deaton and Muellbauer (1980):

$$w_i = (\alpha_1 - \delta_i\alpha_0) + \sum_{j \in C}\gamma_{ij} \cdot \ln p_j + \sum_{k \in D}\gamma_{ik} \cdot \ln p_k + \delta_i \ln\left(\frac{M}{I^*}\right).\qquad(6.3)$$

We then adapt this to capture the effects of household demographic structure, and to take account of the fact that there is no in-sample variation in the

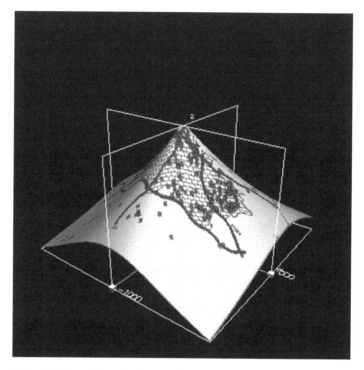

Figure 6.1   Estimated land value surface viewed from southeast

prices of those attributes that are measured in a dichotomous fashion. Some
further discussion is presented in Cheshire and Sheppard (1998) and (2002).
The final demand system to be estimated is presented in equation (6.4):

$$w_i = \overline{\alpha_i} + \overline{\gamma_i} \cdot \ln \hat{P}_j + v_{ai}A + v_{bi}\,B + \delta_i \cdot \ln\left(\frac{M}{I^*}\right) + \sum_{j \in C} \gamma_{ij} \cdot \ln p_j \qquad (6.4)$$

where

w_i	=	expenditure share on attribute i,
v_{ai}, v_{bi}, δ_i and γ_{ij}	=	demand system parameters to be estimated,
$\hat{P}$	=	structure value estimated using the hedonic price function,
$\overline{\alpha_i}$	=	$(\alpha_i - \delta_i\alpha_0) + \sum_{k \in D} \gamma_{ik} \cdot \ln p_k$ (demand parameters to be estimated),
$\overline{\gamma_i}$	=	$(1 - \hat{\psi}) \sum_{k \in D} \gamma_{ik}$ (demand parameters to be estimated),
A	=	number of adults present in the household,
B	=	number of children present in the household,

$\beta_k, \hat{\psi}$ = estimated parameters from the hedonic price function,

M = household income,

I^* = Stone's price index, $\ln I^* = \sum_i w_i \ln p_i$,

p_j = price of house attribute or local amenity estimated from the hedonic price function,

C = indices of attributes that are 'continuously' variable,

D = indices of dichotomous attributes.

In order to estimate this demand system using single-market data we construct instruments for attribute prices using the prices faced by the two nearest observations in the sample, plus the distance between the observation and these 'nearest neighbors'. The estimated demand system parameters are presented in Tables 6A.3 and 6A.4. Particularly for those variable attributes whose demand structure plays a central role in our analysis the models work well.

4   BASELINE LEVEL OF DEVELOPMENT CONTROL

Having estimated a demand system we have access to an indirect utility function and expenditure function based on the estimated parameters. We use this for analysis of policy alternatives, calculating new urban equilibria,[4] and evaluating the welfare consequences of these policies. The first step in our analysis is to establish the baseline utility and structure of development control. We do this by constructing a 'representative agent' urban economy in which all households in the urban area are of a single household type whose demographic structure and income is equal to the sample mean for these variables. Letting land be indexed as good 1, with its price represented as r, the expenditure function associated with the demand system implies that the common utility level achieved by all of these households is

$$u = \left(\frac{\ln(M - t(x,\theta)) - \ln(I^*) - A \cdot \sum_i v_{ai} \ln p_i - B \cdot \sum_i v_{bi} \ln p_i}{r^{\delta_1} \prod_{i \geq 2} p_i^{\delta_i}} \right). \quad (6.5)$$

All variables are as defined in equation (2.4), M is the (common) household income level, and the transport costs (with operating costs as estimated by the Automobile Association) are given by

$$t(x,\theta) = \left(\tau_1 + \frac{\tau_2}{\tau_3 + \tau_4 \cdot x} \right) \cdot (1 + \tau_5 \cdot \sin(3 \cdot \theta + \tau_6)) \cdot x, \quad (6.6)$$

with

τ_1 = 2.5, operating cost of £2.5 per 10 meters,

τ_2 = 7200, annual cost of a one-hour daily commute at mean income levels (pounds sterling),

τ_3 = 500, speed (tens of meters per hour) at edge of CBD,

τ_4 = 4, increase in travel speed as distance from CBD increases,

τ_5 = 0.0922 matches asymmetry in land rent function estimated from the hedonic price function,

τ_6 = 3.2674, based on estimated land rent function in the hedonic price function.

Using these transport cost parameters generates a land rent function derived from the expenditure function that matches the estimate obtained from the estimated hedonic price function. With these parameters we then obtain an estimated common utility level for the representative household in equilibrium. The expenditure function implies a land rent function for each utility level:

$$r(u,x,\theta,p,M) =$$

$$\left(\frac{\ln(M - t(x,\theta)) - \ln(I^*) - A \cdot \sum_i v_{ai} \ln p_i - B \cdot \sum_i v_{bi} \ln p_i}{u \cdot \prod_{i \geq 2} p_i^{\delta i}} \right)^{\frac{1}{\delta_1}}. \quad (6.7)$$

We solve for the utility level that generates a land rent function providing the best approximation to the observed pattern of land rents obtained in the sample. This provides an estimated status quo utility level of u = 15.0631.

We model development controls as consisting both of restrictions on the fraction of land within the urban area made available for development, denoted by ω, and of an urban growth boundary modeled as a maximum extent of allowed development. We capture the urban growth boundary by constructing a border at which residential land values fall to a particular level that would be set by the planning authority. Not only does this provide a representation of the status quo policy that closely matches the observed physical pattern of development, but it can also be justified by noting that defense of the urban growth boundary is itself a costly process. Allocation of resources within the Town and Country Planning system will then be focused on those parts of the periphery under the most pressure for development. The result tends to produce a uniform value of residential land along the effective urban growth boundary, which itself then exhibits the same asymmetries as exist in the land value function.

The observations that are furthest from the CBD in our sample have estimated land rents that translate to a purchase price for land as pure space of approximately £88 600 per acre (note this compares to a value of vacant agricultural land at the time of approximately £2000 per acre). We use this value to define the urban growth boundary for our simulation.

The final status quo planning parameter we require is an estimate of the share of land available within the built-up area for private residential consumption, ω. We can solve for this from the standard equilibrium condition for an urban land market. Let N be the number of households; r is the rent function defined in equation (6.7), h represents the compensated demand for land, χ_1 is the radius of the CBD and $\chi(\theta)$ represents the distance (in each direction θ) from the CBD at which land value falls to the value that defines the urban growth boundary. Then we have

$$\omega = \frac{N}{\int_0^{2\pi\chi(\theta)} \int_{\chi_1} \frac{x}{h(u,r(u,x,\theta,p,M),p)} dx \, d\theta} \tag{6.8}$$

Using the status quo utility level and taking sample mean prices for other attributes, we obtain an estimated internal space availability of $\omega = 0.2568$.[5] This implies that just over a quarter of land within the urban growth boundary is actually made available for private residential consumption. In our analysis below, we assume that the parameter ω remains unchanged. The urban growth boundary represented by $\chi(\theta)$ implies that the total area within the urban growth boundary is about 52 553 acres. In solving for equilibria under alternative policies we impose the constraint that the total area of land devoted to urban uses remains unchanged.

5 POLICY ALTERNATIVE: TRANSPORT TAXATION

The first alternative policy we consider is an ad valorem tax on the operating cost of transport. We model this by changing the transport cost function to

$$t(x,\theta) = \left(\tau_1 \cdot (1 + tax) + \frac{\tau_2}{\tau_3 + \tau_4 \cdot x} \right) \cdot (1 + \tau_5 \cdot \sin(3 \cdot \theta + \tau_6)) \cdot x. \tag{6.9}$$

and then letting the boundary of the built-up area be defined by the point at which land value falls to the price of agricultural land, taken to be £2000 per acre. Land consumption and land rents are those that would characterize our representative agent approximation of the Reading urban area using the demand system estimated from the sample collected from that area.

After allowing for changes in the spatial distribution of population, we calculate the total revenue generated from the tax and distribute this to households as an income transfer so that M becomes $M + \dfrac{\text{total revenues}}{N}$ This income transfer increases the demand for land (and other house attributes in our demand system) and requires a further adjustment in the tax and utility level to accommodate all households. What we seek is an equilibrium in which the total tax revenue is distributed back to households, urban equilibrium is achieved and the total land used in the urban area is equal to the land area devoted to urban uses in the status quo. Such an equilibrium will be characterized by a tax rate and an equilibrium utility level. The spatial density of households and land value function will in turn follow from these.

Such an equilibrium does exist and is described by utility = 14.6179, tax = 6.21884. That is, to achieve the same level of urban land use using only a tax on the 'operating cost' portion of transport would require a 622 per cent tax on such costs. As a result of this, the utility level of the representative agent would fall from 15.0631 to 14.6179. We stress that this is not because the tax revenues are spent within the urban area itself. Indeed, discarding the revenues altogether would achieve the same sized total urban area with a lower tax rate but actually result in an even lower utility level.

The spatial structure of the equilibrium is illustrated in Figure 6.2 below. The bold line indicates the maximum extent of urban land use under a

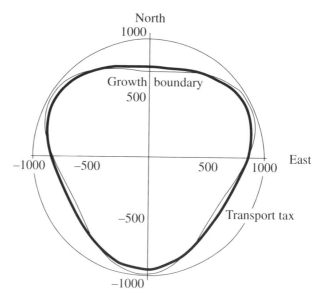

Figure 6.2   Urban development with a transport tax

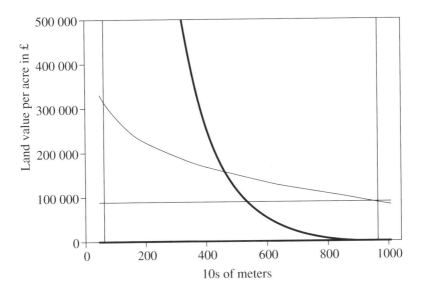

Figure 6.3   Land values with a transport tax

policy of transport taxation, allowing the boundary to be set by the true agricultural land value. The thin line indicates the maximum extent in the status quo policy of an urban growth boundary. The circular line is for reference set at the distance of the furthest observation in our sample.

Imposing a tax on operating costs alone results in a somewhat more 'circular' pattern of land use because it increases the relative importance of part of transport costs that are less sensitive to travel speed. This was chosen for the simulation because it provides a better approximation to the type of fuel taxes or road user charges that have been proposed.

The pattern of land values produced in this equilibrium is illustrated in Figure 6.3. Again the thin line represents the equilibrium pattern of land values in the status quo, while the bold line represents the land value in equilibrium with a transport tax. Note that the vertical scale is truncated. Under the transport tax the land value at the edge of the CBD rises to approximately £3 million (about a tenfold increase relative to that observed under the urban growth boundary).

Finally, Figure 6.4 presents the changes that would occur in the density of land use. As expected from such a severe change in land values, the change in equilibrium densities is substantial. The number of households per acre at the edge of the CBD would rise from the current value of just over 20 to more than 100. The revenues raised from this tax would be considerable. In equilibrium the tax would raise over £558 million. All of these

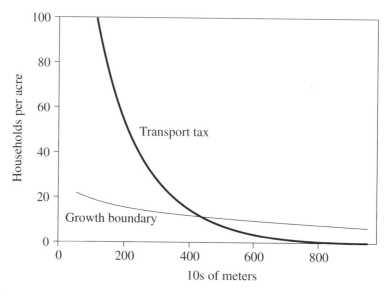

Figure 6.4   Residential density with a transport tax

calculations are based on the final equilibrium. Obviously, transformation of land use of this order of magnitude would take many years to achieve, and its political acceptability is problematic.

6   POLICY ALTERNATIVE: LAND TAXATION

We next turn attention to a policy alternative based on differential taxation of land that assigns a per acre tax (in addition to the current rates) on all land in urban residential use. This tax can be avoided entirely by keeping the land in agricultural use and would serve to increase the opportunity cost of urban residential land.

Our microsimulation[6] is again based on a representative household model of the Reading urban area, and we further assume that the incidence of the property tax is fully borne by the residents. As before, we assume that all tax revenues are spent within the community and model this by rebating to each household an equal share of the total revenues collected by the pure land tax on residential land.

Equilibrium will be a standard urban equilibrium in which households must pay the value of land plus the tax, and the distance at which land value falls to the value of agricultural land plus the present value of the tax burden determines the boundary of development. Such an equilibrium

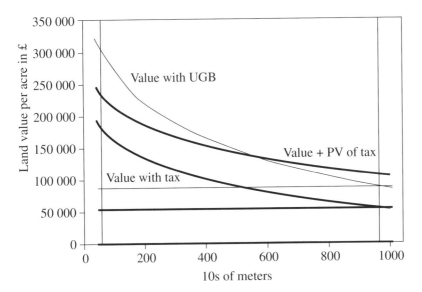

Figure 6.5 Land value and cost with a land tax

does exist and is described by:

$$\text{utility} = 15.3515, \text{tax} = £3624.15 \text{ per acre.}$$

Thus the land taxation equilibrium that achieves the same level of urban land use as the status quo would actually increase household welfare levels. The tax that would achieve this represents a significant increase over existing rates, but could be argued to be manageable. At typical residential densities of 10–12 households per acre, the tax on residential land would represent an increase of approximately 50 per cent in current council tax levels. The associated increase in local expenditures could, at least, result in an increase in overall levels of welfare.

   The pattern of equilibrium land values (and effective cost of land including the present value of the tax) is illustrated in Figure 6.5. The thin line indicates the pattern of land values that prevails under the existing urban growth boundary policy. The lower bold line indicates the equilibrium pattern of land values, and the upper bold line indicates the equilibrium land cost to households (land value plus the present value of the stream of required tax payments).

   Figure 6.6 shows the equilibrium pattern of residential densities that emerge in equilibrium with a tax on land. While all policies achieve the same total amount of land in urban uses, the land tax produces a flatter

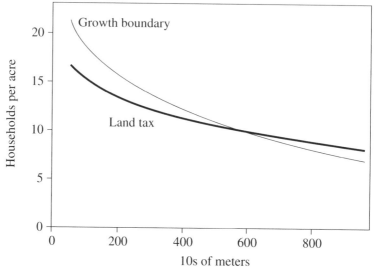

Figure 6.6   Residential density with a land tax

density gradient than the urban growth boundary and one much flatter than the transport tax. The tax on residential land would produce less revenue than the transport tax – in equilibrium, approximately £190.5 million per annum. Since the land tax increases the welfare level of the average household it seems reasonable to argue that it provides a more feasible policy alternative and dominates the existing policy based on urban growth boundaries.

We next provide some evaluation of the distributional effects of a land tax compared with maintaining the urban growth boundary. For this we must move away from our representative household model so that we can take account of the differences in income levels among households.

Using equation (6.5) above we obtain an estimate of the utility each household achieves in the status quo. From our calculations using the representative household model we have an estimate of the average change in utility level and the tax rebate received by each household. We assume that each household achieves the same proportionate increase in welfare level and the same income rebate. This allows us to calculate, using equation (6.7) the bid rent that could be expected of each household in an equilibrium with the land tax.

We then calculate, for each household, the amount of extra income that would be sufficient to generate the same utility level as they would, under these assumptions, achieve in an equilibrium where they faced the higher effective cost of land (land value plus tax) but received the benefit of the

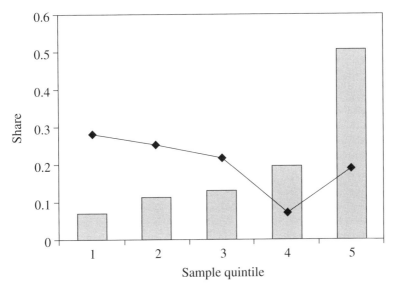

Figure 6.7   Distributional impacts of land tax

local tax expenditure. This equivalent variation in income will be positive on average, but not necessarily positive for each household. If a household's demographic structure, for example, leads it to demand large amounts of land then the local tax expenditure may be insufficient to compensate for the more costly land.

We calculate the average equivalent variation in income to be approximately £422 per annum. This ranges from a high of a gain of £11 525 to a low of a loss of £10 400. These are not small quantities, given that the sample mean income after taxes is £29 560. Figure 6.7 presents a summary of the distributional impacts of the land tax. The sample households are divided into income quintiles, and the vertical bars show the share of total sample income accruing to each share. The line indicates the share of total equivalent variation in income accruing to each quintile. Each quintile receives a positive net benefit (relative to the urban growth boundary) from the land tax policy. Furthermore, the poorest quintile receives the largest share, so that the policy change is significantly progressive.

It should be stressed that the income quintiles represented here are for our sample, which is already restricted to owner-occupiers and hence drawn disproportionately from the most affluent two-thirds of the population. Nevertheless, it appears that switching from a land use policy based on an urban growth boundary to one based on land taxation could also contribute to a goal of reducing inequality.

7 CONCLUSIONS

There are a variety of policies that societies might consider to limit the extent of urban development. Much recent interest has been devoted to urban growth boundaries and other 'smart growth' policies. Many British urban areas have been subject to such policies for long periods of time. We have collected data from one such area, estimated the structure of demand for land and other house and neighborhood attributes, and used this estimated structure as the basis for a microsimulation of alternative land use policies to achieve the same total area of urban land.

We have considered two alternative policies: taxation of transport and taxation of land. We found that both policy alternatives were capable of achieving the same level of urban land use as the status quo policy based on an urban growth boundary. While both policies could be used, there are very striking differences between them. A policy of transport taxation would require very high levels of taxation to achieve the land use goals achieved by the urban growth boundary. Furthermore, it would actually reduce welfare levels relative to the status quo. It would modify the built form of the urban area to generate very much higher densities closer to the fringe of the CBD. A policy of land taxation, on the other hand, could improve welfare levels and achieve the same levels of urban land use. While this would require significant increases in local property taxes, the levels required remain modest by the standards of many communities in North America. We also find that the land taxation policy would be strongly progressive relative to the urban growth boundary.

Our analysis suggests that communities in the UK and those in the USA considering urban growth boundaries may well benefit from giving serious consideration to the use of land taxation as an alternative. This should not necessarily be taken as a positive recommendation for introducing such taxes, however. The analysis presented here takes as its 'datum' the status quo of very tight development constraint. As is shown in Cheshire and Sheppard (2002) this appears to represent a substantial net welfare cost relative to a more relaxed regulatory constraint on urban land supply – even allowing for the loss of open space amenities that would result. Nevertheless, the results in the present chapter do strongly suggest that attacking the perceived problem directly with a pure land tax would achieve a given growth constraint at lower welfare costs compared either to the present regulatory system or to a tax on the operating costs of vehicles. Since this latter tax might possibly generate additional social benefits over and above those of increasing the supply of unbuilt open space (such as a quasi-tax on congestion and atmospheric pollution) it cannot be dismissed as strictly less efficient. The size of the tax necessary and the loss of welfare entailed are nevertheless suggestive.

APPENDIX

Table 6A.1 Estimated hedonic price function

Continuous attributes		Dichotomous attributes		Continuous attributes		Dichotomous attributes	
Variable	Estimate	Variable	Estimate	Variable	Estimate	Variable	Estimate
Constant	0.430174	$\beta_{CentralHeat}$	0.053347	$\beta_{InaccessOpenSpace}$	0.000843	$\beta_{DoubleGarage}$	0.081925
t	3.897	t	2.891	t	1.049	t	2.334
$\beta_{Bedrooms}$	0.029933	$\beta_{Detached}$	0.221032	$\beta_{Elevation}$	0.000464	$\beta_{ThamesFrontage}$	0.339446
t	1.884	t	4.614	t	0.496	t	4.618
β_{WC}	0.061056	$\beta_{Semi\text{-}detached}$	0.118829	*Land value function*		$\beta_{LocalConstruction}$	0.007666
t	4.115	t	3.436	β_1	0.064091	t	0.416
β_{SqFt}	0.007858	$\beta_{Terrace}$	0.02785	t	3.210	$\beta_{Year\,2}$	0.027767
t	4.184	t	1.102	β_2	−0.00083	t	1.338
$\beta_{SchoolGCSE}$	0.003901	$\beta_{Wide\,through\,street}$	0.023627	t	−2.304	$\beta_{Year\,5}$	0.047747
t	3.051	t	1.206	β_3	−0.00014	t	2.711
$\beta_{BlueCollar}$	0.02778	$\beta_{B\text{-}Class\,road}$	0.016329	t	−1.113	$\beta_{Year\,6}$	0.110903
t	2.350	t	0.153	β_4	−3.26736	t	3.096
β_{Ethnic}	0.010976	$\beta_{A\text{-}class\,road}$	0.035196	t	−4.623		
t	2.163	t	0.679	*Box–Cox parameters*			
$\beta_{Industrial\,Land}$	0.004154	$\beta_{Parking}$	0.033803	γ	−0.06941		
t	2.686	t	1.498	t	−0.893		
$\beta_{AccessOpenSpace}$	0.003223	$\beta_{SingleGarage}$	0.043101	λ_1	0.840378		
t	1.338	t	1.863	t	12.919		
				λ_3	0.208264		
				t	1.766		
				α	0.119181	Log likelihood	−712.489
				t	5.774	Observations	461

Table 6.4.2   Descriptive statistics, prices and expenditure shares for sample

Variable	Mean	Std. dev.	Min	Max	Description
ADULTS	1.897106	0.618811	1	4	Number of adults
CHILDREN	0.858521	1.080285	0	4	Number of children
MHAT	3.478157	2.757165	0.481737	13.70793	Income adjusted for hedonic
ESTPRICE	9.309626	5.241151	3.5389	45.36409	Structure price estimated from hedonic
SLAND	2.553258	1.332589	0.347236	7.96668	Expenditure share on land
SBEDS	2.203248	1.225636	0.164506	5.710995	Expenditure share on bedrooms
SWC	2.629387	1.744641	0.268627	8.951286	Expenditure share on WCs
SSQFT	9.142989	5.501154	0.735887	28.10168	Expenditure share on sq. ft. interior space
SBCOL	4.020366	2.107541	0.573379	12.98416	Expenditure share on avoid blue collar neighborhood
SAFIN	2.49594	1.446089	0.177507	7.706844	Expenditure share on avoid ethnic neighborhood
SINDU	5.416209	2.783108	0.741677	15.00779	Expenditure share on avoid local industrial land use
SAMEN1	1.144407	0.638904	0.10858	3.811946	Expenditure share on accessible open space
SAMEN2	0.327002	0.296338	0.009194	1.868709	Expenditure share on inaccessible open space
SALT	0.162774	0.128151	0.00366	0.760515	Expenditure share on local elevation
SGCSE	2.450426	1.51033	0.14816	9.290032	Expenditure share on school quality
SST2	0.077652	0.243186	0	1.457162	Expenditure share on street being wide through road
SST3	0.003255	0.040939	0	0.578579	Expenditure share on street being a 'B' class road
SST4	0.021408	0.144846	0	1.450225	Expenditure share on street being an 'A' class road
SSING	2.568107	3.61862	0	13.69357	Expenditure share on detached house
STERR	0.201016	0.411929	0	2.110691	Expenditure share on terrace house
SSEMI	0.822254	1.59143	0	8.925956	Expenditure share on semi-detached house
SCENTH	1.274579	0.877165	0	4.043052	Expenditure share on central heat
SOSPARK	0.157154	0.399491	0	2.521592	Expenditure share on off-street parking
SSINGAR	0.675341	0.791927	0	3.26653	Expenditure share on single garage
SDBLGAR	0.269837	0.814473	0	4.713673	Expenditure share on double garage
SYEAR2	0.099402	0.291666	0	1.720246	Expenditure share on structure built in 1915–45
SYEAR5	0.419968	0.723346	0	3.59282	Expenditure share on structure built in 1976–90
SYEAR6	0.116884	0.669945	0	6.458597	Expenditure share on structure built after 1990

Variable					Description
SUNBLIT	0.171402	0.131037	0	0.580989	Expenditure share on avoid local construction
STHAMES	0.134007	1.175906	0	13.66355	Expenditure share on Thames frontage
SOTHER	60.44173	21.16822	0.616958	95.73976	Expenditure share on all other goods
ESTRENT	0.002552	0.001153	0.000365	0.010029	Price of land
PBEDS	0.018549	0.010449	0.007092	0.093752	Price of bedrooms
PWC	0.041927	0.022667	0.016158	0.198166	Price of WCs
PSQFT	0.002865	0.001505	0.001265	0.013277	Price of sq. ft. interior space
PBCOL	0.015259	0.009119	0.005348	0.079487	Price to avoid blue collar neighborhood
PAFIN	0.00555	0.003279	0.00216	0.028853	Price to avoid ethnic neighborhood
PINDU	0.001508	0.000921	0.000561	0.008065	Price to avoid local industrial land use
PAMEN1	0.001508	0.000928	0.000533	0.008111	Price of accessible open space
PAMEN2	0.0004	0.000228	0.000145	0.001819	Price of inaccessible open space
PALT	0.000225	0.000131	0.000073	0.001086	Price of local elevation
PGCSE	0.001639	0.000983	0.000585	0.008516	Price of school quality
PST2	0.017755	0.010922	0.006253	0.095678	Price of street being wide through road
PST3	0.012271	0.007549	0.004321	0.066124	Price of street being a 'B' class road
PST4	0.026449	0.016271	0.009314	0.142526	Price of street being an 'A' class road
PSING	0.166099	0.10218	0.058494	0.89507	Price of detached house
PTERR	0.020928	0.012875	0.00737	0.112779	Price of terrace house
PSEMI	0.089296	0.054933	0.031447	0.481199	Price of semi-detached house
PCENTH	0.040089	0.024662	0.014118	0.216029	Price of central heat
POSPARK	0.025402	0.015627	0.008946	0.136885	Price of off-street parking
PSINGAR	0.032389	0.019925	0.011406	0.174538	Price of single garage
PDBLGAR	0.061564	0.037873	0.021681	0.331756	Price of double garage
PYEAR2	0.020866	0.012836	0.007348	0.112443	Price of built in 1915–45
PYEAR5	0.03588	0.022073	0.012636	0.193352	Price of built in 1976–90
PYEAR6	0.08334	0.051269	0.02935	0.449102	Price of built after 1990
PNEWBLI	0.005761	0.003544	0.002029	0.031043	Price to avoid local construction
PTHAMES	0.255083	0.156921	0.089831	1.374588	Price of Thames frontage
DISTANCE	404.2577	194.6626	55.97321	964.3506	Distance to city centre
DIST1	24.55523	28.47504	1	220.0364	Distance to closest observation
DIST2	36.69851	34.67988	2.828427	288.3834	Distance to next closest observation

Table 6A.3 Demand system for variable attributes

Coeff.	Land	Bedrooms	WCs	Sq. Ft.	Blue Collar	Ethnic	Industrial	Acc. Open	Inac. Open	Elevation	Schools	Other
C	250.3682	−47.6037	−1.306	−362.6823	164.3365	139.1039	179.1604	20.308	−50.2145	32.3625	−62.8509	−681.9516
t	1.3649	0.3453	0.007	0.5549	0.7678	0.9564	0.5762	0.2703	0.9776	1.3878	0.3527	0.3127
Adults	0.0363	−0.0287	0.1001	−0.0396	−0.0833	−0.0033	−0.1297	−0.0139	−0.0355	−0.0137	−0.0922	0.533
t	0.276	0.3051	0.8586	0.0894	0.5737	0.0323	0.648	0.2796	0.9731	0.9762	0.7687	0.3667
Children	0.0883	0.018	0.0655	0.0881	0.0927	0.0839	0.1163	0.0249	0.0166	0.0059	0.039	−0.4953
t	1.2616	0.3532	0.8736	0.3695	1.167	1.5623	1.041	0.9374	0.8339	0.6757	0.5708	0.6483
Phat	−36.445	4.5796	0.1468	28.9345	−21.042	−20.261	−29.2063	−3.855	4.9479	−4.7004	5.9514	146.4294
t	1.5431	0.2607	0.0062	0.3508	0.7538	1.0622	0.721	0.3983	0.7626	1.5793	0.2598	0.5249
Real Income	2.0194	1.8234	2.338	6.9748	3.6654	2.3693	4.692	1.0074	0.2765	0.1432	1.9106	−33.2789
t	7.4843	9.4239	7.8117	7.6723	11.6022	10.8266	10.8891	9.0705	3.5874	4.6293	7.0187	11.0157
P_{Land}	0.3821	−0.0312	−0.0806	−0.8273	−0.3391	−0.2663	−0.3662	−0.0474	−0.2173	−0.0537	−0.4481	1.3333
t	1.3209	0.1708	0.2962	0.8066	1.1556	1.2365	0.8867	0.4532	2.3411	1.2746	1.8736	0.4942
P_{Beds}	7.4977	−4.2708	8.0073	31.9157	2.8372	1.7733	−2.1743	−1.7504	5.039	−0.0332	3.9589	−57.6321
t	1.0253	0.8045	1.1852	1.2806	0.3497	0.3249	0.1902	0.5727	2.2865	0.0349	0.5747	0.7112
P_{WC}	7.1198	−0.033	−13.7845	0.2672	2.4272	3.5608	3.9743	1.0942	−1.606	1.0369	−6.1229	3.4064
t	1.2801	0.0087	3.155	0.0153	0.3587	0.7564	0.4228	0.4783	1.0961	1.5731	1.2927	0.0529
P_{SqFt}	0.7494	−7.5801	−3.4602	−91.0117	11.0336	10.6504	19.4912	4.4751	−5.5513	1.322	−1.4425	49.9913
t	0.0582	0.7861	0.2644	1.9575	0.785	1.126	0.9767	0.8793	1.4112	0.8205	0.1199	0.3343
P_{BCol}	1.8003	1.6741	1.4696	3.1319	−19.0582	−0.6488	2.4029	0.1854	−1.5957	0.5293	0.6219	−35.594
t	0.4521	0.6207	0.3988	0.2298	4.0659	0.2044	0.393	0.1299	1.5816	1.2131	0.2001	0.8136
P_{Ethnic}	3.1507	0.2874	1.9638	−0.9811	4.8826	−4.1688	4.6694	0.8886	0.6669	0.5855	−0.2271	−15.8936

t	1.0569	0.1315	0.7441	0.0984	1.3231	1.8113	0.8933	0.8559	1.6761	0.0978	0.4673
P_{Indus}	9.9519	3.4031	0.0068	17.253	11.7468	4.525	−7.5015	−1.6852	1.3887	3.3691	−41.9581
t	1.2414	0.6167	0.001	0.6184	1.3363	0.8397	0.6112	0.7749	1.4616	0.501	0.4821
$P_{AccOpen}$	−0.3671	−0.2673	2.3505	−0.6418	1.6524	1.2179	1.28	0.5458	0.0195	0.2695	−4.1436
t	0.1815	0.2037	1.2459	0.1002	0.6868	0.7156	0.3899	0.9769	0.0808	0.164	0.1903
$P_{InaccOpen}$	0.4555	−0.3792	−0.4597	−2.4429	0.1399	0.0034	0.5406	−1.4005	0.0256	0.1553	5.9263
t	0.6372	0.781	0.7268	1.0676	0.1834	0.0068	0.5107	6.8727	0.3299	0.2586	0.7949
P_{Elev}	−0.0484	0.1389	0.6505	0.8137	0.4105	0.5121	0.1706	0.186	−0.5309	0.3418	−8.2304
t	0.1001	0.3958	1.3478	0.484	0.7867	1.4323	0.2284	1.3268	7.6841	0.7767	1.4976
P_{School}	3.7819	0.0762	0.4119	3.0036	0.9203	0.3846	1.2126	0.0161	0.2206	−9.449	−6.8173
t	3.4264	0.0865	0.3118	0.7517	0.7058	0.4623	0.6604	0.0552	1.733	9.0378	0.5208
R-squared	0.6645	0.816	0.8239	0.784	0.8251	0.8231	0.8137	0.4438	0.528	0.8183	0.8449
Adj. R-square	0.6474	0.8066	0.8149	0.773	0.8162	0.8141	0.8042	0.4155	0.504	0.8091	0.837

Table 6A.4   Demand system for dichotomous attributes

Coeff.	Street2	Street3	Street4	Detached	Terrace	Semi	CentHeat
C	35.7739	−20.061	47.233	−44.0347	26.1281	4.2479	−94.4885
t	*0.4361*	*1.2461*	*1.4618*	*0.0707*	*0.2138*	*0.0095*	*0.4701*
Adults	0.0305	0.0102	−0.028	0.1702	0.0344	−0.2905	0.0834
t	*0.713*	*1.1535*	*1.4682*	*0.3947*	*0.4588*	*1.0428*	*0.6456*
Children	0.0137	−0.0011	0.033	−0.1277	0.0102	0.0095	0.0622
t	*0.4444*	*0.3158*	*2.0019*	*0.4972*	*0.225*	*0.0548*	*0.8901*
Phat	−4.6456	2.4285	−5.4224	9.0864	−1.7345	−11.0788	7.8477
t	*0.4472*	*1.2258*	*1.314*	*0.1143*	*0.1101*	*0.1961*	*0.3093*
Real Income	0.0774	−0.0118	−0.0212	2.4503	0.1516	0.4488	0.9769
t	*0.8931*	*0.8958*	*0.4723*	*2.5464*	*0.739*	*0.8421*	*3.1335*
P_{land}	−0.14	0.0255	0.0121	−0.4107	0.3287	−0.5932	0.0404
t	*1.3755*	*0.9296*	*0.1746*	*0.4033*	*1.9468*	*0.8959*	*0.1218*
P_{beds}	0.3296	0.4904	−0.1419	5.4514	−3.9888	0.6614	8.3736
t	*0.166*	*1.0226*	*0.1048*	*0.2183*	*1.0336*	*0.047*	*1.1822*
P_{WC}	−0.0762	−0.2904	−0.1757	−17.1066	0.5384	12.896	0.5641
t	*0.0446*	*0.9589*	*0.2096*	*1.037*	*0.2063*	*1.1827*	*0.1115*
P_{SqFt}	0.7581	−1.2345	2.6449	4.6832	4.7574	−28.1767	−13.8193
t	*0.1389*	*1.2122*	*1.1464*	*0.105*	*0.5924*	*0.9179*	*0.9813*
P_{BCol}	1.1129	−0.0889	−0.0156	−2.8658	−3.4337	25.2739	0.5282
t	*0.9095*	*0.4906*	*0.0277*	*0.2174*	*1.9913*	*3.0549*	*0.1697*
P_{Ethnic}	−0.298	−0.1582	−0.1798	6.6238	0.1323	−6.7524	0.5479
t	*0.3496*	*0.9962*	*0.3077*	*0.8395*	*0.0882*	*1.2477*	*0.2083*
P_{Indus}	0.7882	−1.1475	2.3728	−10.7632	4.1007	7.484	−2.0792
t	*0.2995*	*1.3212*	*1.5725*	*0.4298*	*0.9897*	*0.4341*	*0.2684*
$P_{AccOpen}$	0.7908	0.0132	0.4418	3.0891	−0.066	−3.2463	−2.9233
t	*1.1302*	*0.1471*	*1.1974*	*0.4997*	*0.0674*	*0.6943*	*1.4656*
$P_{InaccOpen}$	0.4817	−0.0985	0.1659	−4.3366	0.0194	1.8522	−0.7596
t	*1.8999*	*1.3233*	*1.3215*	*1.7383*	*0.0516*	*1.2253*	*1.0794*
P_{Elev}	0.2515	0.0722	−0.1156	2.2318	−0.3891	0.1956	0.8207
t	*1.5504*	*1.2897*	*1.4735*	*1.1207*	*1.5346*	*0.1724*	*1.6431*
P_{School}	0.267	0.0164	0.4609	4.8599	−0.3753	−1.5614	−0.4804
t	*0.6844*	*0.3664*	*1.6709*	*1.2879*	*0.5521*	*0.6906*	*0.4412*
R-squared	0.0829	−0.5947	−0.1741	0.4653	0.1461	−0.0969	0.3306
Adj. R-square	0.0363	−0.6758	−0.2337	0.4381	0.1027	−0.1527	0.2966

Parking	1Garage	2Garage	BldYr2	BldYr5	BldYr6	LocalBld	Thames
38.0601	229.9393	−179.2325	−12.1724	−216.9441	112.6463	21.4531	572.4215
0.2962	0.9737	0.776	0.1265	1.07	0.5442	0.703	1.5773
0.0135	0.0541	−0.1203	0.0174	−0.0411	−0.1292	−0.0266	−0.0075
0.1566	0.3983	0.943	0.2898	0.3248	1.5778	1.2896	0.0499
0.0153	0.0716	−0.1583	−0.0072	−0.0218	−0.0274	−0.0051	−0.0109
0.2914	0.8776	1.8956	0.208	0.2629	0.5761	0.4358	0.1083
−7.4301	−29.2275	22.0454	0.2151	30.9535	−12.9613	−3.4658	−72.0905
0.4573	0.9726	0.7421	0.0175	1.1802	0.5104	0.8963	1.563
0.3367	0.7277	0.1786	0.071	−0.1082	0.3205	0.1967	0.2639
1.8436	2.3956	0.5219	0.8242	0.3584	1.3197	3.9938	0.7197
0.1713	−0.1569	−0.1989	0.1098	0.4299	0.1784	−0.0859	1.2513
1.0948	0.4411	0.4756	0.7722	1.4309	0.566	1.7111	2.2631
3.9863	−7.1051	0.9016	2.0229	−5.3317	−0.6946	1.1038	−1.2271
1.0191	0.9684	0.117	0.6523	0.7171	0.0904	0.936	0.123
3.0213	3.841	−1.5161	1.7121	−11.2445	−2.7244	0.9126	8.308
1.2147	0.7011	0.2312	0.6335	2.1072	0.5118	1.2449	0.7101
−0.562	21.9872	−18.6337	−4.0858	3.8208	7.6341	−2.6623	34.2212
0.059	1.3685	1.2295	0.6485	0.2935	0.503	1.1797	1.5225
1.701	5.3142	0.3937	0.8826	2.5076	2.5213	0.2568	10.993
0.8012	1.4514	0.0941	0.6108	0.6594	0.8688	0.3967	1.8285
0.34	1.2591	−0.9515	0.0106	−3.8333	1.9708	0.1419	5.3224
0.2084	0.4304	0.327	0.0097	1.5716	1.005	0.3201	1.2928
−1.9988	3.1139	−1.4945	−1.583	−10.4509	−0.4287	2.3716	6.0798
0.4879	0.3738	0.1704	0.4375	1.3543	0.0528	1.8871	0.4738
0.0839	0.6476	−1.0636	0.2452	−2.1847	3.0344	0.1418	4.4352
0.0794	0.3137	0.5019	0.2856	1.0591	1.0384	0.446	1.4997
−0.1327	0.59	−0.5968	−0.1241	−1.1469	0.1312	0.1184	1.3194
0.3301	0.8063	0.7438	0.3608	1.6632	0.1997	1.1149	1.2913
0.0138	−0.1078	0.4943	0.0714	0.0163	0.7242	−0.0184	1.3773
0.0538	0.2032	0.7198	0.3561	0.0311	1.0568	0.188	1.2946
0.5766	−0.3154	0.2515	0.5465	−2.5471	0.7894	0.6177	2.9461
0.7879	0.2653	0.2084	1.2702	2.2317	0.7321	3.3581	1.6869
0.0005	0.0229	−0.1887	−0.0817	−0.2649	−0.0026	0.0836	−0.0369
−0.0503	−0.0268	−0.2492	−0.1367	−0.3292	−0.0535	0.037	−0.0897

NOTES

1. We would like to thank the Leverhulme Foundation for its support for the work underlying this chapter.
2. Microsoft, Oracle, Hewlett-Packard and others.
3. In the data studied in Cheshire and Sheppard (1998) the amenity values were greater by a factor of up to eight.
4. The evidence in relation to the empirical realism of assuming equilibrium in this urban land market was discussed in Cheshire and Sheppard (2002). In general the evidence was consistent with the land (housing) market being in or very close to equilibrium. Equilibrium, apart from being implicit in the estimation of any hedonic price function, has the further useful property for the present analysis that it implies that all land made available for occupation by the planning system is in fact 'consumed'. As discussed below, this allows us to infer the planning-determined supply of housing land and model alternatives to that supply which would be consistent with the observed values of other relevant variables.
5. This value differs from that reported in Cheshire and Sheppard (2002) primarily because of the difference in the way the UGB is estimated here. This difference, since it is consistent, only affects absolute values and means that those for the welfare costs cannot strictly be compared with the values reported in Cheshire and Sheppard (2002).
6. All microsimulation calculations are done with *Mathematica* and the notebooks containing the models and calculations are available from the authors.

REFERENCES

American Farmland Trust, 1997, *Saving American Farmland: What Works*, Northampton, MA.

Brueckner, Jan, 2001, 'Urban Sprawl: Lessons from Urban Economics', *Brookings–Wharton Papers on Urban Affairs*, 65–89.

Brueckner, Jan and Hyun A. Kim, 2000, 'Urban Sprawl and the Property Tax', unpublished paper, University of Illinois at Urbana-Champaign.

Cheshire, Paul and Stephen Sheppard, 1995, 'On the Price of Land and the Value of Amenities', *Economica,* 62, 247–67.

Cheshire, Paul and Stephen Sheppard, 1998, 'Estimating Demand for Housing, Land, and Neighbourhood Characteristics', *Oxford Bulletin of Economics and Statistics*, 60, August, 357–82.

Cheshire, Paul and Stephen Sheppard, 2002, 'The Welfare Economics of Land Use Planning', *Journal of Urban Economics*, 52, 242–69.

Deaton, Angus and John Muellbauer, 1980, 'An Almost Ideal Demand System', *American Economic Review*, 70, 312–26.

Department of Environment Transport and Regions, 2000. 'Rate Relief for Farm Diversification Enterprises Consultation Paper' (*http://www.local-regions.dtlr. gov.uk/consult/raterel*).

Downs, Anthony, 2001, 'What does "Smart Growth" Really Mean?', *Planning*, April, 20–25.

7. Land use regulations and the property tax: cost–benefit analyses

John F. McDonald

1 INTRODUCTION

The purpose of this chapter is to develop theoretical analyses of several land use and property taxation policies that are employed by local governments. The goals of each model presented are twofold: to gain understanding of the effects of policies as they operate in the relevant markets, and to formulate reasonably simple methods for cost–benefit analyses of these policies. Numerical examples or empirical results are employed to illustrate the possible use of each model.

The chapter begins with an examination of zoning. Zoning ordinances allocate land to uses and regulate the intensity of land use. The first model examines the allocation of a parcel of land to a particular use by land use zoning. The parcel in question is subject to property taxation, and it is assumed that there is unemployed labor residing in the jurisdiction. The next section continues the examination of zoning by studying the effects of land use intensity regulations. This section is followed by a study of the effects of changes in property taxation (the tax on land and structures) on the intensity of land use. Earlier versions of these models were published in McDonald (1979;1983; 2001). McDonald (1983) discussed property tax changes applied only to capital or land.

The next model covered in the chapter examines the property tax and the size of the tax base at the local jurisdiction level. The final model studies land use zoning at the block level and explicitly introduces external effects into the model. Earlier versions of these models were presented in McMillen and McDonald (1993) and McDonald (1993). The chapter concludes with a summary. The appendix contains a more complex version of the first model (land use zoning model).

2   COST–BENEFIT OF LOCAL LAND USE ALLOCATION DECISIONS

State and local governments are making extensive use of policies and programs that are intended to stimulate economic activity. Among those programs is land use allocation decisions for the purpose of generating economic activity. For example, the book by Rast (1999) recounts the recent history of the decision by the City of Chicago to attempt to stimulate industrial growth by designating 'protected manufacturing districts' in which changes in zoning to permit residential development are prohibited. These districts were created in spite of the fact that the value of the land in residential use was much higher than that in industrial use. A suburban example is found in a recent newspaper article by Orr (2000), in which 'Naperville residents seek study of city's last vacant land'. Here the issue is whether land that had been designated for a business park instead should be allocated to residential development.

Bartik (1990) and Courant (1994) advocate the use of conventional cost–benefit methods to assess local economic development policies. The purpose of this section is to devise some methods through which the principles of cost–benefit analysis can be applied to land use allocation decisions. The central point is to make the connection between policies and economic outcomes in the urban land and labor markets. The model shows that land use allocation policies have impacts that can be measured in the urban labor and land markets: changes in employment, land values and the intensity of land use. Procedures for the estimation of benefits and opportunity costs are derived. The benefits in this model fall into three categories: employment of previously unemployed or underemployed workers (including possible multiplier effects), increases in local tax revenue in excess of the cost of additional local public goods and services required, and higher value of land. Local economic development policies considered in this chapter have no benefits if there is no unemployment, if users of local public goods pay taxes equal to the value of the benefits of those goods (as in Tiebout, 1956, and Hamilton, 1976), and if land is already allocated to its 'highest and best' use. In short, the benefits exist in a world with distorted markets. This section previously appeared in McDonald (2001).

One crucial assumption in this chapter is that involuntary unemployment (or underemployment) may exist in the jurisdiction in question. Workers may be available at a reservation wage that is lower than the market wage; the opportunity cost of labor is less than the value of its marginal product. The plan is to proceed through a sequence of models. The first model is devised to study the benefits and costs of land use allocation

decisions and other economic development policies for a small, 'open' jurisdiction. All input and output prices are exogenous to the jurisdiction, and
the economic efficiency of policy is examined from the point of view of that
jurisdiction and from the point of view of the larger society. The next
model, which is presented in the appendix, examines the case in which the
jurisdiction is not completely open, but faces demands for its industrial
(export) product and for housing that are of finite elasticity. In this model
the estimation of benefits and costs is a more complex task than it is in the
case of the open jurisdiction.

This chapter does not consider the question of the timing of economic
development programs. Mauer and Ott (1999) have considered this issue in
the context of a model of firm location (and relocation). In their preliminary discussion of the model (ibid., p. 425) they state that 'The benefits may
include a reduction in the direct and indirect costs of unemployment, an
increase in tax revenue, and the multiplier effect of an increase in economic
activity.' They take these benefits as given and do not consider them further.

The fundamental points of the section can be made with a simple model
of land use and land value. Consider a small, one-unit parcel of land that
might be allocated to either housing or industrial use by a local jurisdiction
that is open; it is assumed that the opportunity cost of industrial land is its
use for housing. All output and input prices (except for land rent) are exogenous to the jurisdiction. This model would usually be applied to the case
of a jurisdiction that allocates another unit of land to businesses that
produce goods for export outside the jurisdiction. The possibility of externalities (negative or positive) is ignored here. All markets are assumed to be
perfectly competitive.

Housing services are produced by combining the services of land and
capital. The market price of a unit of housing services is p_h, which is exogenous both to the parcel in question and to the jurisdiction. Capital services
have an exogenous opportunity cost r per unit, so the annual benefit of allocating the unit parcel of land to housing is

$$R_h = p_h H - r K_h, \qquad (7.1)$$

where H is units of housing services produced, K_h is unit of capital services
allocated to housing and R_h is land rent calculated as a residual. If housing
services are produced with constant returns to scale, R_h is also the value of
the marginal product of land in housing. The assumption of constant
returns will be made.

Industrial activity involves combining the services of land, labor and
capital to produce output (value added). The market price of output p is
exogenous both to the parcel and to the local jurisdiction in question, as

is the opportunity cost of capital services r. The cost of labor to industrial firms is w. However, in this instance it will be assumed that some labor is involuntarily unemployed at wage rate w. The opportunity cost of labor (reservation wage) is assumed to be $w^* < w$. An increase in land allocated to industrial use will shift the demand for labor to the right, and the resulting increase in employment will have a benefit to the worker and to society of $(w - w^*)$ per additional worker employed. As Mishan (1982, pp.68–71) points out, the benefit to society will also include the worker's unemployment compensation or other forms of income support that are eliminated when the person is hired. In other words, society gains additional output that has a value of w at a cost of w^* minus the annualized value U of the unemployment compensation and other income maintenance that the worker received. However, if we are considering the costs and benefits from the point of view of the local jurisdiction, only the portion of U that is paid by the local jurisdiction (and denoted C) is counted. In other words, it is necessary to impute to the local jurisdiction its share of the marginal cost of the unemployment compensation and welfare programs of the state.

The increase in industrial employment is simply

$$dN/dL = N/L, \tag{7.2}$$

where N is industrial employment and L is land. In the long run, each parcel of industrial land of standard quality and accessibility will have the same ratio of labor to land, N/L. Therefore, assuming that the unit parcel in question is of standard quality and accessibility, its employment density will be N/L as well. The addition of the parcel in question to industrial use has resulted in a net gain of (N/L) jobs for the jurisdiction. No jobs located on this parcel have 'moved' from other locations within the jurisdiction. However, as Bartik (1991) points out, many of the jobs will be taken by workers who are not original residents of the jurisdiction. In Bartik's typical case, original residents take 23 per cent of the increase in employment, and 77 per cent of the jobs are taken by workers who move to the jurisdiction.

The benefit *to the local jurisdiction* from allocating the parcel in question to industrial use can be found as follows. It is assumed that the parcel is owned by someone in the jurisdiction (or that, by definition, the owner of the parcel is a member of the jurisdiction). The market rent of the unit parcel in industrial use captures the value added by labor and capital, and is

$$R_m = pQ - rK_m - w(N/L), \tag{7.3}$$

where Q is output and K_m is units of capital services allocated to industry on the parcel; R_m is only part of the benefit because the increase in employment has generated benefits equal to $f(w+C-w^*)(N/L)$, where f is the fraction of jobs taken by original residents or the jurisdiction. The first-round benefits of allocating the unit parcel to industrial use are therefore $R_m + f(w+C-w^*)(N/L)$. As Sridhar (1996) points out, benefits to society as a whole include benefits that arise from the movement of workers to the jurisdiction.

Cost–benefit experts such as Mishan (1982) point out that the net addition to income generated by the industrial use (compared to the residential use) may generate a multiplier effect that should be counted as a benefit. The multiplier effect that counts as a net benefit for the local jurisdiction is the extent to which there is any additional employment of heretofore unemployed workers who are original residents of the jurisdiction. Felsenstein and Persky (1999) provide a more detailed analysis of the multiplier effect by using the 'chain of jobs' approach. Each added worker values his/her employment at $(w-w^*)$, and C is saved in income maintenance payments per worker. In this chapter it is assumed that the multiplier effects are small enough to have no effects on market prices or land use allocation. See McGregor *et al.* (2000) and Merrifield (1987) for more complex neoclassical economic base multiplier models.

The benefits to the local jurisdiction of allocating the unit parcel to industrial use minus the cost, or net benefits NB, can now be written

$$NB = R_m - R_h + fM(w+C-w^*)(N/L) - P, \qquad (7.4)$$

where M is the local employment multiplier effect and P is the (annualized) cost of the program itself. Net benefits of industrial use are positive if

$$R_h - R_m + P < fM(w+C-w^*)(N/L); \qquad (7.5)$$

that is, if the benefits to labor exceed the differential in land rent plus program costs. It is assumed that, because of local zoning and other constraints on land use allocations, R_h does not necessarily equal R_m for the site in question.

Thus far the reservation wage has been assumed to be a constant unknown w^*. Clearly, the level of the reservation wage is a critical variable in the model, but there are few recent empirical studies that can serve as a guide. A survey of older reservation wage studies by Gordon (1973) shows that the average reservation wage varied from 72 per cent to 98 per cent of the previous wage, and the average wage accepted on the new job varied from 59 per cent to 105 per cent of the previous wage. More recent studies by Feldstein and Poterba (1984) and Jones (1989) show that the reservation wage is a function of sex, the cause of unemployment, the length of unemployment and the generosity of unemployment benefits. In the study by Feldstein and Poterba (1984), people who had voluntarily left the previous job and who had been out of work for less than five weeks had a reservation wage that was 112 per cent of the previous wage, but that those who had lost their jobs (and were not on layoff) and had been out of work for at least 50 weeks had a reservation wage that was 91 per cent of the previous wage. The study by Jones (1989) has the result that prime-aged males (aged 25–54) have a reservation wage that is essentially equal to the previous wage until they have been unemployed for more than 24 months, but the reservation wage for the men who have been unemployed for more 24 months is 79 per cent of the previous wage. The reservation wage in the Jones (1989) study for females was equal to the previous wage regardless of the duration of the unemployment spell. The studies by Fishe (1982), Kasper (1969), Kiefer and Neumann (1979), and Stephenson (1976) also show that the reservation wage decreases with the length of unemployment. Sridhar (1996) found that the reservation wage is negatively related to the local unemployment rate. In short, the benefits of increasing employment may depend critically upon local labor market conditions and characteristics of the unemployed workers who are hired as a direct or indirect result of the local economic development program. It is also clear that more empirical studies of reservation wages are needed to facilitate the evaluation of local economic development policies.

Land and capital are subject to real estate taxes and receive benefits in the form of local public goods, so a more realistic version of the model should include the local public sector. Introduction of the real estate tax also provides another variable that can be manipulated by local officials to influence market outcomes. If the real estate tax is a benefits tax as contemplated in the Tiebout (1956) model literature (for example, by Hamilton, 1976, and many others), then the model reduces to equation (7.1) above. In the more general case, the land rent will include the net benefit of local public sector activity. Because capital and households are perfectly mobile with respect to the unit parcel in question and because the demand for output is perfectly elastic, the incidence of the net local real estate tax is entirely on land. In other words, if the local public sector confers benefits in excess of real estate taxes, that net benefit will be reflected in land rent. For residential use this net benefit will usually be positive, and it represents the value of local public services that are costly to produce. Therefore this net benefit (net cost) to the residents of the site should be *subtracted* from (added to) land rent. The benefits to the local jurisdiction of allocating the unit parcel of land to housing are

$$p_h H - r K_h = R_h + T_h, \qquad (7.6)$$

where T_h is the net contribution (taxes minus value of services) of the parcel to the local public sector. The case of industrial use is similar to the residential case. The net benefit of local public goods will be capitalized into land value. In the case of retail use, local taxes include sales taxes as well as real estate taxes. However, given the assumptions of this model, sales taxes are also fully capitalized into land value. Ordinarily the costs of public services attributable to commercial and industrial activity are less than those for residences, largely because of the cost of public schools (Netzer, 1966), so the taxes will exceed the value of the benefit of local public goods for industrial or commercial use.

The net benefit of allocating the unit parcel to industrial or commercial use in the presence of the local public sector can now be written:

$$NB = (R_m - R_h) + (T_m - T_h) + fM(w + c - w^*)(N/L) - P, \qquad (7.7)$$

where T_m is the net contribution of the parcel in industrial or commercial use to the local public sector. (Note that it is probable that $T_m > 0$ and $T_h < 0$).

Equation (7.7) can be used as the basis of a cost–benefit analysis of a local economic development program from the standpoint of the local jurisdiction provided that the assumptions of the model are satisfied; the allocation of the additional parcel of land to employment activity does not subtract from the amount of employment at any other location in the local jurisdiction (because output and input prices are exogenous) and the local multiplier effect increases employment but has no effect on prices or land use allocation.

Assuming that all output and input prices are exogenous, the net benefit of the local economic development program to the larger society includes all of the employment increase (not just fraction f), the national multiplier effect and all income maintenance costs that are avoided (U). Net benefits to the nation are

$$NB_n = (R_m - R_h) + (T_m - T_h) + M_n(w + U - w^*)(N/L) - P, \qquad (7.7')$$

where M_n is the national multiplier effect of the program. In this model the rest of the nation benefits from the local economic development program in the amount

$$NB_n - NB = (M_n - fM)(w - w^*)(N/L) + (M_n U - fMC)(N/L). \qquad (7.8)$$

Assuming $w > w^*$, in this basic model the rest of the nation has an incentive to encourage local jurisdictions to allocate land to industrial use.

A numerical example can serve to illustrate the cost–benefit analysis proposed. Some of the data used in the example are drawn from a Chicago case study discussed by Rast (1999, pp.144–5). In 1994, a developer proposed to build 330 townhouses on an 11-acre largely vacant site that is zoned for manufacturing. The value of the land was $5 per square foot as industrial space and estimated at $15 per square foot as residential space. The issue is whether the City should accept this development plan, or market the property to an industrial user.

Assume that the townhouses have a market value of $250000 each, so the total value of the residential development would be $82500000. Residential property taxes in Chicago are 1.8 per cent of market value, which would be $1485000 annually. Assume that the development would contain 200 children who attend the public schools. At $5000 per child, the necessary expenditure per year would be $1000000. Assume that an additional $1000000 will be needed per year to cover the other public services, so the net contribution of the site to the local public fisc is −$515000. With land value of $15 per square foot and, assuming a 10 per cent interest rate, annual land rent for 11 acres would be $718740.

It is assumed that the site is in demand as industrial space at a market price of $5 per square foot. At this price, with an interest rate of 10 per cent, annual land rent is $239580. Data from McDonald (1985) for Chicago in 1970 indicate an industrial floor–area ratio of 0.59, so there would be 282700 square feet of industrial space on 11 acres. The data also show 840 square feet per industrial employee, so the projected employment for the site is 337. Assume a salary of $30 000 per year. The reservation wage is estimated to be 80 per cent of that salary, and the local share of welfare and unemployment benefits avoided is negligible. The market value of the industrial facility is estimated to be $33700000. If the capitalization rate is 10 per cent, then the annual rent for the facility is $3370000 (and the share of labor is 75 per cent). Of this the land rent is $239580 and the rent for the capital is $3130420 ($11.07 per square foot). The property tax rate on industrial property in Chicago averages 5 per cent, but property tax incentives would be used to reduce that rate to 3.5 per cent. Annual property tax collections would therefore be $1180000. Recall that costs for public services other than schools are $1000000. Following Bartik (1991), assume that $f = 0.23$ (the share of jobs filled by Chicago residents), and assume that the local employment multiplier is 1.15.

These data permit the terms in equation (7.7) to be filled in as follows:

$$\frac{R_m - R_h}{T_m - T_h}$$

$$fM(w + c - w^*)(N/L)$$

Annual net benefits of industrial use

$\$239\,580 - 718\,740$	$= -479\,160$
$180\,000 + 515\,000$	$= 695\,000$
$0.23(1.15)(4800)(337)$	$= 427\,855$
	$= 643\,695$

In this example the use of the site for industry is indicated on efficiency grounds. The loss of annual land rent in residential use is more than made up by the fact that, in this model, industrial use does not require the provision of public schools and that the wage exceeds the reservation wage. Note that the annual net benefit of residential development is $\$718\,740 - 515\,000 = 203\,740$, while the annual net benefit of industrial development is $\$847\,435$.

It has been pointed out correctly that performing the cost–benefit analysis described in this section presents some difficult empirical issues. The variables needed include land rents, reservation wages, the local employment multiplier, the proportion of jobs created that will be held by local residents, net contributions of each land use to the local fisc, and so on. These are the sorts of problems one faces in any detailed cost–benefit analysis, and a standard method is to perform sensitivity analysis with alternative estimates of the important variables.

3 COST–BENEFIT ANALYSIS OF LAND USE INTENSITY REGULATIONS

This section examines the effects of the direct regulation of the intensity of land use at the level of the individual parcel. The model is developed for the housing market, in which (as in the previous section) stocks of land L and capital K produce housing real estate according to a linear–homogeneous production function

$$H = f(L, K_h). \tag{7.9}$$

In this section the local property tax is assumed to be a benefits tax that has no effect on the intensity of land use. This assumption is relaxed in the next section.

The current system of zoning in the city of Chicago, which was enacted in 1957, contains a system for the zoning of residential land that controls the intensity of land use directly. The crucial provision in the ordinance controls the 'floor–area ratio', which is the ratio of usable floor area to the area of the lot. The allowable floor–area ratio ranges from 0.5 for R-1 zoned land to 10.0 for R-8 zoned land. For example, R-1 zoning permits the construction of a two-story house that covers 25 per cent of the lot, and R-8 zoning allows the construction of a 40-story building that occupies 25 per cent of the lot. The zoning ordinance also controls minimum lot area per housing unit, minimum front, side and back yard widths, and minimum parking spaces. What is important from a theoretical standpoint is the limitation on the floor–area ratio. This provision is very nearly a direct control on the ratio of capital to land. Of course, structures of equal floor area can contain different capital inputs by variations in the quality of construction, number of bathrooms and so on. However, the building code places limitations on allowable variations of this kind.

Consider housing production on a unit parcel of land with exogenously fixed accessibility and other amenities. Assume that the land market contains many sites with identical characteristics, so that competition fixes the land rent (and value) of the site in question. The rental price of capital is also exogenous to the site and the producer (or producers) who occupy the site. Only one level of output is consistent with long-run equilibrium. This output can be produced and sold because competition in the output market establishes the exogenously fixed price of housing (given the accessibility and other amenities of the site). The value of the marginal product of land is simply

$$R_h(\mathbf{a}) = p_h(\mathbf{a})MP_L, \qquad (7.10)$$

where $R_h(\mathbf{a})$ is the rent on land, $p_h(\mathbf{a})$ is the price of a unit of housing services, $\mathbf{a}$ is a vector of site amenities, and MP_L is the marginal product of land. The usual approach in land value studies is to make the observation that $p_h(\mathbf{a})$ and $K_h(\mathbf{a})/L(\mathbf{a})$ are both functions of $\mathbf{a}$, $p_h(\mathbf{a})$ and $k(\mathbf{a}) = K_h(\mathbf{a})/L(\mathbf{a})$ are perfectly correlated. One thus only needs to examine land rent (or value) as a function of the variables in $\mathbf{a}$, or $R_h(\mathbf{a}) = g(\mathbf{a})$.

The introduction of zoning to regulate the floor–area ratio potentially breaks the perfect correlation between $R_h(\mathbf{a})$ and MP_L. If the allowable capital–land ratio Z is less than the market-determined capital–land ratio k^*, then MP_L is less than it otherwise would be, but $p_h(\mathbf{a})$ is unaffected. Now land rent can be expressed as

$$R_h(\mathbf{a}) = g(\mathbf{a})[h(k^*/Z)]^D, \qquad (7.11)$$

where $D = 1$ if k^*/Z is greater than one (and $D = 0$ if k^*/Z is less than or equal to one). In other words, land value is equal to $g(\mathbf{a})$ unless Z is less than k^*, in which case land value is less than $g(\mathbf{a})$ by an amount that is a function of the extent to which Z is less than k^*. This point can also be expressed in the language of nonlinear programming. For an individual land parcel,

$$\Phi(Z-k)=0,$$

where Φ is the shadow price of the zoning constraint (which equals zero if Z is greater than k, where k is the actual capital–land ratio).

For purposes of empirical estimation, the zoning variable is relevant only if Z is less than k^*. Furthermore, the appropriate variable to use is k^*/Z, and not Z. The equation to be estimated is

$$\ln R_h(\mathbf{a}) = \ln g(\mathbf{a}) + Dh(k^*/Z) + u_1, \qquad (7.12)$$

where u_1 is a normal error term. Failure to include the term $D\ln h(k^*/Z)$ will lead to a potentially serious omitted variable bias in the coefficients of the $\ln g(\mathbf{a})$ function. However, k^*/Z cannot be measured directly because k^* is not observed if Z is less than k^*. Furthermore, as is seen below, there are problems with determining D on the basis of a comparison of actual k and Z. One further point about (7.12) is of interest. If we assume that the production function for housing has a constant elasticity of substitution (CES), then the functional form of the equation is simplified to

$$\ln R_h(\mathbf{a}) = \ln g(\mathbf{a}) - (D/\sigma)(\ln k^* - \ln Z) + u_1, \qquad (7.13)$$

where σ is the elasticity of substitution. This follows because, by definition of the elasticity of substitution, $\sigma = \partial \ln k / \partial \ln R_h$.

The measurement of $\ln k^* - \ln Z$ can be formulated as a standard Tobit problem. Suppose that

$$\ln k^* = \Omega(\mathbf{a}) + u_2,$$

where u_2 is a normal error term. It is necessary to assume that the error terms u_1 and u_2 are positively correlated because of unobserved factors that increase $R_h(\mathbf{a})$ and increase k^*. The value of the error term u_2 determines k^* and D, so both k^* and D are correlated with u_1 in (7.12). A solution to the problem is straightforward. From the definition of $\ln k^*$ above,

$$\ln k^* - \ln Z = \Omega(\mathbf{a}) + u_2 - \ln Z. \qquad (7.14)$$

We observe $\ln k - \ln Z$, where

$$\begin{aligned} \ln k - \ln Z &= \Omega(\mathbf{a}) + u_2 - \ln Z \qquad &&\text{if RHS} < 0 \\ &= 0 \qquad &&\text{if RHS} > 0. \end{aligned}$$

Estimation of this Tobit model provides an estimate of $\Omega(\mathbf{a})$. Predicted values of $\ln k^* - \ln Z$ can be imputed for all parcels on the basis of the Tobit index as $\Omega(\mathbf{a}) - \ln Z$. This eliminates the correlation between $\ln k^* - \ln Z$ and u_1. Also the correlation between D and u_1 can be eliminated by replacing D with the probability that $D=1$. This probability is based on the estimates of $\Omega(\mathbf{a})$ and the standard deviation of u_2, or

$$\text{prob}(D=1) = \text{prob}[\ln Z - \Omega(\mathbf{a}) < u_2].$$

The cost of an effective zoning restriction can be written simply as

$$\ln R_h(\mathbf{a}) - \ln g(\mathbf{a}) = (1/\sigma)[\ln Z - \ln k^*]. \tag{7.15}$$

For example, suppose that $\sigma=1$ (McDonald, 1981) and that the zoning ordinance reduces the floor–area ratio from $k^*=2$ to $Z=0.5$. We have

$$\ln R_h(\mathbf{a}) - \ln g(\mathbf{a}) = -1.38; \text{ that is,}$$
$$R_h(\mathbf{a})/g(\mathbf{a}) = e^{-1.38} = 0.25.$$

In other words, if the elasticity of substitution equals 1.0, the 75 per cent reduction in the allowable floor–area ratio reduces the land rent by 75 per cent. If $\sigma>1$ ($\sigma<1$), this 75 per cent reduction in the allowable floor–area ratio reduces land rent by less than (more than) 75 per cent. There are no other costs in this model because, while the supply of housing is reduced, the demand for housing on the site is of infinite elasticity.

4   A MODEL OF URBAN PRODUCTION

This section presents a Cobb–Douglas model of production for an industry in an urban area that can be used in conjunction with the models in the previous sections. The Cobb–Douglas production model will also be used in the next section for an examination of local industry subsidy programs, and in other sections of the chapter.

Output is a Cobb–Douglas function of land, labor and capital; that is,

$$Q = aL^\alpha N^\beta K^\varepsilon. \tag{7.16}$$

Constant returns to scale are assumed; $\alpha + \beta + \varepsilon = 1$ with $\alpha = 0.075$, $\beta = 0.70$, and $\varepsilon = 0.225$. The assumption of competitive markets implies that factor prices are equal to the value of the marginal product:

$$R_m(1 + \tau) = pQ_L, \tag{7.17}$$

$$w = pQ_N, \tag{7.18}$$

$$r(1 + \tau) = pQ_K, \tag{7.19}$$

where Q_i is the marginal product of the ith factor and τ is the real estate tax rate as a percentage of rent. Differentiation of the production function with respect to N and substitution into (7.17) gives

$$N^{\beta - 1} + K^\varepsilon = (w/a\beta)p^{-1}L^{-\alpha}. \tag{7.20}$$

Similarly, differentiation of the production function to obtain Q_K and substitution into (7.18) leads to

$$K^{-\alpha-\beta} + N^\beta = [r(1 + \tau)/a(1 - \alpha - \beta)]p^{-1}L^{-\alpha}. \tag{7.21}$$

Substitution for K in (7.20) generates the demand for labor as a function of w, $r(1 + \tau)$ and L. Several manipulations are required to obtain the result that

$$N^{-\alpha/(\alpha + \beta)} = (w/a\beta)[r(1 + \tau)/a\varepsilon]^{\varepsilon/(\alpha + \beta)}p^{-1/(\alpha + \beta)}L^{-\alpha - [\alpha\varepsilon/(\alpha + \beta)]}. \tag{7.22}$$

The addition of one unit of land will increase the demand for labor according to

$$d\ln N/d\ln L = -[(\alpha + \beta)/\alpha][(\alpha(\alpha + \beta - 1)/(\alpha + \beta)) - \alpha] = 1. \tag{7.23}$$

This last result implies that

$$dN/dL = (N/L), \tag{7.24}$$

or that the change in employment is employment density.

5   PROPERTY TAXATION

The provision of sites to industry is only one of many methods used by local governments in the effort to induce growth in the economic base. Other programs include tax cuts, low interest loans, outright grants for employee training and technical assistance. See McDonald (1997, p. 420) for a reasonably complete catalog of these policies. Often some of these other inducements are offered in conjunction with the provision of industrial sites. Sometimes other inducements are needed just to make the site provided equal in quality to alternative locations, but in other cases the idea is to channel industrial growth to the site provided. In this section the model is used to examine this latter case. Assume that the site in question has been made into a standard site in terms of quality and accessibility, and that property tax inducements are offered to *increase* the utilization of the site. Netzer (1966) provided a classic discussion of the economics of the local property tax.

A reduction in the real estate tax rate is often used to stimulate economic activity. See McDonald (1983, 1993) for further analysis of property tax reductions. From (7.22) the employment increase on the site in question can be written

$$-[d\ln(N/L)/d\ln(1+\tau_i)][d\ln(1+\tau_i)/d(100+100\tau_i)] = (\varepsilon/\alpha)(1/100(1+\tau_i))$$

$$= 3/100(1+\tau_i), \tag{7.25}$$

where τ_i is expressed in decimal form (for example, $\tau_i = 0.25$). A unit change in the real estate tax rate divided by 100 would, for example, reduce the tax rate from 25 per cent to 24 per cent of market rent on capital. The reduction in the real estate tax rate also applies to land, but this portion of the tax cut will be fully capitalized into the value of the land and result in no employment increase. Equation (7.25) can be rewritten:

$$-0.01d(N/L)/d(1+\tau_i) = [3/100(1+\tau_i)](N/L). \tag{7.26}$$

For example, if N/L in the absence of the tax cut is 100 workers per acre and $1+\tau_i = 0.25$, then a tax cut of one point to 24 per cent will increase employment by 2.4 workers.

The benefits and costs of the real estate tax cut for the local jurisdiction can be computed. The benefit of the employment increase is $fM(w + C - w^*)[3/100(1+\tau_i)](N/L)$. On the cost side, the tax cut applies to all capital on the site as well as to the land, or, from (7.7),

$$(1/100)(dT_i/d\tau_i) = (1/100)(rK + R_m). \tag{7.27}$$

The tax cut is fully capitalized into the value of the land.

The net benefits for the local jurisdiction of a unit real estate tax cut equal the benefits of the increase in employment:

$$NB = fM(w + C - w^*)[3/100(1+\tau_i)](N/L). \tag{7.28}$$

The net benefits for the nation of a unit real estate tax cut are

$$NB_n = M_n(w + U - w^*)[3/100(1+\tau_i)](N/L). \tag{7.29}$$

This section has considered a subsidy to a particular site in the form of a reduction in the property tax rate without regard to distributional effects. In this model of the 'open' local jurisdiction, the direct costs of subsidies are fully capitalized into the value of the land, so subsidies are redistributions from local taxpayers in general to the owner of the parcel of land. The local jurisdiction must decide whether the benefits of the employment gains can justify the redistribution that takes place.

6 PROPERTY TAXATION, ZONING AND THE SIZE OF THE LOCAL TAX BASE

This section presents a basic model of commercial and industrial real estate demand and supply that can be used to determine the effects of a change in the property tax rate on the market value of real estate and on property tax revenue in a local jurisdiction such as a county or municipality. As usual, it is assumed that real estate is an input into commercial and industrial production processes, and is a function of stocks of land L and structure capital K. The real estate input Θ is assumed to be weakly separable from other inputs such as labor and equipment. All actual or potential real estate developers of a site have identical CES production functions with constant returns to scale, written

$$\Theta = \Theta(L,K), \tag{7.30}$$

with σ denoting the elasticity of substitution.

The first task in establishing the links between the property tax and market value is to set out the relationship between the property tax as a percentage of market value and as a percentage of market rent. The market value of a unit of real property (one unit of Θ) of infinite life is

$$V = (\rho - tV)/i, \tag{7.31}$$

where ρ is the constant annual rent paid per unit of Θ, t is the property tax rate as a percentage of market value, and i is the real discount rate. This equation implies that $V/\rho = 1/(i + t)$, or that $i + t$ is the capitalization rate in this model. Define τ as the property tax rate as a percentage of annual rent, so

$$\tau \equiv tV/\rho = t/(i + t). \tag{7.32}$$

For example, if $t = 0.02$ and $i = 0.06$, then $\tau = 0.25$. Further, define rent received as $\acute{\rho} \equiv \rho - tV = \rho(1 - \tau)$.

The basic result of the model can be illustrated using a simple model of supply and demand for real estate in a local jurisdiction such as a county. Assume that the supply of real estate is expressed as a function of V, the market value per unit. This supply is influenced by zoning regulations. The demand for real estate would usually be expressed as a function of ρ, rent paid, but at a given capitalization rate it can also be expressed as a function of V. An increase in the property tax rate increases the capitalization rate and reduces the demand (as a function of V) because a given rent paid now translates into a lower market value per unit. Assuming that the supply curve has a positive slope, this shift in demand results in reductions in market value and the quantity of real estate in the county. Rent paid (ρ) will tend to adjust upwards, of course. Since both V and Θ decline in response to an increase in the tax rate, the effect on the tax base ($V\Theta$) can be sizable. Tax collections rise or fall, depending upon the size of the decline in the tax base. A mathematical model can be used to determine a rough estimate of these effects.

Define the demand and supply elasticities in quantity–rent space as

$$d\ln\Theta/d\ln\rho = \varepsilon_d < 0, \text{ and} \tag{7.33}$$

$$d\ln\Theta/d\ln\acute\rho = \varepsilon_s > 0. \tag{7.34}$$

A change in the property tax rate τ will change both ρ and $\acute\rho$, and cause the change in Θ, written

$$d\ln\Theta = \varepsilon_d d\ln\rho = \varepsilon_s d\ln\acute\rho. \tag{7.35}$$

From the definition of $\acute\rho \equiv \rho(1-\tau)$,

$$d\ln\rho = d\ln\acute\rho - d\ln(1-\tau). \tag{7.36}$$

These two equations imply that

$$d\ln\rho = -[1/(1 - \varepsilon_d/\varepsilon_s)]d\ln(1-\tau), \text{ and} \tag{7.37}$$

$$d\ln\Theta = -[\varepsilon_d/(1 - \varepsilon_d/\varepsilon_s)]d\ln(1-\tau). \tag{7.38}$$

Since V is the market value per unit of Θ, the market value of property is

$$V\Theta = \rho\Theta/(i+t). \tag{7.39}$$

Property tax collections are

$$t V \Theta = t \rho \Theta /(i + t) = \tau \rho \Theta. \tag{7.40}$$

The change in the market value of property in response to an increase in the property tax rate t in natural log form is

$$d\ln V\Theta/dt = [d\ln\rho/d\ln(1-\tau)][d\ln(1-\tau)/d\tau]d\tau/dt - d\ln(i+t)/dt +$$

$$[d\ln\Theta/d\ln(1-\tau)][d\ln(1-\tau)/d\tau]d\tau/dt. \tag{7.41}$$

Note that this change in market value consists of three parts: the effect on rent paid ρ, the effect on the capitalized value of rent paid, and the effect on quantity Θ. The effect on rent paid will be positive (or zero, as Wheaton, 1984, found in an empirical study of office rents). The effect on the capitalization rate $(i + t)$ is obviously positive, so the capitalized value of rent paid will fall. Finally, a higher tax rate will reduce quantity Θ to the extent that capital is mobile across counties in the metropolitan area.

Given that

$$d\tau/dt = i/(i + t)^2, \tag{7.42}$$

substitution into the equation for $d\ln V\Theta/dt$ produces

$$d\ln V\Theta/dt = [1/(1 - \varepsilon_d/\varepsilon_s)][1/(1-\tau)][i/(i+t)^2] - 1/(i+t) + [\varepsilon_d/(1 - \varepsilon_d/\varepsilon_s)]$$

$$[1/(1-\tau)][i/(i+t)^2] = [i/(i+t)^2(1-\tau)][\varepsilon_s(1+\varepsilon_d)/\varepsilon_s - \varepsilon_d)] - 1/(i+t). \tag{7.43}$$

The sign of the second term in brackets is determined by the demand and supply elasticities. Assuming $\varepsilon_s > 0$, this sign depends upon whether $\varepsilon_d < -1$. An elastic demand produces a negative sign. Indeed, if demand is elastic, the (negative) magnitude of $d\ln V\Theta/dt$ can be quite large. It is possible that there is elastic long-run demand for commercial or industrial real estate in a single county that is part of a large metropolitan area because it is easy to move activities across county boundaries without reducing appreciably access to markets for final output.

The effect of a change in the tax rate on tax collections can be found easily as

$$d\ln t V\Theta/dt = d\ln t\rho\Theta/(i+t) = (1/t) + d\ln V\Theta/dt. \tag{7.44}$$

Zoning regulations influence the elasticity of supply of commercial or industrial real estate in the long run, especially if the tax rate is *reduced*. A reduction in the tax rate creates incentives both to increase the amount of land devoted to the use that receives the tax reduction and to increase the intensity of land use in that sector. Muth (1964) shows that the supply of real estate for the sector in question is

$$\varepsilon_s = [\sigma(\Omega_L e_L + \Omega_s e_s) + e_{Ls}]/(\sigma + \Omega_s e_L + \Omega_L e_s), \qquad (7.45)$$

where Ω_i is the share and e_i is the elasticity of supply of the ith input (land or structure capital). It will be assumed that restrictive land use zoning means that $e_L = 0$, the elasticity of supply of land for the sector in question is zero. Likewise, restrictive land use intensity zoning means that $e_s = 0$, the elasticity of supply of structure capital is zero. If both types of zoning are in place, both input supply elasticities are zero. If neither type of zoning is used, the elasticity of supply of structure capital in the long run is infinite ($e_s = \infty$), and the elasticity of land supply is some finite positive number such as 1.0. These assumptions permit an examination of the possible effects of a cut in the tax rate on the tax base and tax collections under different zoning regimes.

In the numerical results that follow it is assumed that $i = 0.06$ (real interest rate), $t = 0.02$ (property tax rate of 2 per cent of market value), $\tau = 0.25$ and $\Omega_L = 0.2$ (share of land equals 20 per cent), and $\Omega_s = 0.8$. Empirical evidence reviewed by McDonald (1983) indicates that the elasticity of substitution in the office real estate sector exceeds 1.0 (assume $\sigma = 1.2$), but that σ is about 0.7 in the manufacturing and commercial real estate sectors. Additional empirical work is still needed on production functions with land included. The change in t is 0.01.

The numerical results for various cases are shown in Table 7.1. Results are shown separately for the office and manufacturing/commercial sectors for the four zoning regimes under three alternative demand assumptions. In the first set of results the demand for real estate in the jurisdiction is assumed to be of infinite elasticity. In the second set of results the demand is assumed to be elastic (ε_d set at -2), and in the third set of results demand is inelastic ($\varepsilon_d = -0.5$). The magnitude of this demand elasticity is unknown, but presumably smaller jurisdictions face highly elastic demand in the long run. Indeed, a small jurisdiction located in a larger metropolitan area may face a very elastic demand indeed. Whether large jurisdictions face elastic demand is not known, so the case of inelastic demand is included for illustration. It turns out that the results for the two sectors are very similar, so the following discussion refers only to the office sector.

The results in Table 7.1 show clearly that a decrease in the property tax rate will increase the tax base and in most cases reduce tax revenues in the long run, and that the nature of the zoning regime has a sizable influence

Table 7.1   Effects of marginal decrease in the property tax rate

	Tax base		Tax revenue	
	Office	Man./Comm.	Office	Man./Comm.
No zoning ($e_s = \infty, e_L = 1$)				
Perfectly elastic demand	135.00%	110.00%	85.00%	60.00%
Elastic demand (-2)	22.88	22.45	-27.12	-27.55
Inelastic demand (-0.5)	6.55	7.77	-43.45	-42.33
Land use zoning ($e_s = \infty, e_L = 0$)				
Perfectly elastic demand	72.50	47.50	22.50	-2.50
Elastic demand (-2)	21.32	19.79	-28.68	-30.21
Inelastic demand (-0.5)	6.84	7.20	-43.16	-42.80
Density zoning ($e_s = 0, e_L = 1$)				
Perfectly elastic demand	14.38	13.62	-35.62	-36.38
Elastic demand (-2)	13.37	13.04	-36.63	-36.96
Inelastic demand (-0.5)	11.06	11.55	-38.94	-38.45
Both types of zoning ($e_s = 0, e_L = 0$)				
Nonzero demand elasticity	12.50	12.50	-37.50	-37.50

Note: Computations assume $i = 0.06$, $t = 0.02$, $\tau = 0.25$, $\sigma = 1.2$ for office and 0.7 for manufacturing/commercial. Given these assumptions, $-d\ln V\Theta/dt = -12.5[\varepsilon_s(1 + \varepsilon_d)/(\varepsilon_s - \varepsilon_d) - 12.5$ and $-d\ln t V\Theta/dt = -d\ln V\Theta/dt - 50$.

Supply elasticities for real estate are:

	Office	Manuf./Comm.
No zoning	9.8	7.8
Land use zoning	4.8	2.8
Density zoning	0.15	0.09
Both types of zoning	0.0	0.0

See text for supply elasticity formula.

on the outcomes. If demand is infinitely elastic, in the absence of zoning a property tax cut will increase the tax base by such a large amount (135 per cent in the office sector) that tax collections also increase by a large amount (85 per cent in the office sector). The Laffer Curve lives if the tax base is *very* responsive to a tax cut. On the other hand, if zoning prevents the increase in the tax base, then the value of the tax base increases only by 12.5 per cent and tax revenues decline.

If demand elasticity is -2, compared to the jurisdiction with both land use and density zoning, the jurisdiction with no zoning constraints gains almost twice the tax base (22.88 per cent versus 12.5 per cent in the office sector) and loses less tax revenue (27.12 per cent versus 37.5 per cent in the office sector). In contrast, if demand is inelastic, the jurisdiction without zoning constraints gains only about one-half of the tax base that is gained by the jurisdiction with both types of zoning constraints (6.55 per cent versus 12.5 per cent in the office sector). The jurisdiction without zoning constraints suffers the larger loss in tax revenue (43.45 per cent versus 37.5 per cent in the office sector) if demand is inelastic.

The jurisdiction that imposes only land use zoning has outcomes that are very close to the results for the jurisdiction without zoning. As one would expect, then, the jurisdiction with only density zoning has outcomes that differ only slightly from those for the jurisdiction with both land use and density zoning. Density zoning is by far the more effective constraint on development because the long-run supply of structure capital would be infinite in the absence of density zoning, but the long-run supply of land in a jurisdiction for a particular sector is probably finite in the absence of land use zoning (and assumed equal to 1.0 in these computations).

The model presented in this section can be used by jurisdictions to obtain rough estimates of the effects of property tax cuts provided that estimates of the various parameters are available. Clearly, more empirical work is needed. The results in Table 7.1 suggest that the greatest need is for estimates of the elasticity of demand for real estate in various types of local jurisdictions (for example, small jurisdictions versus large jurisdictions, in larger metropolitan areas versus smaller metropolitan areas). The results are less sensitive to assumed alternative values for the elasticity of substitution between structure capital and land in the production of real estate, but further empirical work on this underlying production function may reveal that the range for this parameter is greater than has been assumed here (0.7 to 1.2).

7   COST–BENEFIT ANALYSIS OF ZONING AT THE BLOCK LEVEL

The models developed in this chapter thus far have not considered zoning for the purpose of mitigating the impacts of external effects. This section contains a simple model of land use, land values and zoning in the presence of externalities that has been estimated empirically. The unit of analysis is the 'block', an area that is small enough for externalities to matter, but an area that is larger than the amount of land normally owned by a single owner. The external effects contemplated are localized to the block level and result from the mixing of land uses on the block. In contrast, if the external effects were generated by a large plant, it would be appropriate to represent the harm incurred by distance from a residence to the plant. It is assumed that the externality incurred by residential land users is a function of the proportion of the block that is in nonresidential use.

The model can be formulated as a nonlinear programming problem which extends the model developed by Crone (1983). The presentation here follows McMillen and McDonald (1993). The problem under consideration is the maximization of land on the block with respect to the proportion of land in residential use. The problem is to maximize

$$V = \kappa_r v_r(\kappa_r) A + (1 - \kappa_r) v_c(\kappa_r) A, \tag{7.46}$$

where

V = total land value for the block,
A = area of the block,
κ_r = proportion of the block in residential use,
$v_r(\kappa_r)$ = land value per square foot for residential land (a function of κ_r), and
$v_c(\kappa_r)$ = land value per square foot for nonresidential land.

Because A is a given constant for any particular block, the objective function can be rewritten as

$$V/A = v(\kappa_r) = \kappa_r v_r + (1 - \kappa_r) v_c. \tag{7.47}$$

We therefore maximize average land value subject to $\kappa_r \leq 1$ and $\kappa_r \geq 0$.

Externalities enter because v_r and v_c are functions of κ_r. Designate $v'_r = dv_r/d\kappa_r$ and $v'_c = dv_c/d\kappa_r$. The signs of these derivatives are indeterminate. The usual notion of a negative external effect of nonresidential use on residential use means $v'_r > 0$. However, if residents also value close proximity to jobs and shopping, it is possible that $v'_r < 0$. Nonresidential activities may benefit from close proximity to the residences of shoppers and workers ($v'_c > 0$), or there may be agglomeration economies at the block level that dominate ($v'_c > 0$). It is possible, of course, that none of these effects exists at the block level or that positive and negative external effects offset each other. Also, as Crone (1983) pointed out, the existence of an externality raises the possibility that the production possibility set for the block is nonconvex.

The Lagrangian function is

$$\Lambda = v + \mu(1 - \kappa_r), \tag{7.48}$$

where μ is the Lagrange multiplier. The first-order conditions can be written

$$d\Lambda/d\kappa_r = v' - \mu \leq 0,$$
$$\kappa_r \geq 0,$$
$$\kappa_r(d\Lambda/d\kappa_r) = \kappa_r(v' - \mu) = 0,$$
$$d\Lambda/d\mu = 1 - \kappa_r \geq 0,$$
$$\mu \geq 0,$$

and

$$\mu(1 - \kappa_r) = 0.$$

Three types of solutions for relative extrema can be enumerated: two boundary solutions ($\kappa_r = 0$ and $\kappa_r = 1$) and an interior solution.

Consider first the boundary solution where $\kappa_r = 0$, the case in which land value is maximized with no residential use on the block. The conditions for this solution are that $(v' - \mu) < 0$ and $\mu = 0$, so $v' < 0$. This result implies simply that, at $\kappa_r = 0$, an increase in κ_r from zero will reduce the total value of land on the block. The value of v' can be written

$$v' = v_r + \kappa_r v'_r + (1 - \kappa_r)v'_c - v_c. \tag{7.49}$$

At $\kappa_r = 0$, $v' < 0$ implies that

$$v_c > v_r + v'_c, \tag{7.50}$$

which states that the opportunity cost of residential land (v_c) exceeds the gain from allocating land to residential use ($v_r + v'_c$).

Next consider the boundary solution where $\kappa_r = 1$, the case in which land value is maximized with no nonresidential use on the block. The conditions for this solution are that $v' - \mu = 0$ and $\mu > 0$, so $v' > 0$. The equation (7.49) for v' is shown above, so that $v' > 0$ at $\kappa_r = 1$ reduces to

$$v_r > v_c - v'_r. \tag{7.51}$$

This condition states that the opportunity cost of nonresidential land (v_r) exceeds the gain from allocating land to nonresidential use ($v_c - v'_r$).

Finally, consider the interior solution for the maximization of v. Since $0 < \kappa_r < 1$, the first-order condition reduces to $v' = 0$, or

$$v_c = v_r + \kappa_r v'_r + (1 - \kappa_r)v'_c. \tag{7.52}$$

In other words, the marginal opportunity cost of residential land equals the marginal gain from allocating land to residential use. (Note that the maximization of land value on the block when mixed land use is indicated generally does not occur where $v_r = v_c$.)

The second-order condition for the interior solution can be written

$$v'' = 2v'_r + \kappa_r v''_r - 2v'_c + (1 - \kappa_r)v''_c < 0. \tag{7.53}$$

If $v''_r = v''_c = 0$, the second-order condition reduces to

$$v'_r = v'_c, \tag{7.54}$$

which implies that further increases in κ_r would increase v_c by more than v_r.

The first-order condition for the interior solution can be solved for κ_r:

$$\kappa_r = (v_c - v_r - v'_c)/(v'_r - v'_c). \tag{7.55}$$

The denominator of this expression must be negative and, since $\kappa_r > 0$,

$$v_c < v_r + v'_c \tag{7.56}$$

at an interior maximum.

The global maximum still must be found. If more than one local maximum exists, the values of v for each must be compared. For example, it is possible that both boundary solutions are local maxima. This would occur if, for example, $v' < 0$ at $\kappa_r = 0$, $v'' > 0$ and $v' > 0$ at $\kappa_r = 1$. In other words, v is declining at $\kappa_r = 0$, reaches a minimum at some interior point, and then rises to $\kappa_r = 1$. Assuming that $v''_r = v''_c = 0$, $v'' > 0$ if $v'_r > v'_c$. This is the case of externalities leading to a nonconvex production possibility set that was examined by Crone (1983).

The Competitive Market

Given these solutions to the problem of the maximization of land value, how will the private, unregulated market allocate land? The answer to this question depends upon the ownership, the cost of making transactions and/or the nonconvexity of the production possibility set. Clearly, if the block is owned by one person, κ_r will be chosen to maximize the value of the land on the block. Furthermore, a block with multiple ownership will exhibit the κ_r that maximizes land value so long as the Coase (1960) theorem holds. As Crone (1983, p.169) notes, the Coase theorem states that, if property rights are clearly defined and freely transferable with zero transaction costs, private negotiations will produce the efficient allocation of land, provided that externalities do not generate nonconvex production sets. Note that the efficient allocation of land might involve the mixing of land uses on the block in accordance with the first-order condition for an interior maximum, and that the private market might be capable of achieving this allocation.

Failure of the Coase theorem in the multiple ownership case can produce a κ_r that does not maximize land value. If multiple ownership exists and the Coase theorem fails, the private market will exhibit

$$v_c > v_r \text{ for } \kappa_r = 0,$$
$$v_c < v_r \text{ for } \kappa_r = 1,$$

and

$$v_c = v_r \text{ for } 0 < \kappa_r < 1.$$

The allocation of land can be inefficient because the private owners ignore the external effect of increasing (or decreasing) κ_r on square-foot land values (the v'_r and v'_c terms). As one would expect, the allocation of land in this fragmented ownership case is efficient if $v'_r = v'_c = 0$; in this case both optimal and market values of κ_r equal zero if $v_c > v_r$, and both optimal and market values of κ_r equal one if $v_c < v_r$. Of course, if $v_c = v_r$, any value of κ_r maximizes land values when $v'_r = v'_c = 0$.

In addition, the market allocation of land under fragmented ownership is a local maximum of $\kappa_r = 0$ if $v_c > v_r$ obtains when $v_c > v_r + v'_c$. The market allocation of $\kappa_r = 0$ is locally inefficient when $v_c > v_r$ but $v_c < v_r + v'_c$. Similarly, the market allocation at $\kappa_r = 1$ is locally efficient if $v_r > v_c - v'_r$, and is locally inefficient if the inequality is reversed. In summary, the case of fragmented ownership in the presence of externalities with the failure of the Coase theorem is generally associated with an inefficient allocation of land if land use is mixed. Also, if the market allocates land exclusively to one use, this allocation is (locally) efficient except under the conditions noted.

Zoning to Increase Land Values

Given this model of land use and land values, what might be accomplished by block-level zoning? Two types of zoning are considered. Zoning might be an instrument for 'fine-tuning' the allocation of land to maximize land values, or it might be a blunt instrument that assigns a block to be residential. The zoning as fine-tuning ordinance would alter the market allocation of land only when the market failed to be efficient – the case of fragmented ownership and the failure of the Coase theorem. An improvement in the allocation of land might require a boundary solution, but it also might require mixed land use in accordance with the interior optimality condition above.

The first case in which exclusive residential zoning could increase land values is when the competitive market leads to mixed use on the block, in which case $v_r = v_c$. Let κ_r^* be the proportion of land in residential use when $v_r = v_c$. Exclusive residential zoning can increase the value of land if $v_r(1) > v_r(\kappa_r^*)$. This condition clearly requires that the residential land value function be upward-sloping over some range, although it need not slope upward at either κ_r^* or $\kappa_r = 1$. The global maximum in land value may occur at $\kappa_r = 1$, but it could occur at some other value. Thus a zoning ordinance that assigned a mixed-use block exclusively to residential use could increase, but not necessarily maximize, land value.

There is also a case in which the market leads to exclusive nonresidential use on a block, but the value of land would be higher with exclusive residential use. This case must have $v_c(0) > v_r(0)$ so that there is no incentive for a single owner of a small amount of land to convert from nonresidential to residential use. Also the value of land in exclusive residential use must be higher than existing land value; that is, $v_r(1) > v_c(0)$. Again, this condition implies that the residential land value function must have an upward slope over some range. Also exclusive residential zoning may not maximize land values even if it increases them.

Empirical Evidence

The model discussed in this section implies that a necessary condition for the assignment of a block exclusively to residential use to increase land value is that residential land values rise with the proportion of the block in residential use (over some range). Empirical land value functions were estimated by McMillen and McDonald (1993) for Chicago in 1921, two years before the first zoning ordinance was adopted. This study found that residential land values did not increase with the proportion of land in residential use on the block, so the conclusion was reached that the zoning system that was adopted in 1923 could not have brought about a general increase in land values. However, a subsequent study by McMillen and McDonald (2002) found that land zoned for residential use increased in value more rapidly after 1923 than did land assigned to commercial use. The conclusion that can be reached as a result of these two studies is that residential zoning provided a kind of insurance policy against the invasion of commercial or industrial activity that would create strongly negative external effects, even though such invasion had not generally been the case prior to zoning. Apparently, the value of residential zoning was a value attached to a reduction in a form of risk.

8   CONCLUSIONS

This chapter provides a set of related models of the land market and land use intensity that can be used to assess the effects of a variety of local zoning and property taxation policies on land values, employment, local property tax base and other related variables. The models are applications of conventional microeconomic theory in which urban land is an input into the production of urban goods: housing or commercial or industrial outputs produced on urban land. In each case the goal is to formulate a relevant model that requires only a few parameter values for application to specific situations. Given estimates of parameter values, cost–benefit analyses of particular policy actions can be undertaken.

The models included in the chapter are: (1) cost–benefit analysis of land use allocation decisions, (2) cost–benefit analysis of land use intensity regulations, (3) cost–benefit analysis of a property tax subsidy to an industrial or commercial site, (4) a market model of property taxation and the size of the local tax base, and (5) cost–benefit analysis of zoning at the block level with externalities.

Additional versions of the models can be developed for other uses. For example, McDonald (1983) explored the effects of variations in the property tax rate applied only to capital or only to land on land value, land use intensity and employment at an urban site.

APPENDIX: A MODEL WITH FINITE DEMAND ELASTICITIES

The discussion in section 2 above is based on a very simple model in which all demands and supplies (except for the supply of land) are of infinite elasticity. This appendix presents a somewhat more complex model that permits the demands for housing and industrial output that the local jurisdiction faces to be of finite elasticity. This modification of the model is important because it produces a convenient method for separating the increase in economic activity on a marginal site into the portion that is net growth in the jurisdiction and the part that 'moved' from other locations within the jurisdiction. In this appendix the effects of policy actions are examined only from the standpoint of the local jurisdiction.

First consider the housing market. The local jurisdiction is not perfectly 'open', so the provision of an additional site for housing will result in net increases for the jurisdiction in households and housing produced that are less than the amounts that appear on that site. On a net basis, some households and their housing capital already located in the jurisdiction 'move' to the new site.

Housing is produced in the local jurisdiction according to

$$H = c\, K_h{}^\mu L_h{}^\delta,\tag{7A.1}$$

with $\mu + \delta = 1$, where H, K_h, and L_h refer to the output and inputs for the entire local jurisdiction. The demand for housing faced by the local jurisdiction is

$$p_h = gH^s,\tag{7A.2}$$

where the elasticity of demand is $1/s$. Competitive input markets ensure that

$$r(1 + \tau_h) = p_h H_k \text{ and}\tag{7A.3}$$

$$R_h(1 + \tau_h) = p_h H_L,\tag{7A.4}$$

where H_k (H_L) is the marginal product of capital (land). Substitution for p_h (from the demand function) and for H_k in equation (7A.3) produces the demand function for K_h:

$$[\mu(s+1) - 1]\ln K_h = \ln[r(1 + \tau_h)/\mu g] - (s+1)\ln c - \delta(s+1)\ln L_h.\tag{7A.5}$$

An increase in land allocated to housing causes K_h to increase according to

$$d\ln K_h/d\ln L_h = -\delta(s+1)/[\mu(s+1)-1], \qquad (7A.6)$$

or

$$dK_h/dL_h = -\{\delta(s+1)/[\mu(s+1)-1]\}\,(K_h/L_h). \qquad (7A.7)$$

Clearly, if $s=0$, $dK_h/dL_h = K_h/L_h$ (infinite demand elasticity case).

If demand is less than perfectly elastic, $dK_h/dL_h < K_h/L_h$, which means that the ratio of capital to land declines and the land rent falls as well. For example, if $s=-1$, then $dK_h/dL_h = 0$: the case in which a constant amount of capital is 'spread out' over a (marginally) larger land area. A more general result can be found by solving equation (7A.7) for $k_h = K_h/L_h$, the ratio of capital to land:

$$\ln k_h = [1/\mu(s+1)-1]\ln[r(1+\tau_h)/\mu g] - [(s+1)/\mu(s+1)-1]\ln c$$

$$- [s/\mu(s+1)-1]\ln L_h. \qquad (7A.8)$$

Therefore

$$dk_h/dL_h = -[s/\mu(s+1)-1]k_h/L_h \le 0. \qquad (7A.9)$$

The total change in capital dK_h/dL_h consists of two parts, written

$$d(k_h L_h)/dL_h = k_h + L_h(dk_h/dL_h) = k_h[1 + s/(1 - \mu(s+1))]. \qquad (7A.10)$$

A site that is newly allocated to residential use will have a capital–land ratio of k_h. In the long run the fraction $s/[1 - \mu(s+1)]$ of that capital will have 'moved' from other locations in the jurisdiction. For example, suppose that demand is elastic and equal to -2 ($s=-1/2$) and the share of capital in the production of housing is 80 per cent ($\mu=0.80$). Then

$$d(k_h L_h)/dL_h = k_h[1 - 0.833] = 0.167 k_h;$$

83.3 per cent of the capital on the site in question will have moved from other locations in the jurisdiction. If demand is inelastic and equal to $-1/2$ ($s=-2$), then (with $\mu=0.80$)

$$d(k_h L_h)/dL_h = k_h[1 - 1.67] = -0.67 k_h.$$

The total amount of housing capital in the jurisdiction is reduced.

The change in land rent can be found by solving the system of equations for $R_h(1+\tau_h)$, by substituting for p_h and H_L in equation (7A.4). The result is that

$$
\begin{aligned}
\ln R_h + \ln(1+\tau_h) = \ln(g\delta) &- [(1+s)/\mu(1+s)-1]\ln c \quad\quad\text{(7A.11)}\\
&+ [\mu(1+s)/\mu(1+s)-1]\ln[r(1+\tau_h)/\mu g]\\
&+ [-(\mu\delta(1+s)^2/\mu(1+s)-1)+\delta(1+s)-1]\ln L_h.
\end{aligned}
$$

The marginal effect of L_h on R_h is therefore

$$
dR_h/dL_h = (R_h/L_h)[-(\mu\delta(1+s)^2/\mu(1+s)-1)+\delta(1+s)-1]\le 0. \quad\text{(7A.12)}
$$

With constant returns to scale ($\delta+\mu=1$), this expression reduces to zero if $s=0$ (infinite demand elasticity). But, if $s=-1$ for example, then

$$
dR_h/dL_h = -R_h/L_h. \quad\quad\text{(7A.13)}
$$

The benefits of allocating the unit parcel of land to housing are now

$$
\begin{aligned}
B_h &= R_h + L_h(dR_h/dL_h) + \tau_h[d(p_h H)/dL_h] - dG/dL_h \quad\text{(7A.14)}\\
&= R_h + L_h(dR_h/dL_h) + p_h\tau_h(dH/dL_h) + \tau_h H(dp_h/dL_h) - dG/dL_h.
\end{aligned}
$$

Here the quantity dG/dL_h is the change in expenditures on local public goods and services that are required. The quantity dH/dL_h is found by noting that $d\ln H = \mu d\ln K_h + \delta d\ln L_h$ and inserting the solution for $d\ln Kh/d\ln L_h$ from equation (7A.6) above. The result is that

$$
dH/dL_h = \delta[1-(\mu(s+1)/\mu(s+1)-)]H/L_h, \quad\quad\text{(7A.15)}
$$

which equals H/L_h when $s=0$. Similarly note that

$$
dp_h/dL_h = s\delta[1-(\mu(s+1)/\mu(s+1)-1)]p_h/L_h, \quad\quad\text{(7A.16)}
$$

which reduces to 0 when $s=0$.

The benefits of allocating the unit of land to housing are thus

$$
\begin{aligned}
B_h &= R_h + R_h[(-\mu\delta(1+s)^2/\mu(1+s)-1)+\delta(s+1)-1] \quad\text{(7A.17)}\\
&+ (\tau_h p_h H/L_h)[\delta(1+s)(1-(\mu(1+s)/\mu(1+s)-1)]-dG/dL_h.
\end{aligned}
$$

With perfectly elastic demand ($s=0$), this expression reduces to

$$
B_h = R_h + (\tau_h p_h H/L_h) - dG/dL_h. \quad\quad\text{(7A.17')}
$$

This expression is just $R_h + T_h$, that is, identical to equation (7A.6), for the case of $s=0$. If $s<0$, then R_h falls and the additional taxes collected are less than if demand were perfectly elastic (that is, the second expression in brackets in equation (7A.17) is less than 1). For example, if $s = -1$, then $B_h = -dG/dL_h$, where dG/dL_h is the change in local public expenditures needed to serve the jurisdiction with the added land devoted to housing. The demand for housing must be elastic for the net benefits to exceed zero even if the additional local public expenditures required are zero.

The term dG/dL_h may appear to be innocuous in equations (7A.14) and (7A.17), but careful study of the projected change in local public expenditures will be needed to implement the model. If the local jurisdiction is perfectly 'open', then the number of households located on the site in question equals the net gain in households for the jurisdiction. There is no impact on the number of households (and their demands for local public expenditures) elsewhere in the jurisdiction, so the local public expenditures devoted to the site in question are also the net increase in local public expenditures. However, if the local jurisdiction is not perfectly 'open' (that is, the demand for housing is not perfectly elastic), then the rest of the jurisdiction experiences a loss in households. One could estimate this loss as proportional to the amount of housing capital that 'moved' from other locations in the jurisdiction according to equation (7A.10). For example, in the numerical example following equation (7A.10) with demand elasticity equal to -2, 83.3 per cent of the capital on the site in question 'moved' from elsewhere in the jurisdiction. If the site provides housing for 100 households, we would estimate that 83 of these households moved from elsewhere in the jurisdiction. This net movement of households will likely permit there to be some reduction in local public expenditures in those areas from which these households moved (for example, fewer public school teachers needed). The extent to which local public expenditures can be shifted from one location to another as households move is a crucial empirical issue that must be investigated.

The industrial sector of the jurisdiction in question also faces a demand of finite elasticity, with $p = bQ^e$. The elasticity of demand is $-1/e$. Solution of the model proceeds as in the presentation of the model of urban production in section 4 above, except that bQ^e is substituted for p in equations (7.16), (7.17) and (7.18). Two simultaneous equations can be obtained from equations (7.20) and (7.21), written in matrix form;

$$\begin{bmatrix} \beta(1+e)-1 & \varepsilon(1+e) \\ \beta(1+e) & \varepsilon(1+e)-1 \end{bmatrix} = \begin{bmatrix} \ln N \\ \ln K \end{bmatrix}$$

$$\begin{bmatrix} \ln(w/\beta b) - (1+e)\ln a - \alpha(1+e)\ln L \\ \ln r(1+\tau)/\varepsilon b - (1+e)\ln a - \alpha(1+e)\ln L \end{bmatrix} \qquad (7A.18)$$

Inverting the 2×2 matrix on the left-hand side yields the solution

$$
\begin{vmatrix} \ln N \\ \\ \ln K \end{vmatrix} = \begin{vmatrix} [\varepsilon(1+e)-1]/\Phi & -\varepsilon(1+e)/\Phi \\ & \\ -\beta(1+e)/\Phi & [\beta(1+e)-1]/\Phi \end{vmatrix} \mathbf{E}, \quad (7A.19)
$$

where $\Phi = 1 - (1+e)(\beta+\varepsilon)$ and $\mathbf{E}$ is the matrix on the right-hand side of equation (7A.18). In addition, land rent equals the value of the marginal product, or

$$
R(1+\tau) = ba Q^{1+e} L^{-1} = baa^{1+e} L^{\alpha(1+e)-1} N^{\beta(1+e)} K^{\varepsilon(1+e)}. \quad (7A.20)
$$

The solutions for N and K can be inserted into equation (7A.20), and the effects on R of changes in the exogenous variables can be found. A full set of comparative statics results is displayed in Table 7A.1.

The results for employment change deserve a further look. From Table 7A.1, an increase in land allocated to industrial use results in an increase in employment in the jurisdiction of $na(1+e)/[1-(1+e)(\beta+\varepsilon)]$, where n is employment density (N/L). Note that the employment increase for the jurisdiction reduces to $n = N/L$ with perfectly elastic demand $(e=0)$. The magnitude of the employment increase is very sensitive to the elasticity of demand for the industrial output; if this elasticity is -2 $(e=-0.5)$ the increase in employment is only $0.07n$ (that is, only 7 per cent on the employment on the site represents a net gain for the jurisdiction), but if the elasticity is -10 $(e=-0.1)$ the employment increase is $0.403n$.

It is also true that

$$
dN/dL = d(nL)/dL = n + L(dn/dL). \quad (7A.21)
$$

The change in employment consists of two parts, the increase in employment on the site newly allocated to industrial use (n), and the decline in employment that occurs elsewhere in the jurisdiction $[L(dn/dL)]$. From Table 7A.1,

$$
dn/dL = e/[1 - (1+e)(\beta+\varepsilon)]. \quad (7A.22)
$$

(The two expressions for dN/dL are equal, as the reader can verify.) For example, if $e=-1$ (unitary elasticity of demand), then $L(dn/dL) = -L$ and one worker 'moves' from each unit of industrial land to the additional unit industrial site in question. Total employment in the jurisdiction does not necessarily increase; it increases provided that

$$
n > eL/[1-(1+e)(\beta+\varepsilon)].
$$

Table 7A.1   Comparative statics results: industrial sector

Independent variable	Dependent variable		
	Capital $(\ln K)$	Labor $(\ln N)$	Land rent $(\ln R)$
Land $(\ln L)$[a]	$\alpha(1+e)/\Phi$	$\alpha(1+e)/\Phi$	$\alpha(1+e)-1$
Wage $(\ln w)$	$-\beta(1+e)/\Phi$	$[\varepsilon(1+e)-1]/\Phi$	$-\beta(1+e)/\Phi$
Return to capital $(\ln r)$	$[\beta(1+e)-1]/\Phi$	$-\varepsilon(1+e)/\Phi$	$-\varepsilon(1+e)/\Phi$
Property tax rate $[\ln(1+\tau)]$	$[\beta(1+e)-1]/\Phi$	$-\varepsilon(1+e)/\Phi$	$-\varepsilon(1+e)/\Phi$

Note: [a] As in the text, $\Phi = 1-(1+e)(\beta+\varepsilon)$.

The formula for the computation of the net benefits to the jurisdiction of allocating the unit land parcel to industrial use can now be obtained. The opportunity cost is the allocation of the parcel to residential use (that is, equation (7A.14) or (7A.17)) or leaving the parcel vacant if the opportunity cost of residential use is negative. The benefits generated for the jurisdiction by industrial use are

$$B = R + (dR/dL)L + dT_m/dL + (dN/dL)fM(w+C-w^*), \quad (7A.23)$$

where **L** is the total amount of land in the jurisdiction devoted to industrial use. Industrial property taxes (with a 10 per cent interest rate) are

$$T_m = \tau[(rK+RL)/0.1] - G, \text{ so}$$
$$dT_m/dL = 10\tau[r(dK/dL) + R + L(dR/dL)] - dG/dL. \quad (7A.24)$$

Values for dR/dL, dK/dL and dN/dL can be found by using the formulae in Table 7A.1. In particular,

$$dR/dL = (d\ln R/d\ln L)R/L,$$
$$dN/dL = (d\ln N/d\ln L)N/L,$$

and

$$dK/dL = (d\ln K/d\ln L)K/L,$$

where the elasticities in parentheses are shown in the first row in the table. The quantities R/L, N/L and K/L must be obtained for the local jurisdiction in question. The magnitude of $dG/d\mathbf{L}$ must also be investigated. (As before, any program cost P is included in the computation of net benefits.)

One important result that can be found immediately is that $B=0$ if $1/e = -1$, $B>0$ if $1/e<-1$ (elastic demand) and $B<0$ if $1/e>-1$ (inelastic demand). The jurisdiction must face an elastic demand for its industrial product for the gross benefit of allocating the unit parcel to industrial use to exceed zero. However, recall that a similar condition was found for the housing sector; the opportunity cost in equation (7A.17) above is positive if the demand for housing is elastic. The net benefit of allocating the unit parcel to industrial use is

$$NB = B - B_h - P \text{ if } B_h > 0, \text{ or } NB = B - P \text{ if } B_h \leq 0. \qquad (7A.25)$$

If $B_h < 0$, the better alternative to industrial use is to leave the land vacant, if such an option is possible. Furthermore, if $B<P$ and $B_h<0$, the best option is to leave the land vacant.

To illustrate the results in this appendix, consider the numerical example from section 2 above, modified to include finite demand elasticities for housing and industrial output (value added).

The net benefits of allocating the parcel of 11 acres to 330 units of housing are based on equation (7A.17). Three parameter values are needed; assume that the elasticity of demand for housing faced by the local jurisdiction is -2 ($s = -0.5$), the share of capital in the production of housing (μ) is 0.8, and the share of land (δ) is 0.2. These parameter values mean that

$$B_h = R_h + R_h(-0.833) + (\tau_h p_h H/L_h)(0.167) - dG/dL_h.$$

Recall that $R_h = \$718\,740$ and annual property tax collections on the site are $\$1\,485\,000$, so

$$B_h = 120\,030 + 247\,995 - dG/dL_h,$$

where dG/dL_h is the net increase in expenditures on local public services that are required. Recall from the previous discussion that, if the demand for housing has as an elasticity of -2, 83.3 per cent of the capital on the site 'moved' from other locations within the local jurisdiction. For this example it will be assumed that 83.3 per cent of the households on the site moved from these other locations – and brought all of their local public expenditures with them. The net increase in local public expenditures is therefore 16.7 per cent of the amount in section 3, above; that is, 16.7 per cent of \$2 million. In this case the net benefits of allocating the site to residential use are $28 025 per year, a result that depends critically upon the degree to which local public expenditures can be shifted from other locations to the site in question.

The net benefits of allocating the parcel to industrial use are based on equation (7A.23). Parameter values assumed are as before; an elasticity of demand for the industrial product of -2 ($e = -0.5$), and factor shares for land, labor and capital of 0.075, 0.7 and 0.225, respectively. The change in land allocated to industrial use is 11 acres, the floor–area ratio is 0.59 ($K/L = 0.59$) and employment on the site is 337 ($N/L = 30.64$ employees per acre). Each employee occupies 840 square feet of space ($N/K = 0.00119$). Also, as McDonald (1984) reported, 6 per cent of the usable land area in the city of Chicago is devoted to industry, which means that the total land supplied for industrial use is 8000 acres. At a price of $5 per square foot, each acre is worth $217 800 (annual rent of $21 780 if the interest rate is 10 per cent). Recall from section 2 that the annual rent for capital is $11.07 per square foot.

The terms in equation (7A.23) are as follows:

$$R + (dR/dL)L = 239\,580 - [(11)(d\ln R/d\ln L)R/L]L$$
$$= 239\,580 - 11(0.93)(21,780)$$
$$= 239\,580 - 222\,809 = 16\,771$$
$$dT_m/dL = 10\tau[r(dK/dL) + R + L(dR/dL)] - dG/dL$$
$$= 0.35[(11.07)(11)(0.07)K/L) + 16,771] - dG/dL$$
$$= 0.35[(8.524)(25\,700) + 16\,771] - dG/dL$$
$$= 82\,543 - dG/dL.$$
$$(dN/dL)fM(w + C - w^*) = 11(0.07)(30.64)(1270) = 29\,963.$$

The annual benefit of devoting the 11 acres to industrial use is

$$B = 129\,277 - dG/dL.$$

Recall that $1 000 000 in local public expenditures are supplied to the site annually. We have seen that only 7 per cent of the capital and employment on the site are net gains for the jurisdiction. If $dG/dL = $70 000$ (that is, public expenditures can be perfectly shifted to the new location), then annual benefits are $59 277 (only 7 per cent of the benefits in the case of perfectly elastic demand). If public expenditures are not perfectly shiftable, then the annual benefits of industrial development could be negative.

REFERENCES

Bartik, Timothy, 1990, 'The Market Failure Approach to Regional Economic Development Policy', *Economic Development Quarterly*, 4, 361–70.

Bartik, Timothy, 1991, *Who Benefits from State and Local Economic Development Policies?*, Kalamazoo, MI: W.E. Upjohn Institute.

Coase, Ronald, 1960, 'The Problem of Social Cost', *Journal of Law and Economics*, 3, 1–44.

Courant, Paul, 1994, 'How Would You Know a Good Economic Development Policy If You Tripped Over One? Hint: Don't Just Count Jobs', *National Tax Journal*, 47, 863–81.

Crone, Theodore, 1983, 'Elements of an Economic Justification for Municipal Zoning', *Journal of Urban Economics*, 14, 168–83.

Feldstein, Martin and J. Poterba, 1984, 'Unemployment Insurance and Reservation Wages', *Journal of Public Economics*, 23, 141–67.

Felsenstein, Daniel and J. Persky, 1999, 'When Is a Cost Really a Benefit? Local Welfare Effects and Employment Creation in the Evaluation of Economic Development Programs', *Economic Development Quarterly*, 13, 46–54.

Fishe, Raymond, 1982, 'Unemployment Insurance and the Reservation Wage of the Unemployed', *Review of Economics and Statistics*, 64, 12–17.

Gordon, Robert, 1973, 'The Welfare Cost of Higher Unemployment', *Brookings Papers on Economic Activity*, 4(1), 133–95.

Hamilton, Bruce, 1976, 'Capitalization of Interjurisdictional Differences in Local Tax Prices', *American Economic Review*, 66, 743–53.

Jones, S., 1989, 'Reservation Wages and the Cost of Unemployment', *Economica*, 56, 225–46.

Kasper, Hershel, 1967, 'The Asking Price of Labor and the Duration of Unemployment', *Review of Economics and Statistics*, 49, 165–72.

Kiefer, Nicholas and G. Neumann, 1979, 'An Empirical Job-Search Model, with a Test of the Constant Reservation-Wage Hypothesis', *Journal of Political Economy*, 87, 89–107.

Mauer, David and S. Ott, 1999, 'On the Optimal Structure of Government Subsidies for Enterprise Zones and Other Locational Development Programs', *Journal of Urban Economics*, 45, 421–50.

McDonald, John, 1979, *Economic Analysis of an Urban Housing Market*, New York: Academic Press.

McDonald, John, 1981, 'Capital–Land Substitution in Urban Housing: A Survey of Empirical Estimates', *Journal of Urban Economics*, 9, 190–211.

McDonald, John, 1983, 'An Economic Analysis of Local Inducements for Business', *Journal of Urban Economics*, 13, 322–36.

McDonald, John, 1984, 'Changing Patterns of Land Use in a Decentralizing Metropolis', *Papers of the Regional Science Association*, 54, 59–70.

McDonald, John, 1985, 'The Intensity of Land Use in Urban Employment Sectors', *Journal of Urban Economics*, 18, 261–77.

McDonald, John, 1993, 'Incidence of the Property Tax on Commercial Real Estate: The Case of Downtown Chicago', *National Tax Journal*, 46, 109–20.

McDonald, John, 1997, *Fundamentals of Urban Economics*, Upper Saddle River, NJ: Prentice-Hall.

McDonald, John, 2001, 'Cost–Benefit Analysis of Local Land Use Allocation Decisions', *Journal of Regional Science*, 41, 277–99.

McGregor, Peter, E. McVittie, J. Swales and Y. Yin, 2000, 'The Neoclassical Economic Base Multiplier', *Journal of Regional Science*, 40, 1–31.

McMillen, Daniel P. and John F. McDonald, 1993, 'Could Zoning Have Increased Land Values in Chicago?', *Journal of Urban Economics*, 33, 167–88.

McMillen, Daniel P. and John F. McDonald, 2002, 'Land Values in a Newly Zoned City', *Review of Economics and Statistics*, 84, 62–72.

Merrifield, John, 1987, 'A Neoclassical Anatomy of the Economic Base Multiplier', *Journal of Regional Science*, 27, 283–94.

Mishan, E.J., 1982, *Cost–Benefit Analysis*, 3rd edn, London: George Allen & Unwin.

Muth, Richard, 1964, 'The Derived Demand for a Productive Factor and the Industry Supply Curve', *Oxford Economics Papers, New Series*, 16, 221–34.

Netzer, D., 1966, *Economics of the Property Tax*, Washington, DC: The Brookings Institution.

Orr, Ginger, 2000, 'Naperville Residents Seek Study of City's Last Vacant Land', *Chicago Tribune*, 153(191), 9 July.

Rast, Joel, 1999, *Remaking Chicago: The Political Origins of Urban Industrial Change*, DeKalb, IL: Northern Illinois University Press.

Sridhar, Kala, 1996, 'Tax Costs and Employment Benefits of Enterprise Zones', *Economic Development Quarterly*, 10– 69–90.

Stephenson, Stanley, 1976,'The Economics of Youth Job Search Behavior', *Review of Economics and Statistics*, 58, 104–11.

Tiebout, Charles, 1956, 'A Pure Theory of Local Public Expenditures', *Journal of Political Economy*, 64, 416–24.

Wheaton, William, 1984, 'The Incidence of Inter-Jurisdictional Differences in Commercial Property Taxes', *National Tax Journal*, 37, 515–27.

8. The rise of the private neighborhood association: a constitutional revolution in local government

Robert H. Nelson[1]

For most of American history, the standard form of housing was a single home or apartment that was owned or rented by an individual household. If there was a need for collective action among individual homeowners, this need was met by a local government in the public sector. Local governments provided public services such as the construction and upkeep of streets, picking up the garbage, enforcement of law and order and many others. Following the introduction of zoning in the United States in 1916, they also regulated the interactions among individual properties that could significantly affect the quality of the surrounding neighborhood environment.

Since the 1960s, however, this historic role of local governments has increasingly been privatized at the neighborhood level. About 1 per cent of all Americans were living in 1970 in a private community association.[2] By 2000, more than 15 per cent lived in a homeowners' association, a condominium or a cooperative – and very often these private collective ownerships were of neighborhood size. Since 1970, about one-third of the new housing units constructed in the United States have been included within a private community association. The Community Associations Institute estimates that, nationwide, about 50 per cent of new housing units in major metropolitan areas are currently being built within a legal framework of private collective ownership.

This privatizing of the American neighborhood over the past 40 years represents a fundamental development in the history both of local government and of property rights in the United States. The rise of private neighborhoods, as Steven Siegel declares, is achieving 'a large-scale, but piecemeal and incremental, privatization of local government'.[3] It is significantly altering the basic manner of provision of housing for tens of millions of Americans. As one authority on homeowners' association and condominium law states, the new forms of housing ownership are creating 'a revolution in American housing patterns'.[4] Another states that more broadly there is taking place today a 'massive social transformation represented by restricted-access living' across the United States.[5] An estimated 1.25 million Americans are today participating directly in local governance as members of the boards of directors of their private community associations.[6]

A revival of the neighborhood is seen by many commentators as a key element in a wider effort to re-energize the intermediate institutions of American society.[7] The weakening of these institutions is blamed for a decline in trust, public spirit and generally an erosion of civic values in the United States in recent decades. The rise of the private neighborhood follows in the wake of the rise of the corporate form of business ownership of property in the late nineteenth century, both representing fundamental turns away from individual ownership of private property and towards new collective forms of private ownership. Indeed, the rise of private neighborhood associations represents the most important property right development in the United States since the rise of the modern business corporation. By 1994, the California Supreme Court would declare that 'common interest developments are a more intensive and efficient form of land use that greatly benefits society and expands opportunities for home ownership'.[8]

In 1988, the Advisory Commission on Intergovernmental Relations (ACIR) convened a conference to announce officially the arrival of an important new player on the American governmental scene. In the introductory remarks, the ACIR stated that 'traditionally the intergovernmental system has been thought to include the national government, state governments, and local governments of all kinds'. Such thinking had to be revised now because 'the concept of intergovernmental relations should be adapted to contemporary developments so as to take account of territorial community associations that display many, if not all, of the characteristics of traditional local government'. As a result, the ACIR declared, 'the governance of local communities in the United States can [now] be said to exist increasingly in two worlds, one public and one private'.[9]

Wayne Hyatt, a leading practitioner in the field of community association law, recently predicted that in the future private associations will 'perform more [new] community services for their members' such as transport and education which 'were formerly public services'. This will have increasing 'legal, political, social, and economic consequences . . . [that will] implicate corporate, municipal, constitutional, and other areas of law as well as social and public policy concerns'.[10] Given the much different groundrules under which private governments work, as compared with public governments, it is no exaggeration to say that there is a constitutional revolution in local government taking place in the United States.

NEIGHBORHOOD ASSOCIATIONS

There are three main legal forms of collective ownership of residential property: the homeowners' association, the condominium and the cooperative. In a homeowners' association, each person owns his or her home individually, often including a private yard. The homeowners' association – which any new entrant into the area is required to join – is a separate legal entity that holds formal title to the 'common areas' such as streets, parks, recreation facilities and other common property. It also enforces neighborhood covenants with respect to the allowable uses and modifications of individually owned homes and other structures. The individual owners of neighborhood properties are also automatically the 'shareholders' in the homeowners' association who collectively own the assets and control the actions of the association.

The other leading legal instrument for collective ownership of residential property is the condominium. In a condominium, all the individual owners have title to their own personal units and, as 'tenants in common', automatically also share a percentage interest in the 'common elements'. These common elements can include things like dividing walls, stairways, hallways, roofs, yards, green spaces, golf and tennis clubs, and other parts of the project area exterior to the individually owned units.[11] Despite the somewhat different legal arrangements, the operating rules and methods of management for homeowners' associations and condominium associations are generally quite similar. As shown in Table 8.1, there were 10.6 million housing units in homeowners' associations in 1998, and 5.1 million housing units in condominium associations.

The third instrument of collective property ownership in the United States is the cooperative. Cooperatives are more likely to be a single building. They became popular in New York City in the decades after World War II, partly as a method of avoiding problems that rent control was posing for owners of rental apartment buildings. As of 1995, there were 416 000 cooperative apartments in New York City.[12] A cooperative is the truest form of collective ownership in that the entire property, including the individually occupied housing units, is owned jointly. Individual occupants of apartments have legal entitlements to the use of their units but are not, strictly speaking, the owners even of the interior portions.

The idea of a private community is synonymous in the minds of some people with a 'gated community'. However, although they have attracted wide publicity (and considerable critical commentary), gated communities are a limited part of the total number of community associations. By one recent estimate, there are around 8 million people nationwide living in about 20 000 gated communities.[13] On the basis of such estimates, about 10

Table 8.1   US housing units in neighborhood associations, by type and year

Type of association	1970	1980	1990	1998
Condominium	85000	1541000	4847921	5078756
Homeowners' association	265000	613000	5967000	10562964
Cooperative	351000	482000	824000	748840
Total assoc. housing units	701000	3636000	11638921	16390560
Total number of associations	10000	36000	130000	204882
Total US housing units	69778000	87739000	102263678	111757000
Neighborhood assoc. units, as % of US total	1.22	4.14	11.38	14.67

Source: Community Associations Institute, *Community Associations Factbook*, ed. Frank H. Spink (Alexandria, VA, 1999, p.19).

per cent of neighborhood associations are gated, and 20 per cent of the total residents of neighborhood associations live in a gated community (partly because of the cost of maintaining the gate, gated communities tend to be considerably larger than the average neighborhood association).[14]

The homeowners' association and the cooperative have had a long, if until recently modest place in the history of home ownership in the United States. The condominium form of collective ownership of housing did not arrive in that country until the early 1960s. In describing these several forms of collective ownership, different commentators have grouped them together under terms such as 'residential community association', 'common interest community', 'residential private government'. In the remainder of this chapter I will refer to all such arrangements as a 'neighborhood association', recognizing that in practice collective residential ownerships may be as small as a single building or as large as a mid-size city.[15]

About 80 per cent of neighborhood associations involve the 'administration of territory such that they resemble communities in the broader sense rather than simply buildings'.[16] The average private collective ownership of residential property is of neighborhood size, about 200 housing units.[17] But others are much larger: Reston in Northern Virginia covers 74000 acres, has a population of more than 35000 and contains 12500 residential units and more than 500 businesses. Sun City in Arizona has 46000 residents and 10 shopping centers.[18]

A DIVIDED SOCIETY?

Not surprisingly, given the degree of social change it represents, the shift from individual to collective ownership of residential property, and from public to private forms of local government, is provoking wide controversy today. Political scientist Evan McKenzie, for one, finds the 'astonishing nationwide growth' in private neighborhood associations since the 1960s to be a disturbing trend.[19] One consequence is that those who are wealthy enough to afford a private neighborhood will become 'increasingly segregated from the rest of society'.[20] The private character of the neighborhood associations that dominate many suburban areas, it is said, may divert the attention of the citizenry from pressing national and international matters. Absorbed in their neighborhood issues and concerns, the residents of private neighborhood associations may lose touch with and become indifferent to the broader problems of American society, including poverty, racial discrimination and other urgent national priorities.[21] In the case of gated communities, the severest critics have gone so far as to describe them as 'a return to the Middle Ages, to moats and drawbridges (with modern amenities)' or as 'a gang way of looking at life' that could ultimately even lead to 'the end of civilization' as we know it.[22]

Two hundred years ago, it was common to impose ownership of property as a requirement for voting in American elections.[23] Such practices were gradually abolished, however, as part of the extension of the franchise to every American. Universal voting rights are widely seen as one of the great triumphs of modern democracy. Yet private neighborhoods revert to the earlier systems of allocating voting rights based on ownership of property.[24] As far back as 1969, Albert Foer argued in the *University of Chicago Law Review* that 'a strong case can be made for the position that ... the property basis of political participation in [the private] Reston and Columbia [communities] may violate the equal protection clause' of the constitution.[25] Foer turned out to be wrong constitutionally (thus far at least) but many observers continue to argue that, legal or not, a system of community voting rights based on the ownership of property is unacceptable in present-day America. Stephen Barton and Carol Silverman, for example, label the private governance regimes of neighborhood associations as 'profoundly undemocratic'.[26]

Professor Gregory Alexander of the Cornell Law School considers that 'residential associations ... may represent the dominant aspect of the late twentieth century contribution to American residential group life'. This new social innovation is 'fundamentally different from both traditional fee ownership of the detached house and apartment living. Common unit developments represent attempts to infuse a social experience of groupness into modern ownership of residential property'. Yet, as Alexander finds the empirical evidence, it suggests that 'the vision of self-governance and participatory democracy within these groups is illusory'.[27] Most residents, he contends, are uninterested and uninvolved in the affairs of their association, or worse are actively discouraged and disillusioned. Boards of directors, partly reflecting an ambiguity in their dual role as resident and manager, often fail to take effective charge of enforcement and service provision responsibilities. These are only part of the reasons for the significant gap that 'exists between the Panglossian image of many residential associations and [the] reality'.[28]

PRIVATE SUBURBS

The privatization of the American neighborhood did not begin with the rise of private neighborhood associations. The key development was found much earlier in the public sector in the rise of zoning. It was zoning that first effectively privatized American neighborhoods. Indeed, the differences between a small suburban municipality and a neighborhood association of equal size are not very large. Among the residents themselves, 'a small suburban town is often seen ... as little more than a form of homeowners association'.[29] The significance of the neighborhood association is not that it is accomplishing a brand new privatization of the suburbs; rather, it is formalizing and extending further a process of privatization of long standing.[30]

Sociologist David Popenoe writes of the pervasive 'privatization of space in metropolitan communities' over the years.[31] The well-off suburb in America has a 'deeply private feel' as a place where the households 'live behind the protection of fence, hedge, or wall, venturing forth only within the confines of a motorized enclosed box'.[32] All in all, as Popenoe complains,

> It is in the privatization of space, because it is so tangible and visible, that the breakdown of the public realm in metropolitan life can most clearly be seen. The American suburb is the extreme case, but privatization is a dominant motif in most of the other ecological zones of the metropolis as well. Streets and sidewalks that once provided public pedestrian interaction and even entertainment

have for the most part been abandoned to the utter privacy of the automobile; public parks have fallen into disuse and misuse; town squares have become the mostly ornamental appendages of commercialism. ... Where is the public space in a Houston or a Los Angeles? It does exist, but is overwhelmed by the dominance of essentially private spheres.[33]

The political analyst William Schneider comments similarly that 'to move to the suburbs is to express a preference for the private over the public.... Suburbanites' preference for the private applies to government as well' – and not only in the formation of neighborhood associations but in the very basic structure of municipal organization of suburban governance.[34] Or, as another social commentator wrote recently, 'the suburb is the last word in privatization'.[35] Fully half of all American municipalities have fewer than 1000 people; three-quarters have fewer than 5000 people.[36] The majority of public municipalities in the United States thus are of about the same size as a private neighborhood association.[37]

The courts have often seen suburban municipalities as effectively falling in a private category. Harvard law professor Jerry Frug comments that 'many recent Supreme Court cases suggest that cities can best empower themselves by acting just like property owners'.[38] In one 1980s Supreme Court opinion, Chief Justice Warren Burger wrote that 'I believe that a community of people are – within limits – masters of their own environment. ... Citizens should be free to choose to shape their community so it embodies their conception of the "decent life"'.[39]

Within the American system of de facto 'private' suburbs, zoning functions as the de facto private property right that gives the suburb a legal power to exclude others from the use of its 'common property'.[40] University of Texas law professor Lee Fennell thus recently described a system of 'collective property rights created through zoning. Zoning splits property rights between the individual landowner and the local government by vesting a set of collective property rights in the community'. The practical effect of this arrangement is that

These collective property rights allow the community some degree of control over the landowner's use of her own land. While traditional notions of nuisance grant the community some power to limit land use, zoning shifts certain additional property rights from the landowner to the community. Thus, under current zoning law, the community's interest in maintaining a particular atmosphere or growth pattern is protected by a property rule. A landowner cannot simply choose to violate a land use regulation and pay for the damage caused, as she could under a liability rule, but instead must obtain permission from the community before proceeding with any nonconforming use. As long as the land use regulation furthers a legitimate government interest, the community can refuse to grant this permission.[41]

In a series of law journal articles over the course of the 1990s, Columbia law professor Richard Briffault provided an insightful overview of the basic legal arrangements and the workings of local governments in the United States.[42] As he describes it, zoning was only one aspect of a broader pattern of local government serving as an instrument of the private purposes of the municipal residents. Briffault suggests that there are three basic models for the role of local governments in the United States: (1) the democratic 'polis', (2) 'the firm', and (3) 'the administrative arm of the state' government.[43] Zoning represents the local government acting in its private 'firm' capacity – and the stockholders in this firm are effectively the residents of the municipality.

A local government may be particularly advantaged as a firm because it can employ the coercive powers of government for various purposes – for instance, to impose on individual property owners a new collective regime of control over the use of their properties. Zoning can be seen as the retroactive creation of a de facto collective property right, made feasible only by the use of government powers to overcome free-rider and holdout problems.[44] As Briffault observes, the instrument of local government can be particularly useful because it can serve as a device 'for using the coercive power' of the state for private economic ends'.[45] Moreover, these private ends may also function in a way to serve broader public goals, much as the creation of a system of private property rights can be an essential element in maintaining a viable economic system.[46]

PROTECTING THE NEIGHBORHOOD ENVIRONMENT

The functions of a private neighborhood association include essentially the same purpose as suburban zoning: protection of the environmental quality of suburban neighborhoods. Private neighborhoods differ in two important respects, however. First, by virtue of their private status in the legal system, they have a wider latitude in the manner and extent of regulation of land uses within a neighborhood. They generally exercise a finer degree of control than the typical zoning ordinance (although the example of historic districts shows that similar comprehensive controls can arise in a public setting as well). Neighborhood associations also offer an alternative governance model to the conduct of municipal affairs. They have different voting rules, management systems, taxing methods, boundary setting mechanisms and other governance features. The consequences and social desirability of these private differences will be examined further in later sections of this chapter.

It is clear, however, that many Americans prefer private protection of their neighborhood environmental quality. Although the far-reaching regulatory powers of neighborhood associations may seem intrusive, many people are happy to sacrifice elements of their own personal autonomy in order to obtain greater control over the actions of their neighbors. As one person observed, in a neighborhood association 'your neighbor will probably be prevented from rebuilding his '57 Chevy in his front yard, or parking his recreational vehicle for six months at a time'. A Southern California woman declared that 'I thought I'd never live in a planned unit development but then I realized I wanted a single-family detached home with some control over my neighbors. I looked at one house without a homeowner association. The guy next door built a dog run on the property line. All night long his Dobermans ran back and forth.'[47]

Private neighborhood associations, like zoning, represent yet another form of institutional response to 'the tragedy of the commons', as it was so famously portrayed many years ago by Garrett Hardin.[48] Without the ability to exclude other uses, higher quality neighborhoods would be invaded by lower quality uses. These uses would be able to capture the benefits of the high environmental quality in the neighborhood, while not contributing to and in fact detracting from this quality. Indeed, if prospective creators of high quality neighborhoods knew in advance that they would lack tight controls over incoming uses in the future, they would never create such neighborhoods in the first place. There is thus a potential 'tragedy of the neighborhood commons' to match the better known tragedy of the grazing commons. As Hardin emphasized, a solution to the tragedy of the commons can be found in either a governmental regulation or a private property right.[49] In the suburban neighborhood context, the establishment of zoning has constituted the regulatory route; the establishment of a neighborhood association has been the private property approach.

Judged at least by a market test, neighborhood associations are a resounding success. The rapid increase in the numbers of people living in neighborhood associations over the past few decades offers strong evidence that the tradeoffs among advantages and disadvantages of collective home living is favorable for many Americans. In a survey of more than 750 owners of condominium units in Florida, 81 per cent stated that they would make the same decision to live in their current condominium, if given the choice all over again. More than 92 per cent rated the existence of collective controls over the uses of neighboring properties to have been an 'important' factor in choosing to live in the neighborhood association. Nearly 85 per cent rated the opportunity to participate in neighborhood governance as either 'important' or 'very important' in a positive way to their housing decision.[50]

In the second half of the nineteenth century and early twentieth century, the rise of large private business corporations provoked wide fears about new social divisions in American society, as well as the private power and control over the lives of the employees of these corporations. Despite the public anxieties of that era, Americans have come to accept the shift of ownership of American industry from the small business firm to the large private corporation. Although neighborhood associations are much criticized today, there may well be a similar long-run outcome. The rapid spread of private neighborhood associations suggests a social and economic force that is not likely to be reversed. Americans seemingly want tighter and more direct control over their immediate neighborhood environment than is afforded by the mechanisms of municipal land use regulation, and land developers are simply responding to the demands of the private marketplace.

This is not to say that government has no role. Business corporations have operated under state charters that establish various stockholder rights, disclosure requirements, governance procedures and other features of corporate business operation. Since the 1930s, the federal government has set further ground rules for the functioning of business corporations, including the various requirements of the Securities and Exchange Commission. Neighborhood associations also operate within a legal framework established by state law. Already, California has amended the Davis–Stirling Act – its basic statute for overseeing the activities of neighborhood associations – more than 35 times since its enactment in 1985.[51] Neighborhood associations must comply with existing federal laws prohibiting racial, sexual, age and other forms of discrimination. The proper scope of governmental action in setting limits to and overseeing the workings of collective private rights to residential property is likely to be a leading subject for public policy debate in the future.

'PUBLIC' AND 'PRIVATE' AMBIGUITIES

If the rise of private neighborhood associations has not fundamentally altered the private character of the suburbs that already existed, it has modified it in a variety of significant ways. The legal process for establishing the boundaries and governing authority of a new private neighborhood, for example, is much different from the process for incorporating a new suburban municipality. The courts are being called upon to make various rulings concerning the permissible manner of private regulation of individual actions within neighborhood associations. In making such rulings, the longstanding legal distinction between public and private often plays an important role.[52] In a 1992 opinion, Supreme Court Justice Anthony Kennedy declared that, if something 'is a product not of state action but of private choices, it does not have constitutional implications'.[53] Or, as law professor Gerald Wetlaufer explains, a basic assumption of the American legal system is that 'there is a public sphere and a private sphere, and that the state may act legitimately within the public sphere but not within the private sphere' to anywhere near the same extent.[54]

Given the legal importance of the private–public distinction, and the emphasis on the private character of the neighborhood association in much of the social and legal commentary, it is surprisingly difficult to pin this distinction down. The courts have struggled without much success with the problem of defining legally a 'state action'. One legal commentator says that the doctrine of state action was long regarded as a 'conceptual disaster area' in the law, although more recently new court thinking has meant that it has been 'considerably yet imperfectly narrowed'.[55] Another commentator finds that 'the words public and private may seem distinct enough – and they are used in popular and political discourse as if they were – but they are not'.[56]

It is not only lawyers and judges who have trouble defining the boundaries of public and private. Political scientists, economists and other students of local government have also been unable to offer a clear resolution. Various distinctions and concepts might be proposed but none seems to fit the bill.

Some people might suggest that the definition of 'public' be taken to mean 'governmental'. However, neighborhood associations are themselves forms of government and yet are private.[57] The small suburban municipality may nominally be 'public' but as a practical matter its actions often have more of a 'private' character. As Richard Briffault comments, Americans show a powerful 'ideological commitment to local autonomy' in their public institutions of local government that is similar to the autonomy of a private property status.[58] The US Supreme Court has not only accepted this private autonomy of local governments but in a number of decisions has seemed actively to encourage it.[59]

Yet another possibility would be to define 'public' by the presence of an element of coercion. Only a government, for example, has the power to put someone in prison. However, many actions that fall in the public category do not involve any degree of coercion. A poor person is free to accept or reject an offer of public welfare assistance entirely on a voluntary basis. There is no compulsion for anyone to use the railroad services provided by Amtrak.

On the other hand, a potential element of coercion is also present in many private acts. When a business organization fires an employee for poor performance, or when a private club expels a member for failing to pay his or her dues, it is taking a step backed by the police powers of the state. If a mob engages in vigilante justice, it is a private act of violence. The difference between the mob and a state action is in the legitimacy accorded the state use of coercion. Yet private violence can be deemed legitimate as well, as when someone responds in kind to a direct physical attack on his or her person.

Private neighborhood associations impose the practical equivalent of taxes in the form of assessments that each housing unit is required to pay. If it is always possible to avoid the assessment by moving out of the neighborhood, it is similarly possible to avoid a municipal tax by leaving the municipality. It is even possible to emigrate from a nation-state if its income or other taxes become too high – as the tennis star Bjorn Borg once did in leaving Sweden to become a citizen of Monaco. Thus even taxes are in some sense voluntary.

It might be suggested that 'private' organizations, even when they employ coercive devices, do so as a result of previous voluntary agreements. The objects of the coercion have agreed in advance that a failure to comply with the rules will bring about the use of the powers of the state. The incoming resident of a private neighborhood association, for example, formally agrees to abide by a set of covenants and other foundational documents. No such formal agreement usually exists with respect to the rules of municipal governments in the public sector. Nevertheless, the very act of moving into the municipality amounts to an implied statement of consent, an agreement to accept municipal regulatory and other decisions that have been legitimately reached by the local political process. This 'implicit contract' may be no less meaningful and binding – and may be equally clear in its terms and provisions – than the written contract of a private neighborhood association (which may in any case have many 'fuzzy' aspects). If it could be said that the children that are born and brought up in a municipality may never have formally consented to its rules, this is no less true of children born and brought up in a neighborhood association.

In short, we may make much use of the terms 'public' and 'private' in ordinary speech but it is often in different ways. Knowledge of a specific usage often depends closely on the context and may shift with changing conventions of language. The courts have found it difficult to deal with such definitional ambiguities.[60] With respect to neighborhood associations, David Kennedy finds that 'state courts have reached wildly different conclusions when faced with the argument that a residential association qualifies as a state actor'.[61] All in all, as Dan Tarlock has similarly commented, 'American law has [traditionally] drawn a distinction between public and private associations to decide how power should be allocated between the state and individual', but neighborhood associations clearly 'strain this distinction'.[62]

PRIVATE PREROGATIVES

Despite the difficulty in finding a single general definition of public and private, it nevertheless frequently makes a large difference in American law how a specific activity ends up being classified. If an action is deemed to be private – however that may have been determined – this will often have major implications in terms of the views and expectations of the courts. For example, the range of legally permissible actions and obligations of a private neighborhood association in many areas will be considerably wider than is the case for a municipal government in the public sector (in concept of identical population and geographic size). Some important examples of this wider set of options for neighborhood associations include the following.

1. A private neighborhood association can legally assign voting rights according to the extent of property ownership, or in concept on the basis of a wide range of other possible voting criteria. A general purpose municipal government is legally required under the US constitution – as determined by the US Supreme Court in its 1968 *Avery* decision – to allocate voting rights on the basis of one person/one vote.[63]
2. A private neighborhood association can discriminate in admitting residents to the neighborhood in various ways that would not be acceptable for a municipal government. For example, a neighborhood association for senior citizens can exclude younger people, including any children, from living there permanently. It is doubtful that a municipality in the public sector could legally sustain a similar discriminatory rule to exclude people from the whole municipality on the basis of the age of potential residents.
3. If it wishes, a private neighborhood association can sell for money the rights of entry into the neighborhood. A municipal government could not similarly sell a zoning change, even though the zoning change might have the identical practical consequence of granting entry. In the public sector a direct monetary sale of entry rights – of zoning – by a government would be regarded as an illegal act of 'bribery' or other form of municipal 'corruption'.
4. A private neighborhood association can explicitly enforce precise numerical controls over the total numbers of residents allowed into the neighborhood, or even the numbers allowed by the specific type of

resident (as long as its actions are not based on race or some other illegal category). An identical action by a municipal government in the public sector would be regarded as establishing a local 'immigration' policy. It would be an unconstitutional infringement of the exclusive prerogative of the federal government to control matters of internal and external migration, as established by the Supreme Court in various interstate commerce and 'right to travel' decisions.

5. A private neighborhood association can enter into many forms of commercial activities within (or in concept outside) the neighborhood, such as operating a neighborhood grocery store or gas station, publishing a neighborhood newspaper, or running a restaurant. Under most state laws (although these could be changed), it would at present be difficult or impossible for a municipal government in the public sector to engage in a similar range of commercial activities oriented to the general public and that may be directly competitive with private suppliers.

6. A private neighborhood association can make a commitment to undertake future actions that would be legally binding and enforceable in court for the lifetime of the association; a current municipal government in the public sector would find it more difficult to bind similarly the future actions of a duly elected municipal legislature.

7. A private neighborhood association can hire a new employee, or dismiss an existing employee, under the same legal rules as a business corporation or other private firm. In most public jurisdictions this same action would be subject to different (and typically more exacting) standards of judicial review. Governments generally face greater difficulties in firing their tenured civil servants than businesses do in dismissing the members of their private workforce.

8. A neighborhood association of virtually any size or shape can in principle be created as an exercise of the private rights of the owner of an appropriate parcel of land (subject to municipal regulatory review and approval under zoning). The establishment of a new neighborhood government in the public sector – even one falling on exactly the same geographic lines – would have to proceed in a legally and politically more complicated way, involving compliance with state laws for municipal incorporation. In some states, any such changes in the jurisdictional boundaries of local governments would have to be approved by the state legislature – an involvement of state government that would not come into play for a new neighborhood association.

A private status, as the above examples illustrate, in most cases confers a wider range of possibilities that give a greater flexibility in shaping new institutions of local governance. However, a private status can also create some forms of obligations and burdens that would not fall on a government in the public sector. A private neighborhood association is typically required to pay property and other taxes to municipal governments but a municipal government of neighborhood size in the public sector would have no such financial obligations to any higher level of government. In practice, even if it would be constitutionally permissible, the upward transfer of funds to higher levels of government, in the manner of making private tax payments, is almost never required of a local municipality. To the contrary, such governments typically receive significant transfers of funds from state and federal governments – transfers that in most cases would not be available to a private neighborhood association.

ALTERNATIVE CONSTITUTIONAL REGIMES

On further reflection, then, it seems that perhaps the best way to think about the distinction between 'public' and 'private' is as follows. There is one broad legal framework for the functioning of a government that operates in the United States under the status of a 'public' entity. There is another legal framework for a government that operates under the status of a 'private' entity. These two legal regimes, often grounded in US constitutional requirements as well as statutory law, are often markedly different. A distinguishing characteristic of the 'private' legal framework, relative to the 'public', is the greater flexibility of the 'private' regime.[64] In most of the areas described above, the options available to a private neighborhood association encompass and then go well beyond those available to a municipal government in the public sector of similar size.[65] Or, as Wayne Hyatt comments, 'in the absence of unusual circumstances or perhaps an emotionally driven decision, the United States Constitution does not apply in common interest community situations today' for most issues.[66]

The determination of whether an action falls in a public or private status is not well defined or fixed. It shifts over time with changes in political and economic thinking and shifting court interpretations of the law. Historically, the progressive era in the United States opened up a long period over the course of the twentieth century when many formerly private actions shifted to take on a public status. The Supreme Court initially sought to limit increasing governmental regulation of private actions but eventually capitulated in the New Deal years. As a result, government has undertaken the regulation of many aspects of the use of private property, even when it might deprive the owner of a large part of the value of the property. Such matters as the operation of a restaurant or the renting of housing units in an apartment were once seen as strictly private but have now come to be regarded as coming under the legal requirements of a state action. Most recently, social practices in the workplace that were formerly regarded as private matters between fellow employees are now regarded as matters for state oversight under sexual harassment and other workplace laws.

Nevertheless, although the legal significance of a private status has been much eroded in the past century, important differences do remain, as described above in comparing a neighborhood association with a municipality. The legal authority of a neighborhood association today is similar to that of a private business corporation. Indeed, neighborhood associations are generally organized under state law as a form of private corporation.[67]

As a result of the private status of neighborhood associations, a private land developer has the flexibility to tailor a system of governance according to the individual needs of the neighborhood association membership (just as a business corporation might choose between bonds and stocks as a method of financing, or the issuing of different kinds of stocks with different voting rights). This may allow for institutional innovations in the governance of a neighborhood association that are as important to the success of the private community as its physical design. In the case of the DC Ranch private community in Scottsdale, Arizona, for example, the developer sought to create 'a governance structure as special as the physical qualities the development would offer to community residents. The internal governance system that was created combines a sense of stewardship with enforcement techniques that truly work'.[68]

A CONSTITUTIONAL REVOLUTION

In light of all this, the rise of the private neighborhood association in American life might be described as a grand new experiment in local constitutionalism. The specific provisions of the private constitution of each neighborhood are contained in its founding documents or, legally speaking, its 'declaration'. Like other constitutions, the declaration sets out a governing process for the neighborhood, including the form of the legislature (the board of directors), voting rules and eligibility, the areas of neighborhood government responsibility (as reflected partly in covenants), neighborhood appeal procedures, and the manner of amending the neighborhood constitution. As a leading legal practitioner in this area, Wayne Hyatt, explains, 'the declaration is not a contract but, as a covenant running with the land, is effectively a constitution establishing a regime to govern property held and enjoyed in common'.[69]

Reflecting the constitutional character of the founding documents, law professor Susan French has explored the possible provisions of a local 'bill of rights' for a new private neighborhood.[70] Even if people have moved into a neighborhood association in full knowledge of its ground rules, most neighborhood associations have provisions for changing the rules (usually by supermajority votes). If this process were abused, the power to change the covenants and other controls on individual property in the neighborhood, French says, could 'substantially reduce the value of units to their owners or force them to move'. Inattentive or unlucky owners could face the prospect that 'dreams can turn to nightmares for homeowners who are forced to make a choice of moving or giving up beloved pets, lovers, or even children'. To minimize the likelihood of any such event, French recommends that developers include provisions in the neighborhood founding declaration to guarantee new home buyers 'that the majority cannot unite to deprive them of the liberties they are not willing to sacrifice for the advantages of ownership in the community'.[71]

Unlike the federal constitution that applies a common set of civil rights and other basic rules everywhere in the United States, the terms of a neighborhood constitution – perhaps including a bill of rights – might vary considerably from one neighborhood to another, reflecting local preferences and circumstances. French recognizes that there is a tradeoff to living in a private neighborhood association in which 'Americans have been willing to give up some degree of freedom to secure the advantages of ownership in common interest communities'. Moreover, the tradeoff need not be resolved in the same manner from one neighborhood to another:

> Since different common interest communities are designed to appeal to various segments of the larger community, the contents of the constitution and bill of rights for any particular development should be tailored to the interests and fears of the group the developer intends to target. People who are interested in living in communities designed for special activities or interest groups will obviously be willing to give up more of different liberties than those who simply want good housing in a good neighborhood that will retain its value. Even within the group of those who are simply looking for housing, the degrees of liberty people are willing to give up to acquire various amenities will vary. However, certain fears are likely to appear with sufficient frequency that developers should consider addressing them in the constitutions for any community they create.[72]

Compared with the bill of rights in the US constitution, the provisions in a neighborhood bill of rights might be less restrictive of government actions in some respects and more restrictive in others. For example, requirements for the separation of church and state that make sense at the national level may be undesirable in the case of a private neighborhood. Congress has previously recognized, in one instance, that American Indian tribes on their reservations should face fewer restrictions relating to the combining of church and state. Some of the US constitutional provisions for freedom of speech might properly be limited in their application in private neighborhoods, allowing these neighborhoods, say, to exclude sex shops, X-rated movies or other pornographic land uses that would be offensive to the residents (but could not be constitutionally prohibited over the entire United States). Overtly discriminatory policies based on sex, age, family circumstance, ethnic background, professional status, sexual gender preference, occupation, recreational interests or any number of other specialized categories might be allowed (other than racial discrimination) for a private neighborhood, even though the same policies for a state actor might violate the equal protection clause or other provisions of the US constitution.[73]

Thus one leading authority on neighborhood association law, Katherine Rosenberry, argues that 'attempts to apply [traditional federal] constitutional analysis in common-interest developments' will face major difficulties, if such efforts are directed to neighborhood actions with respect to 'voting rights, discrimination, inverse condemnation, or freedom of speech and religion'. She finds that 'common-interest developments are consensual in nature and [federal] constitutional principles which have evolved in response to actions of state and local governments are not necessarily applicable in the common-interest setting' of the neighborhood association. Indeed, as Rosenberry argues, whenever possible the courts 'should refuse to apply the body of [federal] constitutional law to documents governing common-interest developments', even if private neighborhoods admittedly 'have many of the trappings of government'.[74] Rather, these matters of basic individual rights within the neighborhood can be addressed (perhaps in many different ways) in the separate writing of many private constitutions that set out the specific governing rules for each neighborhood association. If a person does not like the rules, he or she is under no obligation to move into the neighborhood.

There are now more than 200 000 neighborhood associations in the United States, about 10 times the number of municipalities. In its founding declaration, each of these associations sets out a constitutional arrangement for neighborhood governance. The rise of neighborhood associations amounts to a new exercise in constitution writing on a far wider scale than has been seen before in the United States. In the process, the constitutional status of local government in the country is being radically changed today.

An alternative path of this kind of constitutional revolution would have required the Supreme Court to revisit and reinterpret the constitutional status of local governments in the public sector.[75] The wider constitutional constraints on municipal actions – most of them the result of Supreme

Court decisions over the past 150 years – could have been reconsidered and perhaps many of them loosened or abolished.[76] However, any such rethinking of the constitutional status of municipal governments would be a long and slow process with a very uncertain outcome. It has been much easier and simpler to shift the institutions of local government from the public sector to the private sector. By this means, a constitutional revolution in local government could be accomplished in a much shorter time and with much less political stress and strain.

A NEW FIELD OF STUDY

The full social significance of the corporate form of ownership of business property was not widely appreciated by economists until long after business corporations had become a central feature of American society. Indeed, it was not until 1932 that Adolf Berle and Gardiner Means in a celebrated work brought this development to the full attention of the economics profession, announcing that the rise of the modern corporation had transformed the basic relationship between the ownership of business and the managerial control over the instruments of business production.[77] Even today, much of the apparatus of formal economic analysis is still best suited to a market framework of atomistic business firms operated by individual owners and decision makers.

In the area of the collective ownership of residential property as well, economists and other social scientists have been slow to recognize fundamental changes occurring in American life. In their professional writings (and in contrast to their own private housing choices), economists have not paid much attention to the rise of the private neighborhood association.[78] If the rise of private neighborhoods constitutes a social revolution in American housing, property rights and local governance, for most professional economists it has been an unknown revolution.

It is not as though economists do not have a useful set of analytical tools that might be applied to the study of neighborhood associations. As least since the contributions of James Buchanan, there has been a body of economic analysis of the workings of private clubs.[79] Buchanan, Gordon Tullock and others in the public choice school have explored numerous issues of governance and other aspects of collective choice from an economic perspective.[80] A new field of constitutional economics has emerged from these efforts in the past two decades.[81] The insights of Mancur Olson's classic *The Logic of Collective Action* are readily applicable to the collective decision making of neighborhood associations.[82] Economists have shown a longstanding interest in the evolution and role of private property rights in an economic system. Insights from all of these fields of economic literature could fruitfully be applied to neighborhood associations, potentially occupying the time and effort of many economists.

Following the classic article of Charles Tiebout, there has also developed a substantial literature of 'fiscal federalism'.[83] Tiebout in effect argued that a system of local governments could function like a set of private clubs, and that there could in theory at least be a level of economic efficiency in the taxing and service delivery of local governments to match the standard of market efficiency for ordinary private goods and services. Much of the subsequent economic literature has examined the real-world constraints that make it difficult for municipal governments actually to function according to the Tiebout standard. As discussed above, there are many limits imposed on state actors by the legal system that do not apply to private actors. For example, as Bruce Hamilton discussed, local governments must be able to exclude unwanted uses, but these governments are not allowed simply to refuse entry to any party they want to exclude. The economic importance of zoning was that its workings in practice provided a reasonable approximation of the necessary exclusionary power (if with some inevitable 'frictions', as compared with a true private property right solution).[84] One might say that the rise of private neighborhood associations is bringing the real world of local governance into steadily closer conformance with the theoretical requirements for the existence of a true Tiebout world – another potential area for economic research.

As compared with economists, political scientists have given somewhat greater attention to the rise of neighborhood associations. A small band of political scientists in the 1990s began to take note of the great social significance.[85] They often offered criticisms of neighborhood associations as a challenge to American ideals of social equality and national community. For them, the private character of the neighborhood association represented a step backward from the 'progressive' trends of the twentieth century that had extended the government role into more and more areas of life. Progressivism had also focused the attention of Americans on the national community, and on the federal government as the instrument for achieving the common goals of a unified nationwide citizenry. The rise of the private neighborhood association, for many critics, has represented a step back towards parochialism and division, towards an emphasis on the rights of small local communities over the interests of the nation as a whole.

Although the social science literature remains slim, lawyers have been more attentive to the growing social importance of neighborhood associations. This is partly because an estimated 4000 cases involving the actions and rights of private neighborhood associations have already been taken up in the courts.[86] A large body of writings now exists in the law journals that describes the rise of the neighborhood association and the many legal issues raised.[87] The remainder of this chapter – drawing heavily on this legal literature – will examine the workings of private neighborhood associations in further detail.

WHY COLLECTIVE OWNERSHIP?

The 1960s was a period of rapid changes in many areas of American life, from the Beatles in music, to escalating crime rates, to the introduction of coeducation in many colleges, to the rise in general of a counterculture among the young. It was a period of fundamental change in American housing as well. Indeed, the timing was not altogether coincidental. The upheavals in American society in the 1960s coincided with the arrival of the first members of the baby boom generation to adulthood, bringing not only increased demands for housing but also new social values that this generation would soon be advancing in American life.

With a generation less enamored of 'progress', and more concerned about the 'environment' than previous generations, there were new social pressures that acted to limit the availability of housing, including the slowing of new highway construction, tighter suburban limits on land use supplies, demands for more and larger open space areas, and greater pressures to limit growth generally. Such factors contributed to a new tightness in metropolitan land markets and rapid escalation in many areas of the price of land. In 1948 the cost of land represented 11 per cent on average nationwide of the total cost of suburban housing; by the 1970s land costs had shot up to 25 to 30 per cent of the total cost of housing.[88]

Rising land and housing prices meant a growing demand for housing at higher densities of occupancy. Building housing at higher densities allowed for the realization of significant economies in the use of land, including joint provision of parks, green spaces and other common facilities for a whole neighborhood. Townhouses became a form of 'apartment' living adapted to the individual ownership and other circumstances of the suburbs. Home buyers were increasingly confronted with a choice: either purchase a home far out in the distant suburbs where land costs remained low, or give up on the idea of living on an individual lot with an acre or so of land for personal use. Only people in the top part of the income scale could now afford such a level of luxury in well located suburban areas.

As many people found that they would have to accept higher densities in order to economize on the use of land, they also found themselves living in closer proximity to their neighbors. A stereo system blaring music 300 feet away might be barely audible; 30 feet away it could keep you up all night.

The actions of neighbors in general became more important to residents and to the enjoyment of their shared neighborhood environment. A new demand thus emerged for collective controls over the actions of individual property owners within the shared neighborhood environment, accompanied by a greater willingness to sacrifice elements of individual autonomy in order to gain such collective controls.

Zoning had always been a crude device for maintaining neighborhood quality. It could keep out new industrial and commercial uses well enough but traditionally had not regulated 'aesthetic' matters such as the paint color of a house, the placement of shrubbery, the building of a deck and many other fine details of neighborhood land use. If these kinds of things were to be put under collective neighborhood control, the wider regulatory leeway afforded by a private system of regulatory controls might be needed. A private set of controls would also have the advantage – in the case, for example, of future disputes – that each resident had already given his or her explicit voluntary consent to the controls.

As compared with the standard workings of municipalities in the public sector, a higher quality of neighborhood services could also often be achieved by obtaining them privately. Many city neighborhoods were required to negotiate with distant bureaucracies concerning the appropriate levels and manner of service delivery to the neighborhood. These bureaucracies were often unresponsive and insensitive to local needs, as well as inefficient in their delivery of services. Where the option existed, many neighborhoods in the suburbs concluded they could do better on their own, buying the services from private providers operating under the competitive pressures of the marketplace.

Many new neighborhood associations across the United States, for example, were built around golf courses as an organizing feature. Compared with the usual municipal golf course, a private association often limited the levels of golfer use more tightly, and maintained a higher standard of upkeep of fairways and greens. In a privately maintained park, the association members could plant gardens, have the lawn mown regularly and otherwise maintain facilities more attractive than most of their municipal counterparts. Indeed, in the 1970s and 1980s, many common areas of municipal governments appeared seedy and run-down; they often suffered from inadequate maintenance. Private police patrols could be used in neighborhood associations to supplement the level of security already being provided by municipal police. Thus, as Marc Weiss and John Watts comment, neighborhood associations 'continued to enforce deed restrictions [on types of neighborhood uses] but their essential purposes increasingly reflected other priorities: the provision of attractive services and the economical maintenance of common property'.[89]

Changing thinking about urban planning and the appropriate design of suburban land development projects also played a role in promoting the rise of private neighborhoods. The typical zoning ordinance specified that each home should have its own separate lot. The planning ideal underlying the creation of zoning was that each home should be well insulated from negative impacts of adjoining homeowners. As one might say, each person in a perfect world of zoning would be wealthy enough to create his or her own private 'park' for his or her individual enjoyment at home, living in a neighborhood with other residents of similar incomes and lifestyles. Jane Jacobs and other critics, however, argued that such zoning goals were a prescription for sterile, aesthetically unattractive, boring and in general bland and unappealing land development.[90] Zoning emphasized the autonomy of the individual at the cost of less opportunity to live in and among the members of a more diverse and vital community environment. Zoning employed government powers to legally enforce patterns of land use in which neighborly interactions with other people would be held to a minimum.

The new architectural goals of the 'planned unit development' were conceived, and from the 1960s increasingly accommodated by municipalities, in part as an antidote to such concerns about the impacts of zoning. Retail and other commercial establishments might be provided in closer proximity to the homes of residents. Some people might like to walk to a corner convenience store. They might like to get their hair cut at a neighborhood barber shop. Zoning rules had to be changed in order to accommodate such mixtures of uses in new land development projects. Under the concept of the planned unit development, it would be the density of the entire development, and no longer the size of the individual lots, that would count for overall compliance with density controls. The trees and areas of green space were found less on the individual lots and more as part of a common area of open space for the whole neighborhood: a 'public' rather than a 'private' space (or 'public' at least for all the members of the neighborhood association).

The real estate industry is in the business of providing what home buyers want and are willing to pay for. These kinds of economic forces in the land market and the shifting aesthetic preferences in land development required corresponding changes in the legal instruments for the ownership of residential property in the United States. In most planned unit developments, a collective form of private property ownership such as the homeowners' association would be necessary.

The first homeowners' association in the United States was created in 1831 in order to provide for the upkeep of Gramercy Park in New York City. The idea of the mandatory homeowners' association – where each purchaser of a home or lot was required to join the association as an initial condition of purchase – was pioneered in the early twentieth century. Mission Hills in Kansas City, built by a leading American community developer, J.C. Nichols, was one of the first large developments to establish a mandatory association.[91] Nichols sought, among other aims, to transfer the burden of future common property maintenance, and private service delivery, to the residents themselves. In earlier developments, where the developer retained this role long after the homes had been built, there had often been many disputes with residents concerning such matters. The use of homeowners' associations spread further after World War II, as large private developments became more common across the United States. Nevertheless, until at least the 1960s, the predominant form of collective protection of neighborhood environmental quality was achieved by means of public zoning.

CONDOMINIUM OWNERSHIP

The increasing demand for collective private ownership of residential property led to a basic property right innovation of the 1960s. The first condominium development in the United States was the Greystoke in Salt Lake City in 1962.[92] Within 40 years, there would be 2 million people living in condominium units in Florida alone, and condominium units would represent 5 per cent of the total American housing supply.

Outside the United States, forms of condominium ownership have ancient origins. Some of the earliest known antecedents can be found in the Middle Ages in Germany where 'story property' – the separate ownership of different stories within the same structure – is known to have existed as long ago as the 1100s.[93] The modern form of condominium ownership was adopted in Belgium in 1924 and Brazil in 1928 and it spread rapidly to other parts of Latin America. A condominium law was enacted in 1951 in Puerto Rico, and the first condominiums in the United States were built there.

In 1960, partly at the request of Puerto Rican representatives, hearings were held by the Congress on the workings of condominium ownership. The National Housing Act of 1961 extended the availability of FHA mortgage insurance to the purchasers of individual units in condominiums. FHA promptly took steps to promote wider condominium ownership, including the publication of a model condominium statute.[94] By 1967, in part on the basis of the FHA model, almost every state had adopted some kind of legislation setting a legal framework for condominium ownership.

From a starting point of essentially zero in 1960, housing units in condominiums by 1970 represented 12 per cent of the housing units found in neighborhood associations across the United States. Condominium ownership spread particularly rapidly during the 1970s, now further encouraged by high inflation and a period of national economic instability that was creating new financial pressures on state and local governments. Local fiscal deficits meant that local governments were less willing to accept any new responsibilities for building and maintaining streets, collecting garbage and providing other municipal services to new entrants within the community. In 1978, the passage of Proposition 13 in California limited the ability of local governments to raise their property taxes. In California and many other states, providing local services privately through a neighborhood association, and thus relieving part of the fiscal burden on a municipality, was often a condition for municipal approval of a large new planned development.[95] As James Winokur comments, 'there is substantial evidence to suggest that the "load shedding" of local government fiscal responsibilities onto common interest communities has been a conscious governmental strategy for relieving strain on shrinking resources'. Indeed, developers often find that local regulations 'either require or encourage them to create commonly owned property managed by community associations'.[96]

In the mid-1970s, another important form of encouragement for neighborhood associations was the acceptance by the Federal National Mortgage Association (FNMA) and by the Federal Home Loan Mortgage Corporation (FHLMC) of the inclusion of condominium and planned unit development loans in the bundling of mortgages in the secondary lending market. As home buyers then voted with their feet, the number of housing units in neighborhood associations rose from 1 per cent of the total US housing supply in 1970 to 4 per cent in 1980, and then reaching 11 per cent in 1990. By 2000, more than 15 per cent of Americans – more than 40 million people – were living in a private neighborhood association of some kind.

GROWING PAINS

As might have been expected for such a new social institution, increasing complaints about the operation of private neighborhood associations were also beginning to be heard by the 1970s. Developers sometimes did not follow through on their commitments to incoming residents, or misrepresented their intentions. The process of transition from developer control to management by the unit owners themselves was often difficult and confusing. In 1973, a survey of 1760 condominium residents found that most were satisfied with their overall condominium experience but 61 per cent were unhappy with one or another aspect of the specific workings of their association management.[97]

In that same year, leaders in the real estate industry joined together to form the Community Associations Institute (CAI) with the purpose of improving the quality of management of private neighborhood associations. The CAI (now located in Alexandria, Virginia, just outside Washington, DC) over the years has provided a wide range of technical assistance for various aspects of association governance. Besides its numerous written materials, CAI also provides a wide range of instructional programs in the management of neighborhood associations.[98]

Many state legislatures responded to public complaints about neighborhood association operation by passing a second generation of condominium statutes. The number of states adopting new condominium laws increased after the publication in 1977 of a 'Uniform Condominium Act' by the National Conference of Commissioners on Uniform State Laws.[99] Under the recommendations of the model condominium law, the full details of neighborhood land use restrictions and of required assessments to pay for services should to be fully and clearly disclosed to purchasers of units prior to the final closing. New state legislation often provided for improved methods of enforcement to achieve greater compliance of residents with neighborhood rules. The model law recommended a 67 per cent vote of approval for amending the foundational documents of a neighborhood association. As of 1998, new laws in 21 states had been enacted that followed the design (in some cases with considerable modification) laid out in the Uniform Condominium Act.[100]

The National Conference on Uniform State Laws also published a Uniform Planned Community Act (later adopted by Oregon and Pennsylvania) and a Model Real Estate Cooperative Act (adopted by Virginia and Pennsylvania). Given the considerable overlap among the various model laws by then in existence, a consolidated Uniform Common Interest Ownership Act (UCIOA) was issued in 1982. The UCIOA contained various recommendations to set ground rules for the exact legal status and collective decision procedures of neighborhood associations.[101] It suggested, for example, that a quorum requirement should be 20 per cent attendance for meetings that involved all of the unit owners of a neighborhood association, and 50 per cent attendance for members at the meetings of the board of directors. The UCIOA recommends that the builder retain management and land use control within a development until 75 per cent of the units have been sold. At that point, the majority of voting rights – and management control – would transfer to the unit owners themselves. (However, even then, the members of the neighborhood association would be legally required to permit the developer to complete the project according to the plan.)

Various voting rules are recommended in the UCIOA for achieving collective approval of neighborhood association actions, varying by the kind of action. In order to recall a member of the board of directors, a vote of 67 per cent of the unit owners is recommended. A 67 per cent vote is also recommended for approval of most types of amendments to the original covenant restrictions and other founding documents of the association. A higher standard is suggested for some special types of amendments that would represent more fundamental alterations in the basic workings of the neighborhood association. For example, the UCIOA would require an 80 per cent vote to amend the founding documents to allow a new type of use within the neighborhood (to allow say a commercial venture). Full and unanimous consent is required to make any changes in the neighborhood association in the division of voting interests among the unit owners.

NEIGHBORHOOD ENVIRONMENTALISM

The rise of the private neighborhood association since the 1960s coincides with the rise of the environmental movement in the United States. Indeed, the rise of the neighborhood association could accurately be described as representing yet another side to American environmentalism (if with little connection to the official environmental movement). This 'neighborhood environmentalism' is dedicated to the improvement and protection of the quality of the immediate surrounding home environment – the one place where most Americans spend the largest part of their time outdoors.

As described above, the environmental protections in most neighborhood associations go well beyond conventional zoning. Neighborhood association rules also often limit the manner of use of individual property. Some associations require, for example, that garage doors be kept closed when not in use. Rules for the types of motor vehicles allowed – prohibiting house trailers, large trucks or even any kind of truck at all – and the manner of their parking on neighborhood streets and driveways are common features in neighborhood associations. As one judge declared in considering a legal challenge to the powers of a neighborhood association, 'although William Pitt, Earl of Chatham, may have declared, in a famous speech to Parliament, that a man's home is his castle, this is not necessarily true of condominiums' and other private neighborhood associations.[102]

Collective neighborhood control may extend into various realms of social behavior such as the playing of loud music or the holding of late-night parties. Apparently reflecting a residual American Puritanism in some places, a few of them have regulated the wearing of bathing suits and even kissing goodnight in public. One Florida association in the 1970s banned the use of alcoholic beverages in the neighborhood clubhouse.

Many associations have restrictions on the ownership of pets, sometimes based on their size and weight.[103] A common restriction in neighborhood associations is a ban on any home-based businesses, in some cases even personal businesses interior to a housing unit that would generate little or no car traffic or other exterior impacts. Other aspects of the behavior of residents that have been restricted by neighborhood associations include the use of patio furniture, the holding of outdoor barbecues, the frequency of toilet flushing, and the type of soap used in dishwashers.

Green Valley is a master-planned community near Las Vegas, Nevada. As described by one observer, this private community provides for control over the common neighborhood environment in all of the following ways:

> In Green Valley the restrictions are detailed and pervasive. ... Clotheslines and Winnebagos are not permitted, for example; no fowl, reptile, fish, or insect may be raised; there are to be no exterior speakers, horns, whistles, or bells. No debris of any kind, no open fires, no noise. Entries, signs, lights, mailboxes, sidewalks, rear yards, side yards, carports, sheds – the planners have had their say about each. ... [They also regulate] the number of dogs and cats you can own ... as well as the placement of garbage cans, barbecue pits, satellite dishes, and utility boxes. The color of your home, the number of stories, the materials used, its accents and trim. The interior of your garage, the way to park your truck, the plants in your yard, the angle of your flagpole, the size of your address numbers, the placement of mirrored glass balls and birdbaths, the grade of your lawn's slope, and the size of your FOR SALE sign should you decide you want to leave.[104]

COURT OVERSIGHT

The private status of a neighborhood association, to be sure, does not mean an absence of any legal limits to its authority. In the past, for example, some courts have shown a willingness to overturn neighborhood restrictions that affected only the interior portions of an individual housing unit. One neighborhood association, for example, was prohibited from imposing a ban on the installation of a TV satellite dish that would have been placed in a way to be entirely out of sight.

In other cases, courts have simply ruled that actions of neighborhood associations have been too intrusive without any reasonable basis. A court thus overturned a neighborhood rule to ban the parking of a small non-commercial pickup truck in a driveway – although an ordinary car would have been allowed under association rules in exactly the same place. The court reasoned that 'cultural perceptions' change and neighborhoods must adjust; in recent years light trucks have no longer had a 'pejorative connotation' and instead for many people are rather fashionable – perhaps even the contemporary social 'equivalent of a convertible in earlier years'. Hence, as this court ruled, it was altogether unreasonable for the association to ban the parking of a small pickup truck in a driveway within the neighborhood.

Law professor Gerald Korngold argues that, although there will be a few exceptions, the courts should nevertheless respect the autonomy of neighborhood associations to control their own land uses 'in virtually all situations'. He finds that 'in almost every case' the restrictions of neighborhood associations do represent a reasonable effort of the residents to protect an attractive neighborhood environment.[105] As courts across the United States are increasingly asked to review issues of the legal acceptability of the actions of neighborhood associations, this has become a fast-growing area of the law.[106]

For the most part, much as Korngold advocates, the courts have thus far deferred to the private autonomy of neighborhood associations. One should give substantial deference, the courts seem to be saying, to the expressed preferences of many millions of Americans who have already chosen to live under the collective system of neighborhood controls of a neighborhood association. They knew in advance what they were getting into, and explicitly agreed to abide by the terms of neighborhood restrictions. Hence, absent a compelling demonstration to the contrary, the normal decision-making and enforcement procedures of neighborhood associations should be allowed to operate according to the rules of the founding documents – the original 'neighborhood constitution' – with a minimum of judicial intervention.

In one much-cited 1975 case, a Florida court thus upheld the prohibition (noted above) on the use of alcoholic beverages within the clubhouse area of the Hidden Harbor Estate association. The Florida Supreme Court first described the routine workings of neighborhood associations:

> Inherent in the condominium concept is the principle that to promote the health, happiness, and peace of mind of the majority of the unit owners since they are living in such close proximity and using facilities in common, each unit owner must give up a certain degree of freedom of choice which he might otherwise enjoy in separate, privately owned property. Condominium unit owners comprise a little democratic sub society of necessity more restrictive as it pertains to use of condominium property than may be existent outside the condominium organization. The Declaration of Condominium involved herein is replete with examples of the curtailment of individual rights usually associated with the private ownership of property. It provides, for example, that no sale may be effectuated without approval; no minors may be permanent residents; no pets are allowed.[107]

In upholding the restrictive actions of the Hidden Harbor association, this Florida court then declared that 'certainly, the association is not at liberty to adopt arbitrary or capricious rules bearing no relationship to the health, happiness and enjoyment of life of the various unit owners. On the contrary, we believe the test is reasonableness. If a rule is reasonable, the association can adopt it; if not, it cannot'.[108] As a practical matter, this test of 'reasonableness' has amounted to a presumption in favor of the actions of neighborhood associations but with the courts maintaining an option to intervene in particular circumstances that they may perceive as grossly unfair or arbitrary.[109]

AN EVOLVING BODY OF LAW

The California Supreme Court has also sought to flesh out the acceptable boundaries of neighborhood association authority. In one important case a unit owner, Natore Nahrstedt, was keeping three cats in violation of a ban that had been imposed by the Lakeside Village Condominium Association.[110] According to association rules, unit owners were not allowed to have pets. However, Mrs Nahrstedt claimed that, because her three cats were not allowed to go outside her unit, it was arbitrary and unreasonable that she should be forced to get rid of them (or alternatively be forced to move out of the neighborhood). Her neighbors countered that she had known about the association rule banning pets all along, and had blatantly acted to defy the expressed wishes of her fellow unit owners in acquiring the cats. This cat lover lost in the first court to consider the case, then won at an appeals level, but finally lost on further appeal to the California Supreme Court.

Using widely cited language, the California Supreme Court declared that 'subordination of individual property rights to the collective judgment of the owners association together with restrictions on the use of real property comprise the chief attributes of owning property in a common interest development'.[111] That is to say, the collective preferences of the unit owners, as clearly expressed in restrictive use covenants that are included in the founding documents of an association, must not be lightly overthrown.[112] Following the California ruling, the common interpretation of state courts is that a restriction imposed by a neighborhood association should be legally sustained as 'reasonable' if it can meet three tests. It must not '(1) violate a fundamental public policy, (2) bear no rational relationship to the protection, preservation, operation, or purpose of the affected land, or (3) create more harmful effects on homeowners' land use than benefits'.[113] (This third test, it must be admitted, seems to invite rather wide judicial intervention in association affairs, if carried out to the full letter of the court opinion. For the most part, it seems to have been interpreted narrowly in practice.)

Although the courts have supported the enforcement of neighborhood association covenants in the great majority of cases, it is still a developing area of the law. In 1997, the Supreme Court of Washington State showed that the courts are also capable of tighter scrutiny. In 1992, William and Carolyn Riss purchased a home in the Mercia Heights area of the City of Clyde Hill. The Risses later sought the approval of the Mercia Homeowners Association to tear town their existing home and to build a new one. As proposed, the new home would have complied fully with the covenants as recorded by the original developer in the 1950s. The Association board turned down the request and then, after an appeal from the Risses to the full membership, the members of the association voted decisively against their request as well. The Supreme Court of Washington, however, overturned the actions of the Mercia Homeowners Association. In ruling in favor of the Risses, the court declared that the association had acted 'without adequate investigation ... based on inaccurate information, and thus was unreasonable and arbitrary'.[114] The Mercia homeowners were probably objecting most of all to the neighborhood disruptions of demolishing an existing home and constructing a new one but apparently that type of concern was not explicitly addressed in the covenants and the court felt free to interject its own judgment.

The courts often distinguish between land use restrictions that are contained in the founding documents of a neighborhood association and any subsequent rules that have been adopted by the association governing officers (or through an internal referendum vote among all the unit owners in the neighborhood). Each new buyer of a unit in an association knows before the purchase the basic covenants and other land use restrictions of the neighborhood – or has the opportunity to find out. (Simply looking around the neighborhood to observe the homogeneous character of the existing properties will normally also be very informative in this regard.) Hence, as Wayne Hyatt and Jo Anne Stubblefield write, the courts have generally given a 'strong presumption of validity' to restrictions contained in the founding documents.[115] However, when a new rule has been voted by the association governing body at a later date, and thus no claim can be made to unanimous initial consent, the courts have been less deferential. In such cases, 'rational rules and restrictions that are rationally enforced – and that promote a legitimate goal – will generally be considered reasonable', but the courts tend to accept a greater responsibility to scrutinize the actions of a neighborhood association.[116]

The potential range of decisions that the governing officers of neighborhood associations are called upon to resolve can seem almost limitless.

Most of them fortunately do not end up in court. In a neighborhood association in Fairfax County in Northern Virginia, for example, the 30 or so unit owners were recently pondering the following issue.[117] The streets of the association are privately maintained, and some of these streets now needed significant capital improvements, requiring a special capital assessment of around $2000 per unit owner. However, a few members of the association live in housing units that front onto a public road. They make little use – and in theory could make no use at all – of the private road network internal to the neighborhood association and that is used by most unit owners. These outside-facing owners would therefore derive little or no direct benefit from the street capital improvements. Should they nevertheless pay the full amount, or should they perhaps be given a discount, or even complete relief from having to pay for the cost of the internal road improvements for their neighborhood association?

Another thorny issue before this same Northern Virginia neighborhood involved the possibility of placing Christmas lights on a part of the common elements of the association. The large majority of the unit owners are Christian and most of them wanted to put up the lights during the holiday season – involving a cost of no more than a few hundred dollars in total to the association. However, the association also has a few Jewish members. At least one objected, recognizing that the rights to the common elements amount to a form of 'property ownership', that it would be offensive to his religious beliefs for him to pay for Christmas lights on what was, in part at least, 'his' property. The association had to consider whether this was a reasonable view or perhaps an unreasonable objection that would frustrate the will of the majority of the unit owners, people who were simply looking to celebrate in a few small ways the Christmas holiday.

Another issue is the extent of constitutional protection of free speech within the boundaries of a neighborhood association. Under the US constitution the extent of such protections typically differs according to whether the setting is public or private. In a 1990s Pennsylvania court case, an owner had placed a 'for sale' sign in the window of his unit. When the association demanded that the sign be removed (prior written permission for the posting of any signs was mandatory under the rules of the association), the owner claimed that his constitutional rights of free speech under the First Amendment were being abridged. A lower court agreed but on appeal a higher court sustained the actions of the neighborhood association, declaring that freedom of speech in this case would have to give way to the rights of private property as manifested in existing land use covenants within a neighborhood.[118]

WHO CAN LIVE THERE?

Neighborhood associations may also seek to maintain the desired neighborhood environment by means of controls on the age or, potentially, other personal characteristics of prospective entrants. Given the long history of active racial discrimination in the United States, this is a particularly sensitive area of neighborhood exercise of collective control over the neighborhood environment.

Although private restrictive covenants to exclude blacks were once widespread in American housing, they were declared unconstitutional by the US Supreme Court in 1948, in *Shelley* v. *Kraemer*.[119] There is thus no question that it would be unconstitutional for a neighborhood association to deny entry to any prospective unit owner on the basis of his or her race. However, the ability of an association to accept or reject entry of new unit owners based on other personal characteristics is subject to wide current uncertainty. Discriminatory actions that are unconstitutional in a 'public' setting could well be constitutional in a 'private' setting.[120]

Some forms of social discrimination, such as exclusions from a neighborhood based directly on ability to pay, are entirely legal. The level of income required to buy into a neighborhood can often be measured rather precisely (as a savings and loan or other mortgage officer would be able to calculate it). Still other forms of discrimination are not constitutionally prohibited but may be illegal at present under one or another statute. In these cases, the law could be changed, and whether to make such a change is potentially an important subject for public policy debate.

In general, the ability to assert strong values of a community will depend on the ability to exclude people who do not share those values. As Michael Sarbanes and Kathleen Skullney note, '"community" is ... filled with the related tension between cohesion and exclusion. The very self-definition which binds some people within a community is likely to exclude others'.[121] University of Virginia law professor Glen Robinson comments that 'real communities are very selective about whom they include. ... A Jewish community comprised of a mixture of Christians, Jews and secular individuals is a contradiction. An Italian–American community half comprised of Irish or Russians is impossible'.[122]

Since the 1960s, public policy in the United States has often emphasized individual rights over the rights of the community to define its own membership. However, there has been growing concern in recent years, partly stimulated by a new 'communitarian movement', to provide greater encouragement to the local 'intermediary' institutions in American society.[123] This may require a new willingness to permit exclusionary practices on the part of local communities in the interest of sustaining the internal cohesion of these communities. Although the legal acceptability of such practices is in doubt, it remains for the most part to be resolved. As Robinson comments, 'conventional wisdom is that covenants based on such personal attributes as race, religion or ethnicity are unenforceable, though aside from racial restrictions … there is remarkably little case law to support this assumption. There is equally little examination of why it should be so'.[124]

The concept of freedom has always involved a tension as seen in the old debate over whether a person should be 'free to choose not to be free'. We can easily agree that complete freedom is unacceptable when it might extend, for example, to some person choosing to sell himself into slavery. However, maintaining the freedom to choose many other kinds of limits on future freedom of individual action will not involve such obvious tensions with basic social values. Indeed, a 'freedom of association' is also a basic right in the pantheon of American civil rights, one that government should not infringe upon lightly.[125]

AGE GROUP COMMUNITIES

Thus far, the issue of the legal right to discriminate has received the most attention in the case of discrimination on the basis of age.[126] Public policy has been caught between two powerful tends in society. Legislatures in general have been moving to include age as a prohibited category for discriminatory actions. On the other hand, the creation of neighborhood associations that limit residents to certain age groups has proved very popular. Neighborhood associations limited to senior citizens today constitute a significant portion of all private associations.

From the 1960s to the late 1980s, it was not only neighborhoods of senior citizens but many others that limited residents to adults only; their founding documents prohibited entry to families who had children below a minimum age.[127] Such actions were soon challenged in the courts, using the argument that they represented an unconstitutional, or otherwise illegal, form of social discrimination. It seems likely that, if a municipal government in the public sector were to limit residency according to the age of potential entrants, this restriction would be struck down by the courts. In most cases involving private neighborhood associations, however, state courts ruled that their private status allowed them to discriminate on the basis of age. In 1978, for example, a California court of appeals upheld the restrictive requirement of a neighborhood association that required any permanent occupant to be 18 years or older.[128]

In another leading case in this area, the Florida State Supreme Court in 1979 considered the constitutionality of a restriction in the White Egret neighborhood association that denied residency to any child under the age of 12. In upholding this restriction, the Florida court reasoned:

> The urbanization of this country requiring substantial portions of our population to live closer together coupled with the desire for varying types of family units and recreational activities have brought about new concepts in living accommodations. There are residential units designed specifically for young adults, for families with young children, and for senior citizens. The desires and demands of each category are different. ... The units designed principally for families are two- to four-bedroom units with recreational facilities geared for children, including playgrounds and small children's swimming pools. ... We cannot ignore the fact that some housing complexes are designed for certain age groups. In our view, age restrictions are a reasonable means to identify and characterize the varying desires of our population. The law is now clear that a restriction on individual rights on the basis of age need not pass the 'strict scrutiny' test, and therefore age is not a suspect classification. ... We do recognize, however, that these age restrictions cannot be used to unreasonably or arbitrarily restrict certain classes of individuals from obtaining desirable housing. Whenever an age restriction is attacked on due process or equal protection grounds, we find the test is: (1) whether the restriction under the particular circumstances of the case is reasonable; and (2) whether it is discriminatory, arbitrary, or oppressive in its application.[129]

The court in essence reasoned that a neighborhood should have substantial freedom to define its own social as well as physical environment. Indeed, the presence of children in a neighborhood could impose significant burdens on others. The owner of a housing unit did not have any automatic right to impose such costs on the rest of the neighborhood.

THE 1988 FAIR HOUSING ACT

Across the entire United States, the wide range of legislative and judicial arenas means that it is possible to lose in one place and still win in another. After losing in California, Florida and most state courts, the opponents of age restrictions in neighborhood associations finally prevailed in 1988 in the US Congress. The enactment of the Fair Housing Act Amendments in that year significantly altered the legal environment for age discrimination by neighborhood associations. Congress now made housing discrimination on the basis of 'familial status' illegal under federal law. ('Familial status' is defined by the presence or absence of a child under 18 years who is living permanently as a member of the family.) Reflecting the political realities, it was necessary to give neighborhoods for senior citizens an exemption from this new limitation. At present private neighborhood associations can gain senior citizen status, and the legal right to exclude children, if they have at least 80 per cent of their units occupied by at least one person 55 years or older.

The precise extent of legally acceptable exclusions (which kinds of people can be kept out, and when attempts at exclusion cross the boundary to become impermissible forms of discrimination) may arise in many other forms. These issues are being worked out at present in the courts, legislatures and other public policy-making arenas. Whether it would be possible to create a neighborhood association limited, say, to unmarried adults, or to gay people, remains cloudy. Neighborhood association law in general is an area in rapid flux. As law professor Stewart Sterk writes, 'community association law is in its infancy, or at best early adolescence'.[130]

Questions of separation of church and state, for example, will likely come before future courts in considering the actions of neighborhood associations. Under the US constitution, a person is generally free to choose his or her own associates in private behavior, and this freedom of association extends with special force to religion. Churches can legally limit their membership to fellow believers in the faith. When churches become involved in property ownership and management, issues of freedom of religion may then extend into a land use setting. Some churches, for example, operate summer retreats where a declared commitment to the faith is expected among those occupying a cabin. Yet the courts at present might well rule against any similar attempt to restrict full-time residency in a neighborhood association to a particular religion – an attempt by a developer to establish, say, a neighborhood association limited to Mormons or Seventh Day Adventists.[131]

However, it is possible that any tight legal restrictions on the forming of religious groups, including neighborhoods, may in the future come to be seen as an unconstitutional form of state interference in the religious freedoms of Americans. The government might in effect be denying religious believers the right to create the social institutions necessary to sustain their own faith-based convictions, and which may in their view require, for example, that children be raised in a religiously supportive neighborhood environment, one limited to people who share the same faith. As law professor Thomas Berg puts it, 'active, welfare-state government now regulates many areas of life. As a result … maintaining church/state separation or religious liberty requires treating religion quite differently from other activities'. But this treatment may effectively discriminate against religion: 'As government grows, separationist efforts to shelter it from religious influence and to bar it from doing anything that aids religion are bound to push religion into a smaller and smaller corner of public life, violating both religious liberty and the equal status of religion with other ideas'.[132]

Law professor Richard Epstein of the University of Chicago argues for the widest possible legal protections for freedom of association. Indeed, in the private sector he would abolish almost any kind of restraint on freedom of association. As Epstein reasons, for example, the effective expression of a viewpoint often requires the collective efforts of an association of advocates. Denying the right of free association (whatever the reason) is equivalent to denying the right to express some forms of speech. Yet the Supreme Court has in the past protected even odious forms of speech such as the protest marches of American neo-Nazis. Hence, as Epstein writes, 'freedom of association is … a derivative right of freedom of speech' and if the state is to avoid interfering with speech, it 'carries with it the idea that the right to exclude or include can be exercised for private reasons that need no validation by any public body'. It should therefore be 'flatly unconstitutional for the US to force any private organization to adopt a color-blind or sex-blind policy in hiring or admission to membership. One university can go all out for affirmative action; an all-girls school can hire only female teachers; a religious school can admit only co-religionists'.[133] The same reasoning would apply, it would seem, to a private neighborhood association – and with freedom of neighborhood association also a derivative right of freedom of religion (one might say that religion is the most important form of 'speech').

NEIGHBORHOOD 'TAXES' AND SERVICES

As part of protecting and maintaining an attractive neighborhood environment, most neighborhood associations also provide common services of one kind or another. The services provided most frequently include garbage collection, lawn mowing, street maintenance, snow removal, landscaping and management of common recreation facilities.[134] Another important function in many neighborhood associations is to protect the personal security of residents through maintaining internal patrols and other private policing methods. Some neighborhood associations also provide services such as bus transport, child care, nursery schools, health clinics and a community newsletter. The privatization of government functions was a worldwide trend in the 1980s and 1990s, but affected the United States less at the national level because there were many fewer government-owned enterprises at that level.[135] Instead, the leading arena for privatization in the United States has been local government.

Neighborhood associations pay for the administration and delivery of services by levying assessments on members. In a 1995 survey conducted by the Community Associations Institute, the median neighborhood association budget was $165 000; however, the average budget (reflecting the existence of some very high budget associations) was $510000.[136] There is wide variation but a typical association assessment falls in the range of $100 to $300 per month per housing unit. It amounts to a private form of taxation but is typically closer to a 'head tax' – so much money per housing unit per month. Municipalities, by contrast, collect property taxes that are assessed as a percentage of value. However, there is little or no expectation in a neighborhood association that the 'taxing' system will be used for internal redistributive purposes. Each unit owner should pay according to that owner's use of (or the opportunity to make use of) the common grounds and facilities, as well as partaking in other association benefits. A neighborhood association, for example, would be most unlikely to impose an income tax on its members.

The levels of services and assessments will then reflect the collective demands of the residents of each neighborhood association. Just as income redistribution is not part of the revenue-raising plan, it is also excluded from the neighborhood association objectives in the delivery of services. Of course, there may be redistribution in practice because a neighborhood association is a political entity and virtually all political bodies witness coalition formation and group negotiation. However, a main goal in designing the constitution of a neighborhood association will be to preclude the possibility of one group within the neighborhood 'exploiting' another. The ability to achieve such constitutional protection may significantly influence the value of the neighborhood housing units – and therefore also affect the level of profit accruing to the developer. A wealthy person would be very reluctant to join a neighborhood association if there were any prospect of his or her wealth being tapped for the general benefit of the association membership.

Besides the constitutional structure of neighborhood governance, another way to avoid any pressures for internal redistribution within neighborhoods will be to have small neighborhoods with homogeneous populations. The neighborhood assessments collected from unit owners will be the equivalent of a price in the market and the actual levels of neighborhood service provision will correspond to a common level of demand of like neighbors. If everyone wants the same things, there is much less chance of internal redistribution taking place. The process of collective choice will in general be simpler as there is more uniformity of preferences in a neighborhood.

However, the time burdens of democratic governance and other fixed 'transactions costs' in neighborhoods will set a limit to how small a neighborhood can be. It may also be desirable to have a neighborhood greater than some minimum size in order to realize economies of scale in the delivery of services (it is impossible to buy half of a police patrol car). A neighborhood should be large enough to be able to offer a self-contained environment of high quality. On the other hand, larger communities may suffer from other kinds of transaction cost problems, as seen in the well known maladies of bureaucracy. Large city size is also likely to involve greater diversity of population and hence greater differences between the public service demands of individuals and the common levels of city services provided to these individuals.[137] In a metropolitan economic system, there will thus be various economic forces affecting the desirable degree of 'horizontal and vertical integration' within the system of cities, municipalities, neighborhoods and other local governing institutions.

In principle, the sizes of governmental units, like the sizes of business units within a private industry, could be determined by the workings of a competitive process.[138] Indeed, some students of urban affairs have argued that the key to improved metropolitan service delivery lies in a much greater flexibility of city size and a resulting much wider room for competition with respect to forms of governance. It should be possible to create new kinds of local government institutions, perhaps larger ones assembled from building blocks of smaller ones (the latter perhaps specializing in one or a few services). As Ronald Oakerson comments,

> There is no fully objective way of determining an appropriate set of provision units apart from the expressed preferences of local citizens for public goods and services. The ease with which a single provision unit can satisfy individual preferences decreases with the preference heterogeneity of the community. By the same token, the ability to satisfy diverse preferences increases with an increase in the number of provision units in a local public economy – at least up to some point. The creation of provision units is constrained by the expected transaction costs of organizing and operating an additional unit. Transaction costs include the costs of citizen participation. The choice is between greater preference satisfaction, obtained by creating an additional provision unit, and lower transaction costs. Citizens face a trade-off that only they can decide.[139]

That is to say, as Oakerson suggests, there should be much wider opportunity for institutional experimentation in local government delivery of services. He contends that 'of central importance is the authority to create, modify, and dissolve [public service] provision units. The structure of the provision side – including the variety of provision units – depends on who can exercise this authority and under what conditions'.[140] Many economic functions that require collective action within a metropolitan economy involve land use interdependencies that only extend over a small area. Such small areas can be characterized as 'a neighborhood'. Oakerson considers that the lack of neighborhood-level institutions is a major omission in current metropolitan governance. In achieving the greater institutional flexibility among city forms that is needed, as he puts it, 'what is essential is that small-scale communities have the capability to organize themselves to act collectively with respect to common problems. This requires that locally defined communities be able to self-govern, exercising the powers of government within a limited sphere – limited in terms of both territory and the scope of authority'. It includes local assumption of authority for the provision of 'some types of goods and services [that] can [best] be provided on a 'neighborhood' scale'.[141]

At present, however, the organizational arrangements for metropolitan areas 'tend to preclude or inhibit the development of smaller, nested provision units – neighborhood governments – within [larger city] boundaries'.[142] In general, the potential benefits from a process of competition among types and sizes of governments within an existing metropolitan area are limited by the current public status of cities. It is possible in concept to enlarge or contract cities by means of the processes of municipal annexation or de-annexation. But these processes are so slow and so cumbersome that in practice little realignment of city boundaries takes place. Once a metropolitan area has achieved a certain set of city and municipal boundaries, these boundaries tend to remain fixed indefinitely. The metropolitan area is thus like a private industry in which the sizes and boundaries of individual business firms in the industry are largely established at some point and the forces of economic competition and change must thereafter operate within these existing business forms. In this light, it should not be surprising that the organization of metropolitan areas tends toward less and less efficient forms, as compared with the private business sector.

Although he acknowledges the growing importance of private neighborhood associations, Oakerson does not give many specifics concerning the means of neighborhood governance. Yet a private neighborhood is an obvious answer. A major advantage of the private status is a greater ease of integration of neighborhood actions into a market economy. If private neighborhood 'constitutions' are properly designed, they can allow for the ready expansion, contraction, termination or other modification of the boundaries and the internal organizational arrangements of private neighborhoods, as new economic conditions or other changing circumstances may prove to warrant such changes. Neighborhood territories could be altered – creating larger or smaller collective units for service provision – with the consent only of those affected. It is possible in concept that small-scale neighborhood governments in the public sector could have a similar flexibility of adjustment. However, given the existing legal rules that apply to 'state actors', this is less likely in practice.

LEGISLATIVE AND EXECUTIVE BRANCHES

The levels of services delivered, internal assessments and other elements of the management of neighborhood associations are typically determined by elected boards of directors. They serve as the private equivalent of the members of a town council. There may be various subcommittees of the neighborhood association board, such as an architectural review subcommittee that typically oversees enforcement of neighborhood covenants and other land use restrictions. The residents of a neighborhood association choose the members of the board of directors through an election. The terms of members are usually staggered so that only part of the board is elected at any given time. Candidates generally run as individuals without any party labels. A typical term might be two or three years.

Most elections are at large: all the candidates run against one another and the highest vote getters win the allotted number of seats on the board of directors. In some particularly large neighborhood associations, the overall area of the association may be divided into districts (like city wards). Each district may have its own board of directors to oversee the smallest-scale interactions within that area. Districts (or combinations of districts) may also send their own representatives to be members of an association-wide board of directors.

In the normal arrangement, voting rights in neighborhood elections are assigned equally to each housing unit, or votes may be allocated in proportion to square feet or some other measure of the value of the housing units. Hence multiple owners of single units must share a single vote, and renters usually do not have any vote at all. Where two or more adults share a housing unit, it is up to them to find a way to reach a common decision for the use of their one allotted vote.

The board of directors of a neighborhood association deals with the basic management of the neighborhood. More 'foundational' or 'constitutional' issues are likely to require a full referendum among all the members of the neighborhood association. The board will normally have its own voting rules that apply for the standard kinds of decisions it handles. Typically, and like most town councils in municipal governments, a board of directors of a neighborhood association will operate by majority rule.

As in the case of the US constitution, there is a further issue of the division of governance responsibilities between a 'legislature' and an 'executive'. In theory at least, the US Congress determines the budget and sets the broad policy; the executive branch under the leadership of the president then carries out these instructions. In a private neighborhood, the board of directors – the legislature – may hire a professional administrator to handle the daily affairs of the neighborhood. Thus, unlike the case of election of the

mayor of a city, few neighborhood associations choose their chief administrative officer by popular vote of the unit owners. In 1990, 42 per cent of
neighborhood associations contracted with an outside private party for
their management. Another 26 per cent undertook their own management
but hired an onsite staff to perform particular management functions. Most
of the remainder (typically the smaller associations) managed themselves
through voluntary contributions of time and effort of the members.[143]

A manager under contract will normally live outside and otherwise have
no personal connection with the neighborhood. Indeed, it is normally best
that he or she should not be a unit owner. Instead of an election, managerial selection in private neighborhoods thus more closely resembles competitive bidding in a business environment – an economic form of decision
making in which the workings of the market replace the standard political
processes as found in municipal governments. If a change is necessary, the
act of contracting with a brand new private firm to manage the neighborhood association is tantamount to dismissing the mayor and the entire civil
service of a municipal government – and it may be much easier to accomplish this kind of transition when it is done privately in such a fashion.

Within the scope of authority as laid out by the board, the private management firm has the power, in effect, to make certain kinds of collective
choices for the neighborhood. A private manager might, for example, have
the authority to hire and fire neighborhood association employees. He or
she may choose subcontractors to perform specific neighborhood service
functions. The resolution of certain types of internal disagreements among
the residents concerning acceptable land uses within the neighborhood may
also fall to the private manager.

AMENDING THE CONSTITUTION

Existing neighborhoods are already beginning to face significant demands
for amendments to the terms and conditions of their founding documents.
Many neighborhood associations, for example, are now under strong pressure to relax tight restrictions on home-based businesses, reflecting the
communications revolution in the American workplace and the spreading
practice of part-time or even full-time work from home. In one 1995 survey
by the Community Associations Institute, 28 per cent of neighborhood
associations had tried on at least one occasion to amend the land use provisions in their Covenants, Conditions and Restrictions (CC&Rs). Of these
efforts, 67 per cent had succeeded in fulfilling the necessary requirements
for achieving an amendment.[144]

A constitutional change in a neighborhood association generally requires a full vote of the unit owners. The percentage required for approval can vary considerably from neighborhood to neighborhood. Although a requirement of unanimous consent for approving an amendment would be ideal in some respects, in practice there are almost certain to be dissenters and holdouts in any neighborhood group that is larger than a small number. Some of these dissenters may not really object to the changes proposed but may hope to gain personally by pursuing complex bargaining strategies that end up with the whole neighborhood decision resting in their hands. They might then be able to 'sell' their vote for a high personal gain. Other than the initial approval of the founding documents that unit owners must accept on entering the neighborhood, it will thus be difficult for most neighborhoods to operate under a requirement of unanimity for other forms of neighborhood decision making. Nevertheless, a few neighborhood documents lack any explicit procedure for subsequent amendment. In effect, these neighborhoods are operating under a requirement of 100 per cent approval for constitutional revisions.

Most neighborhoods that have explicitly considered the issue have opted for a requirement of less than unanimity. Like the rules for the Congress established by the US constitution, the required vote of approval may depend on the type of decision under consideration (approval of a treaty with foreign nations, for example, requires a two-thirds vote of the Senate). The more radical the departure from the initial neighborhood declaration, and the greater the potential impact on the unit owners, the higher the required percentage is likely to be. For example, the Pennsylvania Uniform Planned Community Act, adopted in 1996, requires a two-thirds vote to amend a founding declaration but a four-fifths vote to sell common property of the association. Termination of the association also can be achieved by a four-fifths vote of the unit owners.[145]

Table 8.2 below shows the distribution of approval requirements for standard types of changes in the governing rules of neighborhood associations, as found in a survey of 199 associations done for the Community Associations Institute. Among many other ways in which neighborhood practices can differ, the base of the voting population may be defined differently. In some neighborhoods, the required number of votes is calculated as a certain percentage of the total eligible votes in the neighborhood. In other neighborhoods, the required vote is calculated as a percentage of those actually participating in the voting. In the former case, the most common requirement for approval is a 75 per cent agreement to the proposed amendment.

In *The Calculus of Consent*, in 1962, James Buchanan and Gordon Tullock explored in a general way the tradeoffs involved in setting a voting percentage for approval of a collective decision.[146] They noted that majority rule was

Table 8.2   Percentage of unit votes to amend a neighborhood constitution

Required vote for approval of amendment	Among all unit owners[1]	Among unit owners actually voting[2]
51	12	10
60	2	8
66	24	31
75	33	27
80	2	4
90	11	4
100	3	0
Other	13	16

Notes:
1. Associations in which the required vote for approval is a percentage of all units in the association.
2. Associations in which the required vote for approval is a percentage of voting units only.

Source: Doreen Heisler and Warren Klein, *Inside Look at Community Association Homeownership – Facts, Perceptions* (Alexandria, VA: Community Associations Institute, 1996, p.32).

the prevailing standard in most legislatures but this was more a matter of tradition than of any logical necessity. Indeed, there might well be different percentages required for different circumstances. The basic tradeoff involved two forms of cost. One was the negotiation and decision-making cost of reaching any required minimum voting percentage. As the required percentage approached unanimity, decision making could in itself become extremely costly. The other form of cost might be labeled the 'losing-side' cost. For every losing voter in an election, this voter would suffer a decline of his or her welfare from the implementation of the decision. As the voting rule for collective decisions approached unanimity, the cumulative losing-side cost would approach zero.

In short, as one form of collective choice cost goes up, the other form of cost will go down. There will be a specific percentage required for a vote of approval that will minimize the total costs, and typically this will not be 51 per cent. Whether they think of it this way or not, many thousands of neighborhood associations across the United States have been making this tradeoff in writing their voting rules into their new constitutions. It has been an application of the principles of 'constitutional economics' to the writing of more new constitutions than perhaps has ever occurred in such a short time before.[147]

TERMINATION

One important type of collective choice that many neighborhoods have not addressed is the possibility of termination of the neighborhood association itself. In the long run, few neighborhoods will last forever. There might be, for example, a future change in economic circumstances that would make the entire neighborhood uneconomic for its existing location. A new subway stop, for example, could open up nearby. As a result, it might make economic sense to demolish the existing structures in order to accommodate, say, the construction of an office tower or large apartment building. A developer might well be willing to offer the unit owners a price equal to two or three times the value of the properties in their current use.

In that case, the great majority of unit owners might prefer to abolish their neighborhood association and to move away – and to be rewarded for leaving by taking large windfall gains with them. It would be desirable to have available some form of neighborhood collective process to approve or disapprove such a sale of the entire neighborhood (presumably as one large block of properties or perhaps as several large packages). It would be in the same spirit as the procedures whereby the stock holders of a business corporation might vote to accept a takeover offer by another corporation, possibly abolishing the corporation outright in return for new stock or other appropriate compensation.

If a private neighborhood association were to vote to abolish itself in this fashion, there would be important issues of the proper voting procedure, the percentage of votes required, exactly how the properties in the neighborhood would be sold, and how the profits would be divided up (in proportion to square feet, to individualized assessments of properties, or in other ways). At present, few neighborhood associations have made any provision in their voting rules for such a radical form of 'amendment' in their founding declarations.

The possibility of neighborhood termination represents one of the important ways in which a land use system based on private neighborhood associations may offer large advantages over the current zoning system. Under zoning, it is virtually impossible to organize an orderly process of transition from one basic type of land use in a neighborhood to another. The city would have to change the zoning in advance to accommodate the new use. However, the existing residents of neighborhoods will almost always resist any such changes. Instead, speculators may have to buy up neighborhood properties one or a few at a time, possibly letting the neighborhood run down during an interim period of transition. Eventually, if enough properties are sold, and enough older residents of the neighborhood move out, it may be possible to change the zoning to accommodate a brand new use of the land. In such a process – which is very disruptive for the older residents – much of the ultimate gain in land value ends up going to the speculators. The financial losers are the original owners who failed to act collectively and were instead picked off one at a time.

In effect, a neighborhood constitution that allows for full neighborhood termination might be regarded as a new system of urban land assembly. Urban renewal was used in the 1950s and 1960s for the purpose of putting together large land parcels that would allow comprehensive redevelopment of a whole neighborhood area. However, urban renewal was involuntary for many participants: the city condemned the properties, often generating great ill will. Also much of the monetary gain then went to the city on the resale of the land, not to the property owners. Neighborhood termination might be described as providing instead a private system for accomplishing the aims of urban renewal (if most likely to be applied at present in suburban areas where neighborhood associations are found). It would not be entirely voluntary because some neighborhood unit owners might vote against termination. However, assuming a large supermajority vote of the neighborhood association (say 90 per cent) were required to approve its termination, the number of such losing voters would be a small percentage of the total units in the neighborhood. And the decision to override their preferences would be in the hands of their fellow unit owners, not some distant municipal officials.

The greatest obstacle to planned redevelopment in existing built-up areas is the land assembly process. In the outer suburbs today, large attractive communities with hundreds of housing units can be planned and built from scratch. These are the same places where neighborhood associations are now being formed to provide for private governance. Lacking a way of assembling large enough units of land, similar planned communities are now very difficult or impossible in areas closer in to big cities. Yet, on the evidence of consumer choice in the market, there is a high demand among Americans for planned developments with new kinds of governing institutions that a private status makes possible.

A POLICY PROPOSAL: NEW NEIGHBORHOOD ASSOCIATIONS FOR OLD NEIGHBORHOODS

In previous writings I have offered a proposal for resolving the land assembly problem in existing neighborhoods that may be facing powerful transitional pressures. Those interested in a more complete explanation can consult these papers for further details.[148] I will merely sketch here the basic concept.

I propose to establish a legal mechanism by which an existing neighborhood could create a private neighborhood association. It would be similar to the incorporation of a new municipality but it would instead result in the creation of a private neighborhood, based on a private property relationship among the property owners of the neighborhood. In order to approve the establishment of the new private neighborhood association, a large supermajority vote would be required. Assuming this supermajority could be achieved, those who voted against forming a neighborhood association would nevertheless be required to become members.

There are many possible ways in which such a concept could be implemented.[149] For the purposes of discussion, I propose that the legislature of each state enact a law to provide for the following six-step process.

1. A group of individual property owners in an existing neighborhood could petition the state to form a private neighborhood association. The petition should describe the boundaries of the proposed neighborhood and the instruments of collective governance intended for it. The petition should state the services expected to be performed by the neighborhood association and an estimate of the monthly assessments required. The petitioning owners should possess cumulatively more than 60 per cent of the total value of neighborhood property.

2. The state would then have to certify that the proposed neighborhood met certain standards of reasonableness, including having a contiguous area; boundaries of a regular shape; an appropriate relationship to major streets, streams, valleys and other geographic features; and other considerations. The state would also certify that the proposed private governance instruments of the neighborhood association met state standards.

3. If the application met the state requirements, a neighborhood committee would be authorized to negotiate a service transfer agreement with the municipal government that had jurisdiction over the neighborhood. The agreement would specify the future possible transfer of ownership of municipal streets, parks, swimming pools, tennis courts and other existing public lands and facilities located within the proposed private neighborhood boundaries (possibly including some compensation to the city). It would specify the future assumption of garbage collection, snow removal, policing and fire protection, insofar as the private neighborhood would assume responsibility for such services. The transfer agreement would also specify future tax arrangements, including any property or other tax credits that the members of the neighborhood association might receive in compensation for assuming existing municipal service burdens. Other matters of potential importance to the municipality and

to the neighborhood would also be addressed. The state government would serve as an overseer and mediator in this negotiation process, and could overrule a municipality as a last resort in order to resolve disputes.

4. Once state certification of the neighborhood proposal was received, and a municipal transfer agreement had been negotiated, a neighborhood election would be called for a future date. The election would occur no less than one year after the submission of a complete description of the neighborhood proposal, including the founding documents for the neighborhood association, the municipal transfer agreement, estimates of assessment burdens, a comprehensive appraisal of the values of individual neighborhood properties, and other relevant information. During the one-year waiting period, the state would supervise a process to inform property owners and other residents of the neighborhood of the details of the proposal and to facilitate public discussion and debate.

5. In the actual election, approval of the creation of a new private neighborhood association would require both of the following: (1) an affirmative vote of unit owners cumulatively representing 80 per cent or more of the total property value within the proposed neighborhood; and (2) an affirmative vote by 70 per cent or more of the individual unit owners in the neighborhood. If these conditions were met, all property owners in the neighborhood would be required to join the neighborhood association and would then be subject to the full terms and conditions laid out in the neighborhood association documents (the 'declaration', or, as it would amount to in practice, the neighborhood 'constitution').

6. Following the establishment of a neighborhood association, the municipal government would transfer the legal responsibility for regulating land use in the neighborhood to the unit owners in the neighborhood association, acting through their instruments of collective decision making. The municipal zoning authority within the boundaries of the neighborhood association would be abolished, except insofar as such zoning served to regulated direct adverse impacts on other property owners located outside the boundaries of the neighborhood association.

As I have argued elsewhere, the creation of private neighborhood associations would create market incentives for the redevelopment of many deteriorated neighborhoods in existing cities and inner suburbs.[150] At the same time much of the monetary benefit of such redevelopment would be received by the current property owners. In outer suburbs, new private 'landowner associations' could be formed along the same lines.[151] This would facilitate a change in democratic voting procedures to allow developers to retain control over the process of development of large parcels of land until it is nearing completion. At present, under the one person/one vote rules that apply to municipal government, residential newcomers obtain political control over land use at a much earlier stage of development. They have often used this control to block the completion of socially desirable and efficient development plans. This has not only been unfair to the landowners but has been socially inequitable from a full metropolitan perspective. It has resulted in the tying up of large areas of undeveloped land in less productive forms of use than are warranted by the quality and location of the land.[152] The biggest losers have been lower and moderate income groups who have been denied access to new housing opportunities in attractive locations within their means.[153]

CONCLUSION

The privatization of the American neighborhood was a continuing process over much of the twentieth century. Most 'private' neighborhoods, however, operated formally until the 1960s under a public status. These neighborhoods were parts of a small suburban municipality that might have one or a few neighborhoods. Entry into such a neighborhood was almost as restricted as today it is in a typical private neighborhood association. Zoning was the key legal instrument in this system. Zoning regulations in effect enforced a collective property right to the local neighborhood environment, operating in the guise of a 'public' action. Fenced off from the outside world by their controls on new land uses, over the course of the twentieth century suburban municipal governments would increasingly become private entities for many practical purposes.

Various legal fictions then had to be maintained to justify the use of zoning for such private purposes.[154] It added another chapter to the long history of the workings of the land laws. Perhaps more often than not in this history, the legal form of the land laws has borne little relationship to the actual practice. Richard Pipes writes of the institution of property that there has been a longstanding 'difficulty of distinguishing law from reality' in this area.[155] Informal understandings on the ground have frequently been more important than any formal codes written in the law books.[156] The judiciary would learn to look the other way when obvious discrepancies between legal theory and practice might arise.[157]

New property rights to land thus are seldom created by legislatures from whole cloth. Rather, such rights typically emerge gradually from informal practice, often at odds with the accepted economic and legal theories of the day. As experience accumulates over many years, the informal practice comes to be better understood and the merits to be more fully appreciated. At a still later point the informal practice may come to be accepted and finally codified by the legislature in the law. In describing the evolution of property rights to land in England over many centuries, Sir Frederick Pollock once wrote that 'the history of our land laws, it cannot be too often repeated, is a history of legal fictions and evasions, with which the Legislature vainly endeavoured to keep pace until their results ... were perforce acquiesced in as a settled part of the law itself'.[158]

This process can take decades or even centuries. In the long transition from medieval property concepts to those of a capitalist economic system, the law of usury evolved in this manner.[159] For many centuries, there were also strong social prohibitions on the sale of land. For much of history, as Pipes writes, 'land was universally considered a resource that one could exploit exclusively but not own and sell'.[160] In England, it took from the thirteenth to the nineteenth century to establish the modern concepts of private property rights with respect to land, including the right to sell the land. As Pollock wrote at the end of the nineteenth century, although 'the really characteristic incidents of the feudal tenures have disappeared or left only the faintest of traces, the scheme of our land laws can, as to its form, be described only as a modified feudalism'.[161]

In the United States, things have not been much different. In the nineteenth century millions of squatters illegally entered the public lands. Although the federal government regarded them as criminal law breakers, it was powerless to do anything on a distant frontier. After a few years, strong political pressures often resulted in the Congress retroactively confirming the original squatter occupancy, granting a formal property right.[162] When the Homestead Act passed in 1862, it was not a new concept but a final recognition by the federal government that a squatting mode of land settlement was a simple fact of life on the western frontier.[163]

The evolution of American land law in the twentieth century has followed once again these ancient patterns. Zoning was a radical departure in American land law but it was justified in terms that served to obscure the real degree of change from traditional practice. The practical effect of zoning, along with other laws and court rulings, was the privatization of the suburban municipality. It became virtually a form of private government. When the various zoning fictions were eventually exposed as such, judges were simply forced to look the other way. Short of a revolution in American land law, they had little choice but to sustain longstanding property arrangements – whatever the legal awkwardness.

It is also typical of the land laws that the informal practice is eventually given greater recognition and, perhaps, at some point official acceptance.

The rise of the private neighborhood association can be seen in this light. It represents a new formal recognition in the law of the longstanding private status of suburban governments as it had developed over the course of the twentieth century. To be sure, private neighborhood associations are not only a matter of bringing the legal form into alignment with the practical realities. As this chapter has explored, the private legal status of the neighborhood association opens up a host of new constitutional possibilities for local government. Zoning and other local laws and practices carried the privatization of local government a long way forward, but the rise of private neighborhood associations has acted to carry it further. The very fact of now officially recognizing the private status of suburban local governments in the United States is likely to have major practical consequences in itself in the future.

During the twentieth century many people were convinced that the world was becoming a more rational place. Society, finally, would deal in the realm of facts; political deceptions would cease; governments would finally be able to say directly what they were actually planning and doing. Whole professions, such as the field of public administration, depended on the assumption that the true goals of society could be stated 'up front' and explicitly, and then the goals realized by a process of rational selection from among the alternatives. However, the history of the American land laws in the twentieth century offers little to support this view. The details were now different but the pattern of evolution in the land laws remained much as it had always been in England and the United States.[164] It was a process of unplanned outcomes and unintended results of the actions of the governments involved.

Today, at the beginning of the twenty-first century, perhaps the time has arrived for a new truth in advertising with respect to the American land system and the processes of land development and local governance. It may be time to dispense with the old zoning fictions and to align the official forms of the law more closely with the actual realities on the ground. Perhaps the true function of zoning should be explicitly recognized for what it long ago became – a private collective right to the common elements of the neighborhood environment The creation of neighborhood associations can accomplish this purpose reasonably well in the outer suburbs, the places where most new development is occurring today. A new legal mechanism is necessary, however, for the privatizing of land use controls and neighborhood governance in inner cities and other existing developed areas. If such a mechanism were established by a state legislature, perhaps along the lines sketched above, private neighborhood government might extend some day to encompass the entire metropolitan area. It would not only be the well off residents of new developments in the outer suburbs but also the poorer residents of existing neighborhoods in inner cities who would gain a much higher degree of control over their own immediate environments.

NOTES

1. This chapter is adapted from a paper originally prepared for a conference on 'The Property Tax, Land Use and Land-Use Regulation', sponsored by the Lincoln Institute of Land Policy, 13–15 January, 2002, Scottsdale, Arizona. Robert H. Nelson is a Professor in the School of Public Affairs of the University of Maryland. He is currently writing a book on private community associations. He is the author of *Zoning and Property Rights* (MIT Press, 1977) and, most recently, *Economics as Religion: From Samuelson to Chicago and Beyond* (Penn State Press, 2001).
2. Community Associations Institute, *Community Associations Factbook*, ed. Frank Spink (Alexandria, VA, 1999, p.19). For additional background data on community associations, see also Community Associations Institute, *Community Associations Factbook, 1993 edn*, ed. Clifford J. Treese (Alexandria, VA, 1993).
3. Steven Siegel, 'The Constitution and Private Government: Toward the Recognition of Constitutional Rights in Private Residential Communities Fifty Years after Marsh v. Alabama', 6 *William & Mary Bill of Rights Journal* (Spring 1998, pp.560–61).
4. Robert G. Natelson, 'Consent, Coercion and "Reasonableness" in Private Law: The Special Case of the Property Owners Association', 51 *Ohio State Law Journal* (Winter 1990, p.42). See also Robert G. Natelson, *Law of Property Owners Associations* (Boston: Little, Brown, 1989).
5. Richard Damstra, 'Don't Fence Us Out: The Municipal Power to Ban Gated Communities and the Federal Takings Clause', 35 *Valparaiso University Law Review* (Summer 2001).
6. Community Associations Institute, 1999, *Community Associations Factbook*, p.9.
7. See Harry C. Boyte, *The Backyard Revolution: Understanding the New Citizen Movement* (Philadelphia: Temple University Press, 1980); and Nancy L. Rosenblum, *Membership and Morals: The Personal Uses of Pluralism in America* (Princeton: Princeton University Press, 1998, pp.112–57).
8. *Nahrstedt v. Lakeside Village Condominium Association* (1994), cited in Katharine N. Rosenberry, 'Home Business, Llamas and Aluminum Siding: Trends in Covenant Enforcement', 31 *John Marshall Law Review* (Winter 1998, p.453).
9. US Advisory Commission on Intergovernmental Relations, *Residential Community Associations: Private Governments in the Intergovernmental System?* (Washington, DC, May 1989, pp.18, 1).
10. Wayne S. Hyatt, 'Common Interest Communities: Evolution and Reinvention', 31 *John Marshall Law Review* (Winter 1998, pp.307–8).
11. D. Clurman, F.S. Jackson and E.L. Hebard, 1984, *Condominiums and Cooperatives* (New York: John Wiley).
12. Richard J. Kane, 'The Financing of Cooperatives and Condominiums: A Retrospective', 73 *St. Johns Law Review* (Winter 1999, p.103).
13. Lois M. Baron, 'The Great Gate Debate', *Builder* (March 1998, p.94), reprinted in Urban Land Institute, *Gated Communities* (Washington, DC, June 2000). See also Edward J. Blakely and Mary Gail Snyder, *Fortress America: Gated Communities in the United States* (Washington, DC: Brookings Institution Press, 1997).
14. In California, gated communities are particularly common. In Orange County, about half of the housing in unincorporated areas of the county is in a gated community. One survey in January 1999 showed that 68 per cent of the houses available for sale in the county were located in gated communities. In 1990, a survey of homebuyers in southern California found that 54 per cent wanted to buy a home in a gated community. One critic

foresees a future of the Los Angeles suburbs in which 'vast, sprawling clusters of gated communities are connected to one another and to fortress buildings, enclosed malls, and sports stadiums by a web of freeways and interchanges'. See Richard Damstra, 'Don't Fence Us Out: The Municipal Power to Ban Gated Communities and the Federal Takings Clause', 35 *Valparaiso University Law Review* (Summer 2001).

15. The term 'neighborhood association' has frequently been used in the past to refer to a group of neighbors who join together well after the neighborhood has been settled. The neighborhood group has no authority to require membership and any dues or assessments are paid on a voluntary basis. Some members of the neighborhood typically do not join. The purpose of the association may be to organize events such as a crime watch or neighborhood barbecue. In this book, 'neighborhood association' is being used in a different sense, to refer to a formal neighborhood arrangement in which all the owners are required to join the association as an initial condition of purchase of their homes, and to agree to the future enforcement of private land use restrictions and to pay association assessments to cover the costs of neighborhood services.
16. David J. Kennedy, 'Residential Associations as State Actors: Regulating the Impact of Gated Communities on Nonmembers', 105 *Yale Law Journal* (December 1995, p.762).
17. This is about the same size, interestingly enough, as the 'deme' in ancient Greece, the 'small, territorially based associations, which formed the basic political unit of the Athenian polity'. Indeed, the deme 'shares many characteristics' with the neighborhood association. There were about 150 demes in ancient Athens, each having from 400 to 1200 residents. Among their key roles, they controlled citizenship and voter registration. See Michael Sarbanes and Kathleen Skullney, 'Taking Communities Seriously: Should Community Associations Have Standing in Maryland?', 6 *Maryland Journal of Contemporary Legal Issues* (Spring/Summer 1995, p.292).
18. Siegel, 'The Constitution and Private Government', p.479.
19. Evan McKenzie, *Privatopia: Homeowner Associations and the Rise of Residential Private Government* (New Haven: Yale University Press, 1994, p.11).
20. Ibid., p.22.
21. Law professor Sheryll Cashin laments that the rise of neighborhood associations has 'put the nation on a course toward civic secession'. The spread of 'secessionist attitudes' is promoting a 'reduced empathy' for people outside the neighborhood association boundaries, a rise of 'regional polarization' and in general a reduced capacity for 'shared sacrifice and redistributive spending' within metropolitan areas. See Sheryll D. Cashin, 'Privatized Communities and the "Secession of the Successful": Democracy and Fairness Beyond the Gate', 28 *Fordham Urban Law Journal* (June 2001, pp.1677, 1685, 1690, 1683, 1686).
22. Glen O. Robinson, 'Communities', 83 *Virginia Law Review* (March 1997, pp.304–5 (describing the views of Roger K. Lewis and quoting from Jane Jacobs).
23. Alexander Keyssar, *The Right to Vote: The Contested History of Democracy in the United States* (New York: Basic Books, 2000).
24. Renters thus are entirely disenfranchised in most neighborhood associations. Yet one 1987 survey in California found that the majority of units were occupied by renters in 15 per cent of the neighborhood associations, and that the median association had 20 per cent of the units occupied by renters. See Steven Siegel, 'The Constitution and Private Government: Toward the Recognition of Constitutional Rights in Private Residential Communities Fifty Years After Marsh v. Alabama', 6 *William & Mary Bill of Rights Journal* (Spring 1998, p.539).
25. Albert A. Foer, 'Democracy in the New Towns: The Limits of Private Government', *University of Chicago Law Review* (Winter 1969, p.412).
26. Stephen E. Barton and Carol J. Silverman, 'Preface', in Barton and Silverman (eds), *Common Interest Communities: Private Governments and the Public Interest* (Berkeley, CA: Institute of Government Studies Press, 1994, p.xii).
27. Gregory S. Alexander, 'Dilemmas of Group Autonomy: Residential Associations and Community', 75 *Cornell Law Review* (November 1989, pp.5, 11, 43).
28. Ibid., p.44.

29. Carol J. Silverman and Stephen E. Barton, 'Shared Premises: Community and Conflict in the Common Interest Development', in Barton and Silverman (eds), *Common Interest Communities*, p.141.
30. Kenneth T. Jackson, *Crabgrass Frontier: The Suburbanization of the United States* (New York: Oxford University Press, 1985).
31. The process of privatization in the suburbs has taken many forms. It seems that, as human beings (or at least Americans) become wealthier, they are willing to expend a considerable part of their additional resources on achieving greater privacy. Despite those who regard 'private' motives as uncivic, these motives appear to have a great strength and staying power. A greater desire for privacy can be found within the design of individual homes, as well as in the choice of neighborhood types. A recent report thus notes that the greatest change in the design of new suburban homes is the increase in the number of bathrooms. Fifty years ago, the typical new home had one bathroom; now it has two or three, and many homes have more. A Harvard University researcher declared that 'the biggest change in housing in the past 60 years has been in plumbing'. There were multiple reasons for the increase in the number of bathrooms but a principal reason was the desire for greater personal privacy. The buyers of new homes today

> want to be alone: That means, if they've got the money, they're not interested in teaching the lessons they learned from their parents about the merits of sharing. They want privacy.
>   'We all shared a bathroom – parents and five children – when I was a kid,' said *Better Homes and Gardens* editor and bathroom maven Joan McCloskey, 'but I have no idea how we did it.'
>   It is ... a far cry from the 1940s. ... It's also far different from the experience of baby boomers who shared [a bathroom] with siblings in the 1950s or 1960s. (Sandra Fleishman, 'Builders' Winning Play: A Royal Flush', *The Washington Post*, 24 November 2001, p.H1)

32. David Popenoe, *Private Pleasure, Public Plight: American Metropolitan Community Life in Comparative Perspective* (New Brunswick, NJ: Transaction Books, 1985, p.117).
33. Ibid.
34. William Schneider, 'The Suburban Century Begins', *The Atlantic* (July 1992, p.37).
35. Andres Duany and Elizabeth Plater-Zyberk, quoted in Schneider, 'The Suburban Century Begins', p.37.
36. Richard Briffault, 'Our Localism: Part II – Localism and Legal Theory', 90 *Columbia Law Review* (March 1990, p.348).
37. Neighborhood associations have been slowest to take hold as a new instrument for collective ownership of housing in the northeast and in the midwest. The role of private neighborhood associations is greatest in places such as California, Florida and Texas, where the largest amount of new housing development is taking place. In order to form a neighborhood association, it is necessary to put the founding documents in place and to require agreement as a condition of initial purchase in the neighborhood, all this occurring prior to development. In older areas of the United States, existing neighborhoods were often built before the 1960s when there was much less likelihood of forming a neighborhood association. These neighborhoods have resorted to public zoning powers to protect neighborhood environmental quality. The small suburb in the northeast or midwest thus is in many ways the functional equivalent of a private neighborhood association in the southeast or the southwest. Perhaps because private neighborhood governance was available, there was less resistance in these regions to annexation laws that favored central city expansion, resulting in cities such as Houston and Phoenix that have spread over vast geographic areas. As Richard Briffault comments, 'Southern and Western metropolitan areas generally have fewer municipalities than their Northern and Eastern counterparts.' In 1967, there were only 14 separate municipalities in the greater San Diego area, and 18 in the Phoenix area, compared with

hundreds of independent municipalities in the New York, Chicago and other northern and eastern metropolitan areas.

The rise of neighborhood associations is thus opening the way for a new pattern of organization of local government in the United States. In the south and west where many areas are newly developing, the small-scale services such as garbage collection and street maintenance are provided privately through the neighborhood association, leaving larger units of local government to focus on those services such as connecting highways, sewage and water that may operate most efficiently on a regional scale. The small muni-cipalities, as found in such large numbers surrounding center cities in the northeast and midwest, have much less of a role to play in this new southern and western pattern of land development and governance. Their role is instead fulfilled privately in these regions. See Richard Briffault, 'Our Localism: Part I – The Structure of Local Government Law', 90 *Columbia Law Review* (January 1990, p.81).

38. Jerry Frug, 'Decentering Decentralization', 60 *University of Chicago Law Review* (Spring 1993, pp.265, 266, 270).

39. *Schad* v. *Mount Ephraim*, 452 US 61 (1981) (Burger in this opinion is dissenting), cited in Frug, 'Decentering Decentralization', p.266.

40. For a comprehensive development of this view of the functioning of the zoning system as a de facto set of collective property rights, see Robert H. Nelson, *Zoning and Property Rights: An Analysis of the American System of Land Use Regulation* (Cambridge, MA: MIT Press, 1977). See also William A. Fischel, *The Economics of Zoning Laws: A Property Rights Approach to American Land Use Controls* (Baltimore: Johns Hopkins University Press, 1985) and William A. Fischel, *Regulatory Takings: Law, Economics and Politics* (Cambridge, MA: Harvard University Press, 1995).

41. Lee Anne Fennell, 'Hard Bargains and Real Steals: Land Use Exactions Revisited', 86 *Iowa Law Review* (October 2000, pp.16–17).

42. Richard Briffault, 'Our Localism: Part I – The Structure of Local Government Law', 90 *Columbia Law Review* (January 1990); Richard Briffault, 'Our Localism: Part II – Localism and Legal Theory', 90 *Columbia Law Review* (March 1990); Richard Briffault, 'Who Rules at Home?: One Person/ One Vote and Local Governments', 60 *University of Chicago Law Review* (Spring 1993); Richard Briffault, 'The Local Government Boundary Problem in Metropolitan Areas', 48 *Stanford Law Review* (May 1996); Richard Briffault, 'The Rise of Sublocal Structures in Urban Governance', 82 *Minnesota Law Review* (December 1997); and Richard Briffault, 'A Government for Our Time?: Business Improvement Districts and Urban Governance', 99 *Columbia Law Review* (March 1999).

43. Briffault, 'Who Rules at Home?', p.419

44. See Nelson, *Zoning and Property Rights*, pp.16–17.

45. Briffault, 'Who Rules at Home?', p.383.

46. James V. DeLong, *Property Matters: How Property Rights Are Under Assault – And Why You Should Care* (New York: Free Press, 1997). See also Dennis J. Coyle, *Property Rights and the Constitution: Shaping Society Through Land Use Regulation* (Albany, NY: State University of New York Press, 1993).

47. Cited in Mike Bowler and Evan McKenzie, 'Invisible Kingdoms', *California Lawyer* (December 1985, p.56).

48. Garrett Hardin, 'The Tragedy of the Commons', 162 *Science* (1968, pp.1243–8).

49. To be sure, Elinor Ostrom and others have since shown that many commons situations are effectively handled without resort to either formal regulatory or property right approaches. In small communities, a powerful cultural bond is often sufficient to achieve voluntary cooperation among users of the common areas of the community. In some of these communities, common resources have been well managed and conserved for hun-dreds of years. See Elinor Ostrom, *Governing the Commons: The Evolution of Institutions for Collective Action* (New York: Cambridge University Press, 1990).

50. In another survey completed in 1990, 95 per cent of the board members of neighbor-hood associations nationwide stated that they believed the full membership of the asso-ciation regarded it as either an 'excellent' or 'good' provider of common services. Only

22 per cent believed that there existed any association services that could be delivered more efficiently by a local government in the public sector. Indeed, some studies have suggested that private neighborhoods are obtaining services at costs as much as 30 to 60 per cent below the costs to municipal governments, partly because they are much more aggressive about contracting out to private providers. See Robert Jay Dilger, *Neighborhood Politics: Residential Community Associations in American Governance* (New York: New York University Press, 1992, pp. 89–90).

51.   Katherine N. Rosenberry and Curtis G. Sproul, 'A Comparison of California Common Interest Development Law and the Uniform Common Interest Ownership Act', 38 *Santa Clara Law Review* (1998).

52.   See Cass R. Sunstein, 'Legal Interference with Private Preferences', 53 *University of Chicago Law Review* (Fall 1986).

53.   *Freeman* v. *Pitts* (1992), cited in Bernard K. Ham, 'Exclusionary Zoning and Racial Segregation: A Reconsideration of the Mt. Laurel Doctrine', 7 *Seton Hall Constitutional Law Journal* (Winter 1997, p.614).

54.   Gerald B. Wetlaufer, 'Systems of Belief in Modern American Law: A View From Century's End', 49 *American University Law Review* (October 1999, p.9).

55.   David J. Kennedy, 'Residential Associations as State Actors', p.782.

56.   A. Dan Tarlock, 'Residential Community Associations and Land Use Controls', in Advisory Commission on Intergovernmental Relations (ed.), *Residential Community Associations*, 1989, pp.123–4.

57.   Many observers do in fact contend that private neighborhood associations – or at least the larger ones – should be regarded legally as state actors. Steven Siegel declares that the rise of neighborhood associations in America 'is an exceedingly important political and legal development that touches core constitutional values'. In his view, many neighborhood associations 'could be deemed state actors by means of a robust application of one or more of the established state-action theories'. In 1946, the Supreme Court had declared that a control over the use of private property could nevertheless be regarded as a state action for constitutional purposes. The City of Chickasaw, Alabama was entirely owned by the Gulf Shipbuilding Corporation. A Jehovah's Witness, Grace Marsh, was arrested and convicted for distributing religious literature on the streets of Chickasaw. In *Marsh* v. *Alabama*, the Supreme Court struck down this conviction on the grounds that a company-owned town was the functional equivalent of a public municipality and therefore should also be treated as a 'state actor'. See Steven Siegel, 'The Constitution and Private Government: Toward the Recognition of Constitutional Rights in Private Residential Communities Fifty Years After Marsh v. Alabama', 6 *William & Mary Bill of Rights Journal* (Spring 1998, pp.563, 557).

58.   Richard Briffault, 'Our Localism: Part II', p.382.

59.   Despite the wide criticisms among traditional zoning scholars of the 'exclusionary' effects of zoning, attempts to challenge zoning practices in the courts over the past few decades generally met with little success. The Supreme Court delivered a ringing endorsement of the use of zoning to protect local environments in its 1974 *Belle Terre* decision. In general, the Supreme Court during the 1970s and 1980s continued its longstanding deference to the actions of local governments in zoning matters. As one legal commentator saw the situation, in the jurisprudence of the Supreme Court during the Burger years:

> community self-determination seemed to attain the status of a penumbral, quasi-constitutional principle that provided substantive protection for local governments against constitutional claims asserted in the federal courts, especially claims premised upon the Equal Protection Clause. Indeed, in some cases the [Supreme] Court even deferred to local government decisions which had severe exclusionary effects or which undercut the important principle of public participation. ... Thus, the Court's general pattern was broad deference toward local government structures and decisionmaking. (M. David Gelfand, 'The Constitutional Position of American Local Government: Retrospect on the Burger Court and Prospect for the Rehnquist Court', 14 *Hastings Constitutional Law Quarterly*, Spring 1987, p.636).

60. The confusions of the courts are illustrated by their efforts to say whether a private shopping center should be treated in the law as a 'public' or a 'private' entity – in legal terms whether or not any of its rules should be regarded as a 'state action'. In 1968, the US Supreme Court seemed to declare that shopping centers in important respects must be regarded as state actors. The court ruled that a shopping center could not invoke its private status to prohibit the picketing by union members against the employment practices of businesses operating in the center. However, four Justices, including Justice Hugo Black, dissented strongly. Then, four years later, the Supreme Court seemingly backtracked, ruling that a shopping center was within its rights to exclude protesters against the Vietnam War from coming on the premises. The majority of the court declared that 'property [does not] lose its private character merely because the public is generally invited to use it for designated purposes' and this fact 'does not change by virtue of being large or clustered with other stores in a modern shopping center'. Then, a few years later, the Supreme Court spoke again, this time overturning its 1968 ruling outright. In a private shopping center, the court declared, 'the constitutional guarantee of free expression has no part to play'.

Finally, in 1980 the Supreme Court confused the matter still further. It allowed a California Supreme Court ruling to stand, even though this California ruling had adopted a position very similar to the 1968 decision of the US Supreme Court (now rejected by that court itself). Even though basic constitutional rights seemed to be at issue, the US Supreme Court declared that California courts could follow the guidance of the California state constitution, which might have a different outcome or standard for state action, as compared with the federal constitution. For discussion of these cases, see Harvey Rishikof and Alexander Wohl, 'Private Communities or Public Governments: 'The State Will Make the Call', 30 *Valparaiso Law Review* (Spring 1996, pp.536–41).

61. Kennedy, 'Residential Associations as State Actors', p.784.

62. A. Dan Tarlock, 'Residential Community Associations and Land Use Controls', p.76.

63. *Avery v. Midland County*, 390 US 474 (1968).

64. As one observer comments, 'one of the main reason why CICs [common interest communities] are so attractive as a housing option is that their contractual underpinnings allow residents to define the norms of their own community. Thus, the retention of flexibility in community association governance is critical; community associations must [continue to] be allowed a relatively free rein over the substantive regulations governing their community. Indeed, a convincing criticism of the position advocated by many concerned with the "illiberal" and anti-communitarian tendencies of CICs, which calls for judicial review of association activities as if they were state action, is that such a [new] standard of review would reduce the membership's flexibility.' See David C. Drewes, 'Putting the "Community" Back in Common Interest Communities: A Proposal for Participation-Enhancing Procedural Review', 101 *Columbia Law Review* (March 2001, pp.343–4).

65. The differences between a public and private status may extend, as one legal commentator has noted, to the kinds of permissible 'limitations on First Amendment rights to freedom of speech and association; the right to travel; due process issues raised by the applications of an association's rules to nonmembers; and equal protection questions raised by discrimination on the basis of race or class'. In almost every case, the neighborhood association now has wider freedoms. See David J. Kennedy, 'Residential Associations as State Actors: Regulating the Impact of Gated Communities on Nonmembers', 105 *Yale Law Journal* (December 1995, pp.790–91).

66. Wayne S. Hyatt, 'Common Interest Communities: Evolution and Reinvention', 31 *John Marshall Law Review* (Winter 1998, p.340).

67. The corporate form of governance of businesses became a prominent feature of American life in the progressive era. Evan McKenzie sees the neighborhood association as an extension of social attitudes concerning business and in this respect as a continuation of the 'progressive' tradition. As he writes, the standard form of neighborhood association is 'a Progressive-era creation. ... Pro-business, anti-politics rhetoric was a staple of the Progressive-era urban reformers and was the ideological basis for creating

the city manager form of government. In other words, the business corporation was the model for the city manager system, and the city manager system then became the model for the CID's [common interest development's] managerial government'. See Evan McKenzie, 'Reinventing Common Interest Developments: Reflections on a Policy Role for the Judiciary', 31 *John Marshall Law Review* (Winter 1998, p.408).

68. Wayne S. Hyatt, 'The Evolution in Community Governance', in Adrienne Schmitz and Lloyd W. Bookout (eds), *Trends and Innovations in Master-Planned Communities* (Washington, DC: Urban Land Institute, 1998, p.48).

69. Wayne S. Hyatt, 'Condominium and Home Owner Associations: Formation and Development', 25 *Emery Law Journal* (1975, p.990).

70. Susan F. French, 'The Constitution of a Private Residential Government Should Include a Bill of Rights', 27 *Wake Forest Law Review* (1992).

71. Ibid., pp.349, 350

72. Ibid., p.350.

73. See Robert H. Nelson, 'Pro-Choice Living Arrangements', *Forbes* (14 June 1999, p.222).

74. Katherine Rosenberry, 'The Application of the Federal and State Constitutions to Condominiums, Cooperatives, and Planned Developments', 19 *Property, Probate and Trust Journal* (1984, pp.29, 30–31, 32).

75. Robert Ellickson has in fact suggested the 1968 Supreme Court decision in *Avery*, applying the one person/one vote rule to municipalities in the public sector, perhaps should be reconsidered. Ellickson would give local governments wider flexibility in designing their institutions of governance, including the possibility of establishing property requirements for voting in some cases. See Robert C. Ellickson, 'Cities and Homeowners Associations', 130 *University of Pennsylvania Law Review* (June 1982).

76. In the early years of American history, the legal status of municipalities gave them considerable formal autonomy, similar in fact to that of a private property owner. Many towns were legally established under the same laws of incorporation as private businesses. Until the mid-nineteenth century, the legal status of New York City under state law, for example, differed little from that of a private business corporation. In the second half of the nineteenth century, municipalities came to be regarded in the law as a 'state actor'. As a public entity, but one never specifically mentioned in the US constitution, a municipality would now be seen as drawing its authority from a higher level of American government that did have a well defined constitutional status, the states.

Strictly speaking, a municipality would now be seen as a part of state government. By the end of the nineteenth century, towns and cities had come to be seen legally and constitutionally in the United States as the 'creations' of the states. Following the principles of 'Dillon's rule', all local powers were delegated powers of state governments, and these powers could be rescinded as well. If a state government wanted to abolish a municipality, curtail its authority, alter its form of government or take other radical steps to change its internal workings, all these actions would fall within its legal authority. The US Supreme Court in *Hunter* v. *City of Pittsburgh* early in the twentieth century went so far as to declare:

> The State ... at its pleasure may modify or withdraw all [city] powers, may take without compensation [city] property, hold it itself, or vest it in other agencies, expand or contract the territorial area, unite the whole or a part of it with another municipality, repeal the charter and destroy the corporation. All this may be done, conditionally or unconditionally, with or without the consent of the citizens, or even against their protest. In all these respects the State is supreme, and its legislative body, conforming its action to the state constitution, may do as it will [with respect to towns and cities], unrestrained by any provision of the Constitution of the United States.

All this is in considerable contrast to the protections afforded by the US Constitution for private property, including private neighborhood associations. Under the Constitution, for example, the federal government or a state government cannot 'take' the private property of a neighborhood association without paying compensation. Higher levels of government are required to observe due process, equal protection and other requirements that constitutionally apply to actions that regulate or otherwise affect private parties. There are no analogous constitutional requirements for actions by higher levels of government as they might affect municipal governments. See Joan C. Williams, 'The Constitutional Vulnerability of American Local Government: The Politics of City Status in American Law', *Wisconsin Law Review* (Issue 1, 1986); and Gerald E. Frug, *City Making: Building Communities without Building Walls* (Princeton: Princeton University Press, 1999).

77. Adolf Berle and Gardiner Means, *The Modern Corporation and Private Property* (New York: Macmillan, 1932).
78. One economic analysis of neighborhood associations is Yoram Barzel and Tim R. Sass, 'The Allocation of Resources by Voting', 105 *Quarterly Journal of Economics* (August 1990); a book-length study of neighborhood associations by an economist is Fred Foldvary, *Public Goods and Private Communities: The Market Provision of Social Services* (Aldershot, UK and Brookfield, US: Edward Elgar, 1994).
79. James M. Buchanan, 'An Economic Theory of Clubs', 32 *Economica* (February 1965).
80. James M. Buchanan and Gordon Tullock, *The Calculus of Consent: Logical Foundations of Constitutional Democracy* (Ann Arbor: University of Michigan Press, 1962); see also James M. Buchanan, 'The Constitution of Economic Policy', 77 *American Economic Review* (June 1987); and Dennis C. Mueller, *Constitutional Democracy* (New York: Oxford University Press, 1996).
81. See James M. Buchanan, *The Economics and the Ethics of Constitutional Order* (Ann Arbor: University of Michigan Press, 1991); and James M. Buchanan, *Choice, Contract and Constitutions: Volume 16 of the Collected Works of James M. Buchanan* (Indianapolis, IN: Liberty Fund, 2001); see also past issues of the journals, *Public Choice* and *Constitutional Political Economy*.
82. Mancur Olson, *The Logic of Collective Action: Public Goods and the Theory of Groups* (Cambridge, MA: Harvard University Press, 1965).
83. Charles M.Tiebout, 'A Pure Theory of Local Expenditures', 64 *Journal of Political Economy* (October 1956); see also Wallace C. Oates, 'An Essay on Fiscal Federalism', 37 *Journal of Economic Literature* (September 1999).
84. Bruce W. Hamilton, 'Zoning and Property Taxation in a System of Local Governments', 12 *Urban Studies* (June 1975).
85. See McKenzie, *Privatopia*; Robert Jay Dilger, *Neighborhood Politics: Residential Community Associations in American Governance* (New York: New York University Press, 1992); and Blakely and Snyder, *Fortress America*.
86. Hyatt, 'Common Interest Communities', p.325.
87. A leading legal casebook in the field is Wayne S. Hyatt and Susan F. French, *Community Association Law: Cases and Materials on Common Interest Communities* (Durham, NC: Carolina Academic Press, 1998). See also Natelson, *Law of Property Owner Associations*.
88. James L. Winokur, 'The Financial Role of Community Associations', 38 *Santa Clara Law Review* (1998, p.1137).
89. Marc A. Weiss and John W. Watts, 'Community Builders and Community Associations: The Role of Real Estate Developers in Private Residential Governance', in Advisory Commission on Intergovernmental Relations (ed.) *Residential Community Associations*, 1989, p.101.
90. Jane Jacobs, *The Death and Life of Great American Cities* (New York: Random House, 1961).
91. William S. Worley, *J.C. Nichols and the Shaping of Kansas City: Innovation in Planned Residential Communities* (Columbia, MO: University of Missouri Press, 1990).
92. Carl B. Kress, 'Beyond Nahrstedt: Reviewing Restrictions Governing Life in a Property Owner Association', 42 *UCLA Law Review* (February 1995, p.842).
93. This history is based in part on Natelson, *Law of Property Owners Associations,* pp. 19–32. See also Robert G. Natelson, 'Comments on the Historiography and Condominium: The Myth of Roman Origin', *Oklahoma City Law Review* (Spring 1987).
94. Natelson, *Law of Property Owners Associations*, p.31.
95. C. James Dowden, 'Community Associations and Local Governments: The Need for

Recognition and Reassessment', in Advisory Commission on Intergovernmental Relations (ed.), *Residential Community Associations*, 1989.

96. James L. Winokur, 'The Financial Role of Community Associations', pp.1139–40.
97. McKenzie, *Privatopia*, p.108.
98. The full range of Community Associations Institute activities can be seen at the web site (*www.caionline.org*).
99. Wayne S. Hyatt and Susan F. French, *Community Association Law: Cases and Materials on Common Interest Communities* (Durham, NC: Carolina Academic Press, 1998, pp.20–21).
100. Hyatt, 'Common Interest Communities', p.320.
101. The provisions of the UCIOA are discussed in Katharine N. Rosenberry and Curtis G. Sproul, 'A Comparison of California Common Interest Development Law and the Uniform Common Interest Ownership Act', 38 *Santa Clara Law Review* (1998).
102. Cited in Michael C. Kim, 'Involuntary Sale: Banishing an Owner from the Condominium Community', 31 *John Marshall Law Review* (Winter 1998, p.430).
103 In one celebrated case, a neighborhood association limited dogs to under 30 pounds. When a resident had a dog of about this weight, the association conducted a weigh-in. It raised the obvious question: what if the dog weighs 29.5 pounds one day, and then 30.5 the next? It raised the specter of dogs being deprived of food and drink in the period before the formal weigh-in, much as human boxers and wrestlers who compete in certain weight categories must often do.
104. David Guterson, 'No Place Like Home', *Harper's* (November 1992).
105. Gerald Korngold, *Private Land Use Controls: Balancing Private Initiative and the Public Interest in the Homeowners Association Context* (Cambridge, MA: Lincoln Institute of Land Policy, 1995, pp.5–10).
106. See Katharine N. Rosenberry, 'Home Businesses, Llamas, and Aluminum Siding: Trends in Covenant Enforcement', 31 *John Marshall Law Review* (Winter 1998, p.486).
107. *Hidden Harbor Estates* v. *Norman*, District Court of Appeals of Florida, Fourth District, 309 So.2d 180 (1975).
108. Ibid.
109. One problem is that neighborhood associations are often very rigid in their enforcement of covenants, even in the face of powerful extenuating circumstances. In 2000, the *St. Petersburg Times* in Florida reported:

> Deed restrictions in Tampa Palms require removal of a treehouse, the only place where a boy with leukemia finds peace and solace. ... To his parents ... the treehouse is a symbol of hope, a reminder of the brief time doctors thought Brage had beaten cancer and he felt well enough to build it with his father. ... Yet, the homeowners association that governs the Tampa Palms community has decided that the treehouse must come down: it violates deed restrictions. ... [The association manager complained that] 'your treehouse structure is in direct violation of the Covenants, Conditions and Restrictions for Tampa Palms'.

In the end, under severe media pressure, the association was forced to back down and to allow the treehouse to remain. This case is described in Paula A. Franzese, 'Neighborhoods: Common Interest Communities: Standards of Review and Review of Standards', included in a Festschrift in honor of Daniel R. Mandelker, 3 *Washington University Journal of Law and Policy* (2000, pp.663–4).
110. See 'The Reasonable Pet: An Examination of the Enforcement of Restrictions in California Common Interest Developments After Nahrstedt v. Lakeside Village Condominium Ass'n, Inc.', 36 *Santa Clara Law Review* (1996).
111. *Nahrstedt* v. *Lakeside Village Condominium Association*, 878 P. 2d 1275, 1282 (Cal. 1994).
112. The California Supreme Court also seems to have been concerned that it was important to establish a strong barrier to prevent the court system from being overwhelmed by a flood of suits involving neighborhood associations. If every losing party in a neighborhood decision sought to reverse this decision in court, the number of suits could be vir-

tually without limit. Thus, as one legal commentary notes, the court saw a need to establish a 'judicial barricade' that spared the court system the significant 'problem of judicial, social, and financial burdens resulting from the detailed factual determinations necessary under the previous, fact-specific standard'. See 'The Reasonable Pet: An Examination of the Enforcement of Restrictions in California Common Interest Developments After Nahrstedt v. Lakeside Village Condominium Ass'n, Inc.', 36 *Santa Clara Law Review* (1996, pp.808–9).

113. The characterization of the California court decision is contained in Kenneth Budd, *Be Reasonable!: How Community Associations Can Enforce Rules Without Antagonizing Residents, Going to Court, or Starting World War III* (Alexandria, VA: Community Associations Institute, 1998, pp.14–15).

114. Casey J. Little, '*Riss v. Angel*: Washington Remodels the Framework for Interpreting Restrictive Covenants', 73 *Washington Law Review* (April 1998, p.435).

115. Wayne S. Hyatt and Jo Anne Stubblefield, 'The Identity Crisis of Community Associations: In Search of An Appropriate Analogy', 27 *Real Property, Probate & Trust Journal* (1993, pp.691–2).

116. Budd, *Be Reasonable!*, p.16.

117. Information related to me by a personal acquaintance living in the association. (Neighborhood associations have become so widespread that doing research on them can be as easy as talking with the random person sitting next to you on an airplane.)

118. *Midlake on Big Boulder Lake Condominium Association* v. *Cappucio*, Superior Court of Pennsylvania, 673 A. 2d (340) (1996). See the discussion of this case in Hyatt and French, *Community Association Law*, pp.228–9.

119. *Shelley* v. *Kraemer*, 334 US 1 (1948).

120. Even racial discrimination is entirely legal in a host of 'private' areas of life. Racial motives, for example, obviously – and legally – enter into private choices of marriage partners for many whites and blacks alike (if race were not a factor, statistically, there would have to be many more interracial marriages than are actually seen).

121. Michael Sarbanes and Kathleen Skullney, 'Taking Communities Seriously: Should Community Associations Have Standing in Maryland?', 6 *Maryland Journal of Contemporary Legal Issues* (Spring/Summer 1995, p.296).

122. Glen O. Robinson, 'Communities', 83 *Virginia Law Review* (March 1997, p.299–300).

123. See, among many examples of this new interest in civic society, Robert D. Putnam, *Making Democracy Work: Civic Traditions in Modern Italy* (Princeton: Princeton University Press, 1993); E.J. Dionne, Jr. (ed.), *Community Works: The Revival of Civil Society in America* (Washington, DC: Brookings Institution Press, 1998); and Robert Wuthnow, *Sharing the Journey: Support Groups and America's New Quest for Community* (New York: Free Press, 1994). See also the summary and working papers of the National Commission on Civic Renewal (1998), available from the Institute for Philosophy and Public Policy, School of Public Affairs, University of Maryland.

124. Robinson, 'Communities', p.302.

125. See Amy Gutmann (ed.), *Freedom of Association* (Princeton: Princeton University Press, 1998); also Rosenblum, *Membership & Morals*.

126. See Nicole Napolitano, 'The Fair Housing Act Amendments and Age Restrictive Covenants in Condominiums and Cooperatives', 73 *St. John's Law Review* (Winter 1999, pp.278–9, 283).

127. Although it was not restricted to neighborhood associations, a 1980 nationwide survey by the Department of Housing and Urban Development found that 25 per cent of all US rental units had rules against occupancy by children.

128. *Ritchey* v. *Villa Nueva Condominium Association*, 146 California Reporter, pp.697–8.

129. *White Egret Condo., Inc.* v. *Franklin*, Supreme Court of Florida, 379 So. 2d (1979).

130. Stewart E. Sterk, 'Minority Protection in Residential Private Governments', 77 *Boston University Law Review* (April 1997, p.307).

131. The only case that seems to have addressed this issue involved the Theosophical Society in America. In 1983, a California court invalidated deed restrictions that limited

residents in a retirement community to members of the Society. The court did not recognize the Society as a religious group but nevertheless invalidated the covenant restrictions as a violation of a state law prohibiting deed restrictions based on race, ethnicity, sex or religion. See *Taormina Theosophical Community, Inc.* v. *Silver*, 190 Cal. Reptr. 38 (California Court of Appeals, 1983).

132. Thomas C. Berg, 'Slouching Towards Secularism: A Comment on Kiryas Joel School District v. Grumet', 44 *Emery Law Journal* (Spring 1995, p.442).

133. Richard A. Epstein, 'Free Association: The Incoherence of Antidiscrimination Laws', *National Review*, 9 October 2000, pp.38–40.

134. Nationally, 69 per cent of neighborhood associations provide swimming pools, 46 per cent clubhouses or community rooms, 41 per cent tennis courts, 28 per cent playgrounds, 20 per cent parks or natural areas, 17 per cent exercise facilities, 16 per cent lakes, 4 per cent golf courses, 4 per cent marinas and 4 per cent restaurants.

135. See *Privatization: Toward More Effective Government*, Report of the President's Commission on Privatization (Washington, DC, March 1988).

136. Doreen Heisler and Warren Klein, *Inside Look at Community Association Homeownership – Fact, Perceptions* (Alexandria, VA: Community Associations Institute, 1996, p.20).

137. Pietro Nivola of the Brookings Institution observes, with respect to systems of municipal service provision in the public sector:

> Disparities in services among jurisdictions commonly reflect not only differential tax bases but varying local tastes for public goods. Inasmuch as unitary governmental institutions help equalize the quality of services within metropolitan areas by effectively sharing revenues on an area-wide basis, these arrangements may level local inequalities, thus promising a distributional adjustment, if not an efficiency gain. But inasmuch as equalization reduces the ability of communities and neighborhoods to choose their own preferred baskets of services, the process interferes with the exercise of consumer sovereignty. The logic of such interference is questionable: If public goods should be everywhere the same at the metropolitan level, why not at the state level? And if equal among states, why not nations? (Pietro S. Nivola, *Laws of the Landscape: How Policies Shape Cities in Europe and America*, Washington, DC: Brookings Institution Press, 1999, p.64).

138. For one vision of such a competitive process, see Bruno S. Frey, 'A Utopia: Government Without Territorial Monopoly', 157 *Journal of Theoretical and Institutional Economics* (March 2001).

139. Ronald J. Oakerson, *Governing Local Public Economies: Creating the Civic Metropolis* (Oakland, CA: ICS Press, 1999, p.115).

140. Ibid., p.81.

141. Ibid., p.127, 85.

142. Ibid., p. 86.

143. Community Associations Institute, *Community Associations Factbook*, 1993 edn, p.26.

144. Heisler and Klein, *Inside Look at Community Association Homeownership – Facts, Perceptions*, p.28.

145. Michael L. Utz, 'Common Interest Ownership in Pennsylvania: An Examination of Statutory Reform and Implications for Practitioners', 37 *Duquesne University Law Review* (Spring 1999, pp. 484–5).

146. Buchanan and Tullock, *The Calculus of Consent*.

147. In another area of recent application, the European Union (EU) is now considering how to deal with the problems of expanding to a considerably larger group with the inclusion of many Eastern Europe nations. Traditionally, many EU decisions have required unanimous consent, but it is now generally accepted that some form of basic changes in the EU 'constitution' will be needed in order to avoid an escalation of transaction costs, and a consequent breakdown in EU functioning. As agreed at a 2000 meeting in Nice, the reaching of EU approval will now require in many cases more than a simple majority vote, but less than unanimity. The significant new cost, however, will be more and more

aggrieved EU nations in the future, as they find themselves compelled to go along with specific EU decisions that adversely affect them.

148. A version of this proposal was first presented in Chapter 8 of my 1977 book, *Zoning and Property Rights* (MIT Press). I have developed it in various other writings over the years, most recently in Robert H. Nelson, 'Privatizing the Neighborhood: A Proposal to Replace Zoning with Private Collective Property Rights to Existing Neighborhoods', 7 *George Mason Law Review* (Summer 1999); and Robert H. Nelson, 'Zoning by Private Contract', in F.H. Buckley (ed.), *The Fall and Rise of Freedom of Contract* (Durham, NC: Duke University Press, 1999). These two articles were both adapted from a paper initially presented at the Donner Conference on Freedom of Contract in Property Law, sponsored by the Law and Economics Center, George Mason University School of Law, Alexandria, Virginia, December 1997. At this conference, the commenters on the paper included Steven Eagle (who organized the conference), William Fischel and Robert Ellickson. Revised versions of their comments on my paper were published in Buckley (ed.), *The Fall and Rise of Freedom of Contract*. An additional set of (different) comments by Fischel and Eagle were included in the Summer 1999 issue of the *George Mason Law Review*.

149. Reflecting a similar goal to encourage private improvement efforts in existing neighborhoods by establishing better property right incentives, Robert Ellickson has offered a somewhat different proposal for new neighborhood governance. He would follow more closely in the line of the successful efforts to create 'business improvement districts' in many American cities, involving a less radical departure from existing governance mechanisms. See Robert C. Ellickson, 'New Institutions for Old Neighborhoods', 48 *Duke Law Journal* (1998, p. 75). For an earlier proposal along these lines, see also George W. Liebmann, 'Devolution of Power to Community and Block Associations', 25 *The Urban Lawyer* (Spring 1993).

150. The proposal offered in this paper to establish a new mechanism for creating new neighborhood associations in inner city areas is discussed in Robert C. Ellickson, 'The (Limited) Ability of Urban Neighbors to Contract for the Provision of Local Public Goods', in F.H. Buckley (ed.), *The Fall and Rise of Freedom of Contract* (Durham, NC: Duke University Press, 1999).

151. A critique of the proposal offered in this paper to create landowner associations in undeveloped areas is given in William A. Fischel, 'Voting, Risk Aversion, and the NIMBY Syndrome: A Comment on Robert Nelson's Privatizing the Neighborhood', 7 *George Mason Law Review* (Summer 1999); additional comments on the proposal are provided in William A. Fischel, 'Dealing with the NIMBY Problem', in Buckley (ed.), *The Fall and Rise of Freedom of Contract*.

152. See Fischel, *Economics of Zoning Laws*; see also William A. Fischel, 'A Property Rights Approach to Municipal Zoning', 54 *Land Economics* (February 1978, p. 64); W. Fischel, 'Equity and Efficiency Aspects of Zoning Reform', 27 *Public Policy* 301 (Summer 1979); and W. Fischel, 'Zoning and Land Use Reform: A Property Rights Perspective', 1 *Virginia Journal of Natural Resource Law* (Spring 1980, p.69).

153. See Sidney Plotkin, *Keep Out: The Struggle for Land Use Control* (Berkeley: University of California Press, 1987).

154. For further discussion of zoning fictions, see Nelson, *Zoning and Property Rights*. See also Robert H. Nelson, 'Zoning Myth and Practice: From Euclid into the Future,' in Charles M. Haar and Jerold S. Kayden (eds), *Zoning and the American Dream* (Chicago: Planners Press of the American Planning Association, 1989).

155. Richard Pipes, *Property and Freedom* (New York: Vintage Books, 1999, p.65). See also Tom Bethell, *The Noblest Triumph: Property and Prosperity Through the Ages* (New York: St Martin's Griffin, 1998).

156. See, for example, Robert C. Ellickson, *Order Without Law: How Neighbors Settle Disputes* (Cambridge, MA: Harvard University Press, 1991).

157. A full laying bare of the large discrepancies between zoning theory and zoning practice was developed, for example, by Richard Babcock – if with little subsequent impact on actual municipal zoning practices. See Richard F. Babcock, *The Zoning Game:*

Municipal Practices and Policies (Madison: University of Wisconsin Press, 1966). For more on this theme, see Carol M. Rose, 'Planning and Dealing: Piecemeal Land Use Controls as a Problem of Local Legitimacy', 71 *California Law Review* (May 1983).

158. Frederick Pollock, *The Land Laws* (Macmillan and Co., 1883, p.62).
159. John T. Noonan, Jr., *The Scholastic Analysis of Usury* (Cambridge, MA: Harvard University Press, 1957).
160. Pipes, *Property and Freedom*, p.89.
161. Pollock, *The Land Laws*, pp.51–2.
162. See Chapter 1, 'Ineffective Laws and Unexpected Consequences: A Brief Review of Public Land History', in Robert H. Nelson, *Public Lands and Private Rights: The Failure of Scientific Management* (Lanham, MD: Rowman & Littlefield, 1995). For more on the public lands, see Robert H. Nelson, *A Burning Issue: A Case for Abolishing the US Forest Service* (Lanham, MD: Rowman & Littlefield, 2000).
163. See Paul W. Gates, *A History of Public Land Law Development* (Washington, DC: Government Printing Office, 1968).
164. Remarkably, Scotland only abolished the last vestiges of feudal land tenure very recently. According to a 2002 report, 'Scotland has kept feudal land laws for 800 years. The feudal system of land tenure, under which all land ultimately belonged to the monarch, at the top of a hierarchical pyramid, was formally abolished only two years ago, in a law establishing absolute ownership and finally abolishing feuduties – the token fees paid to feudal superiors for land titles.' See David White, 'Scots Stake their Claims in Land Shake-Up', *Financial Times* (5 March 2002, p.10).

9. The rise of private neighborhood associations: revolution or evolution?

William A. Fischel

In the previous chapter, Robert Nelson suggests that states should replace municipalities with private community associations. As his data show, his goal seems to be well under way to fruition. Developer-designed community associations have grown astoundingly since 1970. They were led first by the condominium boom, which required a collective body to govern common areas and regulate neighborhood property, but they changed in the 1980s into an enormous and continuing growth in private governance of conventional single-family subdivisions. Nelson suggests that state governments realize that neighborhood associations are replacing municipalities. Municipalities, at least those smaller than counties, should face the music and go out of business, yielding their authority to provide local services and land use regulation to private neighborhood associations.

There is a very different way of looking at private community associations. Positively, neighborhood associations have not displaced any municipality or induced it to give up its regulatory powers. It appears that community associations are not substitutes for municipal governance, but complements to it. The rise of neighborhood associations seems to be a response to an increasing demand for protection of home values. Homeowners appear to want both more zoning and more private regulation. They do not seem to want to substitute private for public regulation.

Normatively, it probably would be a bad idea entirely to replace municipal governance with private governance. This is not because private governance is undesirable, but because municipalities provide an important function in our federal system of governance that neighborhood associations would be unable to fulfill unless they simply became municipalities. The objective of limiting the reach of zoning outside currently built-up areas can be accomplished in ways short of wholesale displacement of one of America's most venerable institutions, municipal corporations.

1   NEIGHBORHOOD ASSOCIATIONS HAVE NOT DISPLACED MUNICIPAL ZONING

Neighborhood associations perform functions that municipalities have traditionally done. They collect garbage and remove snow; they provide local infrastructure such as roads, sidewalks and sewers; they regulate land use and occupancy; and they provide collective services such as recreation and sometimes even health maintenance for their residents. The municipality in which the neighborhood association is located may often contract with it to provide such services and give its residents a break on their local taxes if they use association revenues to pay for them. The city may even have required the developer of the association to provide some municipal services as a condition for a zoning permit.

In all cases, though, the city retains the right to exercise its own powers both within and around the neighborhood association's territory. No city cop can be stopped by a neighborhood association's security guard and be told this is not his jurisdiction. Moreover, the city retains all of its zoning and related land use powers over the association's territory as well as beyond it. Municipalities cannot contract away their police powers even if they wanted to.

Nor is there any evidence that neighborhood associations would prefer that the city they are located in get out of the land use business, at least as it pertains to zoning of territory outside the association's boundaries. Despite the enormous growth in community associations in the past 30 years, there are no known instances in which a municipality has attempted to surrender its zoning authority. Below are some examples that suggest the opposite is true: community associations seem to increase the power of municipal zoning.

Houston, Texas, is famous, at least among land use professionals, as the only big city not to have zoning. Its suburban parts that are within the city's boundaries are typically developed within neighborhood associations. Among the more sizable of these is the Woodlands. Houston would seem to meet Nelson's ideal and be the wave of the future in local governance: a passive city government that allows developers and hence new residents to set up their own local governance structure. Yet events in Houston suggest that community association residents would prefer the city to have zoning. Houston lacks zoning because its residents keep voting down proposals to adopt it. The latest of several referenda was held in 1993. The voting pattern revealed that zoning was most opposed by Hispanics and by lower-income blacks and whites (McDonald, 1995). In Houston, most members of these groups live in areas that are not subject to covenants or neighborhood associations. Those who favored zoning were higher-income whites and blacks. Most upper-income people in Houston live in places that do have covenants and neighborhood associations. It seems likely, then, that zoning was most desired by people who already have the institution that is supposed to displace it.

Another event that illustrates the complementarity between zoning and covenants is the formation of new local governments in the *Seattle* area. Formation of the 10 new cities in King County, Washington, during the 1990s was motivated by the desire to have local control of zoning (Fischel, 2001). But a large fraction of the homes in the new municipalities had long been governed by neighborhood associations. The city that incorporated most recently, Sammamish, is almost entirely composed of gated communities, yet its first order of business after incorporation was to seize the reins of zoning from the county and issue a growth moratorium.

It is commonly regarded as curious, if not ironic, that the Standard State Zoning Enabling Act was promulgated by the US Department of Commerce in 1928 by Herbert Hoover. Zoning is quintessentially local, after all, and Hoover is usually (though not entirely fairly) thought of as a conservative who would oppose infringements of property rights. But the real force behind the Act, if Marc Weiss's (1987) account is to be credited, came from an even more ironic source. Developers in *Southern California* in the early years of the twentieth century were among the first to build large subdivisions of homes. To protect the value of these homes and thus make them more marketable, the developers imposed covenants that regulated the subsequent use of land in the area. But the developers found that their investments were often compromised – and homebuyers repelled – by incompatible uses on the borders of their subdivisions and elsewhere in the community.

To deal with this problem, California developers were among the primary lobbyists in favor of the new legal device of zoning. In order to make it more readily available in other places they operated, developer organizations lobbied the federal government to come up with a standard act. Thus one important phase of zoning, the standardization of its legal structure, was promoted by developers who already had experience with covenants, the predecessor of neighborhood associations. The problem was not that covenants did not work; their problem, in the view of developers (and their customers) was that covenants did not control territory outside their immediate neighborhood. In short, the reason for zoning's popularity was exactly that feature that many find objectionable: its ability to control the use land outside the immediate neighborhood.

Gerald Korngold (2001) found that several *Ohio* municipalities in the early twentieth century were laid out by a single developer, who imposed community-wide covenants. All three of the communities later adopted zoning, but none of them dismantled the covenants. The mayors of the three cities in fact administer the covenants. Korngold found that covenants and zoning law developed side by side in many jurisdictions. The famous Kansas City developer, J.C. Nichols, likewise encouraged the privately governed suburbs that he developed in the early 1900s to adopt zoning (Worley, 1990).

One of the functions of *existing neighborhood associations* is to see to it that zoning laws are enforced outside their own borders. Although this is usually done informally, sometimes associations will go about it systematically (Dilger, 1992, p.27). One of the objectives of the Forest Ridge (Texas) Property Owners Association's Architectural & Land Zoning Committee is to 'monitor zoning changes within 5 miles of the neighborhood' (*http://forestridge.tripod.com*). Another example is the Spruce Hill Community Association, an area within the city of Philadelphia. Among its formal activities (as listed at *http://www.sprucehillca.org/activities.html#appearance*) is this:

> Zoning changes – SHCA has for many years maintained an active Zoning Committee. The Association subscribes to a service that alerts the Committee when any change in Spruce Hill area zoning is requested. The Committee reviews the requested change, determines a course of action consistent with the Association's guidelines and brings to the attention of the SHCA Board of Directors any change that might adversely affect the community.

In sum, then, it seems likely that neighborhood associations, created by covenants (such as Forest Ridge) or simply by voluntary association (such as Spruce Hill) currently act as complements to the zoning process. These associations are interested in what happens to land use outside their boundaries as well as within them. The associations help lower the transaction costs of dealing with sometimes complex zoning issues. They are more effective than individual homeowners because their greater numbers and common interests make government officials pay more attention. It thus seems unlikely that zoning will wither away as neighborhood associations proliferate.

2   EXPLAINING THE GROWTH OF NEIGHBORHOOD ASSOCIATIONS

If zoning and covenants (the zoning of neighborhood associations) are complements rather than substitutes, their rapid growth in the last 30 years could be accounted for by an increase in the demand for land use regulation. There are two explanations for this shift in demand for regulation.

The first is that higher density communities tend to require more regulation. Modern covenants and community associations were pioneered by the developers of condominiums, which are usually high-density apartment houses with individual owners. City zoning and other regulation does little to govern relationships among apartment dwellers within the same building. In traditional apartments, disputes among neighbors are mediated by the landlord. Where everyone is his own landlord, as in the condominium, a collective governance structure was necessary.

Neighborhood associations are now being applied to single-family home developments, though. The interesting question is whether these homes are typically developed at higher densities than other subdivisions that appeal to a similar market. My casual impression from planned and gated communities (in which the existence of a community association can normally be presumed) is that they are developed at higher densities than typical subdivisions. For example, the gross densities (population/total land area) of Reston, Virginia and Columbia, Maryland, are about twice that of other suburbs that were not similarly planned and built by a single development company (Fischel, 1999a, p.161).

A second reason for the growing popularity of covenants and neighborhood associations could be rising concern by homeowners that zoning's 'suburban wall' might soon be breached. Legal attacks on zoning and attempts to override zoning by state or regional governments might make homebuyers worried that the exclusive community they are buying into might soon be peppered with low-income housing developments or uncomfortably close commercial developments. This problem was accelerated by the completion of the interstate highway system and the near universal ownership of cars by 1970. The highway system liberated almost all industrial jobs from central cities, and the reduced cost of cars allowed many of the poor to follow jobs to the suburbs. The 'open suburbs' movement began its legal career as it became clear that the jobs were moving out of central cities (Schill, 1991)

The New Jersey Supreme Court's 1983 *Mount Laurel* decision (456 A.2d 390) has forced some suburbs to take low-income housing they do not want, and the legislatively adopted Massachusetts 'Anti-Snob Zoning' law likewise offers a similar entitlement. Federal law now provides certain groups, such as churches, the mentally handicapped and the telecommunications industry, with ammunition to override local zoning restrictions. As zoning has become more vulnerable to legal attack, developers of housing may have wanted to assure buyers that they would not be subject to such inroads in their neighborhoods by disallowing such uses in their own rules.

There was a parallel to this explanation early in zoning's history. One of the first uses of zoning was to establish legally enforced racial segregation.

Literal apartheid zoning ordinances were becoming popular in southern cities until they were struck down by the US Supreme Court in *Buchanan* v. *Warley*, 245 US 60 (1917). Both the state and federal courts thereafter kept racial zoning off the books. In the meantime, covenants were used in many places as substitutes for racial zoning (Bernstein, 1998). Racially restrictive covenants were not struck down until *Shelley* v. *Kraemer*, 334 US 1 (1948). (I would add that covenants were not an adequate substitute for zoning for maintaining segregation, since many landowners refused to agree to them.)

This account points to an inconsistency in the contention that zoning and covenants are complements, not substitutes. Instead of both advancing arm in arm, one (covenants) advances precisely because the other (zoning) is receding. But, on balance, the complements story seems more plausible. The inroads on zoning have been rather modest in their effects. Even the federal Fair Housing Act that entitles group homes to be put in residential neighborhoods allows localities to spread such uses out so that they do not cause much anxiety in any particular neighborhood. The *Mount Laurel* decisions have built only modest amounts of housing, and most of what is built has been isolated from existing homes (Mitchell, 2000).

Moreover, suburbs have come up with powerful new zoning rules to offset the inclusionary devices. A wide array of exclusionary devices, such as farmland zoning, wetlands preservation (which sometimes includes ground that will not get your feet wet in any weather), urban growth boundaries and historic preservation, have been developed at the same time that the open-suburbs movement was making its inroads into suburban zoning. Despite all the litigation and attempts to regionalize local land use regulation, local control of zoning was at least as strong in 2002 as it was in 1972. Indeed, by extending the ability of anti-development interests to regulate land outside their own communities, regional land use bodies have arguably made zoning more exclusionary, not less. On balance, the rise of community associations and private land use regulation looks like it is strongly complementary with public zoning. We should not, therefore, expect zoning to recede as covenants advance.

3   MUNICIPALITIES ARE IMPORTANT MEDIATING INSTITUTIONS

The exclusionary aspects of zoning and covenants are the unsavory side of local government. They emerge from the excessive amount of financial assets that most people have in their homes and the fact that home values cannot be insured or diversified. Even people who do not care what happens next door have to care what prospective homebuyers think. A negative verdict by the homebuyers' market hurts homeowners badly. Most homeowners do not own any other asset of comparable size.

The upside of homeownership is that it induces people to pay attention to the quality of life in their communities (DiPasquale and Glaeser, 1999). They will vote for reasonable expenditures to improve schools (even if they have no children), patch sidewalks (even if they always drive) and create parks (even if they watch TV all day). As long as prospective homebuyers care about those things, owners have some reason to pay attention to them and help promote them. This is one reason for local governments working as well as they do. Concern about home values makes homeowners into more active, or at least attentive, citizens (Fischel, 2001).

Nelson's normative argument would transfer this source of energy – concern for home values – from local municipal government to the neighborhood association. As argued above, this is less a displacement than an augmentation, since neighborhood associations are active and effective watchdogs of municipal affairs. Nelson's main concern, though, is that municipal zoning extends the power of regulation outside of what he regards as its legitimate bounds, the neighborhood. He is less concerned by the 'Not In My Back Yard' folks than by the 'Not Anywhere In My Community' people. He would like to disfranchise the latter by encouraging community associations to be permitted to displace municipalities so that more pro-development forces could be in control of land ripe for development or redevelopment.

At least in the land use area, displacement of municipalities by neighborhood associations is unlikely. Nelson's program is addressed to a real problem, low-density zoning (Fischel, 1999a). His proposal has been criticized on the ground that it infringes too much on property rights by forcing some landowners to join associations. However, Nelson's proposal is in practice less coercive than many zoning laws (Fischel, 1999b). Nonetheless, active efforts by enthusiasts to displace local governments by neighborhood associations seem misguided.

America's federal system has many layers. The formal, constitutional, layers are the national 'federal' government and the states. The states, however, have numerous geographic layers, too. Counties are ubiquitous, and most are divided into municipalities, school districts and various special purpose districts.

Federalism has a duality to it that is often overlooked. The flows of power go both upward and downward in the federal hierarchy. The downward flow is most familiar. Federal (national) law is paramount for the states. The Supreme Court's occasional exceptions that give states constitutional protections raise much uproar in legal circles, but they do not amount to much as a practical matter. Even less contested is the power of the state government over the local governments. Cities and towns are 'creatures of the state', and their creator can remold or even destroy them pretty much at will (Briffault, 1990).

This downward-flowing hierarchy has much to recommend it as a coordinating device. If a state wants to set out an easily followed system of roads, it is best not to give localities too much discretion in the matter. If the federal government desires a uniform foreign policy, it is best not to let cities and states have embassies in other nations.

The other face of federalism is somewhat neglected. This is the bottom-up version that allows for a variety of experiments in governments. It is most famously expressed in Justice Louis Brandeis's dictum about states being 'laboratories of democracy' (*New State Ice* v. *Liebmann*, 285 US 262, 311 [1932]). The same idea applies to local governments. Local governments have originated many good ideas (and some bad ones) that the states and the national government later adopted.

By most accounts, the primary impetus for free public education came from localities, not the state and national governments (Cubberley, 1919). America's bottom-up, decentralized system of local governance produced the high school decades before most European nations, with their nationally controlled education systems, came around to universal secondary education. According to Claudia Goldin (1998), America's high school success emerged precisely because a few local majorities were able to adopt it before the state and national majority of voters were convinced of its desirability. The success of the high school was then imitated by other localities that wanted the same competitive advantage in attracting households and businesses in a 'race to the top'.

A more recent example of local innovation is the advancement of civil rights. Gay rights did not originate as a national or even state movement. Cities in which gays were a substantial political presence adopted laws to protect their civil rights (Bailey, 1999). From this base, gay activists have been able to persuade state and national legislators and courts of the rightness of their cause and, perhaps more importantly, show that granting gay rights did not upset the social order. Indeed, much of the backlash on civil rights has come from the state level, not from localities, in the form of attempts to limit what local governments can do.

The filtering-up of new ideas is the side of the federal system that would be compromised by the replacement of local governments by neighborhood associations. Municipalities are better at transmitting new norms to the state and national government than private neighborhood associations would be. Municipalities possess most of the trappings of state law. Although municipal governments can be analyzed in ways similar to private corporations, the fact remains that they have the coercive powers of government. This means that they at least partly displace the powers of the state government.

The local police can do most of the things that the state police can do but a neighborhood association's security guards cannot. If security guards displaced city police, the first line of true government authority – the authority that can put you in jail – is then the state. Likewise, displacement of city zoning authority by covenants means that the uncovenanted land that remains is subject to zoning by the state. The state's exercise of this control is apt to be different and not necessarily more efficient or less exclusionary than its exercise by local governments.

The independent exercise of the police power by municipalities is important for social and political experimentation. Independence permits the locality both to keep the state at bay and to exercise its own discretion. If the experiment is a success, other municipalities will imitate it, and the idea may well filter up to the 'higher' governments. If it is a failure, then only a small area has to suffer its consequences. Because neighborhood associations lack the ability to displace the state in its governance function, experiments of interest to higher governments would be less frequent and less persuasive to it.

The other reason for municipalities performing their mediating function more successfully is that higher-government elected officials will pay them more attention. Part of this comes from legislative districting, which at both the Congressional and state legislative level pays attention to local government boundaries. Thus a state or national representative is apt to be responsive to voters in particular towns and cities, since most voters in a given town or cities will be in the same district. Districting in a state with only neighborhood associations would be less likely to collect a community of interest.

The road to becoming a state legislator or achieving a higher office often begins with a local government office. Those who have attained higher office have good reason to pay attention to their origins and to respect the prerogatives of local government. While neighborhood association leaders might follow a similar path up the political ladder, their experience in local politics would be considerably different and on a smaller scale than that of most local politicians.

All of this presumes that neighborhood associations would stay as they are today. A key feature of their governance is that they can (and usually do) allocate votes according to property ownership. This one-dollar, one-vote regime is one feature that proponents believe key to the regulatory limits that promote their efficiency. The one-person, one-vote rule of local governments makes it possible for existing residents to gang up on under-represented landowners and regulate undeveloped land without regard to its most valuable potential use. Displacement of municipalities by neighborhood associations would forestall such redistribution by enabling owners of larger tracts of land to have more votes than smallholders would possess.

But, as Steven Eagle (1999) has pointed out, creating a neighborhood association under Nelson's plan itself requires a degree of coercion. In order to overcome the holdout problems of landowners who decline to join a neighborhood association, Nelson would allow a supermajority of landowners to force those holding out to join the neighborhood association. Even if one regards the supermajority provisions of this plan as adequate protection against majoritarian tyranny, the resulting set of associations would start to look a lot like a government. Several commentators and political figures have already called into question the property-based voting allocations of neighborhood associations (McKenzie, 1994). Their voices would become more numerous and persuasive if such associations became the only local governance mechanism in town. If activist courts did not force the issue, state legislators might start to trim the discretion of neighborhood associations to allocate voting rights. In short, local governments as they are now constituted may provide a useful cover for the less-than-democratic structure of neighborhood associations. Take away that cover, and the populist attack on them would become more persuasive.

In sum, local governments serve as useful mediating institutions in the federal system. Neighborhood associations do, too, insofar as they augment the voices for their members in local government. To merge the two might cause a loss of the chief virtues of both institutions by increasing the local power of the state and compromising the self-ordering nature of neighborhood associations.

4   ALTERNATIVES TO DEALING WITH EXCESSIVE LOCALISM IN LAND USE

The proposal to enable neighborhood associations to displace municipalities is motivated chiefly by the tendency of local governments to zone undeveloped land at inefficiently low and inflexible densities. But the cure, empowerment of neighborhood associations, may have some adverse side-effects. There are alternative approaches to local zoning's excesses that do not require wholesale restructuring of municipal and property law.

The first is to bring the regulatory takings doctrine and related constitutional doctrines to bear on local zoning (Epstein, 1996). There is precedent and doctrinal justification (neither of which is uncontested) for using the Fifth Amendment's 'just compensation' principle to make local government pay landowners when zoning gets too restrictive. This responds to development-minded landowners who are at the front lines of municipal zoning.

At present, most courts are highly deferential to municipalities when regulations are challenged. Courts will hold for developers only when the municipal authorities have perpetrated extreme abuses of zoning authority – and often not even then. One reason for this deference is the judges' anxiety that contrary decisions could be used to overturn desirable regulations along with those that are inefficient and unfair. In response to this concern, several commentators have advanced a legal doctrine that would assist landowners without undermining the legitimate authority of municipalities to protect their residents. At the core of this doctrine is the golden rule: allow owners of undeveloped property to develop it in ways that some previous landowner was allowed to develop the homes in which local resident voters now live (Ellickson, 1977; Fischel, 1995).

This seems consistent with the answer to the question that current residents should ask themselves: if you were not a resident of your community but were considering buying a home there, what sorts of land use policies would you like to see in place? On the one hand, prospective residents would be repelled by overly permissive zoning that resulted in unattractive development. On the other hand, overly restrictive zoning would cause housing prices to be so high that the prospective residents would be unable to afford a home there. The golden mean would presumably be a zoning policy that allowed development much like that in which current residents live, but which also preserved the overall character of the community.

The second and less talked about reform is to promote municipal fragmentation. Breaking up of monopolistic cities is under present state laws almost impossible because the consent of the entire city is usually needed. A more liberal doctrine would allow cities to incorporate more easily in currently unincorporated areas of counties and, more importantly, allow residents of parts of an existing city or town to secede and form their own municipality (Bish, 1971).

Much of the problem of suburban exclusion is caused by the fact that existing residents of a large land area town seek to keep its population small. There are good reasons for this desire. Smaller population towns allow for more citizen control of the government. Local services, including schools, are better because those providing them are more responsive to watchful voters. The way to allow a small town to stay small without excluding others is to allow the residents of the less developed area of town to secede and incorporate as a separate town. The new town can then develop to a reasonable density and still keep its small town character. This is in effect what the proposal to empower community associations would do, too, but secession would not entail creation of a neighborhood association with its share-voting arrangement. The drawback of secession as an option right now is that in most states it requires a vote of the majority of the existing town, and so it hardly ever gets done.

A not-too-radical reform by the state government would allow secession of parts of municipalities with only the vote of those in the seceding parts. There would have to be some state-level oversight of this process so as to discourage secessions that would promote racial segregation or leave the original town in poor fiscal straits or create undesirable spillovers on other towns. But such review is already in place for proposed annexations and incorporations in many states (ACIR, 1992). Having another duty imposed on boundary review boards would not be especially taxing.

Nor would unilateral secession conflict with the one-person, one-vote rule as it is now interpreted. The rule currently does not require that proposed *mergers* of cities be successful if only a majority of the two cities combined approves. (That would allow a larger city to annex a smaller city whose residents opposed it.) The rule insists on per capita voting rights only within general-purpose political jurisdictions as defined by the state, so allowing the state to subdivide existing political jurisdictions by a majority of one of the proposed subdivisions would seem not to violate it.

In sum, there are political and legal approaches to municipal zoning's excesses that do not require subverting the municipality entirely. The reason they have been underplayed is that most municipal reformers want to go the other way. They seek to consolidate local governments in metropolitan governments (Orfield, 1997; Rusk, 1993). Consolidation has not worked well for school districts. In general, the larger the district, the worse the performance (Brasington, 1997). There is little reason to suspect it would be different for municipal functions.

Larger local government is less effective local government, at least when there is already a layer of governments – the state and federal – to provide large area public goods and mediate disputes among the smaller bodies. The Nelson proposal would move to the opposite extreme, eliminating the municipal sector almost entirely. The analysis is a useful counterweight to the centralizers' voices, which are so dominant in the academic and planning world today. As a practical measure, however, it involves Nelson making the same error as those who favor large area government by throwing out the virtues of local government in order to cure one of it vices.

REFERENCES

ACIR (US Advisory Commission on Intergovernmental Relations), 1992, *Local Boundary Commissions: Status and Roles in Forming, Adjusting and Dissolving Local Government Boundaries* (Washington, DC: ACIR).

Bailey, Robert W., 1999, *Gay Politics, Urban Politics: Identity and Economics in the Urban Setting*, New York: Columbia University Press.

Bernstein, David E., 1998, 'Philip Sober Controlling Philip Drunk: Buchanan v. Warley in Historical Perspective', *Vanderbilt Law Review*, 51 (May), 797–879.

Bish, Robert L., 1971, *The Public Economy of Metropolitan Areas*, Chicago: Markham Publishing.

Brasington, David M., 1997, 'School District Consolidation, Student Performance, and Housing Values', *Journal of Regional Analysis and Policy*, 27 (2), 43–54.

Briffault, Richard, 1990, 'Our Localism: Part I – The Structure of Local Government Law', *Columbia Law Review*, 90 (January), 1–115.

Cubberley, Ellwood P., 1919, *Public Education in the United States: A Study and Interpretation of American Educational History*, Boston: Houghton Mifflin.

Dilger, Robert J., 1992, *Neighborhood Politics: Residential Community Associations in American Governance*, New York: NYU Press.

DiPasquale, Denise and Edward L. Glaeser, 1999, 'Incentives and Social Capital: Are Homeowners Better Citizens?', *Journal of Urban Economics*, 45 (March), 354–84.

Eagle, Stephen J., 1999, 'Privatizing Urban Land Use Regulation: The Problem of Consent', *George Mason Law Review*, 7 (Summer), 905–21.

Ellickson, Robert C., 1977, 'Suburban Growth Controls: An Economic and Legal Analysis', *Yale Law Journal*, 86 (January), 385–511.

Epstein, Richard, A., 1996, 'Why Is This Man a Moderate? Review of *Regulatory Takings: Law, Economics, and Politics*, by William A. Fischel', *Michigan Law Review*, 94 (May), 1758–75.

Fischel, William A., 1995, *Regulatory Takings: Law, Economics, and Politics*, Cambridge, MA: Harvard University Press.

Fischel, William A., 1999a, 'Does the American Way of Zoning Cause the Suburbs of US Metropolitan Areas to Be Too Spread Out?', in Alan Altshuler, William Morrill, Harold Wolman and Faith Mitchell (eds), *Governance and Opportunity in Metropolitan Areas*, Washington, DC: National Academy Press.

Fischel, William A., 1999b, 'Voting, Risk Aversion, and the NIMBY Syndrome: A Comment on Robert Nelson's "Privatizing the Neighborhood"', *George Mason Law Review*, 7 (Summer), 881–903.

Fischel, William A., 2001, *The Homevoter Hypothesis: How Home Values Influence Local Government Taxation, School Finance, and Land-Use Policies*, Cambridge, MA: Harvard University Press.

Goldin, Claudia, 1998, 'America's Graduation from High School: The Evolution and Spread of Secondary Schooling in the Twentieth Century', *Journal of Economic History*, 58 (June), 345–74.

Korngold, Gerald, 2001, 'The Emergence of Private Land Use Controls in Large-Scale Subdivisions: The Companion Story to Village of Euclid v. Ambler Realty Co.', *Case Western Reserve Law Review*, 51 (Summer), 617–43.

McDonald, John F., 1995, 'Houston Remains Unzoned', *Land Economics*, 71 (February), 137–40.

McKenzie, Evan, 1994, *Privatopia: Homeowner Associations and the Rise of Residential Private Government*, New Haven: Yale University Press.

Mitchell, James L., 2000, 'Assessing Exclusionary Residential Zoning: A Natural Experiment Approach', PhD dissertation, Woodrow Wilson School of Public and International Affairs, Princeton University.

Orfield, Myron, 1997, *Metropolitics: A Regional Agenda for Community and Stability*, Washington, DC: Brookings, and Cambridge, MA: Lincoln Institute.

Rusk, David, 1993, *Cities without Suburbs*, Washington, DC: Woodrow Wilson Center Press and Baltimore, MD: Johns Hopkins University Press.

Schill, Michael H., 1991, 'Deconcentrating the Inner City Poor', *Chicago Kent Law Review*, 67, 795–853.

Weiss, Marc A., 1987, *The Rise of the Community Builders: The American Real Estate Industry and Urban Land Planning*, New York: Columbia University Press.

Worley, William S., 1990, *J.C. Nichols and the Shaping of Kansas City: Innovation in Planned Residential Communities*, Columbia, MO: University of Missouri Press.

10.   Frontage tax and the optimally compact city

Peter F. Colwell and Geoffrey K. Turnbull

1   INTRODUCTION

It is widely believed among noneconomists that something is inherently wrong with urban sprawl.[1] The 'smart growth' and 'new urbanist' movements generally advocate regulating property markets to check the appetites of housing consumers for large lots and the propensity of speculators for inducing leap-frog development (Burchell *et al.*, 2000). It is widely believed among economists that urban sprawl is inefficient because individuals do not bear the full cost of their property development decisions. In short, the prices are not 'right'. The central question is whether the optimal compactness that would be achieved by getting the prices right would necessarily produce a smaller city. That is, does less sprawl necessarily yield a smaller city?

In this study, we re-examine the relationship between efficient residential land use and city size, focusing on the roles of lot dimensions and the total area of land developed in the market. Some of the sources of urban sprawl are tied to the mispricing of land area by households in the city; others are tied to frontage of developed parcels, or how widely spaced consumers reside along laterals in the infrastructure. Matching the social costs of development with the appropriate decisions generally entails differential tax treatment of lot dimensions, like frontage and depth, and area. We present a simple framework to examine the consequences of differential taxes on lot dimensions and study their relationships with more traditional property and land taxes and their implications for the size of the efficient city.

Urban economists have not been drawn to questions concerning the shape of residential lots.[2] There are a variety of reasons for this neglect. There is the widely accepted notion that lot dimensions are details that can be safely ignored in formal modeling; in a sense, distinguishing frontage from depth simply does not matter. In addition, and perhaps more importantly, the most popular tools employed by urban economists are simply not geared toward dealing with parcels of finite size and integer populations. The standard neoclassical urban model envisions a continuum of consumers residing on parcels of land comprising lengths of arc with infinitesimal width and lot dimensions do not enter such analyses in a meaningful sense. As with all researchers, the perspectives of economists are shaped by their tools, and the demonstrated usefulness of the neoclassical urban model doubtless prompts economists to overlook factors not readily captured within its structure. Regardless of the reasons, economists have paid little formal attention to the relationship between the shape of land parcels and the efficiency of urban land development patterns.

By formally modeling how frontage and depth of residential lots are determined in market equilibrium, this chapter adds to the recent and growing literature concerned with the relationship between taxes and urban sprawl. There is a continuing literature analyzing the effects of property taxes on residential land use and the size of urban areas, especially within the context of the neoclassical urban land market model (Polinsky and Rubinfeld, 1978; Sullivan, 1985; Brueckner, 2000; Brueckner and Kim, 2000). There is even some discussion of the consequences of taxing lot area as a correction for infrastructure congestion or externalities (Brueckner, 2001; Thompson, 1965, p.325). There is, however, little mention to the economics literature of another possibility: a frontage tax. In 1965, Thompson parenthetically suggested the use of a frontage tax as a user charge for the many social services that are correlated with frontage. These services may include such things as street repairs, street cleaning, snow removal, street lights, police patrols, fire protection services, school bussing, water distribution and sewerage collection. Of course, a frontage tax is a comparatively well-known tax, sometimes used as a special assessment to pay for the periodic repair of lateral streets or sewers. An area tax, on the other hand, is virtually unknown in practice. A land value tax is virtually unused, although graded systems of property taxes with different tax rates on land and buildings do exist in a few locales.

Although not fully understood, frontage and area taxes represent feasible policy options for some sources of inefficient land use. The primary purpose of this study is to examine how such taxes affect land use patterns, with particular attention to their effect on city size. The discussion is organized as follows. Section 2 explains the model, introducing the land market comprising residential parcels of finite dimension. Section 3 derives the effects of land area and frontage taxes on the total area developed for residential use in the market. Section 4 looks at the relationship between these land taxes and taxes that have received attention elsewhere in the literature, in particular, property and land value taxes. Section 5 presents our summary and concluding comments.

2   THE RESIDENTIAL LAND MARKET

This section explains the land market model and important relationships that are needed for our analysis in subsequent sections. We begin with an outline of the residential land demand, then turn to a more detailed explanation of the supply of residential land. The section concludes with the structural model of the land market.

Previous analysis of land tax effects on urban form are cast within the context of the neoclassical monocentric urban land market model.[3] As noted earlier, the problem with this approach for addressing land tax concerns is that there is no notion of area or of lot dimensions; all land parcels are lengths of arc of infinitesimal width. Introducing finite lot sizes into the neoclassical monocentric city model is not as straightforward as it might seem. The series of papers by Asami *et al.* (1991), Berliant (1985), Kamecke (1993) and Papageorgiou and Pines (1990) debate the extent to which the neoclassical urban land market model with lots of zero measure can be interpreted as relevant to a land market with finite parcels. In a related vein, Berliant and Fujita (1992) present a proof for the existence of equilibrium in a linear city comprising residential lots of finite length. Turnbull (1997) also presents a finite area model. There are no taxes in that framework and it therefore does not distinguish between frontage and depth, the dimensions that play key roles in our study. While Berliant and Ten Raa (1988) present a model of consumer preferences over the shape of lots, their framework is difficult to operationalize beyond the technical questions concerning equilibrium existence that are the focus of that study. Thus, although there are spatial models that incorporate parcels of finite dimension, none is sufficiently well-developed or tractable enough for conducting the type of comparative static analysis that we pursue here. Instead, we offer a simple land market model, suppressing the complicating differential spatial characteristic of land in order to focus solely on how finite lot dimensions and area are determined in the unregulated urban land market.

This study envisions a rectangular land market situated on a featureless Euclidean plane. The total width of land that is available to the market for residential use is given by $\tilde{F}$ and the depth or length is $\tilde{D}$. Since we are primarily interested in how frontage and area taxes affect urban sprawl, we assume that neither dimension of available land is strictly binding on the market in equilibrium.[4] All developed land is occupied by consumers for residential purposes. The market is closed to migration; the number of consumers in the market is given by the integer N.

All developed plots have finite dimension, frontage F and depth D. We abstract from the location attributes of residential land as the determinant of differential values and assume that all consumers in the market are identical and all land is equally well situated with respect to proximity to job sites, shopping or other attractive locations in the urban area. As a consequence, there are no location rents in the land market. Instead, developed land garners greater rent than undeveloped land solely because of the land improvements (road, sewer, water, utilities and so on) that are put into place in order to make the land capable of accommodating capital improvements in the form of residential structures. We label such land as developable land, to be distinguished from raw land. Given homogeneous consumers and the lack of location rent differentials, all plots of land in the market that are developable have uniform dimension $\{F, D\}$.

We note as an aside that, with the finite number of consumers and the suppression of spatial proximity or other sources of rent differentials, the market depicted in this study need not be densely packed in equilibrium. That is, occupied lots can surround vacant land. Such open spaces do not represent leap-frog development because this is not a dynamic model. In a model with explicit spatial preference or transport costs (that is, a source of location rents), land is not left vacant in the interior of a developed area because consumers will never occupy less accessible land when more accessible land is open in the market (Turnbull, 1997). Nonetheless, we assume without loss of generality that all development is dense; any undeveloped land will be relegated to the margins of the developed space.[5]

Most urban infrastructure is associated with the frontage of lots. Roads, street lighting, sidewalks, pipes and cables tend to be run along the fronts (or backs) of lots to make uniform access feasible. Even side streets may be considered a cost of frontage since they are required by subdivision ordinances to be placed every 800 feet or so. There may be some exceptions such as school capacity that could be more associated with the number of lots, but school bussing is likely also a function of frontage. Similarly, the spatial frequency of fire houses and the associated response times may not be solely related to frontage, but police patrol costs are clearly a function of frontage. Because most urban infrastructure is tied to frontage, we argue that it is frontage that is generally associated with the marginal social costs not borne by private development decision makers.

Consumer Demand for Developable Land

The land demand is derived as a straightforward application of consumer theory, in which the consumer allocates money income to non-housing consumption and housing consumption, which is in turn created by the consumer by combining developable land and capital in the form of structures. We adopt the following notation:

m = money income,
p = price of land consumed,
r = price of housing capital,
k = housing capital applied to developable land in the form of structure,
q = land consumption,
y = nonhousing consumption spending.

Consumer preferences are represented by the neoclassical utility function $u(y,k,q)$ exhibiting the standard properties. This utility function can be thought of as a compound function of housing h and nonhousing consumption y, say $v(y,h)$, in which housing is produced with structures and land consumption, $h = h(k,q)$. The housing production function plays a minor role in most of what follows, however, and so is suppressed.

The Marshallian demands for land consumption capital improvements in the form of structures, and all other goods are defined as follows:

$$\{q(p,r,m); k(p,r,m); y(p,r,m)\} \equiv \arg \max \ \{u(y,k,q) \text{ s.t.}$$
$$m = y + rk + pq\}. \tag{10.1}$$

Using subscripts to denote derivatives, the usual demand properties hold under normality, including $q_p < 0$ and $q_m > 0$.

Further, $q_r \gtreqless 0$ as land and structures are substitutes, unrelated, or complementary inputs in consumer demand. Recalling the role of k and q as inputs in the production of housing services by the consumer, it can be shown that a larger elasticity of substitution between q and k as inputs in the production function tends to increase (algebraically) q_r, the substitutes case. On the other hand, a larger elasticity of substitution between housing and nonhousing consumption in the utility function or a high structural density tends to decrease (algebraically) q_r, the complements case.

Supply of Developable Land

The shape of the residential lot affects the amount of residential services that the consumer garners from the land. Denote the frontage of the parcel F and the depth D. The Euclidean area is $A = FD$, graphically depicted by the hyperbolic iso-area locus A_0 in Figure 10.1. We assume, however, that the consumer cares about the shape of the lot in addition to the physical area encompassed by the lot boundaries. In particular, we assume that the consumer obtains the greatest amount of residential services from the land parcel of area A_0 when it has a depth-to-frontage ratio $(D/F)_0$, and obtains a lower level of service from parcels with equal Euclidean area that increasingly diverge from this configuration.[6] There is hedonic price evidence that households are not indifferent to the dimensions of residential land parcels.

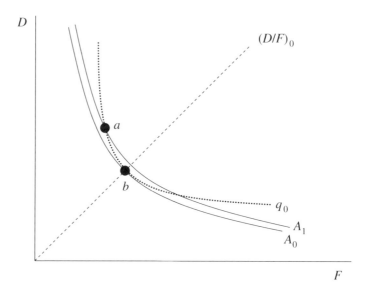

Figure 10.1   Consumer preference for lot dimensions and Euclidean area

Empirical estimates support the notion that frontage, depth and lot shape can have different impacts on property value in the market (Cheshire and Sheppard, 1995; Colwell and Scheu, 1989, 1994; Colwell *et al.*, 2000). The relationship between lot price and frontage and depth appears to increase at a decreasing rate, while the relationship with frontage tends to be more proportional than depth. In any case, the notion that the shape of the lot matters to consumers is intuitively appealing. For example, a longer frontage gives greater distance from side neighbors for a given structure footprint, yielding greater privacy for outdoor activities or even just greater aesthetic appeal for landscape purposes.

Specifically, land consumption is given by the increasing strictly quasi-concave function of lot frontage and depth, $q = \phi(F,D)$. An example of such a function is $\phi(F,D) = FD + \sigma(\|(D/F) - (D/F)_0\|)$ with $\sigma' < 0$. Graphically, the isoquant q_0 in Figure 10.1 is tangent to the iso area locus A_0 where the dimension ratio $D/F = (D/F)_0$. The isoquant rises above the iso area A_0 for lot sizes that diverge from $(D/F)_0$, with $\sigma' < 0$ ensuring that the distance between the two curves increases with greater distance from the radial vector with slope $(D/F)_0$. For example, the total Euclidean area of a long narrow land parcel like a in the figure exceeds that of parcel b, even though a and b yield the same amount of land consumption to the household: $A_1 > A_0$ in Figure 10.1.

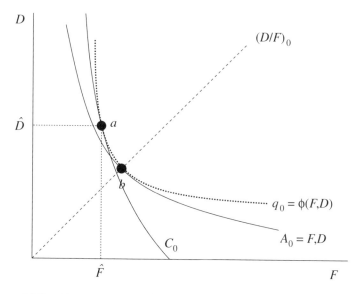

Figure 10.2   Cost minimizing lot dimensions

The choice of lot dimensions

In order to derive the supply of developable land to the market, consider first the cost of preparing a parcel of land for development, that is, preparing the land for the addition of the structural capital. For a parcel of dimension $\{F, D\}$ the cost of such preparation is

$$C = \alpha + \beta F + \delta FD. \tag{10.2}$$

This is the cost of developing a lot; that is, creating developable land from raw land. α represents the fixed cost per lot. This would include such things as surveying and any lump-sum taxes, exactions, fees or permits. β represents the cost per front foot of infrastructure such as streets, sidewalks, street lights and utilities (that is, gas, electricity, phone and cable). δ represents the cost per square foot of raw land.

It is convenient to portray the lot dimension choice problem graphically. To do so, we define the isocost for expenditure C_0 which, when graphed in Figure 10.2, is convex with the slope $-(\beta + \delta F)/\delta D < 0$ for $\delta > 0$, $\beta \geq 0$. As is standard, isocosts to the northeast indicate greater land preparation costs.

In order to construct the development cost function, consider the problem

$$\min_{F,D}\{C \ s.t. \ q = \phi(F,D)\}. \tag{10.3}$$

Denoting the multiplier λ and partial derivatives by subscripts, the cost-minimizing land parcel dimensions $\{F^*, D^*\}$ satisfy the necessary conditions

$$\beta + \delta D - \lambda \phi_F(F,D) = 0 \tag{10.4}$$
$$\delta F - \lambda \phi_D(F,D) = 0 \tag{10.5}$$
$$q - \phi(F,D) = 0, \tag{10.6}$$

where we assume a positive definite bordered Hessian subject to constraint, $B < 0$, so that the relevant sufficient conditions hold locally.[7] The bordered Hessian condition holds for this problem when the curvature of the isoquant q_0 is greater than that of the isocost C_0, as pictured in Figure 10.2.

The conditions (10.5) and (10.4) imply

$$\frac{\beta + \delta D}{\delta F} = \frac{\phi_F}{\phi_D}. \tag{10.7}$$

The left-hand side is the (absolute) slope of the isocost curve C_0; the right-hand side is the (absolute) slope of the isoquant q_0. The solution $\{\hat{F}, \hat{D}\}$ is where the isocost C_0 is tangent to the isoquant q_0 in Figure 10.2.

We can easily assess the role of frontage costs in the model. When the developer is not responsible for frontage costs, $\beta = 0$, and the isocost coincides with the iso area curve. The cost-minimizing lot dimensions are determined by the point of tangency between the iso-area locus and the isoquant, b in Figure 10.2, a lot with dimensions satisfying the crucial ratio $(D/F)_0$. When compared with the $\beta > 0$ case, portrayed by a in the figure, the influence of frontage cost on lot dimensions is as expected: developable land is put on the market with narrower frontage and greater depth. What, perhaps, is not as expected is the larger total area for a given level of land consumption. Of course, the level of land consumption in market equilibrium when $\beta > 0$ generally varies from that when $\beta = 0$, as shown later.

Applying the sufficient condition $B < 0$, there exist differentiable functions for lot dimensions and marginal cost,

$$\hat{F} = F(q, \beta, \delta), \tag{10.8}$$
$$\hat{D} = D(q, \beta, \delta), \tag{10.9}$$
$$\hat{\lambda} = \lambda(q, \beta, \delta) \tag{10.10}$$

Totally differentiate (10.4)–(10.6) and solve for the partial derivative properties of the lot dimension functions, $F(q, \beta, \delta)$ and $D(q, \beta, \delta)$. The effects of the frontage parameter β on lot dimensions are

$$F_\beta = \frac{\phi_D^2}{B} < 0 \tag{10.11}$$

$$D_\beta = \frac{-\phi_F\phi_D}{B} > 0 \tag{10.12}$$

Solving for the effect of δ on the solution yields $F_\delta = D_\delta = 0$ for $\beta = 0$ and while for $\beta > 0$:

$$F_\delta = \frac{\phi_D[D\phi_D - F\phi_F]}{B} > 0, \tag{10.13}$$

$$D_\delta = -\left(\frac{\phi_F}{\phi_D}\right)F_\delta < 0. \tag{10.14}$$

In order to derive the indicated signs of the above results, first notice that

$$\phi_D[D\phi_D - F\phi_F] = \phi_D^2 F\left[\frac{D}{F} - \frac{\phi_F}{\phi_D}\right]. \tag{10.15}$$

Now note that the optimality condition (10.7) implies

$$\frac{D}{F} - \frac{\phi_F}{\phi_D} = -\frac{\beta}{\delta F} \leq 0 \text{ as } \beta \geq 0. \tag{10.16}$$

Together, (10.15) and (10.16) imply that the numerator of (10.11) is negative for $\beta > 0$ so that the signs of (10.11) and (10.12) immediately follow as indicated.

Expansion path characterization
It is useful to take a closer look at the nature of the cost-minimizing lot dimensions before addressing the characterization of the developable land cost function below. The output effects on the lot dimensions are, respectively,

$$F_q = \frac{\lambda[\phi_F\phi_{DD} - \phi_D\phi_{FD}]}{B} > 0, \tag{10.17}$$

$$D_q = \frac{\lambda[\phi_D\phi_{FF} - \phi_F\phi_{FD}]}{B} > 0, \tag{10.18}$$

where the signs follow under the assumption that both dimensions are equivalent to normal inputs in a production function.[8] That is, under reasonable conditions in standard production theory, the expansion path is upward sloped, as in Figure 10.3.

The slope of the isocost curve is $-[\beta + \delta D]/\delta F$, so that the isocost curves flatten, approaching $-D/F$, as we move outward along the ray in Figure 10.4. When ϕ is homothetic, the slope of the isoquants are constant along

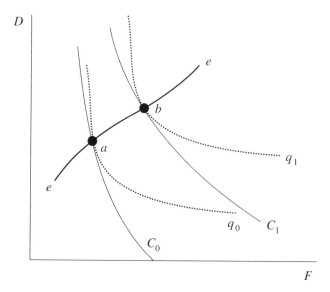

Figure 10.3   Expansion path for lot dimensions

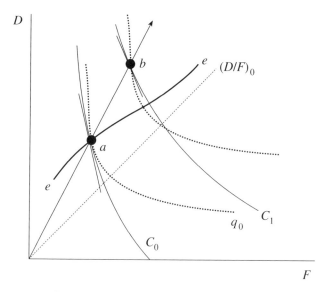

Figure 10.4   Efficient lot size and dimensions with homothetic preferences

the indicated ray. This implies that the tangency between the relevant isocost and the isoquant q_1 lies to the right of the indicated ray. Under homothetic ϕ, the expansion path *ee* approaches the radial vector with slope $(D/F)_0$ as q rises. Since land consumption is normal, this expansion path implies that *higher consumer incomes increase land consumption and therefore yield neighborhoods that comprise residential lots that are less rectangular than lower-income neighborhoods. But notice that this also reduces the Euclidean land area that is required to meet the greater consumer demand for land consumption that comes with higher income. This in turn implies that this finite lot size model of the urban area will predict less spatial expansion arising from consumer income growth than will the neoclassical Mills–Muth infinitesimal lot size model.*

Developable land cost function

We can now construct the cost function for developable land. Substituting the cost-minimizing lot dimensions into (10.2) yields the cost function

$$C(q,\alpha,\beta,\delta) \equiv \alpha + \beta F(q,\beta,\delta) + \delta F(q,\beta,\delta) D(q,\beta,\delta). \qquad (10.19)$$

The properties of this function are key to understanding the effect of land taxes on the land market equilibrium. Differentiating reveals

$$C_\alpha = 1 > 0, \qquad (10.20)$$
$$C_\beta = \hat{F} > 0, \qquad (10.21)$$
$$C_\delta = \hat{F}\hat{D} > 0. \qquad (10.22)$$

Further, the marginal cost of lot size is $C_q \equiv \hat{\lambda} > 0$ where $\hat{\lambda} = \lambda(q,\beta,\delta)$ as defined earlier. Totally differentiate the conditions (10.4)–(10.6) to find the comparative statics λ_β and λ_δ, then rearrange and substitute (10.17) and (10.18) into the comparative statics to obtain the following properties for this marginal cost function as:

$$\lambda_\beta = F_q > 0, \qquad (10.23)$$
$$\lambda_\delta = \hat{D}F_q + \hat{F}D_q > 0. \qquad (10.24)$$

Therefore increases in either the frontage or area cost parameters increase both the average and marginal costs of land consumption under our maintained assumption that both dimensions are normal inputs in producing land consumption.

Market Equilibrium

The consumer's demand for land consumption is

$$q = q(p,r,m). \tag{10.25}$$

The developer's profit-maximizing q satisfies the usual marginal condition that price equals marginal cost,

$$p = \lambda(q,\beta,\delta). \tag{10.26}$$

The equilibrium developed land price is that which ensures that each consumer demands the same quantity of land that the profit-maximizing developer is willing and able to offer.

Finally, since $\{F(q,\beta,\delta), D(q,\beta,\delta)\}$ are the residential lot dimensions chosen by the profit-maximizing developer for land consumption q, the total Euclidean land area that is developed for residential use, T, is therefore

$$T = NF(q,\beta,\delta)D(q,\beta,\delta). \tag{10.27}$$

Conditions (10.25)–(10.27) fully describe the market equilibrium land consumption for each household, developed land price and the total physical quantity of land developed for residential use: $\{q^*,p^*,T^*\}$.

3   LAND TAX EFFECTS

In what follows we use the neutrality of taxing the value of raw land, a standard outcome in static models, as our benchmark.[9] This section analyzes the effects of land taxes on the market equilibrium. To do so, differentiate the system of equations describing the market equilibrium to get

$$
\begin{bmatrix} 1 & -q_p & 0 \\ -\lambda_q & 1 & 0 \\ -N\lambda_\delta & 0 & 1 \end{bmatrix}
\begin{bmatrix} dq^* \\ dp^* \\ dT^* \end{bmatrix},
$$

$$
=
\begin{bmatrix} q_r & q_m & 0 & 0 \\ 0 & 0 & \lambda_\beta & \lambda_\delta \\ 0 & 0 & N(F_\beta D + FD_\beta) & N(F_\delta D + FD_\delta) \end{bmatrix}
\begin{bmatrix} dr \\ dm \\ d\beta \\ d\delta \end{bmatrix}, \tag{10.28}
$$

where $F_qD + FD_q = \lambda_\delta$ is used to simplify the left-hand side. The Jacobian determinant of the system of equations describing market equilibrium is $J = 1 - q_p\lambda_q > 0$. This determinant is positive under the standard Marshallian market stability condition that the demand curve cuts the marginal cost curve from above.

Frontage Tax

Solve the system (10.28) directly to find the effects of frontage and area taxes on the land market equilibrium. An increase in the frontage tax increases β in the improvements cost function (10.19), yielding

$$\frac{\partial q^*}{\partial \beta} = \frac{q_p\lambda_\beta}{J} < 0, \tag{10.29}$$

$$\frac{\partial p^*}{\partial \beta} = \frac{\lambda_\beta}{J} > 0. \tag{10.30}$$

Thus the frontage tax decreases land consumption and increases the price of improved land. These results are intuitively appealing in the context of our examination of the cost-minimizing frontage–depth relationships. The frontage tax increases the marginal cost of improved land ($\lambda_\beta > 0$), thereby driving up the price and reducing the quantity of improved land demanded in the market, (10.29) and (10.30).

The effect of the frontage tax on the total Euclidean area, however, requires some additional attention. Solving (10.28) for the comparative static prediction and simplifying yields

$$\frac{\partial T^*}{\partial \beta} = N(F_\beta D + FD_\beta) + \frac{Nq_p\lambda_\delta\lambda_\beta}{J}. \tag{10.31}$$

The second term is unambiguously negative from $q_p < 0$, (10.23), (10.24), and $J > 0$. The first term, on the other hand, is not so clear-cut. Substituting (10.13) and (10.14) into the first right-hand side term gives us

$$F_\beta D + FD_\beta = \frac{1}{F\phi_D B}\left[\frac{D}{F} - \frac{\phi_F}{\phi_D}\right] \geq 0 \text{ as } \beta \geq 0,$$

using $B < 0$ and (10.16). Clearly, the first right-hand side term in (10.31) is non-negative so that the tax effect on area is in general ambiguous. In the special case in which there are no frontage costs associated with the land, $\beta = 0$ initially, and introducing a frontage tax unambiguously decreases the total area of land used for residential purposes.

To understand why the effect of the frontage tax on total area is ambiguous in general, recall our earlier result (10.13): for given land consumption, an increase in the frontage tax reduces the cost-minimizing frontage (and increases the lot depth). But this increase in frontage also increases the total Euclidean area that is required to maintain a given land consumption (see, for example, Figure 10.1). This is the dimension substitution effect of the tax. At the same time, of course, the decrease in land consumption demanded by itself tends to decrease Euclidean area. This is the output effect. The net effect is ambiguous: the lower land consumption tends to decrease T (the second term in (10.31)) while the effect of a smaller frontage tends to increase T (the first term in (10.31)).

Nonetheless, as shown in the appendix, Cobb–Douglas consumer preferences ensure that the lot dimension substitution effect that increases total area is stronger than the offsetting output effect so that the frontage tax increases the Euclidean area occupied by the market.

Area Tax

An increase in the area tax increases the parameter δ in the improvements cost function. Since by $\lambda_\delta > 0$ this increases the marginal cost of developed land to the market, it is not surprising that this tax decreases land consumption by each household and increases the price of developed land:

$$\frac{\partial q^*}{\partial \delta} = \frac{q_p \lambda_\delta}{J} < 0, \tag{10.32}$$

$$\frac{\partial p^*}{\partial \delta} = \frac{\lambda_\delta}{J} > 0. \tag{10.33}$$

Once again, the effect of the tax on the total area of developed land requires additional manipulation. The system (10.28) yields, with simplification,

$$\frac{\partial T^*}{\partial \delta} = N(F_\delta D + FD_\delta) + \frac{N q_p \lambda_\delta^2}{J}. \tag{10.34}$$

The second term is unambiguously negative. To evaluate the first term, note that substituting (10.11) and (10.12) into the parenthetical expression reveals

$$F_\delta D + FD_\delta = \frac{F_\delta}{F}\left(\frac{D}{F} - \frac{\phi_F}{\phi_D}\right) \leq 0 \text{ as } \beta \geq 0,$$

where the inequality condition follows from (10.16). This result and (10.34) establishes that

$$\frac{\partial T^*}{\partial \delta} < 0 \tag{10.35}$$

and the area tax unambiguously reduces the total Euclidean area of land developed in the market.

The intuition for the area tax draws from our earlier analysis of cost-minimizing lot dimensions. An increase in an area tax leads to relatively wider and shallower residential lots for a given amount of land consumption. This tends to decrease the Euclidean area of land used to generate the given amount of land consumption for each household. At the same time, a greater area tax increases the marginal cost of improved land, driving up the equilibrium price of developable land and thereby reducing the household's demand for land consumption. This reduction in land consumption by itself leads to less land area developed. Together, these effects are reinforcing, leading to (10.35), a smaller total area of developed land.

Shifting from Area Tax to Frontage Tax

Let $d\beta$ and $d\delta$ reflect changes in the exogenous frontage and area tax rates for improved land, respectively. An equal-revenue movement away from the area toward heavier use of the frontage tax requires $Fd\beta + FDd\delta = 0$, where the constraint is understood to be imposed at the initial equilibrium. The effect of shifting from the area to the frontage tax can be found from (10.28) subject to the constraint, which gives

$$\frac{dq^*}{d\beta} = \left(\frac{\partial q^*}{\partial \beta}\right) - \left(\frac{1}{D}\right)\left(\frac{\partial q^*}{\partial \delta}\right)$$

$$= \frac{q_p\lambda_\beta}{J} - \frac{q_p\lambda_\delta}{DJ}$$

$$= \frac{q_p}{J}\left(\lambda_\beta - \frac{\lambda_\delta}{D}\right)$$

$$= -\frac{q_p FD_q}{DJ} > 0, \qquad (10.36)$$

where the last equality follows from substituting $\lambda_\beta = F_q$ and $\lambda_\delta = DF_q + FD_q$ and simplifying. Note that $d\lambda/d\beta = (\lambda_\beta - \lambda_\delta/D) = -FD_q < 0$ under the constraint; the shift away from the area tax toward the equal-revenue frontage tax decreases the marginal cost of land consumption. It is this lower marginal cost of land consumption that increases land consumption in equilibrium. The effect on the value of improved land is similarly found:

$$\frac{dp^*}{d\beta} = \left(\frac{\partial p^*}{\partial \beta}\right) - \left(\frac{1}{D}\right)\left(\frac{\partial p^*}{\partial \delta}\right)$$

$$= \frac{\lambda_\beta}{J} - \frac{1}{D}\frac{\lambda_\delta}{J}$$

$$= -\frac{FD_q}{DJ} < 0. \tag{10.37}$$

Again, it is the decrease in marginal cost that lowers the price of developable land.

How does this shift affect the total Euclidean area of land developed for residential use in the market? Solving (10.28) subject to the constraint, we find

$$\frac{dT^*}{d\beta} = \left(\frac{\partial T^*}{\partial \beta}\right) - \left(\frac{1}{D}\right)\left(\frac{\partial T^*}{\partial \delta}\right)$$

$$= \left(N(F_\beta D + FD_\beta) + \frac{Nq_p\lambda_\beta\lambda_\delta}{J}\right) - \left(\frac{1}{D}\right)\left(N(F_\delta D + FD_\delta) + \frac{Nq_p\lambda_\delta^2}{J}\right). \tag{10.38}$$

Substituting for λ_β and λ_δ and rearranging:

$$\frac{dT^*}{d\beta} = N\left\{(F_\beta D + FD_\beta) - \left(\frac{1}{D}\right)(F_\delta D + FD_\delta)\right\}$$

$$+ \frac{Nq_p}{J}\left\{F_q(DF_q + FD_q) - \left(\frac{1}{D}\right)(DF_q + FD_q)^2\right\}. \tag{10.39}$$

Now substitute for F_q and D_q in the first bracketed expression while multiplying out the terms in the second bracketed expression and simplify to get

$$\frac{dT^*}{d\beta} = N\left\{\frac{\phi_D^2 F}{B} - \left(\frac{F_\delta}{DF}\right)\right\}\left[\frac{D}{F} - \frac{\phi_F}{\phi_D}\right] - \frac{Nq_p F^2 D_q^2}{J}. \tag{10.40}$$

Use $B < 0$, $F_\delta > 0$, and (10.16) to show that the entire first right-hand side term is positive. Similarly, $q_p < 0$ and $J > 0$ imply that the second right-hand side term is positive. Therefore

$$\frac{dT^*}{d\beta} > 0, \tag{10.41}$$

and shifting from an area to a frontage tax increases the total amount of land developed for residential use.

Although it might seem strange at first, this last result does have intuitive appeal upon reflection. Since $\lambda_\beta - \lambda_\delta/D < 0$, shifting from the area tax to the frontage tax reduces the marginal cost of improving land, thereby increasing the demand for land consumption. By itself, increasing land consumption leads to a greater Euclidean area. At the same time, though, the shift to the frontage tax decreases the optimal frontage for the consumers. This by itself leads to a greater Euclidean area in order to just keep the land consumption constant. The two effects, greater consumption and smaller frontage, are reinforcing on total land area, leading to the larger amount of land used by the fixed population in the market.

This is a key result. Among the other things, it reveals why *frontage and area taxes are not perfect substitutes*, a result that has escaped the attention of economists. How land is taxed matters. Although it seems reasonable to suppose that shifting to a frontage tax to fully capture the marginal social cost of publicly supplied services tied to frontage would lead to a more compact and efficient city, the above result reveals that this city shrinkage need not occur. If efficiency can be enhanced by shifting from an area to a frontage tax then not only is the city larger, the larger city is more efficient. To this extent, the larger city does not exhibit wasteful sprawl but rather efficient expansion: *Reducing inefficient sprawl does not reduce the size of the city in this case; in contrast, it makes the city larger. More generally, the optimal amount of urban sprawl is tied to the social cost of frontage relative to area. The greater the social cost of frontage relative to area, the greater the amount of land required to house the given population efficiently.*

Of course we need to consider changes in tax regimes other than shifting from the area to the frontage tax, and it is to this task that we now turn. Nonetheless, the above relationship helps to understand the results that follow.

4   AD VALOREM TAXES

The analysis thus far concentrates on taxing the physical dimensions of residential lots. It is also useful to consider how value taxes affect the outcome, and especially, how shifting from value-based taxes to physical dimension taxes like area or frontage taxes affects consumption and sprawl.

To introduce value tax into the model, denote the ad valorem tax rate on structures by θ and the tax rate applied to the market value of improved land by τ. From the household's perspective, the total cost of housing with capital k and land consumption q is therefore $(1 + \theta)rk + (1 + \tau)pq$. Suitably modifying the consumer's problem (10.1) and using the gross-of-tax prices $R = (1 + \theta)r$ and $P = (1 + \tau)p$, gives the consumer's demands $k = k(P,R,m)$, $y = y(P,R,m)$ and

$$q = q(P,R,m). \tag{10.42}$$

Replacing the household's demand in the market model with the above and totally differentiating yields the system

$$
\begin{bmatrix}
1 & -(1+r)q_P & 0 \\
-\lambda_q & 1 & 0 \\
-N\lambda_\delta & 0 & 1
\end{bmatrix}
\begin{bmatrix}
dq \\
dp \\
dT
\end{bmatrix}
$$

$$
=
\begin{bmatrix}
rq_R & q_m & 0 & 0 & pq_P \\
0 & 0 & \lambda_\beta & \lambda_\beta & 0 \\
0 & 0 & N(F_\beta D + FD_\beta) & N(F_\delta D + FD_\delta) & 0
\end{bmatrix}
\begin{bmatrix}
d\theta \\
dm \\
d\beta \\
d\delta \\
dr
\end{bmatrix}.
\quad (10.43)
$$

Clearly, all of the earlier results established for the area and frontage taxes still pertain.

Tax on Structures

As a point of departure for this section, we first look at the ad valorem tax on buildings. A tax on structures increases the gross price of housing capital. The effects on consumption, land price and total area are

$$
\frac{\partial q^*}{\partial \theta} = \frac{rq_R}{J} \gtreqless 0 \text{ as } q_R \gtreqless 0,
\quad (10.44)
$$

$$
\frac{\partial p^*}{\partial \theta} = \frac{-rq_R\lambda_\delta}{J} \lesseqgtr 0 \text{ as } q_R \gtreqless 0,
\quad (10.45)
$$

$$
\frac{\partial T^*}{\partial \theta} = \frac{rNq_R\lambda_\delta}{J} \gtreqless 0 \text{ as } q_R \gtreqless 0.
\quad (10.46)
$$

When structures and land are complementary in demand, $q_R < 0$ and a tax on structures leads to lower land consumption, a higher price of improved land and less total land developed. When they are substitutes in demand, however, the opposite results obtain.

The fact that these comparative statics hinge upon the ambiguous cross-price effect of capital on land consumption is not surprising. Brueckner (1986), for example, shows that the effect of a structures tax on land demand hinges upon the elasticity of substitution between structures and land in the production function. And in a study more closely related to ours, Brueckner and Kim (2000) show in a spatial model that the impact of a structure tax on the size of the urban area depends upon the substitutability between housing and non-housing consumption in the household's utility function. At one extreme, Brueckner's (2000) assumption of fixed dwelling sizes can be shown to lead to demand substitutes ($q_r > 0$) in our model. In this case, the consumer's response to the tax on buildings only induces a production substitution effect (since total housing, h, is assumed fixed). The structure tax increases the demand for land consumption, leads to a lower price and unambiguously increases the city size. The city size result is consistent with his conclusion.

The other extreme case considered by Brueckner and Kim (2000) assumes fixed structure per acre. Since we use land consumption as our measure of the effective land input into the production of housing services, this is equivalent to assuming a fixed input ratio k/q in our framework. It can be shown that this leads to the complements case ($q_r < 0$), with the outcome that the tax decreases land consumption, increases land price and decreases the overall size of the city. This last result is consistent with Brueckner and Kim's special case.

Tax on Developable Land Value

Our interest now concerns how a tax on the value of improved or developable land alters the market outcome. This is a differential land tax, as it is not levied on unimproved property. It can nonetheless be thought of as the outcome of a uniform tax on the value of all land, developable and raw. Since the portion of the tax that is levied on the underlying value of the raw land is neutral, the only effects of the tax observed in the market will be those arising from the portion on the improvements that have been put into place to make the land developable.

Solving the system (10.43) for the land value tax effects gives us the following new results:

$$\frac{\partial q^*}{\partial \tau} = \frac{p_{qP}}{J} < 0, \tag{10.47}$$

$$\frac{\partial p^*}{\partial \tau} = \frac{-pq_p\lambda_\delta}{J} > 0, \tag{10.48}$$

$$\frac{\partial T^*}{\partial \tau} = \frac{pNq_p\lambda_\delta}{J} < 0. \tag{10.49}$$

The tax on the value of urban land decreases the demand for land consumption, leading to lower land value and a smaller area of land developed.

The tax on developable land value increases the gross price of land to households, which in turn decreases the demand for land consumption. The decrease in land consumption reduces both demanded lot frontage and depth as the market equilibrium pushes consumers down the expansion path in Figure 10.3. The net effect of the reduced lot dimensions leads to a smaller overall urban area. And, since the tax on raw land is neutral, our conclusion further implies that *shifting from the tax on developable land value to a tax on raw land value leads to a lower price of developable land, greater land consumption by households, and a larger urban area.*

Property Tax

For a property tax levied uniformly on buildings, developable land and raw land, we impose $\theta = \tau$. The above comparative static results immediately imply that shifting from such a tax to an equal-revenue raw land value tax has an ambiguous net effect on the Euclidean area of developed land. This much is consistent with Brueckner and Kim's (2000) general conclusions, although the incremental value of urban land in their analysis arises from location rents rather than the developable state envisioned here. *When land and structures are complements in demand, however, $q_R < 0$ so that reducing the property tax while increasing the tax on raw land value unambiguously increases the total size of the urban area.*

Brueckner and Kim (2000) offer a numerical example of a shift from the property tax to a land tax that leads to a smaller urban area, but admit to it as a special case. Given that our conclusion rests upon the general characterization of structures and land consumption as complementary goods, our result at least suggests that their example of a sprawl-inducing property tax will not generalize too broadly. As a consequence, it appears that, contrary to their conjecture, the property tax itself is not a very likely source of urban sprawl.

On the other hand, our treatment of developable versus raw land points out another relevant comparison not considered before, that of shifting away from a tax on structures toward an equal-revenue tax on developable land. To examine this possibility, we consider an equal-revenue shift in taxes from structures to improved land satisfying the constraint $rkd\theta + pqd\tau = 0$. Solving the system (10.43) for the land consumption effects subject to this constraint yields.

$$\frac{dq^*}{d\tau} = \left(\frac{\partial q}{\partial \tau}\right) - \left(\frac{pq}{rk}\right)\left(\frac{\partial q}{\partial \theta}\right) = \frac{pq_P}{J} - \frac{pq}{rk}\frac{rq_R}{J}. \tag{10.50}$$

Substituting the Slutsky equations for the Marshallian price terms using upper case Q and K for Hicksian demands, $q_P = Q_P - qq_m$ and $q_R = Q_R - kq_m$, so that $q_P/q - q_R/k = Q_P/q - Q_R/k + q_m - q_m$ and the above expression reduces to

$$\frac{dq^*}{d\tau}=\frac{pq}{J}\left[\frac{Q_P}{q}-\frac{Q_R}{k}\right]=\frac{pq}{J}\left[\frac{Q_P}{q}-\frac{K_P}{k}\right]=\left(\frac{pq}{PJ}\right)\frac{d\ln(Q/K)}{d\ln P}, \quad (10.51)$$

where Slutsky symmetry, $Q_R=K_P$, is used to obtain the second equality. Using H to denote the level of housing services holding utility constant, $H=h(Q,K)$, we have

$$\frac{d\ln(Q/K)}{d\ln P}=\left(\frac{d\ln(Q/K)}{d\ln P}\right)_{dH=0}+\frac{d\ln(Q/K)}{dH}\frac{\partial H}{\partial \ln P}. \quad (10.52)$$

Under the assumption of a homothetic housing production function $h(q,k)$, the input ratio is invariant to scale and the second term in the right-hand side of the above equation is zero. The first term is recognizable as the production substitution effect in elasticity form and is unambiguously negative. Thus $d\ln(Q/K)/d\ln P<0$, so that

$$\frac{dq^*}{d\tau}<0. \quad (10.53)$$

The demand for land consumption declines when shifting from the property tax to the tax on urban land value.

The effects of the tax shift on land price and total size are similarly found from (10.43) subject to constraint. Similar manipulations reveal

$$\frac{dp^*}{d\tau}=-\lambda_\delta\left(\frac{dq^*}{d\tau}\right)>0. \quad (10.54)$$

The change in total area is

$$\frac{dT^*}{d\tau}=N\left(\frac{dq^*}{d\tau}\right)<0. \quad (10.55)$$

The shift from the property tax to the urban land value tax increases land price and decreases total area.

Shifting from Developable Land Value Tax to Frontage Tax

Now consider some other new results relevant to our treatment of developable land. Suppose we shift from a land value tax to a frontage tax. The above comparative statics reveal that reducing the land value tax increases land consumption and land price, and increases the total area of developed land. Increasing the frontage tax decreases land consumption, increases land price and has an ambiguous effect on the total area of land developed. To examine the net effect of an equal-revenue shift in the taxes, as indicated, solve (10.43) for $d\beta>0$ subject to the constraint $pqd\tau+Fd\beta=0$. So doing yields

$$\frac{dq^*}{d\beta} = \left(\frac{\partial q^*}{\partial \beta}\right) - \left(\frac{F}{pq}\right)\left(\frac{\partial q^*}{\partial \tau}\right) = \frac{q_P\lambda_\beta}{J} - \frac{F}{pq}\frac{pq_P}{J} = \frac{q_P}{J}\left(F_q - \frac{F}{q}\right). \quad (10.56)$$

This result hinges upon the size of F_q along the expansion path relative to the frontage intensity F/q. The above result appears to be ambiguous at this level of generality. The price effect is similarly ambiguous.

How does shifting from the land value tax to the frontage tax affect the overall land area occupied by residents? Again solving (10.43) subject to constraint,

$$\frac{dT^*}{d\beta} = \left(\frac{\partial T^*}{\partial \beta}\right) - \left(\frac{F}{pq}\right)\left(\frac{\partial T^*}{\partial \tau}\right)$$

$$= \left(N(F_\beta D + FD_\beta) + \frac{Nq_p\lambda_\delta\lambda_\beta}{J}\right) - \left(\frac{F}{pq}\right)\left(\frac{pNq_p\lambda_\delta}{J}\right)$$

$$= N(F_\beta D + FD_\beta) + N\lambda_\delta\lambda_\beta\left(\frac{dq^*}{d\beta}\right). \quad (10.57)$$

The first term is positive. When $dq^*/d\beta \geq 0$, the second term is non-negative and this tax change increases overall size of the city. Clearly, however, if the conditions hold for the more intuitively appealing outcome $dq^*/d\beta < 0$, then the second additive term above is negative, and leads to an overall ambiguous total area response to the shift from value to the frontage tax. This possibility also makes sense. If land consumption declines in response to the shift toward the frontage tax from the value tax then this by itself leads to a lower Euclidean area. On the other hand, the decrease in frontage demanded by consumers tends to increase the total land area needed to obtain a given level of land consumption, providing an offsetting effect on total size of the market.

Recall that an increase in the frontage tax increases Euclidean area for the Cobb–Douglas preferences case in the appendix. Since a decrease in the land value tax unambiguously decreases total area, the shift away from a land value tax toward heavier reliance on the frontage tax increases total area.

Shifting from Developable Land Value Tax to Area Tax

As a last comparison of land tax regimes, we consider a shift from the tax on improved land value to an area tax. Again imposing a local equal-revenue constraint, such a shift requires $pqd\tau + FDd\delta = 0$. Solving for the comparative statics using (10.43) subject to this constraint, we have

$$\frac{dq^*}{d\delta} = \left(\frac{\partial q^*}{\partial \delta}\right) - \left(\frac{FD}{pq}\right)\left(\frac{\partial q^*}{\partial \tau}\right)$$

$$= \left(\frac{q_P \lambda_\delta}{J}\right) - \left(\frac{FD}{pq}\right)\left(\frac{pq_P}{J}\right)$$

$$= \frac{q_P}{J}\left(\lambda_\delta - \frac{FD}{q}\right)$$

$$= \frac{q_P}{J}\left(DF_q + FD_q - \frac{FD}{q}\right)$$

$$= \frac{q_P}{J}\frac{FD}{q}\left(\frac{\partial(FD)}{\partial q}\frac{q}{FD} - 1\right). \tag{10.58}$$

The term $\dfrac{\partial(FD)}{\partial q}\dfrac{q}{FD}$ in the above expression is the elasticity of Euclidean area with respect to land consumption along the expansion path in Figure 10.4. For $\beta > 0$, as noted above, the dimension ratio $D/F \to (D/F)_0$ as q increases, ceteris paribus. Thus $q \to FD$ as q increases. This, with $q < FD$, implies that the area FD increases at a slower rate than does the land consumption q along the expansion path, and the Euclidean area elasticity of land consumption is less than one in the relevant range. By this argument, the above expression reveals

$$\frac{dq^*}{d\delta} > 0 \tag{10.59}$$

and the shift from a developed land value tax to an area tax increases each household's land consumption.

So, how does this increase in land consumption affect the overall size of the land market? Recall that the demanded lot dimensions change as well as land consumption. The net effect on total area is

$$\frac{dT^*}{d\delta} = \left(\frac{\partial T^*}{\partial \delta}\right) - \left(\frac{FD}{pq}\right)\left(\frac{\partial T^*}{\partial \tau}\right)$$

$$= N(F_\delta D + FD_\delta) + \frac{Nq_P\lambda_\delta\lambda_\beta}{J} - \frac{FD}{pq}\frac{pNq_P\lambda_\delta}{J} \tag{10.60}$$

$$= N(F_\delta D + FD_\delta) + N\lambda_\delta\left(\frac{dq^*}{d\delta}\right),$$

where the last equality follows by substitution. Given that the first term is always nonpositive,[10] it follows that $dq^*/d\delta > 0$ as determined above leaves the net effect on Euclidean area ambiguous. Thus, while it is generally presumed that shifting from land or property taxes to an area tax will reduce the size of the urban area, this need not be so. On the other hand, the appendix shows that an equal revenue shift from the land value tax to the area tax decreases Euclidean area for the parametric model with Cobb–Douglas utility.

5   CONCLUSION

In this chapter we have developed a closed urban land market model in which all lots are identical and rectangular. There are no location rents, but rent differentials arise between developable and raw land as a result of improvements such as roads, sidewalks, sewers, water and access to other utilities. We find that, as income increases, the frontage-to-depth ratio of residential lots increases. This change reduces the actual area required to meet the higher demand; this model therefore predicts less growth in total area than would be predicted by the standard neoclassical monocentric urban model with a continuum of consumers and infinitesimal lot sizes. In addition, a frontage tax decreases land consumption (that is, effective land area), increases the price of urban land and has an ambiguous effect on the total actual land area. For reasonable parameterization with Cobb–Douglas utility, though, the frontage tax increases total land area. An area tax also decreases the effective area and increases the price of land, but it unambiguously decreases the total land area developed. Shifting from an area tax to a frontage tax while holding revenue constant lowers the marginal cost of land consumption, which in turn decreases land price, increases land consumption and increases the total area occupied by the city.

   While the area tax leads to a smaller total area, it does not produce an optimally compact city because the area tax results in a city that is too small overall but with too large an aggregate investment in infrastructure. Therefore the main normative conclusion of this study is that, when frontage is associated with many social costs of development, a frontage tax is appropriate for eliminating inefficient sprawl, even though it results in a larger city relative to the area tax.

   We have also examined other tax instruments. In addition to taxes on frontage and area, a tax on the value of buildings is considered, along with a tax on the value of land, developable and raw. Shifting from an ad valorem tax to an equal-revenue tax on raw land leads to a larger area of developed land. Somewhat surprisingly, shifting to a frontage tax has an ambiguous effect on the total size of the city in the general case. The Cobb–Douglas utility model, however, reveals a reasonable situation in which shifting from the land value to the frontage tax increases city size. On the other hand, the parameterized model also reveals that shifting from a land value tax to an area tax decreases city size.

APPENDIX

This appendix derives the frontage tax comparative statics for the model with consumer utility $u = x^\gamma q^{1-\gamma}$ and the land consumption function $q = FD - \sigma|D - F|$. The cost minimization conditions become

$$\beta + \delta D - \lambda(D + \sigma) = 0, \tag{10A.1}$$

$$\delta F - \lambda(F - \sigma) = 0, \tag{10A.2}$$

$$q - FD - \sigma(D - F) = 0, \tag{10A.3}$$

using $D > F$ in equilibrium. The inverse demand function (with the developable land value tax τ) is

$$(1 + \tau)p = \frac{(1 - \gamma)m}{q}. \tag{10A.4}$$

The equilibrium condition for developable land remains $p = \lambda$ and the total Euclidean area is $T = NFD$.

The slope of the marginal cost of developable land is, from (10A.1)–(10A.3),

$$\lambda_q = \frac{(\delta - \lambda)}{2(F - \sigma)(D + \sigma)} < 0,$$

using $\delta - \lambda < 0$ from (10A.1) and $F - \sigma > 0$ from (10A.2). The Marshallian stability condition for equilibrium requires that the demand curve cut the marginal cost curve from above, or

$$J = \frac{(1 - \gamma)m}{q^2} + \frac{(\delta - \lambda)}{2(F - \sigma)(D + \sigma)} > 0,$$

where J is the Jacobian determinant of the equilibrium. Differentiating the equilibrium conditions and simplifying, the effect of the frontage tax on the Euclidean area is

$$\frac{\partial T^*}{\partial \beta} = \frac{N}{J}\left\{ -F(\delta - \lambda) - \frac{\lambda(1 + \tau)\sigma}{q}(F + D)(F - \sigma) \right\} > 0.$$

In the case of Cobb–Douglas preferences, the dimension substitution effect outweighs the countervailing output effect of the frontage tax on total area so that area increases with greater frontage tax.

The constant-revenue shift from the developable land value tax to the frontage tax increases total area is

$$\frac{dT^*}{d\beta} =$$

$$\frac{N\{F(\lambda - \delta)[q(1 + \tau) + F(D + \sigma) + D(F - \sigma)] + \lambda\sigma(1 + \tau)(F + D)(F - \sigma)\}}{qJ} > 0.$$

The constant-revenue shift from the developable land value tax to the area tax decreases total area is, similarly,

$$\frac{dT^*}{d\delta} = -\frac{\sigma N\lambda F(D - F)(D - \sigma)}{qJ} < 0.$$

NOTES

1. This research was supported by the Lincoln Institute of Land Policy. The authors are grateful for the helpful comments and suggestions of Karl Case and participants at the Lincoln Institute conference, 'Property Tax, Land Use, and Land Use Regulation', held in Scottsdale, AZ, January, 2002. All errors or omissions remain the responsibility of the authors.
2. This is not meant to imply that there has been no interest in lot dimensions per se. There is, for example, a separate literature that deals explicitly with lot dimensions in the context of subdivision development. For example, see Cannaday and Colwell (1990).
3. See, for example, Brueckner (2000), Brueckner and Kim (2000), Polinsky and Rubinfeld (1978), Sullivan (1985).
4. Given the lack of location differentials in the model and the assumption that the extent of available land is not binding on the market, any partial lots on the end of developed 'rows' of parcels will be left unused in equilibrium.
5. For example, if vacant land held in the interior of the market cannot be used for agricultural, forestry or other purposes that generate the opportunity rent, then developers will always be drawn to any vacant interior parcels before pursuing development on the fringe of the market.
6. The assumption that a single ratio $(D/F)_0$ represents the most desired configuration regardless of lot size can be relaxed to allow for different key ratios as lot area rises or even for a range of ratios $[(D/F)_l, (D/F)_u]$. We adopt the single $(D/F)_0$ value for all q in order to simplify the derivation of results presented in the chapter.
7. The consumer's preferences over lot dimensions are not trivial in land market models with finite dimensions. In this model, for example, if the consumer is indifferent over lot dimensions then the land developer's problem becomes one of choosing dimensions to minimize C subject to the constraint $A = FD$. It can be shown, however, that no finite solution exists for this problem when $\beta > 0$.
8. The normality result holds for dimensions that are complementary or neutral in the land consumption function, that is, for $\phi_{FD} \geq 0$. When substitutes ($\phi_{FD} < 0$), normality holds when each dimension is a better substitute for itself than the other dimension in producing land consumption.
9. The effects of different types of land value taxes (for example, current use and best use) can differ in a dynamic context, however. See, for examples, Bentick (1979), Mills (1981) and Turnbull (1988) for related discussion. Feldstein (1977) introduces a different source of dynamic land tax effects.
10. From (10.11) and (10.12), $F_\delta D + FD_\delta = [(D/F) - (\phi_F/\phi_D)]F_\delta F \leq 0$ as $\beta \geq 0$ from (10.16).

REFERENCES

Asami, Y., M. Fujita and T.E. Smith, 1991, 'On the Foundation of Land Use Theory', *Regional Science and Urban Economics*, 20, 473–508.

Bentick, B.L., 1979, 'The Impact of Taxation and Valuation Practices on the Timing and Efficiency of Land Use', *Journal of Political Economy*, 87 (4), August, 859–69.

Berliant, M., 1985, 'Equilibrium Models with Land: A Criticism and an Alternative', *Regional Science and Urban Economics*, 15, 325–40.

Berliant, M. and M. Fujita, 1992, 'Alonso's Discrete Population Model of Land Use: Efficient Allocations and Competitive Equilibria', *International Economic Review*, 33, 535–66.

Berliant, M. and T.Ten Raa, 1988, 'A Foundation of Location Theory: Consumer Preferences and Demand', *Journal of Economic Theory*, 44, 336–53.

Brueckner, J.K., 1986, 'A Modern Analysis of the Effects of Site Value Taxation', *National Tax Journal*, 39, 49–58.

Brueckner, J.K., 2000, 'Property Taxes and Urban Sprawl', in W.E. Oates (ed.), *Property Taxation and Local Government Finance*, Cambridge, MA: Lincoln Institute of Land Policy.

Brueckner, J.K., 2001, 'Urban Sprawl: Lessons from Urban Economics', *Brookings Papers on Urban Affairs 2001*, Washington, DC: Brookings Institution Press.

Brueckner, J.K. and H.-A. Kim, 2000, 'Urban Sprawl and the Property Tax', Department of Economics, University of Illinois at Urbana-Champaign.

Burchell, R.W., D. Listokin and C.C. Galley, 2000, 'Smart Growth: More than a Ghost of Urban Policy Past, Less than a Bold New Horizon', *Housing Policy Debate*, 11 (4), 821–80.

Cannaday, R.E. and P.F., Colwell, 1990, 'Optimization of Subdivision Development', *Journal of Real Estate Finance and Economics*, 3 (2), June, 195–206.

Cheshire, P. and S. Sheppard, 1995, 'On the Price of Land and the Value of Amenities', *Economica*, 62, 247–67.

Colwell, P.F. and T. Scheu, 1989, 'Optimal Lot Size and Configuration', *Journal of Urban Economics*, 26, March, 90–109.

Colwell, P.F. and T. Scheu, 1994, 'A History of Site Valuation Rules: Functions and Empirical Evidence', *Journal of Real Estate Research*, 9 (3), Summer, 353–68.

Colwell, P.F., C. Dehring and N. Lash, 2000, 'The Effect of Group Homes on Neighborhood Property Values', *Land Economics*, 67 (4), November, 615–37.

Feldstein, M.S., 1977, 'The Surprising Incidence of a Tax on Pure Rent: A New Answer to an Old Question', *Journal of Political Economy*, 85, April, 349–60.

Kamecke, U., 1993, 'Mean City – A Consistent Approximation of Bid Rent Equilibria', *Journal of Urban Economics*, 33, 48–67.

Mills, D.E., 1981, 'The Non-Neutrality of Land Value Taxation', *National Tax Journal*, 34 (1), March, 125–9.

Papageorgiou, Y.Y. and D. Pines, 1990, 'The Logical Foundations of Urban Economics are Consistent', *Journal of Economic Theory*, 50, 37–53.

Polinksy, A.M. and D.L. Rubinfeld, 1978, 'The Long-Run Effects of a Residential Property Tax and Local Public Services', *Journal of Urban Economics*, 5, 241–62.

Sullivan, A.M., 1985, 'The General-Equilibrium Effects of the Residential Property Tax: Incidence and Excess Burden', *Journal of Urban Economics*, 18, 235–50.

Thompson, W.R., 1965, *A Preface to Urban Economics*, Baltimore, MD: Johns Hopkins Press.

Turnbull, G.K., 1988, 'The Effects of Local Taxes and Public Services on Residential Development Patterns', *Journal of Regional Science*, 28 (4), November, 541–62.

Turnbull, G.K., 1997, 'Revealed Preference and Location Choice', *Journal of Urban Economics*, 41 (3), May, 358–76.

Index

development rights, transfer/purchase
    of 77–9
development timing effect 70–71
developmental control, baseline level
    of 155–7
Dilger, R.J. 276
Dipasquale, D. 91, 279
discriminatory actions 241–2
dispersion parameter 12
Dorgan, Senator 64
Downs, A. 89, 90, 124, 148
Dunford, R.W. 66
Dye, R.F. 37–60
dynamic market equilibrium 17–20
dynamic model of real estate markets
    6–35, 139–41
    comparative static analysis 32–4
    conventional tax 21–3
    fortran code 31
    multinomial logit calculus
        29–30
    optimal taxation problem 24–8
    structure of model 10–20
        basic assumptions 10–13
        consumers 13
        dynamic market equilibrium
            17–20
        investors 14–17
        vacant land tax 23–4

Eagle, S.J. 282
'edge cities' 129
Ellickson, R.C. 283
empirical evidence 71–3, 197
employment centers 128–30
Entreken, H.C. Jr 66, 77
environmentalism, neighborhood
    235–6
Epstein, R. 244–5, 282
equalized assessed value 38–46, 49,
    51–4, 55–6, 57–8
equilibrium with multiple locations
    131–3
equity insurance market 141
Escondido 94
Euclidean area 289, 291–2, 297–303,
    306, 308–10, 312
Europe 280
Ewing, R.H. 89, 90–91
executive branches 249–50

expansion path characterization 295–7
extensive margin 9

F statistic 111
factor taxes *see* zoning and factor taxes
Fair Housing Act (1988) 243–5, 278
Fairfax County 240
Fansler, D.A. 93, 98, 102, 111, 117
Federal Home Loan Mortgage
    Corporation 233
Federal National Mortgage
    Association 233
federalism 279–80
Feldstein, M. 178
Felsenstein, D. 177
Fennell, L. 215
Ferguson, J.T. 66
FHA mortgage insurance 232
Fifth Amendment 282
finite demand elasticities model
    199–206
first-order condition 81, 193–4, 195,
    196
Fischel, W. 122, 123–4, 127, 140, 141,
    273–84
Fishe, R. 178
floor–area ratio 122, 131, 134–7, 138,
    141
Florida 66, 77, 80
    private neighborhood associations
        217, 232, 235–6
    Supreme Court 237–8, 242–3
Foer, A. 213
Forest Ridge (Texas) 276
fortran code 31
French, S. 225
frontage tax and optimally compact
    city 287–313
    ad valorem taxes 303–10
    land tax effects 298–303
    residential land market 289–98
Frug, J. 215
Fu, Y. 130, 139, 141
Fujita, M. 289

Gatzlaff, D. 140
general equilibrium model 84
generalized least squares random
    effects model 54
George, H. 6, 7, 65